MEDICAL STORYWORLDS

Medical Storyworlds

HEALTH, ILLNESS, AND BODIES IN RUSSIAN
AND EUROPEAN LITERATURE AT THE TURN
OF THE TWENTIETH CENTURY

Elena Fratto

Columbia University Press
New York

Columbia University Press
Publishers Since 1893
New York   Chichester, West Sussex

Copyright © 2021 Columbia University Press
All rights reserved

Library of Congress Cataloging-in-Publication Data
Names: Fratto, Elena, author.
Title: Medical storyworlds : health, illness, and bodies in Russian and European literature at the turn of the twentieth century / Elena Fratto.
Description: New York : Columbia University Press, 2021. | Includes bibliographical references and index.
Identifiers: LCCN 2021016642 (print) | LCCN 2021016643 (ebook) | ISBN 9780231202329 (hardcover) | ISBN 9780231202336 (trade paperback) | ISBN 9780231554503 (ebook)
Subjects: LCSH: Literature and medicine. | Medicine in literature. | Health in literature. | Death in literature. | Russian literature—19th century—Themes, motives. | Russian literature—20th century—Themes, motives. | Italian literature—20th century—Themes, motives. | French literature—20th century—Themes, motives.
Classification: LCC PN56.M38 F73 2021 (print) | LCC PN56.M38 (ebook) | DDC 809/.933561—dc23

Cover image: General practice leather doctor's bag,
1890–1930, © SSPL / UIG / Bridgeman Images
Cover design: Chang Jae Lee

A papà

CONTENTS

ACKNOWLEDGMENTS ix

Introduction 1

Chapter One
The Grand Finale: Death as the Revelatory Ending 13

Chapter Two
End of Story: Temporality and the Prospect of the Ending in *Ivan Ilych*, *Anna Karenina*, and (Potential) Cancer Patients 45

Chapter Three
Medical Enlightenment in the Early 1920s: Rhetoric and Diffused Authorship in Jules Romains's *Knock* and Soviet Public-Health Campaigns 89

Chapter Four
Time, Agency, and Bodily Glands: Metabolic Storytelling in Italo Svevo and Mikhail Bulgakov 159

AFTERWORD 189

NOTES 195

BIBLIOGRAPHY 233

INDEX 249

ACKNOWLEDGMENTS

The daughter of a lithographer and an operating-room nurse, I was exposed at a tender age to different systems of representations for understanding the human body. However, it was only when I moved to the United States as an adult and had my first close encounters with a healthcare system that is substantially different from the one to which I was accustomed in Europe that the interpretive nature of medicine was revealed most vividly to me. A narrative-theory enthusiast, I felt the urge to chart that territory with my critical tools in order to parse it. It takes a village, and, indeed, I am grateful to many colleagues, mentors, and friends.

This book began in the Department of Comparative Literature at Harvard University, where William Mills Todd III, David Shumway Jones, Tom Conley, and Jeffrey Schnapp encouraged it from the beginning. I am first and foremost grateful to them; their thought was formative in the manuscript's earliest stages, and their influence on my work only grows with time. My thanks also go to Svetlana Boym—in memoriam—probably the most bodily and embodied scholarly mentor I have ever encountered, and to Christopher D. Johnson, who encouraged my epistemological explorations of science–literature configurations before I embarked on this specific avenue of research. Bruce Moran's history-of-science seminar on early modern curiosity allowed me to test my methodology. I am also grateful to Federica Pedriali for igniting my interest in early twentieth-century endocrinology and to Marta Puxan-Oliva for our conversations on narrative reliability. Serving as an assistant instructor in David Jones's, Arthur Kleinman's, Nate Greenslit's, and Karen Thornber's courses on the medical humanities exposed me to different methodological approaches within that vast field.

This project would not have been possible without the generous support of Harvard's Department of Comparative Literature. Publication was subsidized in part by Harvard Studies in Comparative Literature. Initial sketches of the chapters originated in conversations with Dennis Tenen, Clara Masnatta, Anders Engberg-Pedersen, Louise Nilsson, Curt Shonkwiler, Wei Hu, Marco Romani Mistretta, Raphaël Koenig, Guy Smoot, Katie Deutsch, Juan Torbidoni, Kathryn Heinzman, Yvan Prkachin, Evgeny Morozov, Leah Aronowsky, Allyssa Metzger, and many others who called Dana-Palmer House and the fourth floor of the Science Center their home. A year-long residence at Project Narrative at Ohio State University provided me with the time and scholarly environment necessary to fine-tune the theoretical basis of my argument. My deep gratitude goes out especially to James Phelan, Brian McHale, Amy Shuman, and Sean O'Sullivan in that leading research group in narrative theory. As I prepared the manuscript, several Slavist scholars offered invaluable remarks and suggestions on portions of it, if not the full work, at different stages. For their time, engagement, and intellectual generosity, I am indebted to Eric Naiman, Kevin M. F. Platt, Catriona Kelly, Thomas Seifrid, Donna Orwin, Olga Peters Hasty, Ellen Chances, Ilya Vinitsky, Riccardo Nicolosi, Michael Wachtel, Justin Weir, David Horn, Cathy Popkin, Jacob Emery, and Massimo Maurizio. This book came to fruition at Princeton University. As I worked through my manuscript drafts, I benefited immensely from conversations with and feedback from several colleagues on the Princeton campus, especially Maria DiBattista, Peter Brooks, Brooke Holmes, Katja Guenther, Erika Milam, João Biehl, Rachael DeLue, Judith Hamera, Dan-el Padilla Peralta, Keith Wailoo, Michael Gordin, Ruha Benjamin, He Bian, Alessandro Giammei, Guangchen Chen, and the working group Bodies of Knowledge, which I co-convened with inspiring colleagues—Tala Khanmalek, Amy Krauss, and Natalie Prizel—and which provided an important forum for several of the book's chapters. I thank all of the participants and presenters throughout the four iterations of the

ACKNOWLEDGMENTS

working group. I am also grateful to the Princeton Department of Slavic Languages and Literatures for its unflagging support of all my research and teaching initiatives related to this book. Beyond my Princeton community, a heartfelt thanks goes to Joseph Dumit, Jeremy Greene, Carol Any, Galya Diment, José Alaniz, Irina Sirotkina, Michael Finke, Alec Brookes, Kathryn Montgomery Hunter, Catherine Belling, Marie-Claire Picher, Stefania Sini, Roberta Sollazzi, and Marina Connelly; to Julia Vaingurt for the medical-humanities symposium she organized at the University of Illinois in Chicago in the spring of 2017; and to the two anonymous reviewers for their insightful remarks on my book manuscript.

To obtain images and publication permissions during a worldwide pandemic was no easy task, but I was able to count on the solidarity and guidance of many. I am grateful to Tricia Starks, Catherine Gran, Riccardo Cepach at the Svevo Museum in Trieste, and Corbin Apkin at the National Archive for their generosity; to Marco Franceschetti, Francesca Tramma, Margherita Zanoletti, and Natalia Plagmann (née Klimova) for their assistance in retrieving high-resolution images and documents from archives and special collections in the midst of the winter holidays. "Copyright is not for the squeamish," the research librarian Janice Pilch warned me at the onset of my search for publication permissions. I thank her, Thomas Keenan at the Princeton University Libraries, and Marina Balina for their invaluable help navigating that unfamiliar terrain and obtaining all the necessary information through all kinds of channels. Special thanks also go to Michael McBain for his assistance with medical terminology and to Dexter Palmer, Tess Rankin, and Manuel Vignati for their work on the more technical aspects of manuscript preparation. Philip Leventhal and his team at Columbia University Press expertly guided this book to publication.

The year 2020 was exceptional for me in many ways—pandemic, pregnancy, parenthood, publications—with my brainchild and my newborn son, Alessandro, coming along around the same time, while the world as we knew it was being disfigured by natural and human-made disaster. No achievement would have been possible without my loved ones, near and far, and I am indebted to them.

Earlier iterations of portions of chapter 4 appeared in "Narrative Time and the Thyroid: Hormone Secretions and Storytelling in Italo Svevo's *Doctor Menghi's Drug*," in "Narrative and Medicine," ed. Elena Fratto, special issue of *Enthymema* 16 (2016): 60–73 (revised version included here with permission from the journal); "Endocrine Glands and the Anthropocene: Metabolic Storytelling in Mikhail Bulgakov's *Heart of a Dog*," in "Anthropocene and Russian Literature," ed. Alec Brookes and Elena Fratto, double special issue of *Russian Literature* 114–115 (June–July 2020): 45–65 (revised version included here with permission from Elsevier).

INTRODUCTION

The field of medicine generates a remarkable variety of stories belonging to different genres. Among them, case reports, journal articles, public-health campaigns, patient blogs, and educational websites are but the tip of the iceberg. One can detect an inherent narrative structure in the way medical knowledge is formulated and transmitted, in medical practice as a set of protocols and procedures, in the reasons for which research is funded and furthered, and in the goals that medical specialists and public-health officials set for their societies. One can argue that patients tell their stories (their anamneses or chief complaints) to physicians, nurses, and paramedics in hopes of having them retold by these specialists in better-informed iterations that are likely to seem more plausible to other medical professionals (diagnoses, case reports, clinical charts). Differential diagnoses are the result of the competing plots into which different specialists order a single set of symptoms and data; more broadly, patients, doctors, caregivers, insurance companies, pharmaceutical groups, legislators, and religious leaders all claim authorship and authority over matters of illness and healing. The ordering of scattered events and phenomena into causal-temporal chains is a cognitive necessity not only for the physician but also for any patients who wish to make sense of what they are experiencing by authoring a story and achieving that split of subjectivity established by the author-hero dichotomy. And in the case of long-course treatment with an uncertain outcome, such a "plot" is updated every step of the way—after each laboratory test, visit, or cycle of treatment. The contested notion of "patient empowerment" suggests something akin to a postcolonial gesture on the part of the patient, who strives to repossess a body that has been colonized by medicine and its language. As part of that gesture, patients google their diagnoses as soon as they receive them, learn to speak in technical language in order to be taken seriously and sound reliable, and reauthor the story of their illness in the form of blogs and autobiographies, which serve as a counterpoint to case reports and clinical charts. Governmental and political agendas often go hand in hand with public-health goals, whereby the state is described as a body that needs to be protected from infections that threaten it from the outside (otherness in the broadest sense) as well as from the social and societal illnesses that undermine it from the inside (nonconformism). As a result, invasive public-health campaigns regulate and micromanage citizens' everyday behavior, including the most private aspects of their lives. Diffused and segmented agency ensues, which is at times displaced onto nonhuman actors—be they prosthetics or other devices we host in our bodies—or attributed to chemicals that are either produced by our organisms, such as hormones, or introduced from the outside, such as pharmaceuticals.

While diagnostic labeling, medical tools, and pharmaceuticals leave traces on patients' bodies, those patients, in turn, as they move from one hospital room to the next, from registration to the physician's office or an ER cot, from the ER to the operating room, from a room in the ward to the surgical ICU, leave inscriptions that take disparate forms. They may include notes about the patients' chief complaints that the registration-desk staff enter into a template as patients talk, checked boxes in the self-assessment pain-scale form that patients fill out in the waiting area or the nurse types into a "computer on wheels" at the patients' bedsides, clinical charts, nursing assessments, anthropometric measurements, data reported from laboratory tests, insurance billing codes, and indexical images yielded by X rays, MRIs, and CT scans. Hospitals have been investing considerable resources into streamlining this information and creating order within these monstrous hypertexts composed of paratactic and heterogeneous bits and clusters of data, images, and fragmentary prose that are painfully redundant and at times even contradictory.

INTRODUCTION

The groundbreaking work of Rita Charon and other seminal texts in the field of the medical humanities have eloquently demonstrated that medicine—as a system of representation and a set of practices steeped in the times and cultures that produce it—can be especially productively mapped and comprehended with the rich apparatus of tools and definitions that are commonly applied to the production, transmission, and reception of literary texts or works of art.[1] No longer understood entirely within the hermeneutical domain of the *Erklären* (explanation), medicine emerges from that body of scholarship as belonging to the *Verstehen* (understanding), an ultimately interpretive discipline that relies on the sciences. Questions of authorship, plot construction, narrative time, space, and perspective constitute a privileged framework for analyzing the constellation of expressive forms that characterize a field—medicine and healthcare—that features delocalized epistemologies and a vast plurality of actors.[2]

This book builds on the assumption that the endeavor of plot building represents a necessity that is certainly cognitive and often also existential. Plot provides structure and meaning to the world that surrounds us and to our experience of it. In the words of Paul Ricoeur, plot constructs "meaningful totalities out of scattered events"[3] by ordering a set of otherwise unrelated elements into causal-temporal chains. By embracing this tenet of literary theory that has accompanied us since Aristotle, this book argues that authoring a story bestows a tremendous degree of agency on individuals, allowing them to turn standardized and reductive narratives on their heads and recast them on their own terms. In particular, literary texts are compelling because they undermine public and scientific narratives that seek to generalize about human bodies and human lives. This book examines literary works that were produced in Russia at the turn of the twentieth century and conceived in response and resistance to medical and public-health tenets of that epoch and in dialogue with other European cultures, especially those of France and Italy. Their authors and characters rub against the grain of official and seemingly unassailable biomedical truths by claiming their own agency in telling the story of mortality, illness, and well-being, whether it is a matter of personal or public health. And such agency, I argue, can be attained only through authorship by recasting the monolithic and inescapable narratives produced in the fields of medicine and public health in different terms—by manipulating and reversing narrative temporality, by transforming endings into new beginnings, by defamiliarizing established plots in order to question them profoundly, by reconfiguring hierarchies of humans vis-à-vis nonhumans. The aesthetic, ethical, and existential mandate of the authors and characters I examine in the pages that follow was to claim at once authorship, authority, and agency over the stories told about individual bodies and collectives. Each chapter analyzes a crisis of and challenge to human agency, one posed by no less than death and the prospect of death in chapters 1 and 2, by constrictive biopolitical discourse in chapter 3, and by nonhuman entities in chapter 4. In the face of such challenges, Fyodor Dostoevsky, Leo Tolstoy, Viktor Shklovskii, Jules Romains, Italo Svevo, and Mikhail Bulgakov complicate limited and limiting biomedical truths, put them in perspective, and undermine their undisputed authority. They do so by constructing plots, mobilizing time and perspective, articulating a plurality of voices, and exploring and expanding the semantic and aesthetic possibilities of words. In their indefatigable endeavor of storytelling as the act of attaining agency, those voices, which reach us from more than a century ago and belong to a cultural tradition largely understudied in the medical humanities, speak to major current debates in the field, extending beyond the cultural horizon of the texts and the intentions of their authors. In resounding tones, those voices address concerns such as the end of life, the question of "risk," the time horizon in long-course treatment with an uncertain outcome, biopolitics, and nonhuman entities in our bodies, in the process contributing fresh perspectives and insights.

Consider Bulgakov's novella *The Heart of a Dog* (1925, discussed in chapter 4 along with Italo Svevo's story "Doctor Menghi's Drug," 1904), at once a scathing satire of New Economic Policy–era Russian society and a cautionary tale against the biomedical experiments that the Bolshevik authorities were conducting with the help of scientists in all fields—from physiology to endocrinology—in order to forge the so-called New Soviet Person. This canonical text is generally interpreted along two exegetic lines—as anticommunist satire (the case of most Cold War–era literary scholarship) and as a variation on the Frankenstein theme. However, when we look closely at how a seemingly innocuous pituitary gland drives the unfolding of the plot—something we can detect only by examining the novella's style, structure, and semantic choices—in spite of all the plans made by the brilliant surgeon protagonist and by the state, unexpected insights emerge forcefully. We can discern how our current understanding of chemical imbalance, the microbiota, body ecologies, and nonhuman entities within the body is shaped and informed by the way perspective, temporality, and language are employed to describe these phenomena, which prompts us to reconsider our views on human and nonhuman agency. Most likely, Bulgakov, who articulated deep existential, ethical, and aesthetic concerns about official representations of the human and the social body in his epoch, could not have predicted the impact that his story would have on our current debates in the medical humanities. Today, a century after the publication of the novella, questions regarding nonhuman agency have been raised by the increasingly widespread use of mechanical body parts and devices (artificial limbs, cardiac defibrillators, hearing aids) and are at the center of debates in disability studies. These questions are further articulated in the recent reassessment of the biota (see, for instance, the renewed attention directed at the gut) and in the use of concepts such as "chemical imbalance" and "sugar blues" that are now widely employed by laypersons and health professionals alike. By the same token, examining the novella's relevance to medical humanities debates opens up a new interpretive avenue into that canonical text for literary scholars, one that hinges on nonhuman narrative agents in order to add new dimensions to Bulgakov's broader concerns about human agency in the new Soviet state.

That same unintended yet sizable impact on today's debates from texts penned in the late nineteenth and early twentieth centuries as an act of resistance to normative and seemingly objective scientific discourse of the times characterizes all of the literary works examined here. As described in chapter 1, Dostoevsky and Tolstoy expose and reject, on ethical grounds, the limits of deterministic approaches to the human condition backed up by positivistic science. Their powerful claims regarding what it means to be human, which uphold human agency and free will, weigh in forcibly on our current nature–nurture debate, especially in determining whether biological determinism or the social environment lies at the roots of certain syndromes and behavioral disorders. Chapter 2 stages Tolstoy's writing afflatus as the attempt to reach two major goals—to plumb the depths of human mortality and vulnerability and grasp the meaning of illness and death beyond unsatisfactory medical-biological definitions as well as to gain the illusion of control over the passage of time and exorcise his fear of death by developing an unparalleled mastery of narrative time and skillful management of his characters' and readers' expectations. That same obsession and necessity—at once existential and cognitive—to author one's story as a way to own it, honor it, and distill its meaning informs end-of-life protocols and procedures in our times and spurs reflections on what constitutes a good death by both doctors and patients, who often resort to Tolstoy, if only for thematic and ethical inspiration. The urgency to engage with temporality by constructing and sustaining plots that may develop over long and uncertain timeframes and thus to intervene in one's authorial agency to provide meaning and direction to otherwise overwhelming experiences characterizes those at genetic risk of developing a frightening illness, the so-called previvors. These potential patients resort to plot to come to terms with the risks and responsibilities entailed in the prospect of an undesirable ending. From the physician's perspective, the emplotment of events and phenomena in long-course treatment with an uncertain outcome is a constitutive component of oncology protocols to manage patients' expectations and time horizons, even if oncologists do not necessarily describe that important part of their work in terms of emplotment. As shown in chapter 3, both Jules Romains and Viktor Shklovskii wrote with the urgency of interwar public intellectuals who sought to lay bare the rhetoric of public-health campaigns in order to warn their readers against the state's control over citizens' bodies that went hand in hand with the rise of totalitarianism. Their defamiliarizing techniques empowered reader-citizens to step out of the plot that the state had constructed for them, to question public-health rhetoric and its scientific legitimization, and to formulate their own stories instead. Their active warning against biopolitics and state or corporate intervention in and surveillance of human bodies rings loud and clear in our time, as does their vehement exhortation to react to and resist dangerous and constrictive top-down distinctions between the normal and the pathological. We are prompted to reconsider the notion of "patient empowerment" as slippery and double-edged, and we are invited to analyze closely the rhetoric of medical and public-health discourse that can deeply influence our perception of being healthy or ill.

The wealth of literary texts written in Russia in the late nineteenth and early twentieth centuries in response to rapid, structural changes in the field of medicine and in the definition of health and illness makes that specific era and geographic area particularly fecund for my purposes. At the turn of the twentieth century, Europe witnessed a deep transformation in the medical episteme, procedures, and institutions, with groundbreaking advancements in diagnostics, prophylaxis, and therapeutics.[4] Not only was medicine defining itself as a profession, but what constituted medical *knowledge* was also rapidly changing. In the nineteenth century, medical discourse and practices evolved at different speeds in different regions. At the turn of the twentieth century, Russia was still largely a peripheral and modernizing European society that was responding to developments in the West in terms of both medical advancements and literary aesthetics. Russian authors and artists absorbed and reacted to the medical theories and discourse that were coming from western Europe and that Russian scientific institutions were quickly adopting.[5] Quantitative assessment tools had come to characterize the positivistic approach to the human body; large-scale wars and the resulting battlefield wounds provided a new impulse for the development of surgical techniques and pharmaceuticals; groundbreaking developments, from germ theory to the discovery of endocrine glands, contributed to redefining and redistributing agency in medicine; and, naturally, psychoanalysis, although it did not really take off in Russia until the 1920s, questioned the physician's authorship and previously undisputed perspective. Massive public-health campaigns that sought to regulate both the human organism and the state-as-body appeared in interwar Europe in tandem with new political systems and their totalizing rhetoric. The extraordinary advancements in the medical field that were taking place all over Europe coincided in Russia with times of rapid and profound political and social changes in which the human organism became the testing ground for the Soviet experiment and the utopias it was to bring about.[6]

Although offering a historical account of Russian medicine is clearly beyond the scope of this book, which firmly situates itself within the field of literary studies and literary theory, I rely on existing works by historians who have examined Russian and Soviet medicine and medical institutions as well as medicine, the body, and public-health discourse in connection with the rise of totalitarianism in the time period in which the works I investigate were produced—Dan Healey, Susan Gross Solomon, Frances Lee Bernstein, Nancy Frieden, Irina Sirotkina, and Nikolai Krementsov, on the one hand, and Giorgio Cosmacini, Ruth Ben-Ghiat, and David Horn, on the other. Histories of Russian medicine and medical institutions have detailed Russia's long-term scientific relationship with Germany, a country where Russian physicians often trained. German neurology, the rise of chemical-pharmaceutical groups, biomedicine, and the interwar medical discourse that emerged under Nazism are commonly addressed in historical accounts of Russian medicine in the late nineteenth and early twentieth centuries. The Vienna psychoanalytic tradition is sometimes mentioned as well, although Freudian psychoanalysis did not establish itself in Russia until decades after its emergence in the Mitteleuropean milieu.

It is not my intent to suggest an overarching teleology or to highlight points of origin of our current debates, but to examine powerful earlier iterations of today's most urgent questions. For this reason, I have chosen to conduct my inquiry along conceptual axes, which has prompted me to analyze less commonly studied connections between Russian literary works written in an era of deep transformations in medicine and texts from France and Italy.

The association between literature and medicine naturally brings psychoanalysis to mind. In the 1990s, literary theory devoted considerable attention to the process of meaning making at work in the so-called talking cure by scrutinizing the palimpsest of narrative voices that this remedy entails. This emphasis on authorship revealed the inescapable literariness of Sigmund Freud's works. More recent works that complicate the concept of "narrative reliability," originally formulated by Wayne Booth in *The Rhetoric of Fiction* (1961) to describe instances in which the author gives the reader hints to suggest that the narrator cannot be trusted, also draw on mental illness and autism-spectrum conditions to refine that category in literary studies—the narrator is sick or fallible rather than plain untrustworthy.[7] Examples include Alexander Luria's and Oliver Sacks's patient-characters as well as Christopher, the young adult protagonist in Mark Haddon's *The Curious Incident of the Dog in the Night-Time* (2003).[8] This side of the complex interconnections between literary theory and medicine has been addressed at length. In Russian literary studies, this vast and fascinating territory is explored in Angela Brintlinger and Ilya Vinitsky's edited volume devoted to literary representations of "madness and the mad in Russian culture"; Harriet Murav's book on Dostoevsky's revisiting of the Russian medieval tradition of the Holy Fool; Cathy Popkin's examination of early Russian psychiatric case histories (most notably on hysteria); and Rebecca Reich's work on psychiatry, literature, and dissent after Stalin.[9]

My choice not to address mental health springs in part from the fact that Freudian psychoanalytic practice became popular in Russia in only the 1920s,[10] whereas other western European trends were adopted quickly there—germ theory, vaccines, Gall's phrenology, pharmaceutical compounds, battlefield surgical procedures, and endocrinology. More crucially, my goal is to show that in fact it is not only the fields of psychology, neurology, and psychiatry that share imagery and structural features with the production of literary texts, as one might expect. Rather, the whole field of medicine and healthcare—understood as a complex system of practices, knowledge, procedures, and protocols—lends itself to be parsed and illuminated by the methodological apparatus of literary studies. By highlighting the stylistic patterns, tropes, and storytelling devices that are essential to the medical field, we can release additional meaning from literary texts and the processes, conditions, and goals that underlie their composition, transmission, and reception. This latter avenue represents one of largely untapped potential; to pursue it by introducing materials from Russian culture at the turn of the twentieth century affords us a new perspective on medical and storytelling practices alike.

The examination of storytelling as agency in the face of deterministic and constrictive official narratives about the body makes literary texts from more than a century ago speak with arresting force to discussions of modern-day medical humanities. By the same token, an interdisciplinary, medical-humanities approach to literary works reveals new interpretive avenues for Slavic literary scholars and changes our understanding of well-known texts and cultural phenomena from the turn of the twentieth century.[11] By looking at specific authors and their texts, most of which are canonical and "dusty," in conjunction with the medical definitions, theories, and procedures with which they engage in great depth, we can reveal new facets of their aesthetics. By reading Tolstoy through contemporary notions of "risk," oncological protocols in revealing prognoses, and the concept of "previvors," we cast new light on the author's celebrated mastery over narrative time. By examining Romains's play *Knock* and Shklovskii's writings from the mid- and late 1920s through the prism of institutionalized medical rhetoric, we see signature characteristics of the two authors' aesthetics—unanimism and defamiliarization, respectively—taking on new meaning. When we read Bulgakov's novella through the lens of gland grafting and metabolism, his discussion of agency suddenly acquires broader, existential implications, thus emerging as more layered and richer than is recognized in traditional readings of *The Heart of a Dog* as anti-Soviet satire.

The methodology of this book is bifocal, the analysis constantly moving between the medical humanities today and Russian culture at the turn of the twentieth century as well as between literary tropes and devices, on the one hand, and medical practice, discourse, and policies, on the other. Two concepts from Russian literary theory—"defamiliarization" (*ostranenie*) and "outsideness" (*vnenakhodimost'*)—inform my inquiry, which aims to highlight structural patterns and stylistic and aesthetic traits shared by these seemingly unrelated epochs and epistemes. As the Russian formalists maintained, defamiliarization is the main goal of artists and literary scholars.[12] This book sheds a radically new light on questions, practices, phenomena, and texts that are familiar to both scholars of Russian and comparative literature and scholars of the medical humanities. "Outsideness," according to Mikhail Bakhtin, is a factor of utmost importance in the study of cultures because "it is only in the eyes of *another* culture that foreign culture reveals itself fully and profoundly."[13] In the mutually productive dialogues this study advances, literary aesthetics and the field of medicine can observe and illuminate one another in powerful and generative ways.

To foreground the conceptual juxtaposition of literature and medicine along the axes of specific topics—from death and dying to "risk" and potential prognoses, from public-health rhetoric to the body's porosity with respect to prostheses and nonhuman organisms—each chapter of this book examines literary texts alongside medical concepts or procedures. From chapters 1 and 2, which discuss individual, discrete bodies, we move in chapter 3 to the collective and the social, the state-as-body understood as a continuum of all citizens' bodies, regulated by legislators through pervasive public-health campaigns. From there, in chapter 4 the discussion moves beyond the human to include nonhuman actants. Although no overarching teleology is implied, the overall analysis tracks a switch in narrative agency as we move from one chapter to the next. In chapter 1, which analyzes endings and postmortem examinations along with treatises from Paul Broca and Cesare Lombroso, Dostoevsky's *Brothers Karamazov*, and Tolstoy's *Resurrection*, the surgeon is the sole author because the body is dead and therefore voiceless. In chapter 2, previvors, who are potential patients, claim authorship and authority over a story that is steeped in the contingency of "risk" and thus shaped by a constantly shifting time horizon. There, I read previvor Masha Gessen's book *Blood Matters* and Tolstoy's works *Anna Karenina* and *The Death of Ivan Ilych* alongside the notions of time horizon and virtual plot in long-course treatment and serialized narratives. Agency bestowed by authorship is no longer individual but becomes collective, diffused, and refracted in chapter 3 and its discussion of public-health campaign rhetoric—real in the Soviet propaganda play *When the Babka Treats the People, She Ruins Them* and fictional in Jules Romains's *Doctor Knock, or the Triumph of Medicine*, both read alongside public-health campaigns and pharmaceutical advertising. Finally, in chapter 4, in which I discuss Bulgakov's *The Heart of a Dog* and Svevo's "Doctor Menghi's Drug" in the context of posthuman theories, narrative agency spills beyond the boundaries of the human and is negotiated with nonhuman agents. Agency claimed through authorship thus emerges as the book's through line or leitmotiv, and the four chapters can be seen as the four movements of that symphony. This order of chapters follows a structural progression, which is especially well suited for a transhistorical inquiry, while the texts and phenomena analyzed follow a chronological order. I chose this arrangement not because I wish to suggest historical causality but because intertextuality and literary evolution make it more productive to discuss Bulgakov after Tolstoy and not vice versa.

There is no doubt that health and healthcare are global phenomena. The medical humanities have been somewhat slow in acknowledging the planetary scale of its traditional questions and concerns. The field is still overwhelmingly Anglophone in scope and would benefit immensely from different cultural perspectives. As a Slavist and comparatist, I introduce texts that belong to my fields of expertise, and I hope that other non-Anglophone traditions will soon be brought into the conversation as well. Social historians and public-health researchers have turned to Tolstoy in their discussions of the cultural history of death and its accompanying rituals;[14] neurologists, including Oliver Sacks, and psychoanalysts have devoted attention to Dostoevsky's epilepsy and his characters' mental health and neurodiversity;[15] generations of Western physicians have read Anton Chekhov's medical stories, which William Carlos Williams admired.[16] Beyond those three macroareas, however, there seems to be little to no awareness of the Russian tradition. The medical humanists who have written on those authors are generally not literary scholars, nor are they Slavists, so their analysis inevitably relies on translations.

The examination of texts and phenomena from time periods and cultural traditions other than the ones I have chosen may have served my inquiry just as well. Russian culture can certainly be set in productive dialogue with traditions other than the French or the Italian. The structural and conceptual comparisons chosen for this study are those that work best to illustrate my points and articulate my argument. The cross-disciplinary and transhistorical interconnections that this book highlights contribute to current debates in both the medical humanities and the Russian and comparative literature. Other cultures, too, can be set fruitfully in dialogue with Russian culture, especially within the framework of a comparative cultural and epistemological analysis. This study encourages and lays the groundwork for more research informed by such a methodological approach.

Chapter One

THE GRAND FINALE
Death as the Revelatory Ending

It was November 24, 1959, and Boris Eikhenbaum, a leading figure of the Russian formalist school of the 1910s and 1920s, was giving the introductory talk to a play by Anatolii Mariengof at the Leningrad House of Writers (Dom pisatelei). Eikhenbaum was replacing the previously designated speaker, Igor' Gorbachëv, who was stuck in Riga, and the audience looked quite disappointed by this change in the program. Decades of deep and abrupt transformations on the political and cultural scene as well as the end of the formalist enterprise, despite leaving Eikhenbaum's prestige unchanged, had still pushed him to the periphery of the writers' association. Given the mood of the audience, Eikhenbaum decided to cut down his speech substantially. He talked for about fifteen minutes and closed his intervention by remarking that the most crucial virtue of a speaker is the ability to understand when it is time to conclude.

As somebody who had devoted the first half of his career to revealing the formal features in literary texts and their function in literary evolution, Eikhenbaum was aware of when and how the ending should occur and of the ways to build up to it effectively. He had discussed this specific issue in his essay *O. Henry and the Theory of the Short Story* (*O. Genri i teoriia novelly*, 1925). For instance, he points out the differences between short and long literary forms in the way a story ends, and he celebrates O.

Henry as a master of short-story writing by virtue of his well-crafted closures:

> By its very essence, the story, just as the anecdote, amasses its whole weight *toward the ending*. Like a bomb dropped from the airplane, it must speed downwards so as to strike with its war-head full-force on the target.... Short story is a term referring exclusively to plot, one assuming a combination of two conditions: *small* size and *plot impact on the ending*. Conditions of this sort produce something totally distinct in aim and devices from the novel.... The culmination of the main line of action must come somewhere *before* the ending. Typical for the novel are "epilogues"—false endings, summations setting the perspective or informing the reader of the *Nachgeschichte* of the main characters (*cf. Rudin, Voyna i mir* [*War and Peace*]).... [T]he short story, on the contrary, gravitates expressly toward maximal unexpectedness of a finale concentrating around itself all that has preceded. In the novel there must be a descent of some kind after the culmination point, whereas it is most natural for a story to come to a peak and stay there. The novel is a long walk through various localities with a peaceful return trip assumed; the short story—a climb up a mountain the aim of which is a view from on high.
>
> ... [F]or O. Henry this quality of the unexpected constitutes the very heart of the construction and bears a perfectly specific character. His endings are not merely a surprise or contrary to expectation, they appear in a sort of lateral way, as if popping out from around the corner; and it is only then that the reader realizes that certain details here and there had hinted at the possibility of such an ending.... [T]he ending not only serves as the dénouement but also discloses the true nature of the intrigue, the real meaning of all that has occurred.[1]

Eikhenbaum concluded his speech at the House of Writers promptly and with witty remarks on timing and endings; he went back to his seat in the audience, next to his daughter's, and as the applause ended, he died, reclining his head on her shoulder,[2] as though loosely following a script he had outlined in his literary scholarship and in his very last words. The whole scene could well have been authored by O. Henry: all elements tend toward the climactic moment of the powerful finale, which sheds new light upon those events that have preceded and gradually prepared it, in a sophisticated construction.

Moreover, Eikhenbaum's death, in which the scholar seems to embody his own theoretical principles in a powerful synthesis, may well be read as the ultimate example of what Aage Hansen-Löve defines as "formal behavior": not only did formalism and formalist critics make their way into the literary production of their time, both as authors and as characters, but the formal method was also internalized by its creators on a deeply existential level, which blurred the borders between life and the concepts of the formalists' literary theories.[3] In a move analogous to the so-called structural behavior of the Tel Quel group in France in the 1960s, Russian formalists often described their lives in strictly theoretical terms: "in reality there is no *siuzhet*, but only *fabula*" (Shklovskii, *Tret'ia fabrika*); "life became an artistic device" (Eikhenbaum, *O chtenii stikhov*); "our current life has no *siuzhet*" (Shklovskii, *O Pil'niake*).[4]

Death indeed is a plot trigger, a prime mover of story lines; it allows for the possibility of authorship by suggesting ways in which events may be ordered in causal-temporal chains. By virtue of this epistemological function, death brings together medicine and theories of narrative in powerful ways, as the circumstances and the framing of Eikhenbaum's "ending" seem to illustrate. This chapter draws on established theories of narrative in order to reveal the ways in which death, be it real or fictionally staged, creates the conditions for an ordering, a structuring, of signs and events into a coherent story line by allowing the clinician to examine the body with an acute gaze and steady hands. The exploration of the body's interiority casts a retrospective light on the course and development of diseases, on the "backstory" that lies behind superficial symptoms, but also on bodily configurations, functions, and discrete parts. The discussion of death as an event that bestows sense on what has previously occurred, of the unmatched revelatory power it derives from its irreversible character, of the way it illuminates gray areas in medical knowledge and settles diagnostic controversies by finally unveiling truths of which the body was the one and only repository during life leads to a brief incursion into contemporary case studies in the *New England Journal of Medicine*. This incursion aims to demonstrate the plot-building endeavor set in motion by death and evaluated in the light of the postmortem interrogation and intends to highlight how the medical-biological authorship of illness narratives largely continues to prevail in our times. I wed medical epistemology with categories from literary theory through the exploration of death as the ending. Michel Foucault has already given scholarly attention to these interdisciplinary correspondences in *The Birth of the Clinic* (1963), a groundbreaking study on the rise of the clinical method and its portentous consequences in the human sciences. Foucault's theories inform the final part of this chapter, which is devoted to the late nineteenth century as the celebratory moment of the clinical gaze in a true positivist spirit, with readings of Paul Broca and Cesare Lombroso, on the one hand, and of Dostoevsky's and Tolstoy's responses to Broca's and Lombroso's medical approaches, on the other hand—an overview that is more thematic than stylistic or structural. Throughout the chapter, the analysis of sources belonging to distinct geographic areas highlights epoch- and culture-specific inflections of one and the same emplotment process, which features the physician—or the writer who anatomizes and explores fictional bodies—as the sole storyteller.

Not only does the event of death reorder past events into new hierarchies and causal-temporal chains, as this chapter aims to show, but it also actively shapes the unfolding of the future and, interestingly, is amenable to numerous "emplotting" solutions, as Hayden White would define them.[5] The event of a death or of multiple deaths often determines the future trajectory of an individual, a family, a community, a state. An obvious example is provided by mourning practices, more- or less-elaborate rituals that are automatically set in motion when somebody passes away: they allow for meaning building as through them a community makes sense of its identity by taking stock and determining goals. In a similar fashion, a will or informal requests or instructions voiced by a dying person during a deathbed speech—a moment that encompasses past, present, and future—can deeply influence the course of events for years after the death of the person who expressed them. The medical anthropologist Cheryl Mattingly builds on this concept when she contends that these plots not only anticipate future events but also determine how those events will be understood as they unfold.[6] A line from the Italian director Marco Bellocchio's film *The Wedding Director* (*Il regista di matrimoni*, 2006), "In Italy the dead rule," underlines the binding power of the dead person's will, which forecloses the goals and desires of those who survive. Bellocchio's provocative statement pales in comparison to the official proposal advanced in the spring of 2016 by Aleksandr Ageev, the director of the Russian Institute of Economic Strategy (Institut ekonomicheskikh strategii RAN), a major research institution. Ageev proposed to extend to the twenty-seven million Russian citizens who died during World War II the right to vote in all elections; they would do so by proxy through their families and progeny. Because those deceased individuals had been crucial to the rescue and growth of their country, they should continue to influence every turn in its present and future trajectory.[7] Addressing this phenomenon, Mikhail Epstein has coined the term *necrocracy* (*nekrokratiia*).[8] Eccentricities aside, the complex meaning-making process that death generates is acknowledged by Arthur Kleinman in *The Illness Narratives* when he argues that "death is an awesome process of making and remaking meaning through which we come to constitute and express what is most uniquely human and our own."[9]

If death has plot-building power over the past and the future, it should also be noted that the very process of dying lends itself to a process of emplotment. With the establishment of intensive-care units and with the advanced medical technology available in our hospitals, the event of death allows for competing descriptions, a cluster of different narratives, each springing from a specific agenda or ethical standpoint. Whereas determining the moment when death occurred was a straightforward process until after the 1950s, today that moment has to be picked quite arbitrarily along the continuum of dying. When a patient is put on life support and kept alive for an undetermined period of time, the family, authorities, religious groups, insurance companies, organ-transplant supporters can have their say, and as of now there is no unified procedure to abide by but instead quite a few, each equally legitimate and based on a different definition of "death." In order to sidestep this hurdle, physicians have had to coin and precisely define concepts such as "irreversible coma"; ad hoc committees have been formed to create a common set of criteria to determine what counts as death; and conceptually problematic if not contradictory entities, such as "brain-dead bodies" and "living cadavers," still pose numerous questions, both philosophical (the Cartesian split between body and mind seems to be still at work) and ethical.[10] Brain death and cardiopulmonary death can surpass each other in importance depending on the legislator. Not only have discursive practices been introduced in both medicine and law to define the status of death, but after the introduction of organ transplant, protocols and procedures are now followed and enacted, not unlike theater scripts, to determine with legal certainty that the patient is dead but that the person's organs are still alive. To describe such a convoluted process, historians of medicine have coined the phrase *choreographed death*. An example of choreographed death is provided in a *New York Times Magazine* article:

> To authorize D.C.D. [donation after cardiac death], doctors must follow a strict procedure. Amanda would be taken, technically alive, to an operating room, where her breathing tube would be removed. If her breathing ceased naturally and her heart stopped quickly (within an hour), she would be moved to an adjacent room and [Dr.] Kleinman would count off precisely five minutes, during which time Amanda would be prepped for surgery with antiseptics and surgical drapes, while Kleinman carefully watched for signs of a returning heartbeat. If there were none, Amanda would be declared legally dead; the stoppage would then be considered "irreversible." Before her organs were seriously damaged by the lack of oxygen (every minute counts), the surgeons would rapidly open Amanda's torso and remove them for transplant.[11]

All of these procedures are dictated by conventions and are therefore arbitrary; the way death is defined, enacted, and described is often a result of a negotiation among conflicting actors, each with a different agenda, each with a different narrative. As the scope of this analysis is death's emplotment of the past, which is, however, never disjointed from its emplotment of the present and the future, it is now time to return to our opening parallel between death and endings and to address narrative theories on closure and finitude.

As literary theorists have consistently argued from the fourth century BCE (Aristotle) to today (Genette, Ricoeur, Booth, Brooks, Mink), plot provides a narrative with an underlying structure, which defines stories and experience as unfolding over time. In other words, plot constructs "meaningful totalities out of scattered events"[12] by ordering a set of otherwise unrelated elements into causal-temporal chains. In *Reading for the Plot* (1984), Peter Brooks defines narrative as "one of the large categories or systems of understanding that we use in our negotiations with reality, specifically ... with the problem of temporality."[13] Narrative truth rests not on actual events alone but also on closure: the ending of stories gives significance to previously unnoticed details and coherence to the whole story in retrospect, as Eikhenbaum points out in his essay on O. Henry.

Not only is medicine one of the fields that most remind us about our mortality, but its daily practices—such as tracking the trajectory of a disease, investigating its causes, and trying to predict how the clinical picture is expected to progress, or how the "story" will unfold—amply characterize the discipline as steeped in temporality. Because clinical thinking and diagnostic reasoning depend on time sequences and suggest causal links, they can be conceived of as fundamentally narrative enterprises, with the clinician as the sole author.

Although temporality is the founding pillar of any narrative, one should not underestimate the spatial dimension as its complementary component. Paul Ricoeur identifies two distinguishing features of plot: succession and configuration.[14] Succession, on the one end, inscribes all the events and threads of a story within a timeline, and as such it is closely engaged with temporality. Configuration, on the other end, is related to spatial knowledge and metaphorics, and it can be seen as making sense of the world through the mutual relationship (or the mutual position) of different elements in a given moment. In modern medicine, configuration corresponds to a snapshot assessment of the patient's condition and of the progress of the disease—in other words, to the clinical picture.[15] With an understanding of these concepts, we can now direct our analytical gaze to the process by which death allowed physicians and surgeons to shed light on these two main tenets of plot—the temporal and the spatial, succession and configuration—in the late nineteenth century.

SUCCESSION: STORYTELLING EX POST FACTO AND THE NARRATIVE STRUCTURE OF THE CPC

> It is a capital mistake to theorise before one has data. Insensibly one begins to twist facts to suit theories, instead of theories to suit facts.
>
> —ARTHUR CONAN DOYLE, "THE ADVENTURES OF A SCANDAL IN BOHEMIA"

Cesare Lombroso, Paul Broca, and all the clinicians and criminal anthropologists of their times extensively produced and heavily relied on case reports, which constituted the largest portion of clinical writing, for the sake of the formulation and transmission of medical knowledge. The case report as a genre had been around since Hippocrates, and the detailed classification of diseases begun in the seventeenth century and later described by Foucault drew on the case reports of Thomas Sydenham (1624–1689) and his followers. Case taking, however, did not become a systematic practice until clinical institutions and medical schools manifested their need to produce and codify a professional discourse.

In his article on the "humanitarian narrative" (1989), the historian Thomas W. Laqueur brings the clinical report, the autopsy, the parliamentary inquiry, and the realist novel under a unifying genre label and points out that these kinds of writings developed and flourished around the same time in a rising trajectory that began in late eighteenth century and reached its highest point in the late nineteenth century.[16] Another historian, Carlo Ginzburg, further reinforces the analogy between medical writings and one of the most realistic literary subgenres, the nineteenth-century detective story, in "Clues: Roots of an Evidential Paradigm" (1986). Both are informed by the "evidential paradigm" that, according to Ginzburg, had characterized medical semiotics well before the humanities adopted it.[17]

Whereas at the turn of the twentieth century literary evolution led the realist novel to extinction, the case report as a genre has persisted until our times. Although twentieth-century debates on the legitimacy of generalization from an individual to a whole population have gradually confined the case report to accounts of the rare or the new, its structure, as taught to medical students—first, symptoms or complaints; second, signs or objective manifestations found during a physical examination; third, laboratory and other findings—has not changed since the 1890s. A celebration of diagnostic reasoning and a cognate of the realist novel, the case report presents its own narrative implications. To examine how death illuminates the element of succession (as opposed to configuration) in plot construction, I focus on a specific subgenre of the case report, one that always features death as the main character and a catalyst of storytelling, using the "clinical-pathological conference" section in the *New England Journal of Medicine* as a typical example.

Richard Cabot instituted the section of the *New England Journal of Medicine* entitled "Case Records of the Massachusetts General Hospital" in 1910. Even today, in a journal that presents cutting-edge medical research in the driest and most codified style, this section, which stands out for its idiosyncratic genre, still persists. Although its layout has evolved over the decades, with the addition of section titles, with more and more sophisticated attachments, including videos accessible in the online version, and with a constant tweaking of the patient description in accordance with rapidly changing privacy policies, the main structure has remained almost unchanged.

The clinical-pathological conference (CPC) is conceived as a word-by-word transcription of the academic event that bears the same name. In a form that highly resembles the script of a drama, it describes the process of diagnostic reasoning with all the actors involved and in all its stages. The names of all the physicians are reported in italics before their direct speech, and their interaction is captured in full, with the illusion of a one-to-one narrative-time-to-real-time ratio. The conclusion toward which the text is headed is an ultimate, finalized diagnosis.

A puzzling, distinctive medical case—that is, one that from a literary perspective is "eventful" (as Yuri Lotman would define it) and "narratable"—opens the section and allows for the plot to unfold. A very short description is given of what has taken place. For instance: "An American student of twenty-four entered March 26, 1923, complaining of pain and dyspnea," or, more recently, "A 34-year-old man was brought to the emergency department at this hospital because of multiple traumatic injuries that he sustained when a bomb exploded while he was watching the 2013 Boston Marathon."[18] This part is presented in a succinct fashion by an unspecified narrator, who does not correspond to any of the actors involved, as in a voice-over. In later issues of the *Journal*, where the different subparts of the CPC are labeled, this part is entitled "Presentation of Case." After the opening, a quite wordy and not-so-dynamic play begins. The two main parts here are "Differential Diagnosis" and "Pathological Discussion." The former is authored by an expert unfamiliar with the patient and identified by title and last name (i.e., "Dr. Richard Cabot") and provides a number of viable diagnoses for the case. Most times this section offers one diagnosis on which those who have given medical assistance to the patient have reached consensus, a second diagnosis given by the expert, and sometimes a third one offered by residents or medical students. This part of the CPC provides in fact a wonderful opportunity to medical students from all over the world to try their luck and gain visibility. It is however the anatomopathologist who has the last word, after cutting the body open and revealing how things really went.

The clinical consultant enters the scene in medias res and tries to solve the puzzle by offering the best course of investigation and treatment—that is, by emplotting the available data in the way that makes the most sense. Details given in the case presentation may be relevant, but they may also be misleading. For instance, in case 9433, "An American barber of sixty-two entered July 21, 1923, complaining of pain in the stomach," how crucial are the patient's profession, his nationality, his age? Or in case 32-2006, about a three-year-old girl who was admitted to the hospital because of fever "after a visit to Africa," how fundamental should one deem the patient's age, gender, and recent trip to Africa?[19] As if in a detective story, the expert weighs all these elements in making emplotment choices that are assessed against the foil of how the medical staff at Massachusetts General Hospital actually proceeded in that case and that also provide an assessment of that course of action. The "clinical diagnosis," arrived at consensually, is given right afterward in a very laconic fashion—usually in one or two sentences (i.e., "Bronchopneumonia. Septicemia, staphylococcus")—and it is followed by the clinical expert's opinion ("Dr. Richard C. Cabot's Diagnosis: Bronchopneumonia"). After further discussion of the pathology by local clinicians, the text concludes with the part titled "Anatomical Diagnosis."[20] There is no metareflection, no moral to these narratives, which are meant to be educational tools as well as appraisals of the brilliant inductive reasoning clinicians display in challenging cases. The former aspect was emphasized by the editorial as early as 1923, when the journal was facing the threat of the discontinuance of the case reports:

> Too often in current medical literature we get accounts of brilliant successes, rather than of failures in diagnosis and treatment, which are of far higher educational value. Harbors are made safer for mariners not by records of prosperous voyages, but by buoying the dangerous reefs and sunken ledges that have caused disasters. If for nothing else, these Case Records are of exceptional value because of their honest acknowledgment of mistakes. In them one may either follow step by step the reasoning of the diagnosticians, or with the evidence that was in their possession he may make his own independent diagnosis. In either case, on turning the page,

he has before his eyes the autopsy findings.... The complete indexes of each volume make it possible, where one fears a fatal malady, to compare his patient's history and symptoms with the records of cases of the dreaded disease. This is as often a comfort as otherwise; for our fears as well as our hopes are often misleading.[21]

However, the structural detail that is most relevant to my present analysis is the settling, finalizing function of the part titled "Anatomical Diagnosis." After the whole discussion, it is for the anatomopathologist and nobody else to unveil the truth by cutting the body open. This has remained unchanged over the past hundred years: the postmortem examination provides the final authorial word on illness narratives, despite the supposedly rising importance of the patient's perspective. What has changed is the much lower frequency of cases ending with the death of the patient. The evolving subtitle of the CPC section in the journal speaks to this change: until May 1943, it was "Ante-Mortem and Post-Mortem Records as Used in Weekly Clinico-Pathological Exercises," and it clearly stated a juxtaposition between two distinct diagnostic realms; from then until July 2003, the subtitle was simply "Weekly Clinicopathological Exercises"; since then, the section has had no subtitle at all.

One could advance many hypotheses to explain this progression: advanced medical technology certainly makes it possible for diseases to be correctly diagnosed through the mere removal of a piece of tissue and to be cured in time; in addition to that, anthropologists or historians of medicine, such as Philippe Ariès, would probably argue that this shift is also due to an increasing denial of the final event in life that is considered a medical failure in our society, death. Valuable accounts of this fascinating debate can be found in the specialized literature.

From my point of view and for the sake of this analysis, the CPC, in both its traditional and its present form, represents a contest and a superb exercise in the emplotment of a medical narrative, in which each of the involved physicians superimposes a unifying story on the elements available, with death allowing for the release of that additional, ultimate, and previously concealed meaning that confirms, modifies, or dismisses all the previously assumed plotlines. This element is worth examining by virtue of its interesting narratological implications.

The CPC engages the conventional features of both historical and literary writing—that is, of narrative—in the fullest sense. However, far from questioning the reliability of the narrator and the unsettling indeterminacy of interpretation, the format of these case reports suggests that there is only one "correct" emplotment towering above all others and against which all others are measured. Far from fostering the proliferation of meanings, the exercise aims to narrow the margin of error and ambiguity and to quickly move from hypotheses to a firm diagnosis that only death can help attain. Differential diagnoses are given in order to make the case more engaging and to showcase the brilliant inductive reasoning of the physician-actors, but in the end one specific explanation represents the efficient ideal in the eyes of the medical community, embodied by the transparent, effaced narrator who occupies the outermost narrative frames and authors both the opening and the "addendum."

If medical cases are socially and biologically constructed—as will be particularly evident in the discussion of Cesare Lombroso, Paul Broca, and Jean-Martin Charcot later in this chapter—then the reliability of even their ostensibly objective narrators should be questioned, and so should the conclusions they draw. Fiction and the medical case report are clearly two different genres, which serve different purposes and are intended for different audiences. However, when we consider the omniscient author of the CPCs as a history writer, we have to come to terms again with Hayden White's argument in *Metahistory* (1973), which reveals the arbitrariness of the choices history writers make in producing their accounts.

In Henry Fielding's novel *Tom Jones* (1749), the reader stumbles upon the following statement by the narrator: "I am not writing a system, but a history, and I am not obliged to reconcile every matter to the received notions concerning truth and nature."[22] The crux of the problem lies right in this remark. The physician-narrator is not in the position to make a statement along those lines because every "matter" needs to be "reconciled" or to be assigned a function in the diagnostic process. The case report has to default necessarily to an unproblematic narrative, which looks more like a detective story, where every detail makes sense in light of the solution, with no room for indecision. In the case report's clearly narrative structure vis-à-vis its rigid refusal of emplotment as an open-ended process, which lends itself to questioning and is entangled in myriad equally valuable interpretive endeavors, lies the contradiction of the case study as scientific prose as well as its complexity and fascination as a genre.

CONFIGURATION: MEASURE FOR MEASURE

The (Literally) Speechless Patient in Late Nineteenth-Century Neurology

In *The Birth of the Clinic*, Foucault indicates the seventeenth century as the epoch in which the early modern medical episteme is gradually overturned and replaced by a new system of representation characterized by abstract, quasi-botanical classification. Foucault then outlines the transition from that new episteme to eighteenth-century medicine as a "grammar of signs" and then to the clinical method, which rises and establishes itself in the nineteenth century and which constitutes the primary focus of his analysis. In describing the surgeon as a reader and an author/authority, Foucault reveals the profound epistemological implications of the clinical gaze cast on the dissected body. No reading is objective and unbiased, Foucault tells us, and the clinic as an institution where a number of interests intersect (medical research, state legislation, social control) "owes its real importance to the fact that it is a reorganization in depth, not only of medical discourse, but of the very possibility of a discourse about disease."[23]

The clinic inaugurates a new perception of the body, a new use of language, new dynamics among disease, life, and death. Foucault entangles illness in many different discourses and outlines for it a picture in which structures are spatial, determinations are causal, phenomena are anatomo-physiological. In ways previously unknown, the clinical gaze determines with uncontested rigor the definition of illness and the normal/pathological distinction, generates power dynamics, and shapes the healing space. It unmakes and remakes the world. Among the most crucial practices available to physician-readers and their trained eyes, the postmortem examination occupies a prominent position in Foucault's argument: "The constitution of pathological anatomy at the period when the clinicians were defining their method is no mere coincidence: the balance of experience required that the gaze directed upon the individual and the language of description should rest upon the stable, visible, legible basis of death. This structure, in which space, language, and death are articulated—what is known, in fact, as the anatomo-clinical method—constitutes the historical condition of a medicine that is given and accepted as positive."[24] If finitude is a structure in which "space, language and death are articulated," the postmortem examination becomes the privileged tool for the formulation and the advancement of medical knowledge. In this picture, the patient's voice is silenced, and the clinician retains full authorship over the illness narrative.

In the history of neurology, the last quarter of the nineteenth century represents a golden age characterized by a positivist optimism toward unstoppable medical progress. Scientists embraced the machine model of the brain as an organ that operates in discrete functional parts.[25] In their renowned works on language loss and speech disorders, neurologists Carl Wernicke (1848–1905) and Paul Broca (1824–1880) took a spatial approach to the study of the brain and postulated and developed theories of cerebral localization:[26] language functions, in all their complexity, were supposedly controlled by one specific area of the brain. It is, of course, no accident that the same decades in which localization theory was established in neurology also witnessed the predominant role of cell theory in biology, atomic theories in physics, cellular pathology in medicine, and "idea particles" in psychology.[27] The prevailing approach to understanding a complex phenomenon consisted in breaking it down to its essential components; holism would develop only in the early twentieth century in response to this method.

The classificatory imperative of the time led to the proliferation of diagrams and to the establishment of the case study: patients, far from being considered in their individuality or "phenomenologically," with no prejudgment, were turned into an archive of cases, from which neurologists were to extract general norms and patterns to be applied for diagnostic purposes in a hermeneutic circle. Neurologists strived to find a "case that would provide a 'veritable schema' of a particular form of aphasia,"[28] and patients, deprived of their individuality, were considered little more than medical commodities.[29] Interestingly enough, in the study of speech disorders, patients' words were considered relevant only to determine the underlying pathology; no effort was made to understand what patients actually wished to convey. Aphasic patients were speechless in the broadest possible sense. As Anne Harrington points out, "In this non-dialogue, the final doctor–patient encounter generally occurred at the patient's autopsy, when the neurologist would check the accuracy of his predictions against the revealed physical state of pathology or injury in the patient's brain."[30] In the face of diseases that could not be cured, classificatory and diagnostic purposes came before any therapeutic goal, and dissection proved an irreplaceable tool for physicians to map the different areas of the brain and their mutual interactions as well as to learn about the origin and evolution of pathologies the dead individual had happened to be the host of. If we were to apply Ricoeur's definitions to that era of medical history, diagrams and the mapping of the brain show that "configuration" was the feature of plot that death revealed most vividly; "succession" and causality were derived from configuration.

An illuminating example of the era's predominant approach, heavily reliant on the postmortem examination, is provided by the case of Paul Broca's patient Lebrogne, more famously known as "Tan." Broca reports that Lebrogne was transported to the Bicêtre Hospital on April 11, 1861, and that "to the questions that I addressed to him the next day on the origin of his malady, he responded only with the monosyllable tan, repeated two times in sequence, and accompanied by a gesture of his left hand."[31] In a humiliating synecdoche, the patient is named after his pathological utterance, which in a clinical context encompasses his whole being and alone becomes his full identity. After the examination, "the probable diagnosis was therefore: original lesion in the left anterior lobe, propagated to the striate body of the same side. As for the nature of this lesion, everything indicated that it was a matter of a progressive, chronic softening, but extremely slow, for the absence of all phenomena of compression excluded the idea of an intracranial tumor."[32]

The eagerly awaited death of the patient occurs only six days later, and it allows Broca to finally prove or disprove his assumptions—literally to unveil the truth, confirm configurations that he had only assumed, and solve the mystery: "The patient died on 17 April, at eleven o'clock in the morning. The autopsy was done as soon as possible, that is to say, at the end of twenty-four hours."[33] Here follows a detailed description of the direction of the cuts and the progressive unveiling of interesting features of the brain as well as an account of the damaged organs and of how the disease had progressed spatially and temporally. These findings are then compared to the symptoms that the patient had shown when he was alive: "Having said this, it is impossible not to recognize that there had been a correspondence between the two anatomical periods and the two symptomological periods."[34] Everything that was assumed is now grounded in evidence; the surgeon is now able to make sense of all the symptomatic phenomena that manifested themselves in Tan while he was alive.[35]

In the diagnostic endeavors of late nineteenth-century neurology, death was the agent that allowed for an emplotment process, whereby surgeons, with their objectifying gaze and trained judgment, would determine the story one-sidedly. Whatever meaning patients might have conferred on their experiences was irrelevant. This was the time when photography as a diagnostic tool and as objective proof had just been introduced in the medical field (for instance, by Charcot in his Tuesday lessons on hysteria at the Salpêtrière), which further enhanced the importance of the surgeon's gaze and the reliance on sight as a privileged sensorial experience in medical research. Visual observation seemed to yield an unproblematic revelation of truth. The failure to grasp the limitations of this approach and its inevitable subjective charge laid the foundation for a shift in prominence from the communicative function of visual observation to its flip side—that is, an objectification of the patient, a scientific approach not unfamiliar to Cesare Lombroso.

Cesare Lombroso's "Social Anatomy" of Dostoevsky and Tolstoy

The theories of Cesare Lombroso (1835–1909), professor of forensic medicine and public hygiene at the University of Turin and later chair of psychiatry (1896), bear the mark of their times. Obsessed with quantitative data, classification, and standardization, Lombroso maintained that madness, genius, and criminality could be measured. Among other instruments, he used the craniograph devised by Paul Broca; the induction coil, derived from the work of Alessandro Volta, Luigi Galvani, Michael Faraday, and Heinrich Daniel Ruhmkorff, to measure sensitivity to electric discharges; and Thomas Edison's "electric pen" for graphological measurements. All throughout his career, Lombroso collected skulls and other anatomical specimens from all sorts of criminals, brigands' clothes, objects used by murderers, writing samples by criminals, and the wax death masks of convicts who died in prison. In 1898, he founded a museum of psychiatry and criminology in the anatomical institutes building of the university. His office was there as well, and the two areas—the workspace and the displayed collection—semantically complemented and illuminated each other. Today the Cesare

THE GRAND FINALE

Lombroso Museum of Criminal Anthropology, the result of valuable curatorial work, displays additional artifacts, including Lombroso's own skeleton, per his will. Lombroso's discoveries about the skull's internal configuration, which lie at the basis of his success but which were dismissed by the scientific community as ungrounded a few decades later, were achieved through countless postmortem examinations.

Among Lombroso's abundant scholarly production, the most relevant work is certainly *Criminal Man* (*L'uomo delinquente*, 1876), published in five editions that follow the evolution of the author's theories. Based on the observation of 3,839 criminals, the book meticulously describes physiognomic, bodily, and behavioral features of the delinquent person.[36] For instance, we learn that a few typical facial traits of criminals include a narrow forehead; an abnormal shape of the skull and asymmetry of the face; a receding chin; enormous frontal sinuses, orbits, and zygomata; bulky mandibles; prominent eyebrows; apelike features. Lombroso did not neglect the criminal behavior of children, plants (especially carnivorous plants), and animals (notable are his descriptions of the violent and criminal actions of Angora cats, male ants, and even doves, birds the reader would probably consider beyond suspicion).[37] Interesting also are the sections of the book devoted to criminal jargon, songs, and tattoos as well as graffiti on prison walls.[38] The language of criminals was treated as a symptom and manifestation of their biologically determined condition, not as words with their own meaning. In this respect, Lombroso's approach was not dissimilar to Broca's (lack of) attention to his aphasic patients' utterances.

All of the remarks that Lombroso based on his observations, set out in his thick volume and culminating in his theory of atavism, amounted to pure speculation and certainly would not have made him famous had it not been for an event that, in Lombroso's view, provided the one piece of evidence, the indisputable proof, of the scientific soundness of his analysis. In December 1870, the anatomy of the skull of a brigand, Giuseppe Villella, showed that the median occipital depression, which accommodates part of the cerebellum, was larger than normal. The wax calque of the cranium showed, instead of a regular posterior cranial fossa, "a perfectly regular trilobed cerebellum." This is how Lombroso described the moment when he saw that depression: "Like a vast plain beneath an infinite horizon, the problem of the nature of the criminal, which reproduced in our times the characteristics of the primitive man all the way down to the carnivores, was illuminated."[39] Because this specific feature appears in lemurs, rodents, and other mammals, Lombroso deduced that primitive biological traits had remanifested themselves in Villella, which undoubtedly constituted the primary cause of his criminal behavior. From that day forth, Lombroso kept Villella's skull right on his desk as the tangible proof of his scholarly success. It has been sitting there ever since, visible to the museum's visitors.

In 1908 in the cave site La-Chapelle-aux-Saints, France, a specimen of Neanderthal man was found in which the facial bones appeared to be preserved. Lombroso had a reconstruction of the face made on the basis of the published photograph. The collection of comparative anatomy in the Lombroso museum displays this and other anatomical specimens that were supposed to "show the presence of the brigand Villella's cranial anomaly in mammals evolutionarily distant from humans."[40]

Once more, the postmortem dissection seemed to Lombroso to provide the decisive proof of a theory he had previously inferred from observation of behavior and superficial traits. After the unveiling of that one characteristic that could generate a pattern and a classificatory criterion, Lombroso could hermeneutically move back to observation of physiognomies and behaviors to further confirm his theory (or to disprove it, provided this was even an option in his mind). In other words, once death had revealed the biological and anatomical bases of criminal behavior in the shape and conformation of a somewhat subhuman skull, then every time we encountered such cranial features shining through in a living person, we could label her or him potentially criminal with absolute certainty.

Lombroso's theory of atavism springs from the anthropologist's engagement with the fields of craniology, physiognomy—founded by Johann Kaspar Lavater (1741–1801) at the end of eighteenth century—and phrenology, developed by the German physician Franz Joseph Gall (1758–1828). Lombroso was also indebted to Charles Darwin's *The Origin of Species* (1859). Physiognomy postulated a correspondence between crime and facial features and other bodily characteristics. The skull had particular importance because the craniological research of that time assumed that crime is a form of behavior controlled by a specific part of the brain. These studies of the criminal mind and body, which retain little or no scientific importance today, lay at the core of criminal anthropology at the time, the basis of modern criminology.[41]

Lombroso coined the term *atavism* (from the Latin *atavus*, meaning "great-great-grandfather") to define the biological condition of people who fail to evolve all the way to a fully human state and therefore show physical features and behaviors that are typical of earlier stages of human evolution.[42] The first notable consequence of such a theory is that criminals can be scientifically differentiated from noncriminals. Furthermore, Lombroso argued in *Criminal Man*, we can distinguish between the born criminal, who is known by his anatomy, and the occasional criminal. Heredity is considered to play a decisive role. Although toward the end of his career Lombroso acknowledged that psychological and sociological factors could be of some relevance in the etiology of crime, criminal anthropometry remained the field that most informed his methodology: in a brusque turn away from previous theories of crime and punishment (most notably, those of Cesare Beccaria [1738–1794]), Lombroso argued that crime is the result of measurable causes, with no room left for free will. This raises the problem of responsibility (or, rather, the lack thereof) for a given crime and, consequently, questions regarding the meaning of punishment. Prison, Lombroso argued, has no effect on the born criminal. One could try treatment or opt for a death sentence because the criminal threatens society as a wild animal does. Born as a medical theory, atavism bears philosophical and legal implications, which expands the scope of Lombroso's work beyond its original fields (biology, psychiatry) into the social sciences. He, his disciple Enrico Ferri (1856–1929), and the other scholars in their circle can therefore be defined as "social anatomists."

Undoubtedly, death as an event allowed Lombroso to proceed in his medical emplotment quite considerably, for better or worse. From the point of view of narrative, the postmortem examination of skulls belonging to criminals allowed the scientist to take that further step along the hermeneutic circle that proved necessary for his career because it supposedly enabled him to determine the temperament of living people and the likelihood of their developing criminal behaviors on the basis of their anatomical features alone. Generalization and typologies, major components of Lombroso's method, made the task even easier.

Lombroso enjoyed prestige and popularity all over Europe, and this was initially due to the popularity of the German and Dutch translations of Ferri's essay on criminals in the arts, which, published in 1896, was based on Lombroso's theories and which drew the attention of those interested in criminology from a variety of perspectives, including a literary one. The interconnections between Lombroso's criminal anthropology and the literature of that time are worth exploring. In particular, Lombroso and his theories can be put in dialogue with the two main Russian writers of the late nineteenth century, Fyodor Dostoevsky (1821–1881) and Leo Tolstoy (1828–1910).

The figure of the artist fascinated Lombroso immensely. Literary production was the output of the writer's mind and therefore came second in importance to Lombroso. In *Genius and Insanity* (*Genio e follia*, 1864), he maintained that the genius and the madman represent two sides of the same neurological condition, degeneration, a state reached either through a regression along the phylogenetic arc or through arrested development at an earlier stage of evolution.[43] The latter description applies to the born criminal, whereas the former holds true for geniuses because their madness is considered a form of neurobiological compensation for intellectual overdevelopment. Postmortem examinations had revealed that geniuses and madmen possess similar cranial stigmata and other deviations. However, compared to a criminal's insanity, in the genius the evolutionary throwback is of modest proportions, and positive qualities are mixed with the degeneration of selected somatic organs. Examples of geniuses whose cranial asymmetry supposedly testified to such reverse evolution are Pericles, Kant, Dante, and Descartes.[44]

This theory alone was extraordinarily influential upon European literature. Max Nordau (1849–1923) dedicated his analytical work *Degeneration* (*Entartung*, 1892) to Lombroso, and the Pre-Raphaelite Brotherhood was among the literary circles that most famously incorporated this originally Lombrosian concept into their aesthetic. The reciprocity between the two fields was acknowledged by criminologists and writers alike. For instance, Émile Zola (1840–1902) declared himself heavily indebted to Lombroso's theories, saying that he constantly referred to *Criminal Man* during the composition of *La bête humaine* (1890), one of the twenty novels composing the Rougon-Macquart cycle (*The Rougon-Macquart: Natural and Social History of a Family under the Second Empire*, 1871–1893), the chief monument of French naturalism, characterized by a documentary, scientific approach to the description of human behavior and by sociobiological determinism as prevailing over free will. Lombroso, in turn, wrote an essay on Zola's novel, "*La bête humaine* and Criminal Anthropology,"[45] and one must note that Paul Broca and Claude Bernard (1813–1878), too, commented on Zola because they considered *Thérèse Raquin* (1867) a source of interesting examples of the medical types they had delineated.[46]

Lombroso demonstrates a peculiar approach to literature. Far from taking into consideration the aesthetic or structural complexity of the masterpieces he analyzes or from showing awareness of any fictional filter, Lombroso reads them as additional proof to support his theories, thus myopically failing to grasp the rich range of significance they offer. *Criminal Man* features numerous examples from literary works—besides criminals' own literary production in the chapter "Criminal Literature"—and its first edition (1876) had a stand-alone chapter on criminals in novels. According to Lombroso, the discoveries of criminal anthropology have been anticipated by brilliant works of literature and can be, in turn, used to better analyze society through literary types. What authors wrote can now be properly diagnosed and interpreted as accurate criminological observations; therefore, literary works provide both relevant proof to support Lombroso's theories and interesting case studies for criminal anthropologists to analyze. *Criminal Man* lists, among other examples, Dostoevsky's *Memoirs from the House of the Dead* and *Crime and Punishment*; Zola's *La bête humaine*; Gerolamo Rovetta's *Baraonda*; Arne Garborg's *Kolbotnbrev*; Henrik Ibsen's *Hedda Gabler*, *The Pillars of Society*, and *Ghosts*; Gabriele D'Annunzio's *The Victim*; Luigi Capuana's *Profumo* and *Giacinto*; and Giovanni Verga's *The She-Wolf*. He does not forget to add a few lines on Max Nordau's *Degeneration*.[47]

To Lombroso, Dostoevsky was a criminal anthropologist *ante litteram*, and excerpts from his literary works are employed quite often to illustrate Lombroso's theses. As Lombroso points out, Dostoevsky's sketches of convicts in Siberia in *Memoirs from the House of the Dead* (*Zapiski iz mërtvogo doma*, 1860) "do not only provide support, but also valuable contributions to the field of criminal anthropology."[48] In *Criminal Man*, the chapter "On the Intelligence and the Instruction of Criminals" reports Dostoevsky's descriptions as examples of lighthearted, carefree, and merry criminals, of the dreamers among them, and of their educations (more than half of the convicts Dostoevsky describes could read and write).[49] In his analysis of political crime, Lombroso reports on Dostoevsky's "mattoid" characters in *Demons* (*Besy*, 1872).[50] He also remarks that all of Dostoevsky's characters who fall into his category of "born criminals" are quite tall and well built, which, he argues, confirms his theories.[51]

Lombroso's employment of Dostoevskian sources finds its most paradigmatic formulation in his analysis of *Crime and Punishment* (*Prestuplenie i nakazanie*, 1866),[52] in which the author, in the character of Raskol'nikov, "has splendidly portrayed an occasional criminal as a variant of the born criminal."[53] Lombroso points out that Raskol'nikov is devoid of special physical features, whereas Svidrigailov, a "born" murderer and rapist, has "hair fairer than normal and eyes exaggeratedly cerulean."[54] In a simplifying summary of the plot, Lombroso underscores that Raskol'nikov hesitates before committing the crime, that he is deeply shocked afterward, that he ends up confessing his guilt and feels relieved after doing so, and that he goes back to being an honest man. Lombroso totally fails to see Dostoevsky's critique of the legal system and of those same deterministic ideas promoted by criminal anthropologists. Dostoevsky reaffirms the role of free will vis-à-vis social or biological determinism. He portrays the issues of responsibility, blame, and free will as existing in a complex relationship, but Lombroso completely disregards that complexity. There is no decisive proof of Raskol'nikov's guilt, but the magistrate Porfirii Petrovich plays a subtle psychological game (the moth and the flame) with him and finally gets him to confess. Finally, Lombroso neglects that the punishment that Raskol'nikov inflicts on himself is in fact more relevant than the court's decision to send him to Siberia. Lombroso fails to see that it is precisely through this self-inflicted punishment and through subsequent suffering that the criminal frees himself and reconnects with humankind. A sign of Lombroso's reductionist reading of the novel is his conclusion, in which he seems to find a "perfect concordance" between himself and Dostoevsky in the words that Svidrigailov, the born criminal, speaks to Raskol'nikov, the occasional criminal: "we are fruits of the same tree."[55]

By the 1880s, Lombroso's criminal anthropology was well known in Russia, mostly through French translations, while philosophical determinism and the positivist urge to apply quantitative methods to the social sciences came directly from France. Dostoevsky was familiar with physiognomy as well as with the phrenology of Franz Joseph Gall. As much as Dostoevsky opposed nihilism and reductionism in the social sciences, his proneness to epileptic fits kept him alert to new developments in the field of neurology.[56]

Moved by curiosity to learn what his own cranium revealed about his character, Dostoevsky once asked his friend Stepan Ianovskii, a physician and amateur phrenologist, to interpret his skull for him. Ianovskii traced a correspondence between Dostoevsky's physical features and Socrates's, especially the shape of the cranium and his "tightly clenched lips." Apparently, this similarity was the mark of a common understanding of "man's soul."[57]

We know from Konstantin Barsht's analysis of Dostoevsky's manuscripts that the writer frequently sketched faces parallel to delineating his characters in words.[58] However, in his prose none of the protagonists (unlike Tolstoy's) is ever given a detailed face. This holds true for the Underground Man, Raskol'nikov, Prince Myshkin, the Demons, and the Karamazovs. The reader gets acquainted with their nature, their general constitution, perhaps specific details of the face (Rogozhin's eyes), or the effect that their faces have on observers (Nastasia Filippovna's photograph), but one never finds a full description of a character's face. Tolstoy instead dwells on detail, even including comments on the facial hair on Princess Bolkonskaia's upper lip, and is more likely to repeat it, and over the course of his narrations one acquires a composite image of the characters.

Nevertheless, faces in Dostoevsky's works communicate emotions from character to character and are mirrored. For instance, in *Crime and Punishment*, after killing the pawnbroker and her sister, Lizaveta, Raskol'nikov recalls the latter's childish expression, and he automatically reproduces it on his face ("s toiu zhe *detskoiu* ulybkoi" [with that same *childish* smile], part 5, chapter 4).[59] Similarly, in book 2 of *The Idiot* (1868), just when Rogozhin is about to stab Prince Myshkin, the latter's face, especially his eyes, suddenly assumes a horrifying look ("chrezvychaino iskazhaetsia litso, osobenno vzgliad") as his epileptic fit begins (part 2, chapter 5).[60] A feeling of terror is communicated to Rogozhin, who stops his hand as if frozen, which saves the prince's life.

Although Dostoevsky's characters are struck by the faces they have seen, they seem to find their depiction challenging. In book 1 of *The Idiot*, Prince Myshkin is at the Epanchins', and he suggests that Adelaida paint the face of a man who has been sentenced to death one moment before the guillotine's blow:

"Paint the scaffold so that only the last stair can be seen clearly and closely; the condemned man has stepped on to it: his head, white as paper, the priest holding out the cross, the man extending his blue lips and staring—and *knowing everything* [*vsë znaet*]. The cross and the head—that is the painting, the face of the priest, of the executioner, of his two assistants and a few heads and eyes from below—all that may be painted on a tertiary level, as it were, in a mist, as a background.... That's what the painting should be like."[61]

Dostoevsky powerfully conveys to the reader the emotional charge of a face but refrains from outlining an exact description, as if caught in the territory of the uncanny.

The poetics of faces in Dostoevsky is much more complex and nuanced than Lombroso argues. The influence of the environment, both social and biological (Dostoevsky was familiar with Claude Bernard's concept of milieu),[62] on Dostoevsky's characters is prominent: we constantly read about the unhealthy Petersburg air and the sense of oppression and crooked ethics associated with it. However, Dostoevsky strongly argues for the importance of free will and often ridicules supporters of determinism and their limited views. In the 1860s, a new generation of thinkers and literary critics led by Nikolai Chernyshevskii (1828–1889) and Nikolai Dobroliubov (1836–1861) dominated Russian intellectual debate. Deeply informed by French rationalism, utilitarianism (Jeremy Bentham), Ludwig Feuerbach's atheism, Charles Darwin's evolutionary theory, and Claude Bernard's biological determinism, these radical thinkers considered themselves critics not only of literature but also of society. Because stringent censorship did not allow them to address social topics directly, they did so indirectly by analyzing literary depictions of society. This approach was aesthetically acceptable because, according to Chernyshevskii in *What Is to Be Done?* (*Chto delat'?*, 1863) and to Dobroliubov in his abrasive pamphlets, works of art have the purpose of explaining life and passing judgment on it, besides representing or illuminating it. With their lack of literary perspective and in their consideration of fictional characters and situations just as amenable to social diagnosis as real ones, these new intellectuals took an approach that was not so remote from Lombroso's. Even outside Russia, literary critics were at times blind to these nuances. For instance, Émile Hennequin describes Dostoevsky's writing as a direct product of his social and biological environment:

> He disowned his intelligence, abjured reason, and exalted madness, idiocy, imbecility, the candor of idiots and the goodness of criminals; he became a mystic.... This troubled, loving, and restless man was thin, sickly, and deathly pale. Sick with epilepsy, having undergone in his youth the frightful shock of a condemnation to death, and having been pardoned on the scaffold only to drag out years in a Siberian prison, with all the vermin of a primitive society, he lived subsequently under the "ink-saturated" sky of Saint Petersburg.... In this obscure life and in this snowy and torrid city, the vacillating intelligence and sick sensibility of Dostoevsky were reused and deployed.[63]

Nihilism, faith in progress, reductionism, and, as Chernyshevskii puts it, "rational egoism," constituted the core values of the new Russian cultural elite. The best-known literary depiction of the clash between the old and the new generations is probably Ivan Turgenev's *Fathers and Children* (*Ottsy i deti*, 1862). In his oeuvre, Dostoevsky repeatedly rejected and opposed the rising reductionism, nihilism, and sociobiological determinism. Both his nihilist characters and his "underground men," such as Svidrigailov in *Crime and Punishment* and Kirillov in *Demons*, often commit crimes or suicide, *Demons* showing us the extreme consequences of this new ideology. In the epilogue to *Crime and Punishment*, nihilism and radicalism are presented as a plague of massive proportions. A delirious Raskol'nikov dreams about a pestilence brought on by viruses from Asia and "endowed with intelligence and will" (odarënnye umom i volei), spreading wider and wider and eventually annihilating humankind with the purpose of "renew[ing] and cleans[ing] the earth" (obnovit' i ochistit' zemliu) (epilogue, chapter 2):[64]

> Never, never had any men thought themselves so wise and so unshakable in the truth as those who were attacked. Never had they considered their judgments, their scientific deductions, or their moral convictions and creeds more infallible.... each thought he was the sole repository of truth.... They did not know how or whom to judge and could not agree what was evil

and what good. They did not know whom to condemn and whom to acquit. Men killed one another in senseless rage.... In the towns, the tocsin sounded all day long, and called out all the people, but who had summoned them and why nobody knew, and everybody was filled with alarm.[65]

Conflagrations and famine cause everybody and everything to perish. It is in this closing part of the novel that Raskol'nikov understands the fallacy of his theories to the fullest degree and reconnects with humankind after the profound separation he had created by killing the pawnbroker and her sister in part 1.

Dostoevsky's most direct and polemical response to the criminal anthropology of his time can be found in book 12 of *The Brothers Karamazov* (*Brat'ia Karamazovy*, 1880), which is entirely devoted to the account of Mitia's trial. In chapter 3, "Medical Expertise and a Pound of Nuts," we are confronted with the competing assessments offered by three different medical experts of the gaze of the accused as he entered the law court. In this chapter, Dostoevsky offers a bitter satire of the contemporary trends in criminal psychology and anthropology, which casts shadows on the real possibilities of the new forensic psychiatry to come to solid conclusions about accused persons and their connection to the crime. The different meanings that the three experts attribute to Mitia's gaze spring from the preexisting opinion that each has before the observation and from each one's attempt to find further confirmations of that opinion.

The first expert to express a pronouncement is Doctor Herzenstube, who postulates a discontinuity between Mitia's general character and his specific behavior on that day as a sign of psychotic dissociation. He "roundly declared that the abnormality of the defendant's mental faculties was self-evident."[66] This abnormality is demonstrated by the fact that although Mitia was an admirer of women, he looked straight in front of him instead of looking to his left, where women were sitting. Underlying this discrepancy is a more relevant one, which the old physician sees between Mitia's generous heart (he recalls an episode from the accused's childhood) and the crime of which he was accused.

The second opinion is offered by a very famous lawyer, who came to the provincial town Skotoprigonevsk, where the trial is taking place, from no less a city than Moscow. He also maintains that "the defendant's mental condition [is] abnormal in 'the highest degree,'" and he claims that this condition is the result of an obsession and the highly irritable state Mitia had been showing in the past weeks anytime anyone discussed the three thousand rubles he owed his father. According to the Moscow specialist, Mitia's gaze further confirmed his theory: one would have expected him to look to his right, where his defense counsel, "on whose help all his hopes rest," was sitting.[67] This physician considers this obsession to be the first sign of Mitia's impending madness.

Third comes Doctor Varvinskii's pronouncement. Contrary to the opinion expressed by the Moscow specialist, Varvinskii believes that the defendant was lucid and mentally healthy both in the days when the murder occurred and in the law court. He maintains that Mitia's "exceedingly excited state before his arrest . . . might have been due to several perfectly obvious causes, jealousy, anger, continual drunkenness, and so on. But this nervous condition would not involve the mental 'aberration' of which mention had just been made." The fact that Mitia had looked straight before him further confirms Varvinskii's hypothesis because it makes perfect sense: he was looking at the judges, "on whom his fate depended." At the end of Varvinskii's testimony, Mitia expresses his satisfaction by crying: "Bravo, apothecary!"[68] Indeed, this physician has given him back full responsibility in the face of the crimes he is being tried for. This is a murder he did not commit, but the fact that he had desired it, Mitia thinks, makes him deserving of punishment.

Dostoevsky most probably knew of Lombroso, but it is not certain to what extent he was familiar with his theories. In all likelihood, he would not have concurred with an interpretation of his characters based on Lombroso's typological categories. If the two had had a conversation, they would probably have disagreed on many fronts. Although Lombroso never had the opportunity to meet his favorite literary criminal anthropologist, he did meet the other titan of late nineteenth-century Russian literature, Leo Tolstoy.

The Twelfth International Medical Conference was held in Moscow in the summer of 1897. Lombroso chaired a session on psychiatry in which, among other contributions, the French psychiatrist Hippolyte-Marie Bernheim (1840–1919) presented a paper on hypnotism and its uses in legal medicine. Lombroso took the occasion to take a trip to Iasnaia Poliana and visit Leo Tolstoy on his estate. Although he did not draw much on Tolstoyan works to illustrate his theories, he had high expectations of the man: "I had found in Tolstoy's works so many elements in support of my theories (for instance, hereditary burden, eccentric behavior at a young age, epileptic fits, psychic excitement that grows into hallucination) that I could hope to find further confirmations by meeting the greatest living artist and novelist in person."[69] He had expected Tolstoy to follow the physical patterns Lombroso had outlined in his criminological works—that is, to show "a cretinous and degenerate look," as he had described the genius in *The Man of Genius* (*L'uomo di genio in rapporto alla psichiatria, alla storia ed all'estetica*, 1888). Lombroso had even chosen a portrait of Tolstoy to illustrate the physiognomic type of the genius in the sixth edition of the book, and Nordau, too, had devoted a chapter to Tolstoy in *Degeneration*.

When Lombroso arrived at Iasnaia Poliana on August 15, 1897, he was stunned by Tolstoy's strength and well-built figure. He proved to be a sturdy, old peasant type of man—quite contrary to the prototype of the slender, sick-looking genius Lombroso's theory would have him be. He saw Tolstoy play lawn tennis with his daughters for two hours. Then the writer invited his Italian visitor for a horseback ride to a river for a swim. After fifteen minutes, Lombroso was exhausted, and he expressed admiration for Tolstoy's strength while complaining about his own weakness. At that point, Lombroso recalls, the Russian novelist just "protracted his arm and lifted me up enough above the ground, as if I had been a small dog."[70]

Once they were back in Tolstoy's house, Lombroso started explaining his theory of the born criminal, and perhaps he also mentioned his idea of punishment, including the death sentence as social defense against the beastly behavior of underdeveloped born criminals: "But here a spiritual wall was raised between us, which prevented us from accepting each other's conclusions. This wall originated in his curious conviction that neither my theory of criminal law nor the other ones could explain on what human societies based their right to punish a criminal."[71] Tolstoy had been firmly opposed to the death sentence since he had witnessed a guillotine execution in Paris as a young man. Moreover, the garden of his Moscow house was contiguous with the park of a mental health clinic directed by the famous neurologist and psychiatrist Sergei Korsakov (1845–1900), who had organized the Moscow conference. Tolstoy had always looked with admiration upon Korsakov and his clinic for the humaneness and empathy of the treatment they offered. It is therefore no surprise that while

Lombroso expanded on his theories, "[Tolstoy] remained deaf to my argument, knitting his frightening eyebrows, and casting menacing lightning bolts [on me] from his sunken eyes; in the end he responded: 'This is delirious. All punishment is criminal!'"[72]

The encounter did not have a successful outcome, predictably so. On that day, August 15, 1897, Tolstoy wrote in his journal: "Lombroso was here—a naïve little old man" (Byl Lombroso, ogranichennyi naivnyi starichok).[73] A couple of years later, in January 1900, he would add: "I read newspapers, journals, and books, and still cannot get used to ascribing any real value to what is written there, namely: the philosophy of Nietzsche, the dramas of Ibsen and Maeterlinck, and the science of Lombroso.... Surely this represents complete poverty of thought, understanding, and feeling."[74]

In the summer of 1897, Tolstoy had momentarily postponed his work on *Resurrection* in order to write *What Is Art?* (*Chto takoe iskusstvo?*). He resumed his writing of the novel during the fall, and presumably his meeting with Lombroso had an influence on it. In *Resurrection* (*Voskresenie*, published in 1899), Tolstoy ridiculed the theory of atavism and heredity as well as the conclusions drawn by criminal anthropology. It is through the figure of Breve, the public prosecutor in Maslova's trial, that Tolstoy voices his concerns about the new criminology and mocks Lombroso's theory as well as probably Lombroso himself. The main character, Prince Nekhliudov, on a visit to his native town in the Nizhny Novgorod province, is serving on the popular jury for a trial of a prostitute, Maslova, who has been accused of murder. Nekhliudov recognizes in the woman a maid he had seduced and abandoned in his youth, a memory that triggers his guilt and then his attempt to save her as well as the rest of the plot.

Breve, the assistant prosecutor, is a convinced positivist, and in court he speaks about Maslova's degeneration, typical of the corruption of the times (book 1, chapter 21): "Every new craze then in vogue among his set was alluded to in his speech: everything that then was, and some things that still are, considered to be the last word of scientific wisdom [poslednee slovo nauchnoi mudrosti]: heredity and congenital crime. Lombroso and Tarde, evolution and the struggle for existence, hypnotism and hypnotic influence, Charcot and decadence."[75] Breve describes Maslova's accomplice, Kartinkin, as an atavistic product of serfdom and his mistress, Botchkova, as a victim of heredity. Maslova, he says, is just a degenerate.

She is of unknown parentage, her lawyer claims. Nevertheless, the public prosecutor maintains that "the laws of heredity were so far proved by science that we can not only deduce the crime from heredity, but heredity from crime" (book 1, chapter 21).[76]

Nekhliudov disagrees, remaining unsatisfied by the answers provided by criminal anthropology. When asked by Kolosov whether he believes in heredity, he replies that he does not (book 1, chapter 27). Later in the novel (book 2, chapter 30), we encounter him reflecting on the new science in a Siberian prison, where he has followed Maslova after she is found guilty. In that prison, Nekhliudov has seen quite a variety of people. He turns to the famous works everybody quotes, but he finds that they cannot explain "why all these very different persons were put in prison, while others just like them were going about free, and even judging them."

> He obtained the works of Lombroso, Garofalo, Ferri, Liszt, Maudsley, Tarde, and read them carefully. But as he read he became more and more disappointed.... Science answered thousands of other very subtle and ingenious questions touching criminal law, but not the one he was trying to solve. He asked a very simple question: "Why, and by what right, do some people lock up, torment, exile, flog, and kill others, while they are themselves just like those whom they torment, flog, and kill?" And in answer he got deliberations on whether ... or not signs of criminality could be detected by measuring the skull; what part heredity played in crime;... what madness is, what degeneration is ...—and so on. (book 2, chapter 30)[77]

When Lombroso read *Resurrection*, he claimed in frustration that he had found "factual evidence that [he] had spoken to him [Tolstoy] in vain."[78]

Among the most enthusiastic followers of Lombroso's theories in Russia ranked psychiatrist Vladimir Fëdorovich Chizh (1855–1922), a very successful clinician who served as head of psychiatry in the St. Panteleimon Hospital in Petersburg and held a professorship at the University of Dorpat (today's Tartu) as the successor of Emil Kraepelin (1856–1926). Like his contemporaries, Chizh turned to the newly founded discipline of criminal anthropology to investigate possible connections between crime and insanity, and he was the first in Russia to conduct psychological experiments on criminals. In his pathography on Nikolai Gogol' (1809–1852), *Gogol's Illness* (*Bolezn' Gogolia*, 1903), Chizh diagnosed the writer as mentally ill by referring to Lombroso's theory of degeneration as expressed in *Genius and Insanity*. Lying at the basis of Gogol's behavior, Chizh claimed, was his degenerate constitution.[79] On the occasion of the Congress of Criminal Anthropology, held in Paris in 1889 and featuring a debate between the two speakers of honor, Lombroso and the French alienist Valentin Magnan (1835–1916), most Russian physicians opposed the former's biological and anatomical explanation of the criminal "type" and supported instead the latter's theories on the social roots of criminal behavior. On that occasion, Chizh constituted a notable exception; he embraced Lombroso's theories entirely and even compared the Italian medical anthropologist to Charles Darwin on the basis of the impact and bearing of his theories on the field of evolutionary biology.[80] Just like Lombroso, Chizh was fascinated by literary characters, who seemed to confirm his theories better than his patients did and published studies of Dostoevsky's and Turgenev's works, following in Lombroso's footsteps.[81] Specifically, he contended, literature provided the most compelling illustrations of Lombroso's celebrated discoveries: not only is criminal behavior hereditary, but the born criminal also constitutes an evolutionary throwback. In his analysis of Dostoevsky's novels and characters, "Dostoevsky as Psychopathologist and Criminologist" ("Dostoevskii kak psikhopatolog i kriminolog," 1901), Chizh mentions that the direct biological influence of parents' alcoholism on the physical and mental health of their children, of which the novels he examines offer evidence, had been demonstrated by Lombroso's research. From Lombroso's work *Genius and Insanity*, Chizh reports, we learn that among the progeny of one alcoholic Lombroso had identified "200 thieves and robbers, 90 prostitutes, 30 who died in their childhood, and 60 who were sickly, blind or consumptive."[82] Chizh further traces correspondences between Dostoevsky's characters and Lombroso's evolutionary theories of criminal behavior in his examination of *The Brothers Karamazov* and *Memoirs from the House of the Dead*.

In the sources examined in this chapter, death has been outlined as a privileged condition that allows for the releasing of meanings otherwise concealed and offers a rereading and reordering of previous events into a unifying, crystalized plot structure by channeling them into new causal-temporal chains. Along the lines of Ricoeur's distinction between "succession" and "configuration" as the two major functions of plot, death propels storytelling in both directions: on the one hand, postmortem examination unveils the spatial configuration of body parts and their reciprocal position, and, on the other hand, it shows the observer how phenomena and events have unfolded, thus dissipating all initial doubts and dismissing all preceding inaccurate emplotment attempts.

If death is a catalyst for storytelling, the surgeon—an explorer, a detective, a reader, and a writer—represents the only authorial voice. However, when death has not yet occurred but is clearly in sight, the prospect of life's ending shapes the temporality that characters in fiction as well as seriously ill patients in real life inhabit. Not only death but also its prospect generate plots in the present; and although the physician is necessarily the sole storyteller after death has occurred, when we turn to the prospect of death, then the patient's voice comes forcibly to the foreground as well. The following chapter is devoted precisely to this phenomenon. By turning our attention from the author/physician to the reader/patient, we move to a structural and stylistic analysis of teleology, temporality, and endings in Leo Tolstoy's *Anna Karenina* and *The Death of Ivan Ilych* in comparison to oncology patients, real and potential.

Chapter Two

END OF STORY

Temporality and the Prospect of the Ending in *Ivan Ilych*, *Anna Karenina*, and (Potential) Cancer Patients

The tradition of the *ars moriendi* (literally, "the art of dying") dates back to late medieval Christianity; it appeared in the wake of a devastating plague epidemic—the Black Death—that claimed millions of lives in Europe between 1347 and 1351. Instructions and advice on the protocols of a good death, according to Christian precepts, were collected in two texts from the early fifteenth century, titled *Ars moriendi*. After a consoling section that encourages readers not to be afraid of death, the text warns against the temptations that haunt those who are dying—including impatience, avarice, lack of faith, and pride—and mentions Christ's life as a model. The final section is devoted to deathbed interactions with family and lists appropriate prayers. In *The Hour of Our Death* (1981), Philippe Ariès claims that the tradition survived, largely unchanged, through the nineteenth and early twentieth century and spread beyond Europe.[1] It was believed that one should die among family members assembled around the deathbed. It was considered crucial that they witness the death and assess the state of the dying person's soul because these critical last moments of life would epitomize that person's spiritual condition. The end of one's life was charged with final, crystalized significance: those who were dying were at that moment defining their essential selves for eternity. For this reason, a life was seen as an incomplete story without this final chapter and, particularly, without the life-defining last words.

Ariès claims that while having always held a place of prominence in the *ars moriendi* tradition, the deathbed speech assumed by the eighteenth century the explicit secular importance that it still retains today for matters of inheritance and the will of the dying.[2] Across centuries, people believed dying declarations to be the truth because they thought that the dying no longer had any earthly motivation to lie and would not want to bear false witness when they were just about to meet their maker, an experience for which preparedness was considered crucial. In their finality, last words imposed meaning on the life narrative they concluded; they also communicated precious lessons to those gathered around the deathbed, lessons that remained as lingering exhortations and constituted a tie between the living and the dead. Deathbed declarations would also bring reconciliation and settle life's controversies and injustice. When life circumstances prevented the dying from following the *ars moriendi*, the dying would strive to re-create whichever part of the experience was possible. In her account of the U.S. Civil War, *This Republic of Suffering* (2008), the historian Drew Gilpin Faust reports that the suddenness and unpreparedness that characterized death on the battlefield deprived the parents, sisters, wives, and children left at home of the dying soldiers' last words and the sense of connection to them. Those soldiers would therefore dictate their deathbed declarations in letters to be sent home and would carry photographs of their kin in their pockets in order to have them close at the moment of death.[3]

Leo Tolstoy was the writer to whom the Russian formalist Boris Eikhenbaum devoted the most scholarly attention. Fascinated by Tolstoy's literary longevity and his survival at the center stage of the literary scene throughout times of dramatic change in Russian history and culture, Eikhenbaum was interested in studying not only Tolstoy's "devices" at the level of the text but also his fashioning of a literary persona and his choices in both the public sphere and the publishing arena. Ironically, the theoretical question of death and narrative time that Eikhenbaum's own death scene sparked, described at the beginning of chapter 1, is best explored by juxtaposing two works by Tolstoy—*The Death of Ivan Ilych* and *Anna Karenina*—that offer distinctive features in their treatment of endings. We proceed in reverse-chronological order and begin with *Ivan Ilych* for reasons that are structural: in it, temporality is well defined, and the ending is clearly prepared and performed in a compelling teleology, whereas *Anna Karenina*'s endings present an elusive quality. Both texts are paradigmatic for the sake of our discussion in that they allow, I argue, for in-depth exploration of structural patterns shared by storytelling and the biomedical sciences in broaching endings; specifically, their examination allows us to investigate the ways in which it is the prospect of death, rather than death itself, that generates plots.

Tolstoy was writing during monumental transformations of medicine as a discipline and of medical institutions in Russia and throughout Europe that included an increasing classification of diseases and "types," the institutionalization of treatment, the rise of professional organizations of physicians, and great scientific discoveries such as pasteurization and germ theory. In *The Birth of the Clinic* (1963), Michel Foucault describes the epistemic change that took place in medicine from the mid-eighteenth to the late nineteenth century following the formulation and development of the clinical method. Although Russia initially lagged helplessly behind France and Germany in this rearrangement, Alexander II's liberal reforms in the 1860s, which fostered major efforts in the field of public health, and the institution of *zemstvo* doctors, which brought about better healthcare coverage for the population and significant improvements in hygienic conditions even in peripheral provinces, reduced the gap significantly.[4] The second half of the nineteenth century also saw the rise of physicians' awareness of themselves as a professional group; their social importance increased exponentially, and they coalesced into professional organizations. The Judicial Reform of 1864 instituted local self-government units, the *zemstvo*s (*zemstva*), which were put in charge of managing public health. Far from the central bureaucracy, *zemstvo* doctors saw their autonomy increase, even at the time of Alexander III's counterreforms of the late 1880s, while their cooperation during the numerous epidemic waves solidified their corporate consciousness. Among the most fervent promoter of medical *korporativnost'* (corporatism) was Nikolai Pirogov (1810–1881). The first person to use anesthesia on a battlefield, Pirogov established the practice of field surgery and was among the founders of experimental surgery. His anatomic atlas, *Topographical Anatomy of the Human Body* (*Topograficheskaia anatomiia*), published in four volumes with detailed drawings between 1851 and 1859, facilitated the work of surgeons immensely and became famous all over Europe. Pirogov became a professor at the Medical School in Dorpat (today's Tartu, Estonia), where he became acquainted with the local corporate traditions that he wanted to see extended to the Russian academic environment. *Diary of an Old Doctor* (*Dnevnik starogo vracha*), which he wrote in the two years preceding his death in 1881, constitutes a precious record of the rapid changes that occurred in the field of medicine over his lifetime. At midcentury, epidemics were still considered administrative emergencies. The bulk of physicians' work consisted of stressing prevention, improving hygiene, and limiting contagion through isolation and quarantine. With rapid advancements in Western medicine, the etiology of fatal diseases such as cholera became clear, and techniques to reduce their impact were discovered. As a result, physicians gained unprecedented visibility and undisputed authority as experts in antiepidemic measures. Russian physicians were no longer seen as *chinovniki* (clerks). Cognizant of Western medical thought, they applied their knowledge at home and saw their social status grow. The number of Russian medical journals increased considerably, with *Vrach* (The physician) being the most influential, and the Society of Russian Physicians in Memory of Pirogov (Obshchestvo russkikh vrachei v pamiat' N. I. Pirogova) had its first congress in 1885. By the mid-1880s, Russian physicians had become a corporate group—their social status and their authority undisputed.[5] Between 1856 and 1890, the number of physicians doubled, while a reformed medical education enhanced their competence. By the end of the century, Moscow began hosting international conferences on medicine (including the one on psychiatry in 1897, after which Lombroso's encounter with Tolstoy, described in chapter 1, took place).

Such was the state of Russian medical institutions in the 1870s and 1880s, when Tolstoy wrote *Anna Karenina* and *The Death of Ivan Ilych*. The first university clinic in Russia was established in 1884, when the Faculty of Medicine at Moscow University received funds from the city of Duma to erect a twelve-building hospital on vacant land by Devich'e Pole. Undoubtedly a realist writer, Tolstoy veered away from physiological sketches and naturalistic prose (a genre that Dostoevsky explored and that was in many respects the literary counterpart to determinism in medicine). He firmly rejected the new medical approaches on the basis of their scientific, procedural, and ethical shortcomings, as he would state via the character of

Nekhliudov in *Resurrection*. At the same time, he deeply admired neurologist and psychiatrist Sergei Korsakov, head of psychiatry at the Moscow University Clinic, because of the humaneness of his treatment methods. Tolstoy expressed his thoughts on medicine, death, and being ill on many occasions, in both his private writings and his literary works, such as *Childhood* (*Detstvo*, 1852), *Sevastopol Tales* (*Sevastopol'skie rasskazy*, 1855), "Three Deaths" ("Tri smerti," 1859), *War and Peace* (*Voina i mir*, 1865–1867), "Notes of a Madman" ("Zapiski sumasshedshego," 1884), and of course, *Anna Karenina* and *The Death of Ivan Ilych*, which are discussed in this chapter.[6] As Eikhenbaum pointed out, the writer considered all traditional literary representations of dying inadequate and strived to alter that perception quite radically with his own work, making such representations a literary skill to be mastered or a literary puzzle to be solved.[7] However, Tolstoy's experimentation was more than an elegant stylistic exercise. His diaries reveal the extent to which the writer shared with his characters a fear of dying and an anxiety regarding the passage of time that challenged linguistic-literary description or formalization, and he attempted to tame and control that fear and anxiety by anchoring them to the page and capturing their contours.[8]

Although a man with a strong constitution, Tolstoy had numerous dealings with physicians. In 1847 at the age of eighteen, he spent a few weeks in the clinic of Kazan University to be treated for venereal diseases, and there he started writing his diary, an activity he would never abandon. While in the army during the Crimean War, he went to a spa in the northern Caucasus, where he was operated on with the use of chloroform. In 1876, when his wife was ill, he wrote in a letter: "I do not believe in either doctors or in medicine or in the fact that remedies made by people should in the slightest way alter the state of health." Later in life, however, despite writing in his diaries that "everything about medicine is immoral," he thought it essential to have a doctor permanently attached to the household.[9]

"RESPICE FINEM": TELEOLOGY AND EMPLOTMENT IN *THE DEATH OF IVAN ILYCH*

Confronted with the challenges that medical advancement posed and with his own fear of death, Tolstoy addressed in *The Death of Ivan Ilych* (*Smert' Ivana Il'icha*, 1886) questions that today we deem central to both medical epistemology and literary theory, the two fields whose intersections the present analysis reveals and examines.[10] By questioning a reductionist approach to illness and healing, this literary work also anticipated modern theoretical developments in medical ethics and, more generally, the medical humanities. It is no surprise that established authors in the field, such as Philippe Ariès and Atul Gawande, make reference to Ivan Ilych's trajectory in their writings.[11] I have argued elsewhere that Tolstoy's articulation of his thoughts on illness, healing, death, and caregiving in the pages of this novella constitute simultaneously a reflection upon storytelling in its constitutive units—authorship as authority, emplotment, narrative reliability—and, as a consequence, a reflection upon the literary medium.[12]

In *The Death of Ivan Ilych*, Tolstoy describes the final three months in the life of his protagonist, a successful judge. The narration, albeit in third-person singular, is conducted from the point of view of the hero (with the exception of the beginning), which gives the reader privileged access to his thoughts and his reactions both to external stimuli (his doctors' remarks, his family members' words and behavior) and to his bodily symptoms.

The treatment of narrative time in the novella resembles a postmortem examination. Chapter 1 opens with Ivan Ilych's colleagues commenting on the protagonist's recent death and paying a visit to his widow. Like anatomopathologists, the characters voice their final assessment of their colleague and the man, through which we learn about the hypocrisy and greed that used to surround Ivan Ilych: his wife worries that without her husband's income she will not be able to enjoy the same lifestyle; his daughter's main concern is to make a financially advantageous marriage with her wealthy suitor; his colleagues are thinking about the career opportunities that his death has opened up for them and care more about making it to their card game on time than about paying homage to the deceased. The ensuing chapters, from chapter 2 to the end, present the reader with the story of Ivan Ilych's life, from his youth to his last days. Chapter 2 opens with another final assessment of the protagonist's life—this time in a concise and incisive sentence expressed by the author-narrator: "Ivan Ilych's life had been most simple and most ordinary and most terrible."[13]

An account of Ivan Ilych's life follows. We learn about his bourgeois values, his career trajectory, his ambition, his marriage and social life. As the story, along with Ivan Ilych's life, approaches its end, it offers a few flashbacks to his childhood, as though to begin to measure the protagonist's life and set the stage for the moment of death, which will provide the final assessment and yield the ultimate meaning. The very structure of the story seems therefore to echo the idea of death as the ending that reorders past events and confers upon them a final meaning.

In the second chapter, the protagonist falls off a ladder while decorating his newly purchased apartment and is injured. He initially seems to recover, but gradually his mysterious disease becomes more and more serious until he dies amid the indifference of his family and friends. For the majority of the period of Ivan Ilych's disease, the reader is confronted with a clash of paradigms in the definition of being ill and with the plethora of evaluations, interpretations, and explanations that physicians, family, and Ivan Ilych advance in the face of his mysterious illness. In *The Structure of the Artistic Text* (1977), Lotman maintains that "we take an event to mean the smallest indivisible unit of plot construction.... [W]ithin the same scheme of culture[,] the same episode, when placed on various structural levels, *may or may not become an event*."[14] Among the phenomena that surround us, each "author" will choose the ones deemed important and will order them in causal-temporal chains, thus explaining the world through a *fabula*. The process of selection, just like that of ordering, is absolutely arbitrary. In medicine, a similar procedure takes place: from a set of symptoms and the patient's recollections, the doctor proceeds to a diagnosis and to the explanation of the biological phenomenon in its evolution, just as an author or a reporter constructs a story out of a set of scattered events. Ivan Ilych's symptoms ("a sense of pressure in his left side" and "a loathsome taste in his mouth")[15] are interpreted differently by each doctor. In other words, each of them constructs a different story to explain what is happening to the protagonist and comes to a different diagnosis: "That month he went to see another celebrity, who told him almost the same as the first had done, but put his questions differently.... A friend of a friend of his, a very good doctor, diagnosed his illness again quite differently from the others, and ... his questions and suppositions bewildered Ivan Ilych still more...."

A homeopathist diagnosed the disease in yet another way, and prescribed medicine which Ivan Ilych took...for a week."[16] In addition to these many diagnoses formulated by physicians, other characters explain our hero's illness, each in a different way.[17] For instance, Praskovia Fyodorovna, Ivan Ilych's wife, claims that the illness is nothing but her husband's attempt to bring her unpleasantness, while her brother believes from the early symptoms that Ivan Ilych's death is near.[18] The protagonist, too, has his own take on the events and advances his own emplotment, which Tolstoy foregrounds by conducting the narrative from his hero's perspective: for Ivan Ilych, his illness takes on an important heuristic function.

His interactions with those who surround him are portrayed in ways that anticipate numerous modern debates in the medical humanities—from Arthur Kleinman's distinction between "illness" and "disease" to Susan Sontag's remarks on the use of metaphor in the field of medicine to Elaine Scarry's argument regarding the incommunicability of pain. With each of Ivan Ilych's interactions with doctors, the reader is confronted with a clash of paradigms in the definition of being ill. During a visit to a celebrity physician, "to Ivan Ilych only one question was important: was his case serious or not? But the doctor ignored that inappropriate question. From his point of view it was not the one under consideration; the real question was to decide between a floating kidney, chronic catarrh, or appendicitis. It was not a question of Ivan Ilych's life or death, but one between a floating kidney and appendicitis."[19] Particularization, or the emphasis on body parts and organs as discrete entities, is a defining feature of the positivistic approach to the body. This often translates into a single, malfunctioning body organ growing in importance and replacing the patient's identity altogether in the diagnostic process. Ivan Ilych realizes that doctors see him merely as the bearer of a syndrome and therefore conceive of him in a synecdochic fashion—he is no longer a person but a set of kidneys. For him, instead, his illness and the problem with his kidneys constitute a subplot within a much broader life narrative; by no means does his disease define him as a person. Medical reductionism is alienating, and Ivan Ilych's reaction to it is one of estrangement. In a short dreamy passage, Ivan Ilych, on morphine, has a vision in which his organs take on a life of their own, and while the appendix takes the turn the doctors have predicted, he grabs his kidneys floating in the air. In this vignette, which anticipates modernist aesthetics, Tolstoy employs defamiliarization to point to the arbitrariness of medical authority and to deconstruct its dogma.

Medical explanation, which falls into the domain of the *Erklären* of classical hermeneutics, is insufficient to comprehend (*Verstehen*) the protagonist's pain. In this regard, palliative-care physicians have recently coined the concept "total pain" to describe the complex intertwining of physical pain and existential pain that afflicts terminally ill patients.[20] The irreducible gap between Ivan Ilych's perspective and his doctors' also seems to anticipate the distinction between "illness" and "disease" postulated by the medical anthropologists of our times: Arthur Kleinman defines *illness* as a person's unique experience of being ill, in both emotional and physical terms, whereas *disease* indicates the standardized medical definition of that same condition or the description of the biological process that underlies it.[21]

However, entitled as Ivan Ilych feels to construct his own version of the story, he understands that the medical paradigm is the dominant one when it comes to defining and treating his disease and that he lacks the language and knowledge to be able to communicate with his doctors and be taken seriously by his interlocutors. Medical jargon, which the reader experiences through Ivan Ilych's perspective, is just one manifestation of the physicians' authority. For instance: "The doctor said that so-and-so indicated that there was such-and-such inside the patient, but if the investigation of so-and-so did not confirm this, then he must assume this and that, then . . . and so on. . . . All the way home he was going over what the doctor had said, trying to translate those complicated, obscure, scientific phrases into plain language and find in them an answer to the question: 'Is my condition bad? Is it very bad? Or is there still nothing much wrong?'"[22]

Moreover, because Ivan Ilych is a judge in a court of law, he is familiar with the authority that comes with being the repository of knowledge in a certain field. He is aware of the power conferred upon those who pronounce a sentence and compares it to the power that the formulation of a diagnosis entails—in contrast to the feeling of oppression and helplessness experienced by those who are on the receiving end of that power:

> The important air assumed by the doctor . . . was so familiar (resembling that which he himself assumed in court), and the sounding and listening . . .

and the look of importance which implied: "if only you put yourself in our hands we will arrange everything—we know indubitably how it has to be done, always the same for everybody." It was all just as it was in the law courts. The doctor put on just the same air towards him as he himself put on towards an accused person.

And that question the doctor solved brilliantly. . . . All this was just what Ivan Ilych had himself brilliantly accomplished a thousand times in dealing with men on trial. The doctor summed it up just as brilliantly, looking over his spectacles triumphantly and even gaily at the accused.

[Ivan Ilych] remarked with a sigh: ". . . [T]ell me, doctor, in general, is this complaint dangerous, or not?" The doctor looked at him sternly over his spectacles with one eye, as if to say: "Prisoner, if you will not keep to the questions put to you, I shall be obliged to have you removed from the court."[23]

We have here a situation Foucault has analyzed from several perspectives. In *The Order of Things* (1966), he highlights the discursive checks in power dynamics and the employment of scientific discourse as an instrument of power. In *The Birth of the Clinic* (1963) and *Discipline and Punish* (1975), he underscores the clinical gaze as a means of reification and control over the patient.[24] The power of definitions in this context has been explored more recently by the historian of medicine Charles Rosenberg in his article "The Tyranny of Diagnosis" (2002).[25] In the name of functional classification, the clinical method groups patients into categories, defining types and advancing knowledge through case studies. This approach remains at work in our day, especially in public-health interventions meant to contain and defeat epidemics. Generalization further minimizes the individual patient's right to authorship over a specific narrative of illness. Devoid of uniqueness, the patient becomes little more than the physical locus for the manifestation of a disease. In one such scenario, Ivan Ilych recalls his textbooks in school, especially Kiesewetter's textbook of logic:

"Caius is a man, men are mortal, therefore Caius is mortal," had always seemed to him correct as applied to Caius, but it certainly didn't apply to himself. That Caius—man in the abstract—was mortal, was perfectly correct, but he was not Caius, not an abstract man . . . Had Caius kissed his mother's hand like that?. . . Had he noted like that at school when the pastry was bad?. . . Could Caius preside at a session as he did? "Caius really was mortal, and it was right for him to die; but as for me, little Vanya, Ivan Ilych, with all my thoughts and emotions, it's altogether a different matter. . . ."[26]

The hermeneutic circle makes sense only in the abstract world of logic. The experience of illness and healing can hardly be reduced through generalization. It is clear to Ivan Ilych that the doctor has the authority to define the disease and prescribe the cure. Anything the character has to say is dismissed as irrelevant; in other words, although Ivan Ilych is an educated and lucid patient, doctors consider him "unreliable" (according to Wayne Booth's definition of the term) inasmuch as his questions and remarks do not align with the current discourse and the methodological standards of the medical discipline.[27] To this day, from the physician's perspective, physical examinations and laboratory tests often provide more insight than any word a patient may utter. Ivan Ilych's suffering is incomprehensible to doctors, who operate in a different paradigm, as well as to his family: "Those about him did not understand or would not understand it, but thought everything in the world was going on as usual. That tormented Ivan Ilych more than anything. He saw that his household, especially his wife and daughter[,] . . . did not understand anything about it and were annoyed that he was so depressed and so exacting, as if he were to blame. . . . And he had to live thus all alone on the brink of an abyss, with no one who understood him or pitied him."[28]

Ivan Ilych experiences the incommunicability of pain that Elaine Scarry postulates in *The Body in Pain* (1985)—that is, an ontological gap that sets apart those who suffer from those who try to understand (or are supposed to understand) the nature, intensity, and meaning of that pain—physicians, lawyers, family members, legislators. Scarry maintains that "physical pain does not simply resist language but actively destroys it, bringing about an immediate reversion to a state anterior to language, to the sounds and cries a human being makes before language is learned." Moreover, "to be present when a person moves up out of that pre-language and projects the facts of sentience into speech is almost to have been permitted to be present at the birth of language itself."[29] Because of the impossibility of conveying the experience of pain through language, the medical field has introduced pain self-assessment tools and scales that allow patients to locate their pain on a drawing of the human body (*Where Is Your Pain?*, 1975), assign a numerical value to its intensity (Numerical Pain Scale, 1989), and describe it through metaphors pertaining to different semantic spheres—Is the pain stabbing, piercing, burning? Is it cold or hot? and so forth—and such tools have become more detailed over time (from the Wong-Baker Scale, 2001, to the Pain Assessment Quality Scale, 2003). If the experience of pain cannot be communicated, at least patients are invited to draw on a pool of imagery, which, although not completely bridging the gap postulated by Scarry (pain is self-assessed), is somewhat legible to physicians, who tend to resort to similar language to refer to their own experience of pain in everyday life.[30]

However, the roots of Ivan Ilych's difficulties in being understood by those close to him are not solely philosophical or linguistic. His wife is emotionally distant from him and therefore is not in a state to comprehend her husband's suffering. His daughter does not show much interest, either, while his son suffers sincerely but is too young to develop a full understanding of the events. None of his family can comfort him or help him bear the thought of an impending death. Ivan Ilych's interactions with Gerasim, the butler's young assistant, constitute the only exception to his profound existential isolation.

Ivan Ilych is not interested in the exact definition of his condition. His questions are of a different order: "Suddenly he felt the old, familiar, dull, gnawing pain, stubborn and serious. There was that same loathsome taste in his mouth. His heart sank and he felt dazed. . . . Suddenly the matter presented itself in quite a different aspect [*sovsem s drugoi storony*, 'from a completely different angle']. '. . . appendix! Kidney!' He said to himself. 'It's not a question of my appendix or my kidney, but of life and . . . death. . . .'"[31]

Along with Ivan Ilych's body parts, his pain (*bol'*), too, is personified the moment he associates it with the prospect of death: "But suddenly in the midst of those proceedings the pain in his side, regardless of the stage the proceedings had reached, would begin its own gnawing work. Ivan Ilych would turn his attention [*prislushivalsia*, 'listen'] to it [the pain] and tried to drive the thought of it away, but without success [*ona prodolzhala svoë*, 'it continued its activity']. *It* [*ona*] would come and stand before him and look at him, and he would be petrified. The light would die out in his eyes, and he would begin asking himself again whether *It* alone was true."[32] Here Tolstoy depicts the crucial moment in which Ivan Ilych suddenly becomes aware of death as now a concrete prospect by playing with the ambiguity of the feminine pronoun *ona*, which in this context could refer both to the word for pain (*bol'*) and to the word for death (*smert'*), each of them feminine in Russian. In the original text, we have an uninterrupted sentence running from "Ivan Ilych" to "petrified," in which *ona* initially refers to pain but gradually begins denoting death and is italicized.[33] Death is both inside the protagonist, gnawing at his innards, and outside, staring at him as a separate entity.

It is still very common, at least in Western societies, to conceive of illness as an unwelcome alien being in our body that we need to fight. As Susan Sontag points out in her essay *Illness as Metaphor* (1978), the language of public health commonly employs military metaphors—people *fight* cancer by *bombarding* cells and enhancing the body's *defenses*—and such rhetoric exerts a deep influence over our perception of being ill and healing.[34] In Ivan Ilych's epic, "It" is the antagonist to the hero but at the same time his helper by virtue of its heuristic function. Illness prompts Ivan Ilych's incessant authorial endeavor, his continuous reassessment and reordering of events. Alone in his fight against "It," Ivan Ilych is alone in this emplotment enterprise as well. For the sake of this analysis, the passage just examined represents a crucial point in the novella. Until this moment, the focus of the story has been the protagonist's frustration in the face of explanations of his condition that are inescapably imposed upon him. These explanations reveal, on the one hand, the compelling power of medical discourse and, on the other, the incomprehension between him and his family members. It is only now that Ivan Ilych starts considering death to be within the realm of possibility. This realization changes everything in his assessment of his condition. The awareness of approaching the last stop, of reaching the end more quickly than he had imagined, suddenly introduces a new order of things and casts new light on his life trajectory. Inescapably, death reminds Ivan Ilych of itself from within his flesh—through the fetid taste in his mouth and, above all, through that unbearable pain—but it also stands in front of him, stares at him, and forces him to look at his life with no room for veiling, camouflage, or masks. A major tension of the plot thus far—that is, the conflicting stories and explanations that could more or less do justice to Ivan's feelings and could depict his condition more or less accurately—is completely dismissed with the emergence of the ultimate emplotment endeavor triggered by the prospect of death. If in the previous chapter I analyzed how death sets in motion plots about the past, the future, and its own unfolding, here the emphasis is on how the prospect of death—rather than death itself—shapes the act of emplotment.

Tolstoy expressed his views on how awareness and knowledge change over time in a diagram that he drew in his diary on January 24, 1894, and that illustrates the concept of "double-ended immortality" (figure 2.1). In the diagram, he explains, "the straight line is God. The narrow places are the approach to death and birth. In those places God is closer. He is not hidden by anything. But in the middle of life he is obscured by the complexity of life."[35] As Hugh McLean points out, Tolstoy had contended decades earlier, in responding to Jean-Jacques Rousseau's *Vicaire Savoyard* (1762), which mentions "one-directional immortality" (from death onward), "If the concept of immortality requires the memory of a previous life, then we are not immortal. But my mind refuses to comprehend immortality from one end."[36] The moments of birth and of death constitute points of heightened knowledge, Tolstoy maintains, in which we gain deeper insight into life because God is closer and leads us to see the truth.

It is when Ivan Ilych's condition gets serious, his pain will not subside, and he senses that death is fast approaching—he can already see "It" standing right in front of him and staring at him—that he begins reconstructing the chain of events that have led to his present condition in order to make sense of it. Every time he walks home from a doctor's visit or

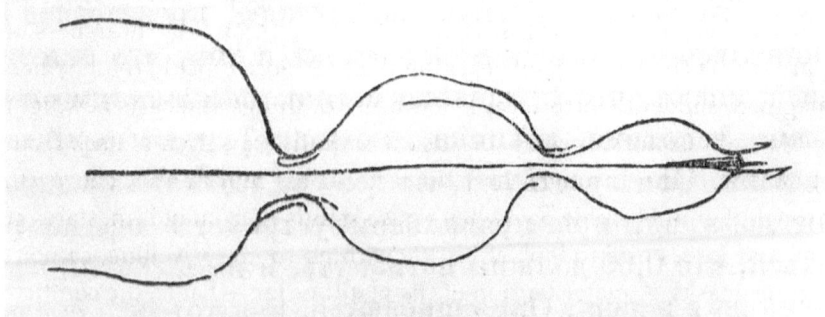

FIGURE 2.1. Tolstoy's diagram of "double-ended immortality." *Source:* Lev Tolstoi, *Dnevniki i zapisnye knizhki, 1891–94*, vol. 52 of *Polnoe sobranie sochinenii*, ed. V. G. Chertkov (Moscow: Khudozhestvennaia literatura, 1952), 110, diary entry for January 24, 1894. Courtesy of the Russian National Library.

experiences another fit of that same old pain, he starts reordering his life into causal-temporal chains, starting from the manifestation of the illness itself:

> "Something must be wrong. I must calm myself—I must think it all over from the beginning." He began thinking again. "Yes, the beginning of my illness: I bumped my side, but I was still quite well that day and the next. It hurt a little, then rather more. I saw doctors, there followed despondency and anguish, more doctors, and I drew nearer to the abyss. My strength grew less and I kept coming nearer and nearer; now I have wasted away and there is no light left in my eyes. I think about my appendix—but this is really death! I think of mending my appendix, and all the while here comes death! Can it really be death?"[37]

This reevaluation of the past prompted by the prospect of an impending death soon extends beyond the clinical realm. Ivan Ilych moves from reconstructing the history of his illness to reevaluating the trajectory of his whole life. After the last visit by a doctor, he is left alone with Gerasim, an uneducated peasant and the only person with whom he feels comfortable. Gerasim performs caregiving tasks for him in a simple and genuine fashion, without empty ceremonies or hypocrisy, which prompts Ivan Ilych to reassess his own life in contrast.[38] Ivan Ilych looks at the young man, and

> the question suddenly occurred to him: "What if my whole life [vsia moia zhizn', soznatel'naia zhizn', 'all my life, my conscious life'] has been wrong [ne to]?" . . . It occurred to him that his scarcely perceptible attempts to struggle against what was considered good by the most highly placed people, those scarcely noticeable impulses which he had immediately suppressed, might have been the real thing, and all the rest false. His professional duties and the whole arrangement of his life and his family, all his social and official interests, might all have been false. . . . He lay on his back and began to pass his life in review in quite a new way. In the morning when he first saw his footman, then his wife, then his daughter, and then the doctor, their every word and movement confirmed the awful truth that had been revealed to him during the night. In them he saw himself—all that for which he had lived—and saw clearly that it was not real at all, but a terrible and huge

deception which had hidden both life and death. This consciousness intensified his physical suffering tenfold.[39]

It is only now, in his last days, that Ivan Ilych realizes how his whole life has been full of hypocrisy and lies:

> What tormented Ivan Ilych most was the deception, the lie, which for some reason they all accepted ... their not wishing to admit what they all knew and what he knew, but wanting to lie to him concerning his terrible condition, and wishing and forcing him to participate in that lie.... Those lies—enacted over him on the eve of his death and destined to degrade this awful, solemn act to the level of their visits, their curtains, their sturgeon for dinner—were a terrible agony for Ivan Ilych.[40]

The prospect of his approaching death reveals the veneer that had coated and stifled the real essence of his life—a veneer that, now that Ivan Ilych can see through it, becomes intolerable. In a conversation with himself, the ill man is able to unmask that frivolousness and superficiality and to trace how it gradually took over his life.[41] After such a powerful and disquieting epiphany, Ivan Ilych can no longer stand the presence of his wife, whose daily gestures (kissing his forehead, insisting on the importance of taking his medications) he now sees are perfunctory and insincere. Even the rituals of doctors' visits seem to Ivan Ilych empty and theatrical:

> [The doctor] begins with a most serious face to examine the patient, feeling his pulse and taking his temperature, and then begins the sounding and auscultation. Ivan Ilych knows quite well and definitely that this is all nonsense and pure deception, but when the doctor, getting down on his knee, leans over him, putting his ear first higher then lower, and performs various gymnastic movements over him with a significant expression on his face, Ivan Ilych submits to it all just as he used to submit to the speeches of the lawyers, though he knew very well that they were lying and knew why they were lying.[42]

It is not by chance that right after this doctor's visit, the stage actress Sarah Bernhardt (1844–1923) is mentioned. An element of insincerity and empty performance is pervasive in the novella. Bernhardt is on tour in Russia, and Ivan Ilych's daughter is rushing to get to her show in time. Recall how, at the beginning of the story, Ivan Ilych's colleagues go about their mourning obligations (bowing, shaking hands, crossing themselves) with superficial and perfunctory movements.

Just as the ending of a story confers new meaning on the events that have led up to it and reorders them retrospectively, the prospect of death possesses a similar emplotting function, becoming the lens through which Ivan Ilych can see anew and reevaluate all the events of his life. The concept of endings being epistemologically charged components of all stories, including one's life trajectory, is further reinforced by Tolstoy's views on birth and death as privileged moments for awareness along the timeline of "double-ended immortality" described in his diaries.

It is also noteworthy that most of Ivan Ilych's reflections about and responses to what happens around him take place in his study, the one room to which the action is confined and in which the protagonist and "It" are alone, while the rest of the story's universe recedes into the background and disappears. Tolstoy's text does not feature the hospital as an institution, and the doctor's office represents an interlocutory stage between the home and the hospital for doctor–patient encounters. When Ivan Ilych is left alone in his study at home, he is able to step out of his role—both as a patient and as a sick relative who is considered a burden—and to look at life with clarity. It is as if spatial isolation were for him the necessary condition to take a step back and rewrite his story in light of his approaching death by reconsidering the validity of established rules: not only the authority of medicine but also the social conventions—the plot that society had outlined for him in all its major steps (wedding, career, wealth, etc.)—by which he used to abide unquestioningly.

In this final step of his long and painful emplotment process, which now includes all his life, past and present, and has assigned a new meaning and a new function to its major events, Ivan Ilych deems it fundamental to have a good death in alignment with the Christian tradition. He takes his sacrament, sees a bright light that makes him think that he will be able to amend his mistakes in the afterlife, and is reconciled with his family through a final look into their eyes. His last words are supposed to be "forgive me" (*prosti*) but come off as "let me pass" (*propusti*),[43] as though to imply that he is now ready to be separated from his mundane world and all those who inhabit it. His mispronunciation of *prosti*, with the addition of a syllable, describes quite realistically the muffled and unclear articulation of our protagonist. Seized by spasms of pain, Ivan Ilych produces additional voiceless bilabial stop consonants, the *p* sound, in the natural movement of his lips as he is taking his last breaths. This detail in word articulation also points to a long tradition of onomatopoeia being employed to express pain that cannot be grasped or conveyed through language or rationalization. One of the earliest iterations (if not the very first) of onomatopoeia employed to denote cries of pain in Western literature is offered in Sophocles's tragedy *Philoctetes* (fifth century BCE). Bitten by a snake and betrayed by his friends Odysseus and Neoptolemus, Philoctetes suffers from pain that is physical and existential. His interactions with Neoptolemus are described as follows:

PHILOCTETES: Ah, ah, ah, ah!
NEOPTOLEMUS: What is the matter?
PHILOCTETES: Nothing grave. Come, my son!
NEOPTOLEMUS: Are you in pain because your sickness is with you?
PHILOCTETES: No, I think I am just getting better. O gods!
NEOPTOLEMUS: Why do you thus groan and call upon the gods?
PHILOCTETES: I am calling on them to come as preservers and be kind to us. Ah, ah, ah, ah!
NEOPTOLEMUS: What is the matter with you? Will you not tell me, but remain silent as you are? You seem to be in some trouble.
PHILOCTETES: I am lost, my son! I shall not be able to conceal my pain in your company. Ah! It goes through me, it goes through me!
O misery, unhappy as I am! I am lost, my son! I am devoured, my son! A-a-a-a-a-h!
I beg you, if you have a sword handy, strike at my heel! Lop it off quickly!
Do not spare my life! Come, my son![44]

Philoctetes resorts to imagery of the sort that we employ today in self-assessment pain scales—"It [the pain] goes through me, it goes through me!" and "I am devoured"—but it is through the onomatopoeia ("Ah, ah, ah, ah!" and "A-a-a-a-a-h!"), appearing as preverbal punctuation constantly interspersed with other words, that the character conveys his condition most effectively, directly, and expressively. It is interesting to note that the onomatopoeia employed in the ancient Greek text, more expressive than in the English translation, is "παπαῖ / ἀπαππαπαῖ, παπαππαπαππαπαππαπαῖ" (papai / apappapai, papappapappapappapai), which features the same voiceless bilabial stop consonant, the *p* sound, that Ivan Ilych utters.⁴⁵

In the moment of his death, Ivan Ilych is described as "struggl[ing] in that black sack [v tom chërnom meshke] into which he was being thrust by an invisible, irresistible force," until he finally breaks through it and sees a bright light.⁴⁶ Critics have associated the black sack both with the intestine, because of Ivan Ilych's illness, and with the uterus.⁴⁷ The latter interpretation, along with the light, makes Ivan Ilych's death resonate even more with Tolstoy's concept of double immortality, whereby birth and death constitute the moments of heightened knowledge made possible by God's nearness. In any event, that Ivan Ilych had a good death was something his colleagues could see by looking at his dead body: "The expression on the face said that what was necessary had been accomplished, and accomplished rightly."⁴⁸

The sentence engraved on Ivan Ilych's watch, "Respice finem" (Consider the end), seems to epitomize the cogent teleology that death as the ending establishes in the novella. The Latin verb *respicere* literally means "to gaze at" (the English word *respect*, intended as "regard," comes directly from it); therefore, the engraving on the protagonist's watch—an object that places emphasis on the passing of time—denotes at once Ivan Ilych's complete reassessment of his life in view of his approaching death and the emplotment in retrospect that death affords. The invitation *respice finem* seems to apply to the circumstances of Eikhenbaum's "ending" as well and to the poignancy he attributed to the finale of a story while uttering what, unbeknownst to him, would be his last words.

STEEPED IN CONTINGENCY? TIME HORIZON IN SERIALIZED NARRATIVES AND LONG-COURSE TREATMENT: ANNA KARENINA AND MASHA GESSEN

> If you want a happy ending, that depends, of course, on where you stop your story.
> —ORSON WELLES, *THE BIG BRASS RING*

We seem to be living in times dominated by long-drawn-out stories that come in installments and both engage and test our guessing abilities, our patience, and our existential and cognitive ambition to get the full picture. Such a turn can be observed in the field of healthcare, where long-course treatment with an uncertain outcome has become quite common with the increase in diagnoses of chronic illnesses and cancer, as well as in the entertainment industry, with the explosion of television series influenced by streaming video, a phenomenon that has raised new questions and posed new challenges to scholars of narrative theories. In both cases, we grapple with a peculiar type of temporality, in which the ending is uncertain, as are the length of the story and the twists of the plot, which is updated each time new information is released—via lab tests and doctors' visits in the medical field and new episodes in a TV series.

Because, as Paul Ricoeur reminds us, we construct "meaningful totalities out of scattered events,"[49] we see our lives as stories unfolding according to causal-temporal connections (Ricoeur's "succession") and the reciprocal positioning of phenomena in space (Ricoeur's "configuration"); oncologists are trained to act like authors or screenwriters and to engage with their patients in what can be defined as therapeutic emplotment. They are taught to manage their patients' expectations and time horizons by making them focus on the present (for instance, with routine tasks, such as scheduling visits and diagnostic exams) and by intentionally blurring the future.[50] One oncologist interviewed by the medical sociologists Mary-Jo DelVecchio Good and her colleagues explains: "You are taught to approach people very cautiously and develop the dialogue or the discussion over time. The first time you meet somebody, it is not necessarily the smartest time to talk turkey. And we are taught to stage things." They employ such images as climbing a mountain "one step at a time," whereby the focus is on the present, while the peak is not visible, hidden somewhere in the clouds.[51] In his autobiography *When Breath Becomes Air* (2016), the cancer patient (and successful surgeon) Paul Kalanithi reports how in the first meeting with Emma, his oncologist, the first piece of information he wanted to learn was where he fell on the Kaplan–Meier survivorship curve. Emma shifted gears by saying, "We can do details later . . . as I know this is a lot to absorb. Mostly, I just wanted to meet you . . . before our appointment Thursday. Is there anything else I can do, or answer—besides survival curves—today?"[52] The oncologist was devoting the first meeting not to talking turkey but, as reported by Good and her colleagues, to "set[ting] the ground for more significant encounters."[53] In the second meeting with her colleague-turned-patient, Emma immediately directed Kalanithi's focus to the here and now: "I know there is a lot to discuss, but first: How are you doing?" She would also refer to a discouraging setback in the course of treatment by saying that it was "a bump in the road, but you can keep your current trajectory."[54] Both metaphors, climbing a mountain day by day in small increments with the peak not yet in sight and traveling on an indefinitely long but linear road, a "trajectory," along which there may be bumps, imply plot and teleology; they instill hope in patients by emphasizing the dimension of immediacy while shaping an ending that is deliberately uncertain and ever receding.

In this section, I discuss endings that are indefinite, ever vanishing, and at the same time undesirable and feared because they threaten to be tragic, and I do so from the point of view of those who inhabit such temporalities. I compare oncology patients and potential ones with both Anna Karenina the character and the novel's readers, whose time horizons and expectations are managed by Tolstoy as masterfully and accurately as oncologists manage their patients'. In order to lay the groundwork for my structural comparisons, I begin by examining, on the one hand, serialization and, on the other, long-course treatment and therapeutic emplotment and by drawing parallels between readers' (or viewers') perspectives and patients' perspectives.

In the current explosion of television series influenced by streaming video, scholars of narrative have been paying close attention to serialization, a mode of storytelling that has a long tradition and that reached its full development, at least in the West, in Tolstoy's times with the nineteenth-century European novel. Reader-response theorists such as Wolfgang Iser, Roman Ingarden, Umberto Eco, and Stanley Fish have closely analyzed the act of meaning making that readers (and viewers of filmed narratives or listeners of oral narratives) constantly perform as the story progresses.[55] Readers try to "uncover the plot" to determine what is really occurring and what is likely to happen as the story unfolds. They thereby construct in response a "virtual text" of remembered pasts and imagined futures that updates and shifts as the action progresses and that represents the "coming together of text and imagination." The "virtual plot" never coincides with the real plot of the text until the reader reaches the end of the story.[56] Scholars of serialized narrative have shown how Iser's concept of "virtual plot" gets further complicated when the story is offered in installments, and they have examined the gap between episodes as a space that generates expectations and grants the readers more room to build a provisional plot.[57]

William Mills Todd III details the publication history and the serialization of *Anna Karenina*, which appeared in installments in the thick journal the *Russian Herald* between January 1875 and April 1877, and he compares the chronology and sequence in the two incarnations of the novel—the serialized version and the book version published in 1878. We learn that in the former each installment presented the reader with some closure, that the division into parts was in fact different in each version, and that the publishers of the *Russian Herald* refused to print part 8, which came out as a separate brochure.[58]

Despite the differences in epoch, technology, and society between Tolstoy's era and ours, certain structural features have defined long-form narratives since Tolstoy's times and are relevant today not only in television series but also, as explained earlier, in doctor–patient interactions. Compared to self-enclosed narratives, series are distinct from the standpoints of authorship, temporality, and reception. Authors of series begin writing with a provisional sense of general plot threads and their developments but without the absolute certainty that self-enclosed narratives grant. This is especially true for today's screenwriters: the first few episodes must be open enough to allow for several options for character and plot development, depending on audience response and periodic feedback from focus groups. The number of episodes over which the story will unfold is not certain at the outset and depends on several factors, including the success of the show and the budget. The modes of reception are particular, too, in that the readership or viewership response—in the form of letters to the journal in the nineteenth century or in more immediately available fan fiction, focus-group reports, and social media debates today—may influence further developments of the story. Of course, in the case of serialized fiction, the readership experience and the process of constructing a virtual plot that is updated as new information is released is even closer to oncology patients' interpretation and understanding of their own therapeutic trajectory. From this point of view—that is, if we compare the oncologist to the author of a serialized narrative who manages the readership's or audience's expectations and time horizons through a careful employment of storytelling devices and if we compare the patient to a reader (although the patient has arguably more investment in the story)—Kalanithi's experience of making better-informed assumptions about his prognosis one bump in the road at a time can be compared to the experience of reading a serialized novel in the nineteenth century. In the case of *Anna Karenina*, we have newspaper reviews of the opening installments of the novel, letters to the author and journal about particular installments, and the author's own reflections on his unfolding novel. Todd reports the experience of Prince Vladimir Mikhailovich Golitsyn (1847–1932), who read *Anna Karenina* as it was appearing in print and recorded in his diary his reactions to the novel's installments. Golitsyn responded to a more sensationalistic novel than the one we know because the divisions between episodes in the journal were not the same as the division into parts in the full novel published as a book: the most shocking parts, such as the consummation of Anna and Vronsky's affair, were placed at the end of an episode. Besides the offense to the prince's sense of propriety, Todd reports Golitsyn's diary entry in response to the third installment, where he hopes for a serious educational function of the novel to emerge in the subsequent parts:

> It would be too hypothetical to assert that this novel will serve to improve society, but one can say with certainty that it will make many people become thoughtful about themselves, and this is already a great deal, especially with us, who are not used to thinking very much, and least of all about ourselves. This denunciatory-educational significance of the novel has come to light most clearly in its third part. I wish from my heart that it will continue this way, develop, and, unsparing and unslackening, reveal, discredit, and condemn certain phenomena of contemporary life, bearing witness to the vulgar decline of our moral force and to the disappearance of our self-awareness.[59]

Todd then shows how midway through the serialization Golitsyn's expectations are left unmet as he reports in his diary that *Anna Karenina* has failed to do what he had hoped. He praises instead the French writer Octave Feuillet for his style: "What a profound knowledge of the human heart . . . the author reveals, and together with this, what subtle taste, what elegant understanding! [His] words contain the profound truth that a soul which has still not completely lost the ability to realize the truth cannot help but be struck by it. I dare say that in *Anna Karenina* there is nothing resembling this in elegance and truthfulness. We Russians have still not attained to such ideas, and we shall not soon attain to them."[60]

Besides and beyond its serialized nature—that is, even as a full book that one can read from cover to cover without temporal gaps—Leo Tolstoy's *Anna Karenina* presents its readers with the unsettling quality of its teleology. A novel without closure, as Gary Saul Morson defines it,[61] *Anna Karenina* unfolds within an unpredictable temporality, in which the ending is regularly anticipated and rehearsed—clearly seen in prospect yet constantly blurred, shifting, and receding. The protagonist's present is shaped by her fatalistic conviction about the tragic death that awaits her, and several events in the novel ring as omens—the deaths of the railroad worker and of the mare Frou-Frou seem to point to a sinister finale in Anna's mind as well as in the reader's; the death of Levin's brother, Nikolai; Vronsky's attempted suicide; the life-threatening complications of Kitty's pregnancy; and Anna's expected death from childbirth (complete with sacraments, a deathbed speech, and Karenin's offering of forgiveness to Vronsky)—all serving as foils for the actual death of the protagonist, which occurs much later in the plot. Tolstoy creates a feeling of tension and uncertainty in both his heroine and his readers, who perceive the ending—not a felicitous one—always hovering over the story. Nonetheless, Anna's death in part 7 does not bring full closure, and the novel continues regardless. Uncommonly and unexpectedly, the ending of Anna Karenina and that of *Anna Karenina* do not coincide. The aftermath of Anna's demise unfolds in the afterlife of the novel, a new part that has little to do with the titular character.

We have seen how *The Death of Ivan Ilych* lays out the linear, if quick, trajectory that the protagonist follows from the day he falls ill to his death: from his superficial and mundane values to his insights about the meaning of life; from isolation and incomprehension to resolution, closure, and redemption in a good death, complete with a postmortem assessment by those who are still leading a life of lies and pretenses. The novella opens ex post facto—the ending is obvious from the first page, if not from the title—and the long flashback follows the protagonist's biography from his youth and culminates in the expected finale. Once the ending of Ivan Ilych's life comes onto the horizon for both the reader and the protagonist, it approaches gradually but steadily until we get to the climax of the novella, whose ending coincides with the death of the protagonist ("He drew in a breath, stopped in the midst of a sigh, stretched out, and died").[62] This powerful, tightened-up closure arrived at by way of a linear trajectory devoid of suspense stands in sharp contrast to the problematic and vaporous sense of an ending that we encounter in *Anna Karenina*. The slippery quality of time and teleology in the novel is to a large extent due to emplotment choices but also in part to serialization, which added to the indefinite temporality in the experience of contemporaneous readers, as each installment of the series offered provisional closure. Through his storytelling, Tolstoy masterfully manages the expectations and time horizon of his heroine, who senses her terrible death from the beginning but does not know when it will occur; of the novel's readers, who partake in Anna's concerns and encounter death—real, anticipated, threatening, and rehearsed—at different points in the plot; and of nineteenth-century readers, who, in addition to the anticipation and expectations that engage readers of all eras, experienced the story in installments, unaware of how many episodes the novel would unfold over or how it would end. Not so differently from physicians who interact with oncology patients, the author of *Anna Karenina* manages the time horizons of both his protagonist and his readers, who in turn construct a virtual plot and update it constantly with every bit of new information (or, in the nineteenth century, every installment that is released), while the prospect of the ending is always present—constantly hovering over the story—but the shape and time of its unfolding are inevitably blurred.

If we look at the novel's temporality in relation to death and endings, we can still detect several traits that make it similar to *The Death of Ivan Ilych*. Among them are the concept of the good death and the prospect of death that casts new light over and confers new meaning on one's life by piercing the veneer of conventions and hypocrisy and allowing one to see things in their true essence. However, all of these elements, although certainly at play in *Anna Karenina*, provide only makeshift closure and fail to bring the plot to completion; therefore, our expectations are constantly betrayed, and the ending is obscured and postponed.

The final stages of Nikolai Levin's illness in the novel introduce the tradition of the good death and caregiving rituals into the story and generate in Levin new insights into the meaning of life (part 3, chapters 31–32).[63] The fearful prospect of Kitty's possible death from childbirth prompts similar epiphanies (part 7, chapter 15). Three deaths—the railroad worker's, the mare Frou-Frou's, and Nikolai Levin's—as well as Vronsky's attempted suicide serve as foils and midway points in the plot that add to the effect of anticipatory tension and pave the way to Anna's suicide. Scholars have underscored the similarities between Frou-Frou's body and Anna's body, such as the "flashing and gay eyes" and a "nimble gait" and the fact that both raise their heads right before dying.[64] Furthermore, in his seminal work on Tolstoy's literary production, Eikhenbaum noticed how the name "Frou-Frou" introduced additional ominous tones for contemporaneous Russian readers, who must have been aware of the tragic story of the titular female character in Henri Meilhac and Ludovic Halévy's play *Froufrou* (1869).[65] Along similar lines, Eikhenbaum pointed out how the novel's epigraph, "Vengeance is mine; I will repay," a major exegetical focus for Tolstoy's contemporaries as well as for generations of literary critics, may be considered the very first omen because it foreshadows Anna's and Vronsky's fates.[66]

The tension builds and deflates again when Anna's death itself is rehearsed thoroughly and in detail but ultimately postponed. Her violent, seemingly fatal fever after Annie's birth becomes the general rehearsal of what would be a good death—one that is instead denied to Tolstoy's heroine—by virtue of all the thoughts and actions it triggers. Anna's deathbed words and exhortations to her husband and Vronsky ironically provide all the closing statements and decisions that characterize the *ars moriendi*: all controversies settled, she is ready to leave in peace with God and humankind, forgiving and forgiven—all of which, quite ironically, she will not have the time to achieve in the moment of her actual death.

At the time of Anna's life-threatening illness, the characters and the readers are prepared for her death and possibly the end of the novel, but within the span of two paragraphs and three days they are repeatedly prompted to recalibrate and update their virtual plot and their expectations (part 4, chapter 17):

> The doctor and his colleagues said it was puerperal fever, which in ninety-nine cases out of a hundred ended fatally [*smert'iu*, "with death"]. All day

she was feverish, delirious, and unconscious. At midnight she lay insensible, with hardly any pulse.

The end was expected any moment. [Zhdali kontsa kazhduiu minutu.]

Vronsky went away, but came again in the morning to inquire.... Toward morning she had become excited and animated, and her thoughts and words flowed rapidly; but again [*i opiat'*] this state lapsed into unconsciousness. On the third day she was just the same, and the doctors gave some hope.[67]

This excerpt is emblematic of the novel's unsettling temporality. The extreme sense of uncertainty and tension as well as the patient's extreme volubility while suffering from a condition that allows for no possible future predictions permeate this passage. The statistics, the use of time expressions such as "any moment" and "rapidly," and the instances of "but again" (*i opiat'*) are indicative of quick and unexpected changes of direction. Vocabulary and syntactic choices amplify the effect: just like the fever, Vronsky "went away, but came again" (uekhal domoi, no utrom on priekhal uznat', "he came back to learn about the developments"). Tolstoy's readers and characters position themselves vis-à-vis the ending in a way that resonates with how many cancer patients experience temporality in reference to the course and outcome of their disease: the timing and quality of the ending are reassessed constantly, and the present scenario is liable to be shattered by any new piece of information that may be revealed in the future (laboratory tests, MRIs, the course of the disease, the body's response to treatment); the patients draw provisional balances that are not conclusive yet must suffice until new information is available, and their expectations about and sense of the outcome are updated at every step.

In the pages leading to Anna's suicide, however, the elements of a good death are offered, if in a blurred, insufficient, and fragmented fashion. In this respect, Anna's final interior monologue leading up to the scene of her actual death, in free indirect speech, can be compared to some extent to Ivan Ilych's end-of-life reflections. Tolstoy employs similar imagery to convey each character's improved understanding of the essence of life, the dissolution of the worldly facade, the clarity with which earthly matters appear, devoid of all conventions and artificiality (part 7, chapter 30):

And now for the first time Anna turned the bright light in which she saw everything upon her relations with him [Vronsky], about which she had always avoided thinking.... She saw it clearly in the piercing light which now revealed to her the meaning of life and of human relations.

The clearness with which she now saw her own and every one else's life pleased her.[68]

Just as Ivan Ilych achieves clarity in the final moments of his life, Anna's approaching death makes her see through the hypocrisy and the deception in which she and those around her had indulged—"a kind of morphia," as she remarked a little earlier in qualifying her morphine use as self-deception (part 7, chapter 12).[69] The light Anna sees at the end of her life evokes Tolstoy's diagram in response to Rousseau that we encountered in the analysis of Ivan Ilych's trajectory—we get closer to God and knowledge at the moments of birth and of death. After all, we see a candle flame is evoked not only at Anna's death but also in the description of the room in which Levin's son is born.

The form of Anna's final reflections is purposely fluid and shapeless, and her stream of consciousness appears to describe what Ivan Ilych parses in clear statements. Liza Knapp has observed that the closer Anna Karenina comes to death, the more acutely she questions language and feels "surrounded by inadequate signs that lack truth." In the hours leading to her death, she feels linguistically isolated, devoid of interlocutors, and no longer sharing a special form of communication with Vronsky.[70]

Interestingly enough, in her final moments Anna clumsily and disjointedly attempts to attain a good death—she crosses herself, asks God for forgiveness, brings up fragments of joyous childhood memories. The feeling of oppression, physical and psychological, has been present from the beginning of the novel and is another trait that Anna has in common with Ivan Ilych. At the end of his life, Ivan compares societal pressure and deception to sitting in a railcar and being confused about what direction one is going: "Suddenly an unknown force crushed against his chest, into his side, and a still stronger force constricted his breathing, he plunged down into the hole, and there, at the bottom, something was shining. What happened to him was like what happens sometimes in railcars, when you think you are going forward but are actually going backward, and suddenly realize your direction."[71]

Up to this point in *Anna Karenina*, readers have been prepared to see Anna's tragic death as the culmination and powerful closure of all the uncertainties, omens, and nerve-racking anticipations, yet Tolstoy decides not to depict the death scene with the solemnity and clarity that the good-death tradition and a more traditional, realistic storytelling technique would require. Once more the readers' expectations are unmet, and the death of the protagonist unfolds within a blurred temporality, dismissed as not the finale but as only one intermediate point of closure within the novel, a major yet partial resolution within a larger story that keeps unfolding without regard to the loss of its heroine.

Besides the structural resonances between the readers of *Anna Karenina* and oncology patients in the way they experience teleology and temporality, another parallel should be highlighted that brings together therapeutic emplotment in long-course, potentially failing treatment and the experience of narrative time in *Anna Karenina*. So far we have focused our attention on the reader's experience. Let's now take a closer look at Anna's own approach to temporality and endings and lay the groundwork for a comparison between such a way of inhabiting time and boundedness and the perception of risk, along with the potential for a tragic ending experienced by so-called previvors in the field of medicine.

Gary Saul Morson, among others, has pointed out the numerous events in the novel that strike Anna and as a consequence the readers as omens—from the death of the railroad worker in part 1, chapter 18, to the deaths of Frou-Frou and of the peasant who appears in Anna's and Vronsky's dreams.[72] The language employed across these discrete events amplifies the resonances in the plot. Among others, the peasant who appears in the dreams pronounces the French saying "Il faut le battre, le fer" ("pendant qu'il est chaud," the saying would continue—"One must strike the iron while it's hot"), and the French for "railroad" is *chemin de fer*, which creates further correspondences between the ominous dream and the suicide scene at the train station. These events and the motif of Anna's unbearable and repeated feeling of oppression—physical, psychological, social—accrue meaning as the story progresses and reveal their full significance in light of Anna's ending. Yet Anna immediately sees them as premonitory signs. Although she has not been diagnosed with an incurable disease, she seems to anticipate with the utmost certainty that she will die under tragic circumstances. She constantly senses that the end is near, and so do the readers. Anna as a character inhabits a peculiar temporality in which an infelicitous outcome is always in sight; she places weight and meaning on the ending to the extent that she interprets and experiences her present in view of a future tragic closure. Morson highlights the strictly binary outcome that the heroine envisions for her trajectory—one utopian, one tragic.[73] Throughout the novel, Anna's stories are often, peculiarly, told from the vantage point of the future (part 4, chapter 3): "'Soon, soon. You were saying that our position was full of torment and should be put to an end.... It will happen soon, but not in the way we think.' And at the thought of how it was going to happen she felt so sorry for herself that the tears came into her eyes and she could not continue." Anna perceives that her tragic ending has been predetermined or that it is fast approaching ("I am near a catastrophe" [part 7, chapter 12]).[74] She feels "sorry for herself" as though reading an already written finale of her story, but her self-destructive tendencies are so powerful that she never considers taking action to avoid such an undesirable outcome. Although she is not physically ill and has no reason to believe that fate has a fatal disease in store for her, her present mood and actions are shaped by the prospect of an unavoidable, terrifying ending toward which her days are unmistakably tending.

When Dolly tries to convince her that a divorce would make things easier (part 6, chapter 23), Anna "d[oes] not listen" and continues expressing her sadness because the "unfortunate" children she may bear out of wedlock "would have to bear a stranger's name! By the very fact of their birth... [they] would have to be ashamed of their mother, their father, their birth!"[75] Anna speaks as though her life were moving through predetermined stages toward a specific ending, as if she were a powerless being in the hands of a cruel puppeteer or a helpless spectator to the sad story of her life. This sensation of spectatorship is well depicted in the scene in which she imagines Vronsky's reaction once she has died (part 7, chapter 26):

> She laid in bed with open eyes, by the light of a single burned-down candle, gazing at the carved cornice of the ceiling and at the shadow of the screen that covered part of it, while she vividly pictured to herself how he would feel when she would be no more, when she would be only a memory to him. "How could I say such cruel things to her?" he would say. "How could I go out of the room without saying anything to her? But now she is no more. She has gone away from us forever. She is...[76]

Here she literally sits back, almost slips into the audience of a play—or a movie, had she been a heroine of our times—and sees her life unfolding on the ceiling that functions as a stage or a screen: she assesses her present condition based on what Vronsky may say or think in the wake of her tragic death.[77]

Although Anna could make active choices in the present that would have an impact on the course of future events and bring happiness to her life, she speaks as though she does not have the option to do so (part 6, chapter 24): "Understand that I love equally, I think, and both more than myself—two beings: Serezha and Alexey... and the one excludes the other! I cannot unite them, yet that is the one thing I desire. And if I can't have that, nothing matters—nothing, nothing! It will end somehow, therefore I can't—I don't like speaking about it."[78]

In Anna's bizarre enterprise of telling stories from the point of the ending, everything becomes a self-fulfilling prophecy as she mitigates her guilt, fends off responsibility, and minimizes the necessity of acting in order to determine her own destiny because she sees herself as a foredoomed tragic heroine. Every attempt other characters make to persuade her to take the reins of her life and make choices fails. Every day of her life is colored by the perception that a terrible fate awaits her. The suicide scene at the end of part 7 is the most emblematic of the complex way in which Anna relates to temporality and makes sense of her present by keeping the ending constantly in sight: "She walked faster away... to the very end of the platform. A goods train was approaching. The platform shook, and it seemed to her as if she were again in the train. Suddenly remembering the man who had been run over the day she first met Vronsky, she realized what she had to do."[79] "She realized what she had to do" (chto ei nado delat'),[80] as though she were following a predetermined script, one that has gradually been revealed to her from the very first omen in part 1 and that she can see clearly and interpret fully now. Every moment in her life has been lived in view of this final scene; all her reflections, explanations, considerations about her present have been articulated from the vantage point of the ending. Ironically, Anna's lifelong emphasis on a powerful and meaningful closure is elided by the general sense of disjointed time segments and missed correspondences that surround her death—unsynchronized communication with Vronsky, among others.

Although readers may be inclined to interpret the chronicle of Anna's haunting thoughts as the expression of an omniscient narrator's point of view, Tolstoy scholars have traditionally warned us against such readings by pointing out how much the novel is concerned with relativization. Among them, Vladimir Alexandrov writes:

> Fictional authority in *Anna Karenina* is... largely dualistic, but without being either dialogic or inconsistent. On the one hand, Tolstoi's typical practice is to portray characters as existing in private worlds that are reflections of their own mental states. In other words, there is relatively little or no "outside" in the novel's world that is independent of a given "inside."... On the other hand, the narrator and some of the characters also make remarks that purport to be expressions of universal and transcendent truths.[81]

The narrator never contradicts Anna when she claims that she sees the truth, and even in the suicide scene we are not certain whether we are experiencing it from the perspective of an omniscient narrator or from Anna's own. There is no evidence that Anna actually notices the shadow of the dead man; we do not know if Anna is seeing anything beyond the limits of her own consciousness; and the narrative here may well be mirroring her fading vision as she is dying.

Based on these premises, we ought to take Anna's considerations and reasoning about the world that surrounds her and the events of her life as potential projections of her subjectivity rather than as insights. Elements in the novel tend to corroborate Alexandrov's point that Anna exists in a world of her own, especially when we see other characters undercutting what she thinks: immediately after she declares that the death of the railroad worker is a "bad omen" (*durnoe predznamenovanie*, with the prefix *pred-* that further emphasizes the foreshadowing, the predetermination), Stiva dismissively responds: "What nonsense!" (part 1, chapter 18). Betsy highlights this mechanism even further by remarking to Anna: "You see a thing may be looked at tragically and turned to a torment, or looked at quite simply, and even gaily. Perhaps you are inclined to take things too tragically" (part 3, chapter 17).[82] Poignantly, Dolly's interpretation of Anna's habit of squinting (*shchurit'sia*) "till only the meeting lashes could be seen," "as if she were blinking at her life so as not to see it all," seems to point to questions of narrative focalization quite literally (part 6, chapters 19 and 21).[83]

Not only is Anna often portrayed reading or writing—the notes and telegrams to and from Vronsky, the novels she reads on the train and at home while Vronsky is away, the children's book she is writing—but she also engages with the world through the filter and according to the rules of the literature with which she is most familiar. She sees herself as a literary character, and she often appears as such to other characters as well in an artful mise en abyme that seems to reassess the very mimetic possibilities of the novel form. Donna Orwin has observed that the word *roman* in the full title, *Anna Karenina: Roman*, means both "romance" and "novel," which speaks directly to that narrative artifice: the title introduces Anna almost as a case study, as the character who best fits the description of a literary heroine. At the same time, Orwin points out, Kitty expresses curiosity about the *roman*—at once the romance and the novel—of Anna's marriage with Alexey Karenin, of whom Kitty had noticed the "unpoetic appearance" (part 1, chapter 30).[84] Along these lines, Liza Merkalova, too, describes Anna as "a real heroine from a novel" (nastoiashchaia geroina romana) (part 3, chapter 17).[85] In revealing the intertextuality of Tolstoy's novel and contemporaneous Western literary prose, Amy Mandelker prompts us to see the Victorian novel both as a tradition to which Tolstoy makes reference and from which at the same time he establishes his distance and as a subtext that constantly runs through *Anna Karenina*. Mandelker reminds us that we cannot understand Anna Karenina's approach to life without bringing such authors as Jane Austen into the picture and that the plot of the Victorian novel that Anna is reading on the train represents a script, "a prolepsis that determines the trajectory of her life."[86] Like Tat'iana Larina in Alexander Pushkin's verse novel *Eugene Onegin* (1825–1832), Anna experiences life, inhabits the world, and interprets events through the filter of Western literary models and conventions, an approach that is further emphasized by the famous sentence in which Tolstoy describes her death and how "the candle by the light of which she had been reading that book [of her life] filled with anxieties, deceptions, grief, and evil, flared up with a brighter light than before, lit up for her all that had before been dark, flickered, began to grow dim, and went out for ever" (part 7, chapter 31).[87]

As we have seen in chapter 1, the act of reordering the events and phenomena that surround us and that we experience into a cohesive plot is a cognitive necessity. Anna Karenina seems to take this approach one step further. Although I will leave the discussion of agency in the novel to Tolstoy scholars, I will remark here that it is striking how deterministically Anna believes that she inhabits a highly semioticized space in which things have been predetermined by some higher, authorial plan where everything holds together and no thread is left hanging. Her approach is similar to that of patients who are trying to make sense of their condition by emplotting symptoms, feelings, and diagnostic information into a cohesive picture and a linear trajectory in which every element is endowed with a specific function and purpose. Yuri Lotman has written eloquently on randomness and contingency in life as compared to events in works of literature, and one of his observations is that "what is asystemic in life is reflected in art as polysystemic." In other words, to convey the illusion of the aleatory chaos and serendipity that characterize real life, authors introduce a particular detail and connect it to many different contexts in their novel—the more disparate the contexts, the more unplanned a detail will appear. Lotman also contends that "everything noticeable in an artistic text is inevitably perceived as meaningful, as something carrying a certain semantic load." Intention and design are what we look for when we are on the receiving end of a story, Lotman remarks: "The listener is inclined to believe that all the elements in a work of art are the result of the poet's designing actions insofar as he knows that there is a certain design in them but does not yet know what that design is."[88] If we apply Lotman's remarks to Tolstoy's novel, then we can certainly claim that Anna acts as though she were immersed in contingency, hence her interpretation of events as omens that must foreshadow some later occurrence. Anna navigates her life as the reader of a novel in which she is the protagonist, a storyworld that is imbued with design and in which all details are meaningful, a book belonging to a genre and tradition with which she is so familiar that she can foresee the plot's turns all the way to the ending, thereby looking at herself in the present from the vantage point of a frightful yet seemingly inescapable future. Ironically, she becomes enslaved to a plot, although all along she is convinced that she is freeing herself from one that had been dictated to her by societal conventions and expectations. Such an existential condition, such a way of engaging with temporality, the unsustainable awareness of a threatening predetermined script that can determine one's life, and the tendency to assess one's present from a possible and undesirable point in the future—all constitute a very tangible and familiar experience for a specific medical demographic, the so-called pre-vivors, in our twenty-first-century society. We now turn to the nonfictional heroine of a contemporary serialized narrative whose way of inhabiting time and teleology has much in common with Anna Karenina's.

To live and interpret the present under the constant influence of an ending that is as terrifying as it is indistinct is not solely an attribute of self-proclaimed doomed tragic heroines. It is also a mode of inhabiting temporality that has become familiar to an increasing number of women in the United States and in other Western countries. It is time to look closely at potential patients—that is, those whose genetic tests show that they are likely to develop cancer sometime in the future and to experience a terrible death preceded by devastating and often mutilating treatment.

In *The Sense of an Ending*, Frank Kermode has shown that our experience and understanding of beginnings and endings as well as our storytelling endeavors are inextricably tied to our being mortal:

> The physician Alkmeon observed, with Aristotle's approval, that men die because they cannot join the beginning and the end. What they, the dying men, can do is to imagine a significance for themselves in these unremembered but imaginable events. One of the ways in which they do this is to make objects in which everything is that exists in concord with everything else, and nothing else is, implying that this arrangement mirrors the dispositions of a creator, actual or possible.... Such models of the world make tolerable one's moment between beginning and end.[89]

Kermode emphasizes human beings' deep need for intelligible ends: "We project ourselves—a small, humble elect perhaps—past the End, so as to see the structure whole, a thing we cannot do from our spot of time in the middle."[90] However, for some, the prospect of the ending—a specific, undesirable one—exerts a particularly strong influence on their self-fashioning, choices, and approach to daily life. This has always been the case for those who are especially fatalistic and deterministic, like Anna Karenina, but the age of genetic testing has changed the way a larger portion of the population conceives of endings and looks at their life's trajectory. Genetic testing has connected possible and undesirable endings with the ultimate beginning by showing how devastating diseases can be inscribed in one's genes. Clinical testing for the BRCA1 and BRCA2 gene mutations, whose presence predicts a vastly increased risk of breast and ovarian cancer, began in the mid-1990s, long before the appearance of direct-to-consumer genetic testing (such as 23andMe and Ancestry). Since then, millions of women in the United States who tested positive have considered undergoing a preventive double mastectomy and oophorectomy to reduce to zero the probability of developing the breast and ovarian cancers they are more likely to experience than most other women.[91] As expected, such a radical decision has generated heated debates, especially after Hollywood celebrity Angelina Jolie underwent the preventive operations between 2013 and 2015. Bioethics experts, patient support groups, physicians, and anthropologists have been grappling with new questions: Is a woman to be deemed irresponsible if she opts out of such major surgeries and their sizeable side effects, deciding instead to be screened regularly, and is she to blame if she then develops an incurable cancer? Or are we dealing, instead, with a form of statistical panic that leads women to drastic self-mutilation and a much lower quality of life? The concept of "risk" in public health has won the attention of anthropologists and social scientists.[92] From the standpoint of narrative theory and for the sake of this chapter, such phenomena stand out when we consider the way in which these *potential* patients engage with temporality. Unlike oncology patients, they have not received a cancer diagnosis, and therefore they are not following any targeted course of treatment. Their position is instead comparable to that of Anna Karenina in that they experience and shape their present life in light of a possibly terrible future. Although we all are mortal, some people's genetic inheritance suggests that they may die of devastating diseases sooner rather than later, and so with the help of genetic testing they decide to change their lives radically, prompted by the prospect of an unbearable ending that they want to avoid at all costs. Their views on and decisions about their present lives are strongly influenced by the risk of a terrible ending that constantly lurks in the background and shapes their thoughts and actions.[93] The slippery, uncertain nature of the ending may generate even more anxieties in the present than a death sentence, with its brutal and brusque certainty, would provoke. In literary history, the transformation of Dostoevsky's death sentence to one of forced labor at the last minute is a powerful incarnation of this type of temporality, and it finds literary expression in *The Idiot* (1868, part 1, chapter 5), when Prince

Myshkin suggests the face of a prisoner condemned to death as a subject for Adelaida Epanchina's painting, as discussed in chapter 1. Myshkin focuses on the condemned man's perception of time between the moment he walks up to the scaffold to the moment the blade of the guillotine falls or right after his death sentence has been commuted to forced labor—in both cases, from the condemned man's perspective every single minute feels like an eternity. That "death-sentence" feeling among those who have tested positive for BRCA1 and BRCA2 is so pervasive that popular culture has coined the term *cancer previvors* to describe those who may become oncology patients in the future as opposed to those who have undergone treatment and become known as "cancer survivors" because they are still alive, even if in remission.

On June 13, 2004, the Russian American journalist Masha Gessen revealed in her *Slate* daily column that she had tested positive for the BRCA1 and BRCA2 genes.[94] Her discovery precipitated the decision to learn as much as possible about the test itself as well as about different types of mastectomy and oophorectomy operations, to seek the advice of several professionals (not all medical doctors), and to determine by the end of that week what she wanted to do. In her daily entries, Gessen shared her background—from her family history to her war-zone reporting to her experience covering AIDS as a journalist in New York City in the 1980s—and documented all the steps that were helping her make an informed decision. She consulted with oncologists, researched surgical procedures and their aftermath, talked with women who had undergone preventive mastectomy and oophorectomy, sought the advice of a Harvard economist who created a formula to compare different scenarios based on probability and risk, and met with a psychologist who studies how and why people make irrational choices, a scholar who examines the role of beauty in evolution, and others. Day after day, her posts showed the decision-making process in all its complexity. Gessen discussed the societal pressure, expectations, and judgments that abound for those who test positive for the mutation and are trying to make a decision; the fact that women in the United States overestimate their risk of getting breast cancer because of how they are told about it by doctors and genetic counselors; and the phenomenon of genetic discrimination on the part of health insurance companies—one more facet of the anxiety that the field of medical genetics tends to instill in people.[95]

END OF STORY

Whether Gessen is reporting her own reflections or those of other patients or physicians, her daily posts are steeped in present urgency, imbued by the anxiety of crucial decision making, and her thoughts, like Anna Karenina's, are heavily influenced by possible future scenarios. "'If you are anything like me,' my doctor says, 'you are looking at your kids and thinking you just want to be around for their college graduation'" (June 13, 2004).[96] Any seemingly insignificant, quotidian gesture, such as looking at one's children, becomes unbearably charged with the variable of a terrible fate inscribed in one's genes (and potentially in those of one's daughters). Thought jumps twenty years ahead and introduces a sinister filter through which Gessen is compelled to look at her present. "Have I mentioned the dread with which the idea of breast cancer fills me?," she asks on June 16, 2004. "Have I mentioned that since I tested positive, I have made mental note of every moment that occurs in the course of every day when it is assumed that I will live a few more decades? Like when we talk about the kids going to college, the kids getting married, my writing many more books, or just getting old. It is amazing, actually, how many references to the uncertain, distant future we make—and now, every time we do, I think of my mutation."

The future is constantly superimposed on the present in inescapable palimpsests that the awareness of her "mutation" prompts her to construct. In Gessen's words, one can detect the unbearable indeterminacy of an abrupt turn of the plot that would quickly lead to an unhappy ending that remains elusive and uncertain in terms of both timing and probability. Planning will work only for the near future as she checks on whether her disease is still only potential, concealed, or now boldly out in the open. It also morphs along with the release of new scientific knowledge that dictates what the new best strategy to keep the genetic time bomb at bay will be. On June 22, 2004, she writes:

> It's not easy, being an empowered patient: I keep putting off calling my doctor and explaining to her that to have the best chance of detecting ovarian cancer early, I want CA-125 tests [early-detection tests] every two to three months and that each time I want to have blood drawn a couple of times in one week, to compensate for the wide variations in levels of this substance. When I do tell her this, I will be passing on the latest thinking, which just

might prove completely erroneous in a couple of years. But if I don't do it, I will be angry with myself and might even be taken to task by other BRCA-mutant women for not being sufficiently empowered.

These entries read like what-if reflections, like an assessment of Gessen's present formulated by an imaginary future self, who is living with the consequences of a very poor choice or perhaps of a very good one or anywhere in between. Guesses and concerns about what meaning the present will acquire from the vantage point of the ending are constantly there as structural components in her act of plot building. The fact that Gessen takes the choices and expectations of other women with the same mutation into account in her decision making confers on her entries the traits of a collective story, as though her condition were entangled in those of a whole group of women, and her decision might have repercussions for them, their rights, and their empowerment.

Gessen's constant superimposition of a daunting ending on her present resonates with Anna Karenina's. Anna, too, when prompted to take action in the present, jumps ahead and looks at it from the vantage point of a possible future (remember her mentioning the "unfortunate" and "ashamed" children she will bear out of wedlock in response to Dolly's simple suggestion that she consider divorcing Karenin in the present). Both Anna's and Gessen's stories are told from the vantage point of their endings. It is precisely the way that cancer previvors such as Gessen inhabit their present and engage with temporality that allows for a comparison with Tolstoy's tragic heroine. Without a doubt, of course, we are dealing with two different contexts and approaches to life. Whereas Anna, with her fatalistic attitude, sees no place for responsibility and pays no attention to the past or present, instead living in view of the tragic future she imagines for herself, the notes written by the previvor Gessen engage prominently with responsibility, with taking one's future in hand and steering it in a direction other than the one it would likely otherwise take. Yet in both cases we encounter decisions that are made (or postponed or altogether avoided) with regard to an ending that is dictated by superstition and fatalism in one case and by statistics in the other.

Written on June 22, 2004, Gessen's last entry, just like the death scene of Anna Karenina, reads like a script:

I know that whatever I decide, it will be irreversible. But I have to make the decision. So, here they are. I plan to get a bilateral mastectomy with immediate DIEP flap reconstruction as soon as my daughter is weaned.... I am not going to get a preventive oophorectomy, at least until I am 40, and will aim to avoid getting one at all, which means staying up-to-date on early-detection research and forcing my physician to do so as well. This means that for the rest of my life I will bear the physical marks of my mutation and will have to stay obsessively on top of medical research and my own health. This is the sort of thing that eventually happens to most people—but for me, like so many other things, it has to happen earlier.

Whereas Anna, prey to her self-destructiveness, follows a script that she considers penned by fate—although in fact she is determining it completely if unconsciously—Gessen actively authors her own script, one steeped in contingency and fear yet based on the information she has collected, on her best judgment, and on her existential reflections.

To witness to Gessen's decision-making process allows readers to plunge into the dimension of an uncomfortable present pervaded with a sense of urgency and uncertainty. Although it is hard to predict if and when cancer will develop, that undesired ending hovers over all the entries, instills anxiety in Gessen and the readers, and shapes every second of her daily life. Years later Gessen collected and edited all these entries into a book. In this new version, Gessen adds a sentence right after reporting her last blog entry: "I wrote that.... Then, secretly, I decided to give myself some time to get used to my decision—or not."[97] Although the sense of tension and urgency that the daily entries conveyed is mitigated in hindsight by means of the reflective narrative that the book form entails, the collection nonetheless constitutes but a partial sum, a subtotal, of the future still manifesting in the everyday dimension in all its weight and uncertainty.

If from the point of view of narrative theory Gessen's mode of engaging with time and the present is structurally comparable to Anna Karenina's, her serialized authorial endeavor puts her in the position of managing the reader's time horizon along with her own as a character. One may therefore argue that Gessen's position in the narrative universe is somewhat similar to Tolstoy's. In this connection, it is crucial to consider Tolstoy's own approach to time, the present, teleology, and endings and how he attempted to tame uncertainty and his fear of death by writing a diary. With a closer look at his way of maintaining authorial control over his life, parallels with Gessen's and Anna's approaches emerge.

Boris Eikhenbaum and Viktor Shklovskii famously drew attention to how Tolstoy used his activity of diary writing to rehearse techniques that he would then develop in full in his literary works. Irina Paperno takes this observation further by contending that young Tolstoy, influenced by Rousseau's ideas, strived to make his life into an open book that could be read as such.[98] In other words, Paperno argues, he fashioned himself as the protagonist of the story he authored day by day in installments in the book of life that was his diary. It was not only concern about how his life would read that influenced Tolstoy's diary writing but also the prospect of his own assessment of today's achievements from the vantage point of tomorrow. For the first half of 1847, from January 27 to June 7, Tolstoy kept a journal of his daily occupations (*zhurnal ezhednevnykh zaniatii*), which served both for assessment and planning. He divided each page in two columns—the one on the left was titled "Future" ("Budushchee"), and in it he listed all the tasks that he planned to accomplish the next day; the one on the right was titled "Past" ("Proshedshee"), and he would comment on the previous day's achievement(s) and would often state "not quite" (*nesovsem*).[99] This habit alone seems to show Tolstoy's difficulty in capturing the present without casting his critical eye forward to the future and looking back from that vantage point in a way that resembles both Anna Karenina's and Masha Gessen's approaches to time and the latter's attempt to fix the past and plan the future in writing as a tool for relief, to manage the anxieties of watching time go by. Moreover, from the 1880s on—that is, for thirty years—Tolstoy expected death every day, as his diaries attest. For some reason, like Anna Karenina and Masha Gessen, he led his daily life under the influence of what he perceived as a hovering threat, an approaching ending. This existential condition was translated in his diaries with a new temporal mapping: the daily account no longer ended with a plan for the next day but with the initials *E. b. zh.*, which stood for *esli budu zhiv*, "if I am alive," and, correspondingly, the account of tomorrow opened with the confirmation *zhiv*, "alive."[100] It is no surprise that Victor Hugo's novel *Le dernier jour d'un condamné* (1829), the fictional journal of a man who has been condemned to death written on his last day alive, provided great inspiration for Tolstoy's experiments in describing the thoughts, impressions, and feelings on the last day of his life, which in turn resonates with Dostoevsky's experience and his attempt to parse it by fictionalizing it, refracted into his characters' recollections, as in the passage on Myshkin at the Epanchins' described in chapter 1. The death-sentence feeling and the sense of an approaching ending colored Tolstoy's own way of inhabiting his present; they provide a foil to read Anna Karenina's insights into and projection onto the world as well as adding a dimension to the act of writing fiction, especially in installments, as an operation by which an author not only manages the readers' expectations and time horizon, as oncologists do with patients, but also relieves anxieties about the present and the future—all narrative coping mechanisms that Masha Gessen employs, too, by conveying her existential condition and gaining control over an unsustainable temporality by authoring her story for an audience and for herself.

In this regard, another, not irrelevant, aspect to consider in the types of storytelling examined here—therapeutic emplotment, Masha Gessen's reports on her thoughts and actions after testing positive for BRCA1 and BRCA2, Tolstoy's writing of *Anna Karenina* in installments—is that the authors themselves, although usually more knowledgeable than the readers (or the patients) about the details of the story, are not completely omniscient. Oncologists base their work on statistics, experience, and approximation; Gessen speaks to us from a position of uncertainty, although she can give us details and describe the recent past and her resolutions for the future; Tolstoy's plans for *Anna Karenina* changed as he was writing it by way of a reassessment mechanism that resonates with those same strategies for taking control over the flow of time that he practiced in his diaries.

The sophisticated architectonics of the final version of the novel, with their intricate "linkings" (*stsepleniia*), of which Tolstoy famously boasted in a letter to N. N. Strakhov on April 23, 1876,[101] appeared clearly to the author in hindsight but were not laid out as such from the very beginning. Not only did Tolstoy's central concern shift over time from Anna's fate to Levin's spiritual trajectory, but Russia's foreign policy also prompted the author to add a whole new part, the eighth, that reads mostly like a pamphlet on the Balkan wars and comes right after what had been intended to be the novel's culmination, Anna's death. Just like his readers, Tolstoy was unaware as he wrote of how the novel would end (the same had been true for *War and Peace*), just as Dostoevsky, when he set out to write *Crime and*

Punishment, did not know whether Raskol'nikov would commit suicide, instead making a decision while writing.[102] Part 8 of *Anna Karenina* therefore reads like an epilogue or, rather, like the aftermath of Anna's ending or a postmortem examination of both the novel and Anna herself. Indeed, we find a final, harsh postmortem assessment by Countess Vronskaia of Anna's life, along with the description of her body,[103] which may have been influenced by Tolstoy's attending the postmortem examination of Anna Stepanovna Pirogova's mangled body. Pirogova was the mistress of his neighbor A. N. Bibikov and threw herself under a train after learning that Bibikov intended to marry another woman.[104] From the diaries of Sof'ia Andreevna, Tolstoy's wife, we learn how this real-life tragic event offered Tolstoy inspiration for the subject of his novel,[105] which would beg for a plot that comes full circle, thus emphasizing endings as generative beginnings. However, the novel does not offer closure or a proper ending.[106] *Anna Karenina* as a literary work does not have a "good death." Tolstoy refuses to make death and endings coincide, and his unusual choice points to an extradiegetic dimension: a broader horizon expands past the novel's storyworld, and Anna's story, although supposedly the centerpiece, is but one facet of the fictional world presented therein and is thus put in perspective.

Therefore, within the map that this chapter has been drawing, Gessen figures as the structural equivalent of both Anna Karenina and oncology patients in that she lives her life under the influence of a feared ending. However, she also plays a role similar to that of Tolstoy and of doctors embarking with patients on long-course treatment in that she spins the thread of the plot in installments, at once managing her readers' expectations and time horizon about the plot and coping with her uncertainty about the plot's ending as well as with her own unbearably indeterminate existential dimension in real life.

The game of narrative nesting articulated in this section on threatening, anticipated, and ever-receding endings further complicates epistemological resonances between narrative closure and end of life. Fear of death, existential anxiety, and the irrational ambition to control the flow of time call for narrative means; they necessitate storytelling devices that allow for the constructing, reading, and reauthoring of one's life as a work of literature and that deeply shape Tolstoy's aesthetics in his personal as well as public writing. By the same token, the use of specific rhetorical and literary strategies to make sense of existential anxieties that result from a slippery temporality proves a helpful tool to parse, on the one hand, the experience of contemporary patients—actual and potential—and, on the other, the way doctors manage and handle uncertainty about a tragic and undesirable ending in long-course, arduous, and potentially unsuccessful treatment.

Relativization and subjectivity; the coexistence of several emplotment choices, all plausible and legitimate, through which different characters inhabit the world and make sense of it; an author's masterful managing of time horizon and expectations—such narrative means underlie the production and reception of serialized narratives, literary and medical alike, and engage with individuals' existential anxieties. This is naturally expected, even of realist novels. However, those same mechanisms are at work in collective narratives as well, including scientific ones, which are not commonly understood to be just as amenable to arbitrary emplotment and relativization. The next chapter closely examines how political and medical authorities lead a joint-authorship endeavor in crafting narratives of health and illness in which citizen-patients, whose expectations are carefully mastered, are initially positioned at the receiving end but gradually become active participants, and diffused authorship ensues. The act of managing the time horizon of individuals and their organisms results in plans and regulations for the collective, for the state-as-body, by way of rhetoric, imagery, and masterful plot construction, medical and political at once.

Chapter Three

MEDICAL ENLIGHTENMENT IN THE EARLY 1920S

Rhetoric and Diffused Authorship in Jules Romains's *Knock* and Soviet Public-Health Campaigns

A case study unlike any other appeared in an issue of the *New England Journal of Medicine* in early 1994. Penned by Dr. Clifton K. Meador from Vanderbilt University, it was titled "The Last Well Person," and it opened as follows:

> Well people are disappearing.... I began to realize what was happening only a year ago, at a dinner party. Everyone there had something. Several had high cholesterol levels. One had "borderline anemia." Another had a suspicious Pap smear. Two others had abnormal treadmill-test results, and several were concerned about codependency. There were no well people. After that, I began to look more carefully. I have not met a completely well person in months. At this rate, well people will vanish. As with the extinction of any species, there will be one last survivor.[1]

These first anecdotal lines give away the speculative nature of the case to follow; although rushing to fictional conclusions, Meador's article serves to scrutinize and question the epistemological premises that inform commonly shared views on health and the established criteria and procedures employed to test it. In other words, the reader is prompted to revisit the very paradigm of health in which Western medical institutions and the general public operate. Here is how the author briefly sketches the pillars that support this system:

> The demands of the public for definite wellness are colliding with the public's belief in a diagnostic system that can find only disease. A public in dogged pursuit of the unobtainable, combined with clinicians whose tools are powerful enough to find very small lesions, is a setup for diagnostic excess. And false positives are the arithmetically certain result of applying a disease-defining system to a population that is mostly well.
>
> What is paradoxical about our awesome diagnostic power is that we do not have a test to distinguish a well person from a sick one. Wellness cannot be screened for. There is no substance in the blood or urine whose level is reliably high or low in well people. No radiologic shadows or images indicate wellness. There is no tissue that can undergo biopsy to prove a person is well. Wellness cannot be measured, yet we seek it with analytic methods.[2]

The constant furthering of medical knowledge and the improvement of diagnostic tools, Meador continues, have led us to think that "if we feel good, stay active, and are comfortable, then we are *probably* well—*at least for the time being*. Clinical medicine can only say, '*With the methods we used*, we found none of the diseases *we looked for*.'"[3] As these qualifiers highlight, because medical knowledge is constantly provisional, the validity of each statement is temporally circumscribed, characterized by built-in doubt, and constantly amenable to being discarded in favor of a better-informed hypothesis or practice. Because the field does not operate with immutable certainties, "no one can measure the absence of all disease." Over the past century, the attainment of deeper and more specialized medical knowledge seems to have translated directly into a higher number of diagnoses, to the extent that "if the behavior of doctors and the public continues unabated, eventually every well person will be labeled sick."[4]

Every person but one, and it is to the description of this last survivor, the titular last well person, that the speculative case study, set in the near future (1998), is devoted. Meador meets him at the Mid-America Health Fair, held in a shopping mall in Kansas and offering screening for all *known* human diseases. The last well person, a professor of algebra at a small college, devotes about seven hours and thirteen minutes a day to staying healthy. He regularly undergoes all kinds of screenings and tests, some of which he has learned to perform himself, such as examining his own vocal cords with a mirror. "With each report of a new potential toxin or food additive or any of the myriad newly discovered health hazards, he narrows his diet, adjusts the humidity in his home, adds extra filters to his heating system, or makes yet another change in his lifestyle." His attention to diet is meticulous, he subscribes to health magazines and journals, and "he is an aerobic wonder." He sees his dentist twice a year and takes excellent care of his dental hygiene daily. He wears a prescription wavelength-adjusted set of dark glasses whenever he goes outside, and he takes Polaroids of the suspicious nevi he spots on his skin and has biopsies performed on them. His lengthy medical workups are repeated regularly, and "every orifice has been subjected to endoscopy at least once, and most of them annually." At no time has any test or procedure yielded a positive or abnormal result that remained abnormal when the test was repeated. Mental health is also actively maintained: "The patient has made many efforts to be screened for every known psychopathological disorder" by practitioners from all leading psychological schools of thought. From this description, the man's lifestyle appears laborious, his mind and body constantly pervaded by doubt and anxiety about staying healthy. Meador does not fail to observe that "in earlier times the man would have been considered to have an obsessive-compulsive neurosis, but that diagnosis has had to be dropped. Obsession is no longer a disease, but an essential attribute of staying healthy."[5]

In closing, Meador expands his analytical lens from the close-up observation of the last well person's lifestyle to the articulation of dystopian big-picture remarks on where humankind is headed within a rapidly changing healthcare landscape: "That is how I suppose the last well person might appear.... In my imagined meeting with the last well person I can hear myself saying, 'Doing all those boring things you do to stay healthy may or may not make you live longer. However, I am sure of one thing: it will make your life seem longer.'" And in reaction the last well person will not smile or see any humor in Dr. Meador's words: "Escaping disease in the 1990s is very serious business."[6]

The concepts "health," "healing," and "disease" have evolved considerably over the past sixty years. As Joseph Dumit argues in *Drugs for Life*, three major trends have profoundly transformed the way we look at illness and health since the 1950s: risk factors have become a major focus of public-health interventions; clinical trials have been increasingly employed to identify smaller and smaller health risks for treatment; and the pharmaceutical industry has grown considerably in power and size. The most relevant transformation in our understanding of health is that illness need no longer be felt.[7] There often is no "chief complaint" on the part of the patient, who—if screening tests and clinical trials so indicate—is considered in need of a cure even though the body is silent. Numbers determine not only a state of illness but also a state of risk that can ideally be reduced by a specific treatment.[8] In *Making Sense of Illness*, the historian Robert Aronowitz has drawn attention to the revolution in diagnostic methods that the emphasis on prevention brought about.[9] If health was once the default condition, occasionally disrupted by diseases (as implied by the expression "to fall ill"), now health is a relative category: one would be healthier if one were on drugs, especially in adulthood. In other words, we are inherently ill, or in the very best of all possible scenarios, as Dr. Meador claims, "we are probably well—at least for the time being."

The epistemological premises of such a view of health were already under scrutiny in the first half of the nineteenth century. In 1943, during the Nazi occupation of France, Georges Canguilhem published *The Normal and the Pathological*.[10] In it he revealed how the definition of each of those titular conditions is, vis-à-vis the other, far from being constant and objective and is constantly reviewed and renegotiated according to the values, the goals, and the historical-epistemological situatedness of any given society that is called to set policies and draw the line between the two.

This two-pronged chapter addresses earlier iterations in interwar Europe of major tenets seen in present-day medical rhetoric—education and enlightenment, patient empowerment, preemptive medicine, and peer surveillance. Such concepts, employed with clearly different goals, characterize state-run public-health campaigns and for-profit medical enterprises alike and entail diffused authorship on matters of health and illness beyond the mere patient/physician dichotomy. I discuss how these narratological-epistemic pillars of medical communication can be traced to conceptions of health and illness that date back to interwar Europe, as articulated in state public-health campaigns as well as in fictional texts, with obvious differentiations that emerge from culture- and genre-specific medical discourse. Specifically, I focus my analytical lens on rhetorical strategies and questions of diffused authorship in Jules Romains's theatrical comedy

MEDICAL ENLIGHTENMENT IN THE EARLY 1920S

Doctor Knock, or The Triumph of Medicine (*Knock, ou Le triomphe de la médecine*, 1923), which stages a physician's successful quest for wealth, and early Soviet public-health campaigns, including a state-commissioned play. It goes without saying that medical-pharmaceutical advertising and public-health campaigns set for themselves very different goals and are informed by quite different values and motivating principles. However, they have in common rhetorical patterns and views on health and illness that, far from being neutral, are shaped by specific agendas—be they political or commercial. Therefore, both types of messages entail a certain degree of arbitrariness and an interpretative endeavor that constructs specific kinds of stories and is thus akin to authorship. From this specific standpoint, one may even argue that propaganda and advertising are fundamentally equivalent. Such forms of widespread and established discourse around health and illness also entail, rely on, and perpetuate power structures that become ingrained in the societies from which they spring, all the more so when power presents itself as legitimized by science. Vivid examples of these configurations emerged in interwar Europe, when the changing language of medicine went hand in hand with the rise of totalitarian dogmas and, in general, of unprecedented state control over the population and its health.

"TOUT HOMME BIEN PORTANT EST UN MALADE QUI S'IGNORE": STORYTELLING IN THE *ÂGE MÉDICALE*

Jules Romains (1885–1972) wrote *Knock* in a handful of weeks during the summer of 1923, and the first staging, with Louis Jouvet as the leading actor, took place on December 14 of the same year at the Comédie des Champs-Élysées. The play immediately saw enormous success, and for years to come Jouvet's theater troupe would stage *Knock* anytime they were in a rough patch and needed a financial boost.[11]

The plot is quite straightforward. A physician of dubious credentials, Knock, arrives in the fictional village of Saint-Maurice in the central-eastern part of France, where he is meant to replace Doctor Parpalaid, who is moving to Lyon. Everybody in the village seems healthy, and therefore the volume of work Knock inherits is very modest. Alarmed by the perspective of a low income, in three months' time Knock, in cahoots with the schoolmaster and the pharmacist, sets out a sophisticated strategy that eventually transforms Saint-Maurice into a place where everybody is aware of all the potential threats that the environment poses to their health on a daily basis, and everyone has been diagnosed with some sort of disease or is considered at high risk and actively seeks treatment, which is offered for as long a time as possible. After everybody is converted to Knock's vision of medicine, the only hotel in the village is transformed into a clinic to accommodate the increasing number of patients coming from the whole valley. When Parpalaid visits Saint-Maurice, he is astonished by the revolution that the new medical age (*l'âge médicale*) has brought about and by the wealth of both his successor and the pharmacist, Monsieur Mousquet. Tired from the journey, he checks into one of the rooms at the hotel, thus immediately and unexpectedly becoming a patient himself.

The play shows how sales rhetoric can be applicable to medicine, which has two contrasting results. First comes the comic effect, built up visit after visit as we learn about the absurdity of Knock's diagnoses and plans. However, a disquieting effect overcomes laughter by the end: when Knock has imposed his reign, everybody complies with his rules, and he claims that he is the creator of the new world that has unfolded before the eyes of the villagers and the audience. Besides the obvious resonances with the historical circumstances of the interwar decades, one should note that the very name "Knock" lends dark nuances to the play's overall tone. In F. W. Murnau's film *Nosferatu the Vampire* (1922), released only a year before Romains's play was staged, the housing agent in league with Count Orlock (Nosferatu) goes by the name "Knock." Nosferatu famously travels on a ship from the Carpathians to Wisborg and kills most of the sailors by spreading the plague. In Jules Romains's piece, we learn that Knock started practicing as a doctor on a ship on which all workers gradually became sick. However, Romains never explicitly acknowledged the connection with Murnau's character.[12]

The idea that medicine is imbued with rhetoric is not at all recent. Aristotle maintains in the *Rhetoric* that "every ... art can instruct or persuade about its own particular subject matter; for instance, medicine about what is healthy and unhealthy."[13] As a work of French literature, *Knock* inscribes itself within a tradition of satirical writing that has doctors and medicine as its targets and that can be traced back to the Middle Ages with the *Fabliau du villain mire* (thirteenth century) and, later and most famously, with Molière's *The Doctor in Spite of Himself* (*Le médecine malgré lui*, 1666) and *The Imaginary Invalid* or *The Hypochondriac* (*Le malade imaginaire*, 1673). More broadly, the rich variety of quack doctors on stage that European literature, theater, and opera have offered—from Palutus's *Menaechmi* (second to third century BCE) to Mozart's *Così fan tutte* (1790)—testifies to the multifarious translations of the pernicious and self-serving fantasies of the quack into various types of artistic fiction.[14] At the same time, Romains veers away sharply from another, more recent tradition, that of Balzac, Flaubert, and Zola, whose doctor characters were champions of scientific progress and whose efforts were directed toward dissipating ignorance.[15] It is precisely ignorance that allows Knock to establish his authority in Saint-Maurice and to instill in its inhabitants a blind faith in science and medicine through his concerted publicity campaigns. Romains himself had explored the complex role of rhetoric and advertising in determining scientific truth in his satirical movie script *Donogoo-Tonka, or The Miracles of Science* (*Donogoo-Tonka, ou Les miracles de la science*, 1920), readapted ten years later for the stage as a play entitled simply *Donogoo*, "a heroic comic epic of modern publicity," as the author defined it.[16]

Knock has enjoyed great success over the years. It has been staged all over the world and translated into many languages, including Afrikaans, Esperanto, and Annamite. A timely piece when it was published, *Knock* continues to appeal to present-day audiences, which may be largely ascribed to the fact that it addresses topics that are still relevant and in doing so emphasizes the role that rhetoric, interpretation, and storytelling play even in a field, medicine, that today is more impersonal and disembodied than ever.

The play opens with Knock driving through the French countryside to the village of Saint-Maurice. He is in the company of Doctor Parpalaid, his predecessor as village doctor in Saint-Maurice, and the doctor's wife, Madame Parpalaid. The car has some mechanical problems, so the travelers have plenty of time to enjoy the views of the valley, perhaps modeled on Saint-Julien-Chapteuil, where Romains spent his childhood, and to engage in conversation. Knock does not waste this opportunity to inquire about the size of the population, its average income, habits, vices, and religious beliefs—questions that other characters as well as Romains's contemporary readers might have found bizarre but that from today's perspective and with our present terminology are clearly aimed at assessing the market size of Saint-Maurice and its growth potentials:

KNOCK: Are there many people suffering from rheumatism in the village?
THE DOCTOR: One would say that there are exclusively people suffering from rheumatism.
KNOCK: Those seem of great interest.
THE DOCTOR: Yes, for him who would like to study rheumatism.
KNOCK: *softly.* I was thinking of customers.[17]

As Knock proceeds in his inquiry, he learns that everybody pays for their doctor visits only once a year, on Saint-Michel Day, at the end of September, which alarms him considerably, given that it is now the beginning of October and the payment date has just passed.[18] One question appears particularly odd to his interlocutors:

KNOCK: So, what do you do with regular customers?
MADAME PARPALAID: Which regular customers?
KNOCK: Well! Those whom you visit multiple times per week, or multiple times per month?
MADAME PARPALAID: *to her husband.* Did you hear what the doctor said? Customers, just as the baker's or the butcher's?[19]

Knock's questions and unusual language ("customers" instead of simply "patients") anticipate his innovative vision, expressed two pages later: "I intended to apply entirely new methods."[20] Right after this programmatic statement, we learn that Knock has never finished his medical school thesis. He has completed only thirty-two pages in octavo entitled *On Purported States of Health* (*Sur les prétendus états de santé*), with the epigraph "Healthy people are sick people who don't know themselves" (Les gens bien portants sont des malades qui s'ignorent), which he has inaccurately attributed to Claude Bernard. Nevertheless, Knock has been practicing as a doctor for twenty years, and most of his knowledge of anatomy and physiology is derived from reading medical ads, which had begun to appear in French newspapers and magazines in the nineteenth century and fascinated him immensely. Before becoming a self-declared doctor on the ship where during a journey, as he reports, a few people died and all the others became ill, Knock had a business selling peanuts.

His views on the medical profession are indeed new and much informed by commerce, which the appearance of the word *réclame* a few lines earlier suggests ("si ... quelque patient ... réclame l'assistance de mon art" [if ... a patient ... requires my professional assistance]).[21] Although *réclame* here is the third-person singular of the verb *réclamer*, "to request" or "to require," when used as a noun it means "advertising." Uttered in act 1, it frames the whole work: Knock sees the domains of health and medicine as an opportunity for business—just like peanuts, health is an industry, and in 1923 this concept is outlandish enough to characterize the play as a comedy. However, Knock has a vision and a mission possessing nearly epic overtones. His plan is solemnly announced toward the end of act 1: "the medical age can begin" (l'âge médicale peut commencer).[22] This new age will entail a profound, epistemic transformation in the villagers' view on health and disease. The grandiosity of this statement, which in act 1 still contributes to a comic effect, appears in retrospect—that is, considering how the play ends—disturbing and totalizing. As we will see, it is not merely the introduction of catchy claims or advertising that makes Knock's plan for health in Saint-Maurice innovative: rather, it is the fact that he sets in motion a complete robust and sophisticated communication strategy that will change the way people conceive of health, and in so doing, he makes rhetorical choices that strikingly point to the path that medicine had begun to take in the previous decade and would further explore in the decades to come.

In act 2, as soon as Knock arrives in Saint-Maurice, he inaugurates his campaign. Upon meeting the town crier to schedule a formal announcement, he immediately requests that he be called "doctor" (*docteur*) and not simply "sir" (*monsieur*).[23] This detail, which Parpalaid had overlooked, is of crucial importance in conferring upon Knock undisputed authority in matters of health in his interactions with the villagers. Labels and definitions greatly shape power dynamics, as Foucault argues in *The Order of Things* (1966);[24] therefore, Knock now has carte blanche to author and construct individual and public-health narratives about his new community. As he chats with the town crier, he informally proceeds to what we would define as his market research by learning what people thought of Doctor Parpalaid.

Among other things, the town crier claims that people are not satisfied when they are not prescribed anything but a natural remedy, such as an herbal tea: "Vous pensez bien que les gens qui payent huit francs pour une consultation n'aiment pas trop qu'on leur indique un remède de quatre sous. Et le plus bête n'a pas besoin du médecin pour boire une camomille" (You can imagine that people who pay eight francs for a visit do not appreciate being given a cheap remedy. Even the most ignorant man does not need to see a doctor to drink chamomile tea").[25]

This new piece of information adds one more detail to the already accurate assessment that Knock has outlined based on his surveys. Now the time has come for him to introduce himself to the whole village, with drums, a crier, and scheduled announcements—that is, precisely the channels and media that still largely characterized advertising campaigns at that time.[26] The tradition of town criers dates back to ancient Greece and Rome, where they were hired on the basis of their pleasant voices and eloquence to advertise auctions of slaves and animals. They were sometimes accompanied by instruments. In Europe through the Middle Ages and early modern period, with the waning of feudalism, the institution of craft guilds, and the emergence of the middle class, criers were paid to advertise a merchant's goods. In early capitalistic societies and up until mass media took over all public communication, this practice remained the most effective way to get the attention of passers-by, which is the first necessary step in a sale.[27]

Here is Knock's announcement:

> Doctor Knock, the successor of Doctor Parpalaid, gives his regards to the population of the town and region of Saint-Maurice. He has the honor to inform you that, in a philanthropic spirit and in order to slow down the alarming progress of all sorts of diseases that have invaded for a few years our once healthy lands [le progrès inquiétant des maladies de toutes sortes qui envahissent depuis quelques années nos régions si salubres autrefois] ... every Monday from 9:30 a.m. to 11:30 a.m. he will offer totally free visits to all the residents of the region. Those who come from outside the region will be charged the ordinary fee of eight francs.[28]

The text is short, sensationalistic, appealing, and informative. It features an alarming moment and a positive resolution, with the intervention of a hero, as in fairy tales—the only difference here is that nobody knows they are in any danger until Knock tells them. Knock presents himself as a knowledgeable and virtuous physician (of "philanthropic spirit"), who will protect the village against horrible threats coming from all directions ("the alarming progress of all sorts of diseases") and will offer free or inexpensive consultations. Basically, he kills the dragon, saves the princess, and gives the residents a good deal, too. The structure of Knock's visits will mirror this announcement, and the first one will be with the town crier himself.[29]

In the second scene of act 2, Knock is busy with one more core component of his campaign—education. He meets the schoolmaster, whose last name is, interestingly, Bernard, like that of the famous physician, and he partners with him in a joint effort to raise awareness about hygiene and disease prevention in schools and among the local population (which he calls "propaganda efforts directed to families").[30]

KNOCK: ... I can heal my patients without you. But the disease—who will help me fight and defeat it? Who will educate these poor people on the threats that besiege their organism every second? Who will teach them that one shouldn't wait till his death before calling a doctor?

BERNARD: They are very negligent. I can't deny it.

KNOCK: *getting more and more heated.* Let's start from the basics. I have here the subject of some popularizing chattering, very detailed notes, good clichés, and a lamp. You'll arrange them as you will. To start, have a small conference, all written, believe me, and very pleasant, on typhoid fever, the unsuspected forms it takes, its numerous vehicles: water, bread, milk, mollusks, vegetables, salads, dust, breath, and so forth ... the weeks and months during which it lurks without revealing itself, the fatal accidents that it triggers suddenly, the frightening complications that it carries; all of which should be complemented by nice pictures: details of typhoid excrements, infected ganglions, intestinal perforation, and not in black and white, but in color—all those various shades of pink, brown, yellow and greenish white that you can imagine. (*He sits back down.*)

BERNARD: *his heart capsizing.* It's that ... I'm very impressionable ... If I immerse myself in that, I won't be able to sleep at night.

KNOCK: That's exactly what we need. I mean: here's the effect of enchantment that we want to penetrate to the marrows of our audience. May they no longer sleep! (*Leaning over him.*) Because their mistake is precisely that they do sleep in a boastful self-assurance from which the thunderbolt of disease wakes them up too late. ...

KNOCK: For those who will be left indifferent by our first conference, I have another one, with a neutral title: "Germs Carriers." There it is demonstrated very clearly by the cases observed that one can walk around with a plump figure, a pink tongue, an excellent appetite and host in all the folds of his organism trillions of bacilli of the highest power, capable of infecting a whole department. (*He stands up.*) On the basis of theory and experience, I have the right to assume that anybody can be a carrier of germs. For instance, nothing proves to me that you are not one.

BERNARD: Me! Doctor...

KNOCK: I would be curious to know of somebody who, coming out of this second conference, would feel in the mood to frolic.

BERNARD: Doctor, do you think that I am a carrier of germs?

KNOCK: Not you specifically. I just took an example. See you soon, dear Mr. Bernard, and thank you for your cooperation, of which I was certain.[31]

This dialogue is crucial because it allows us to pick out a few key concepts that are widely employed in the medical rhetoric of both state-run and for-profit campaigns today: the notion of an asymptomatic body, the emphasis on awareness and information about diseases (Knock employs the verb *instruir*, meaning both "to inform" and "to teach"), the concepts of prevention and risk, and "interpellation" in an Althusserian sense—all of which instill doubt and generates anxiety in the (potential) patient. Knock's wish, "May they no longer sleep!," has come true according to what we read in Dr. Meador's assessment of today's concept of health in "The Last Well Person": "Obsession is no longer a disease, but an essential attribute of staying healthy." This is also true of Knock's default assumption that anybody can potentially be a carrier of germs and that "nothing proves to me that you [Bernard] are not one."

For centuries, it was the patients who would call on the doctor when not feeling well and identify themselves as in need of help and treatment on the basis of the signs and symptoms that their bodies gave out (as in the notion of "chief complaint"). The doctor would then help make sense of those phenomena by visiting the patients and reordering signs and events into a plot that made sense from a medical point of view. In his foundational inquiry *The Normal and the Pathological*, Georges Canguilhem argues that "it is first and foremost because men feel sick that a medicine exists. It is only secondarily that men know in what way they are sick because a medicine exists."[32] In the 1950s, in the face of the increasing reliance of medicine upon statistics and clinical trials, most physicians would still fiercely oppose these developments, "insisting on symptomatic diagnosis, etiological treatment, the ability to personally diagnose, and the idea that drugs were prescribed to cure diseases."[33] Over time we have embraced the concept of an asymptomatic body, on which we cannot rely to determine if we are ill or healthy. The whole grammar of symptoms that we counted on for centuries is now discarded as imprecise. Our body may feel well but in fact be sick. Most times it is not the person who feels sick and calls the doctor, and it is not even the doctor who diagnoses the person with a disease, but rather it is a test or an algorithm (not to mention the genomic spelling mistakes addressed in chapter 2) that determine whether the individual needs treatment.[34]

If certainty and knowledge about our health have left our bodies and now seem to reside in clinical trials, the results are constant doubt and anxiety about our present and future bodily conditions. Health itself, once a default condition occasionally disrupted by diseases, is now a relative condition. Our body is an unreliable narrator: despite our feeling well, it may host all sorts of viruses and diseases. From such a perspective, Knock's words ("one can walk around with a plump figure, a pink tongue, an excellent appetite and host in all the folds of his organism trillions of bacilli of the highest power, capable of infecting a whole department") offers an earlier iteration of a trope that has by now become well established in pharmaceutical rhetoric and public-health rhetoric alike. A fairly recent public-health campaign that promoted colorectal cancer awareness shows how successful the trope still is. A poster from this campaign in 2005 shows a major U.S. TV personality, smiling, looking healthy, and holding up an ornamented picture frame, while the text reads: "Are you the picture of health? You might look and feel fine, but you need to get the inside story. Colorectal cancer has no symptoms, so please get tested. I did." In the Italian equivalent, the visual component creates a particularly striking metaphor: we see a red apple with a slice taken out of it, its fresh-looking surface hiding a small rotten part on the inside, carefully positioned to appear at the apple's "rectum." The "inside story" is unfolding without a sign, independently authored by a body from which we are disconnected (figs. 3.1–3.2).

If the body conceals fatal secrets, then people should be informed not only of epidemics but also of newly discovered diseases and of underestimated threats to their health. Spreading information and awareness is the main goal of today's public-health efforts. People should be made aware of

FIGURES 3.1–3.2. U.S. and Italian campaigns for colorectal cancer awareness from the early 2000s. The one in Italian reads: "Appearances are often deceptive. Colorectal cancer prevention can save your life." *Sources*: Courtesy of the U.S. Centers for Disease Control and the Italian Ministero della Salute.

newly discovered syndromes, of the risk they run of developing one, and of potential diseases they may already have. The goals and motivating principles of such campaigns are undoubtedly distinct from those informing pharmaceutical advertising, yet the views of health and illness that both campaigns and advertising promote display remarkable similarities. In this respect, Knock's definition of "boastful self-assurance" (*trompeuse securité*) stands in stark negative contrast to the virtuous compliance of informed awareness or, as we shall see, "enlightenment."

Another constitutive component of Knock's rhetorical strategies is what Louis Althusser would term "interpellation." "Ideology interpellates individuals as subjects," he claims in his essay "Ideology and State Apparatuses" (1970):

> I shall then suggest that ideology "acts" or "functions" in such a way that it "recruits" subjects among the individuals (it recruits them all), or "transforms" the individuals into subjects (it transforms them all) by that very precise operation which I have called *interpellation* or hailing, and which can be imagined along the lines of the most commonplace everyday police (or other) hailing: "Hey, you there!"
>
> Assuming that the theoretical scene I have imagined takes place in the street, the hailed individual will turn round. By this mere one-hundred-and-eighty-degree physical conversion, he becomes a *subject*. Why? Because he has recognized that the hail was "really" addressed to him and that "it was *really him* who was hailed" (and not someone else) ... yet it is a strange phenomenon, and one which cannot be explained solely by "guilt feelings," despite the large numbers who "have something on their conscience." ... I have had to present things in the form of a sequence, with a before and an after, and thus in the form of a temporal succession. There are individuals walking along. Somewhere (usually behind them) the hail rings out: "Hey, you there!" One individual (nine times out of ten it is the right one) turns round, believing/suspecting/ knowing that it is for him, i.e. recognizing that "it really is he" who is meant by the hailing. But in reality these things happen without any succession. The existence of ideology and the hailing or interpellation of individuals as subjects are one and the same thing.[35]

Similarly, one can argue that in Romains's text Bernard feels interpellated when Knock mentions carriers of germs. Bernard's "Me?" (Moi?) is the response to Knock's words, which in Althusser's scenario could be summarized by "Hey, you!" Medical anthropologists have studied interpellation as an effect of modern direct-to-consumer advertising.[36]

The third and last strategic meeting that Knock schedules is with the pharmacist, Monsieur Mousquet. Knock builds an alliance with him and outlines a medical plan for the region based on projected profits and a radical, innovative vision of medicine and its mission. Money and figures are discussed right away without gentlemanly introductions, while medicine and its protagonists (Knock and the pharmacist) are described as an army carrying out a campaign of expansion. The word *campaign*, we must incidentally note, was initially a military term (from the French *campagne*, the Italian *campagna*, and the late Latin *campania*, meaning "countryside," "open field"—that is, the area where battles used to take place). The fields of politics, communication, and advertising use the word *campaign* as a dead metaphor.

KNOCK: For me, a doctor who cannot rely on a first-rate pharmacist is a general who goes to the battle without artillery.
    ... [A]n organization like yours is certainly rewarding and ... you must make at least twenty-five thousand francs per year.[37]

To Knock's surprise, Mousquet makes much less than that. Therefore, as if undertaking proper marketing research, Knock proceeds to ask about Mousquet's possible competitors, potential enemies, past mistakes, and the previous doctor's volume of prescriptions.[38] Having assessed the situation, Knock is ready to launch his marketing strategy, get Mousquet on board with his enterprise, and explain his vision of the future of health and disease in Saint-Maurice:

KNOCK: I assume by principle that all the inhabitants of the canton are ipso facto our designated clients.
MOUSQUET: All of them—that's asking too much.
KNOCK: I say all of them.
MOUSQUET: It's true that at one moment or another of his life, everybody may occasionally become our client.
KNOCK: Occasionally? Not at all. Regular client, loyal client.
MOUSQUET: Still, he has to fall ill!

KNOCK: "To fall ill" is an old notion that doesn't hold anymore in the face of new scientific data. Health is only a word that we could erase from our vocabulary without causing any harm. I only know people more or less strongly struck by diseases that are more or less numerous and evolving more or less rapidly. Obviously, if you tell them that they look good, they will believe you. In fact, you are deceiving them. Your sole excuse should be that you already have too many patients to heal and you can't take new ones in.

MOUSQUET: At any rate, it is a very good theory.

KNOCK: A very modern theory, Mr. Mousquet—think about it—and a very close relative of the idea of an armed nation that makes our countries strong.

MOUSQUET: You are a thinker, Doctor Knock, and materialists will have a hard time arguing for the contrary: thoughts make the world go round.

KNOCK: Listen to me. (*Both are standing. Knock grabs Mousquet's hands.*) I am perhaps presumptuous. Bitter disillusion may be awaiting me. However, if in one year, day after day, you have not gained the twenty-five thousand francs that are due to you, if Madame Mousquet doesn't have the clothes, the hats, and the stockings that her status requires, you will be authorized to come and complain to me, and I will offer both cheeks for you to strike them.

MOUSQUET: Dear Doctor, I would be ungrateful if I didn't thank you profusely and a miserable man if I didn't help you by doing everything in my power.

KNOCK: Well, well. Count on me as I count on you.[39]

We learn that disease is not a temporary condition we slip into occasionally ("tomber malade") and that we are instead all potentially if not inherently ill. The sole fact of living in that region, if not of merely being alive, makes the villagers patients. This vision of health and disease aligns with the one that prevails in our times, with the exception that now the word *health* does not need to be erased from our vocabulary ("rayer de notre vocabulaire") but has simply acquired a different meaning: surplus health emerges from maximized prevention and treatment. The more screening tests we take and the more drugs we are on, be it for risk prevention or for chronic diseases, the healthier we are considered to be, at least potentially. Knock's statement "I only know people more or less strongly struck by diseases that are more or less numerous and evolving more or less rapidly" resonates with Dr. Meador's observation in the late twentieth century that everybody around him seems to be sick and that he has "not met a completely well person in months."

Canguilhem, with his famous distinction between "physiological" and "pathological," would have been an interesting interlocutor in this conversation. He even refers to *Knock* in *The Normal and the Pathological*: "Certain writers claim continuity between health and disease in order to refuse to define either of them. They say that there is no completely normal state, no perfect health. This can mean that there exist only sick men. In an amusing way Molière and Jules Romains have shown what kind of 'iatocracy' can justify this assertion."[40]

In the play, the military metaphor is developed further and takes on more explicit and aggressive connotations: Knock and Mousquet have to expand the domain of medicine and make everybody a patient, a conquered body. Medicine is compared to a country that embraces arms to grow stronger and larger.[41] How does medicine expand its domains, along which lines, and to what end? Knock and Mousquet set their financial goals for the year and take it from there, instead of considering health their primary goal and making money as only a consequence.

According to Knock, it is also important to keep a strong grip on the market and not lose terrain in their medical-financial empire ("A regular customer is a loyal customer" [Client régulier, client fidèle]), which resonates with the significant share of the market that treatment for chronic disease or risk prevention—that is, long-term prescription drugs—occupy in our days. Knock already shared a founding pillar of his strategy, his focus on long-term treatment, with Doctor Parpalaid during the car ride to Saint-Maurice: "we have to work on the preservation of the diseased" (nous devons travailler à la conservation du malade).[42]

Furthermore, in this conversation with Mousquet, Knock's words—"Your sole excuse should be that you already have too many patients to heal and you can't take new ones in" (Votre seule excuse, c'est que vous ayez déjà trop de malades à soigner pour en prendre de nouveaux)—seem to resonate with Joseph Dumit's claim that there is no set limit to screening or treatment when the goal is not a body free of suffering but one free of risk, as if this were at all realistic.[43] However, in Knock's case, it is all done officially in the interest of public health and not for money. He specifies to the town crier: "You understand, my friend, that what I want more than anything else is people's healing. If I wanted to make money, I would practice in Paris or New York."[44]

MEDICAL ENLIGHTENMENT IN THE EARLY 1920S

When the public announcements have gone out, the partnership with the schoolmaster to carry out public-health campaigns has been confirmed, and the enterprise with the pharmacist has taken off, Knock has laid the foundations for his business. His strategy is in place, and consultations can begin. On his first day of work, Knock visits the town crier, two women, and two village louts. With each of them, we see the same pattern: Knock gauges how much money he can draw from those whom he now designates "patients," and then he makes them aware of a specific syndrome they may have, which scares them enough to generate in them meekness, subordination, and compliance. They are sick, he says, but he will be able to heal them by outlining a treatment plan and prescribing medicines they can purchase at the pharmacist's. The ways in which Knock makes people aware of their disease ranges from drawing pictures to using frightening metaphors and complex language, all of which serves to generate anxiety and place his interlocutors in a vulnerable position in which they feel dis-eased.

In scene 5 of act 2, when Knock visits the Lady in Purple (Dame en violet), he immediately figures out that she is wealthy. She says she feels fine, but as soon as she mentions being kept up at night by some thoughts regarding her estate, Knock seizes the opportunity to transform her into a long-term patient:

KNOCK: There are cases of insomnia that are of utmost seriousness.
THE LADY: Really?
KNOCK: Insomnia can result from a structural problem in the intracerebral circulation, specifically from the alteration of vessels called "pipestems." You may have, madam, pipestem cerebral arteries.
THE LADY: Heavens! Pipestem! Could it be due to my using tobacco?
KNOCK: That's something we will need to look into. Insomnia could also be due to a continuous and deep attack to the gray matter on the part of the neuroglia.
THE LADY: It must be frightening. Please explain it to me, Doctor.
KNOCK: *very composedly.* Imagine a crab, or an octopus, or a gigantic spider as nibbling, sucking, and gently pulling your brain to pieces.
THE LADY: Oh! (*She sinks into an armchair.*) One could faint from horror. This is what I must have. I clearly feel it. Please, Doctor, don't leave me alone. I feel I

am sinking into the most sheer terror. (*Silence.*) This must be absolutely incurable and fatal, is it not?

KNOCK: No.

THE LADY: Is there any hope of healing?

KNOCK: Yes, in the long run,

THE LADY: Don't deceive me, Doctor. I want the truth.

KNOCK: All depends on the regularity and the duration of treatment.... I wouldn't dare give hope to ordinary patients, who wouldn't have the time or the means to be cured with the most modern methods. With you, it is different.

THE LADY: Oh! I will be a very docile patient, Doctor, submissive as a small dog. I will do anything that is required, especially if it's not too painful.

KNOCK: Not at all painful, since we'll resort to radioactivity. The only challenge consists in being patient and constant enough to follow the treatment for two or three years, and having at hand a doctor who will commit to watching the healing process closely, calculating the doses of radioactivity in great detail, and offering almost daily visits.

THE LADY: Do I have to take any medicine today?

KNOCK: Hmm... sure.... Stop by Mr. Mousquet and ask him to prepare this first prescription.[45]

Not only does Knock scare the woman into becoming his patient, but he also employs specialized terminology and mentions a fairly recent medical discovery (radioactivity, just as in an earlier scene he mentions germ theory), which confers power upon him, just as Ivan Ilych's doctors would do to the same end.[46] Although not as obviously as in the case of Monsieur Bernard, this patient, too, seems to be interpellated as she listens to possible causes of her insomnia. As a result of Knock's strategy, the Lady in Purple promises to become a long-term patient and a very compliant one. Knock emerges as the virtuous hero who will save the woman's brain from being feasted on by her neuroglia, almost as if in a fairy tale, while the pharmacist gains from the visit, too. We also learn that Knock's predecessor, Doctor Parpalaid, had only suggested that she read five pages of the *Civil Code* every night when she goes to bed to fight insomnia. Now that the woman is "informed" regarding her condition, Knock, with his detailed descriptions and his treatment plan, appears to be a more concerned, caring, and serious physician than Parpalaid. The Lady in Purple is wealthy, but the two patients Knock sees right after her, a couple of village louts, have no money. It is telling of Knock's strategy that he does not waste any time with them and simply informs them that they will die of an incurable syndrome.

Before the Lady in Purple, we meet the Lady in Black (Dame en noir, act 2, scene 4), who is "reminded" (in an almost psychoanalytic fashion) that she must have fallen on her back in her childhood. Knock frightens her with a drawing of anatomical details of her spine and apocalyptic descriptions of what awaits her in the near future. Once she is in complete shock and thus prone to compliance—but worried that the treatment may be too expensive—he simply suggests a week of observation. If she feels ill after that week, she will have to undergo treatment. However, the recommendations he gives her for the week of observation (lying in bed in absolute darkness and solitude with very little food) will make her feel feeble indeed.

When Knock visits the town crier, the latter feels well in general, but in that very moment he has a bit of an itch. Nevertheless, the doctor assumes a most serious expression—which reminds us of the empty theatricality we have encountered in Ivan Ilych's doctors in chapter 2—and becomes very strict about definitions to determine what kind of itch it is. He also brings out statistics, an established tool for assessing the health of populations and individuals in Romains's times, and asks the town crier if his age is closer to fifty-one or fifty-two before determining that the crier can certainly be cured if he undergoes treatment. The latter detail seems to anticipate risk-oriented diagnosis and treatment.

It is quite interesting to note that present-day direct-to-consumer campaigns are structured somewhat like Knock's initial announcement, his conference on typhoid fever, and his visits—interpellating potential clients and addressing their permanent uncertainty about their health, which results from a divorce between how they feel and what their bodies might actually be concealing. Among other things, pharmaceutical advertising capitalizes on the related notions of an unreliable, asymptomatic body and of "risk factors." In the face of this reality, facts, numbers, and statistics are all we are left with to determine how healthy we are. For Knock to ask the town crier his age before determining whether he should undergo treatment or not may have seemed odd in the early 1920s. However, today's high-cholesterol drug commercials share similar assumptions. Dumit relays a transcript from a Pfizer commercial when he discusses high cholesterol in his article "Prescription Maximization" (2012): "The commercial begins with a scene of middle-aged people on exercise bikes in a gym, working out but looking tired. The only sound is of a ball rolling around, and superimposed above the exercisers is a spinning set of numbers. Finally the ball is heard dropping into place; the number is 265. The cholesterol roulette is over. The text on the screen: 'Like your odds? Get checked for cholesterol. Pfizer.'"[47]

The roulette component further highlights the notion of "risk." Knock's visits generally start with broad questions ("Have you been suffering from insomnia for a long time?"; "Do you suffer from a lack of appetite?"; "Do you experience itching after eating?").[48] No matter the answer, Knock frames the patient's symptoms as potential proof of a serious condition. This rhetorical tactic normally triggers his interlocutors' alarm at being affected by diseases that Knock has described in a terrifying fashion and that they have never before considered. In other words, after a brief exchange, whose content in another context could well be the topic of small talk or a chat with a friend, Knock's serious and frightening revelations offer a new light in which patients can view ordinary episodes in their lives as symptoms; in narratological terms, they can superimpose a medical plot on them. As Yuri Lotman would put it, Knock and his patients have different views of what constitutes an "event."[49] Yet Knock's interpretation, on the surface medically informed and therefore more valuable, prevails and informs the patients' own views. As the conversation unfolds, fear is followed by hope and compliance, which seems to be a reoccurring pattern in our times as well: Dumit shows how direct-to-consumer commercials do not raise a presymptomatic form of awareness, as would be the case for a diagnostic scan or a genetic test that reveals the presence of disease before symptoms manifest themselves.[50] Interpellated people instead find out from watching those commercials that they have been suffering from symptoms of a disease without realizing it. Knock's rhetoric has exactly the same effect on his patients.

In act 3, Parpalaid visits Saint-Maurice three months after he passed the baton to Knock. He finds the town almost unrecognizable. The only hotel, the Hôtel de la Clef, has been transformed into a clinic, the Médical-Hôtel. A great number of patients, most from town but also some who were only passing through, were visited by Knock and ended up checking in for a treatment. If we consider that in French the town hall is called *hôtel de ville*, then it becomes even more interesting to learn that the only *hôtel* in town is now the headquarters of medicine, where it is practiced, institutionalized, and regimented and from where Knock governs the whole region. As in Foucault's clinic, here health, authority, and power are closely intertwined.

Before Parpalaid meets with Knock, he has a short exchange with Madame Rémy, the hotel manager. He expresses his surprise at how sick people have become, compared to in his time as doctor there. Madame Rémy's response testifies to the change in episteme, her view reflecting that of the "new patient," empowered, educated, informed, and compliant.

MADAME RÉMY: People didn't have the thought of finding treatment; all is different now. Some think that in the countryside we are still in a wild state, that we don't have any care for ourselves, that we just wait until the time comes for us to die like animals, and that the remedies, the diets, the equipment and all the progress is for big cities. This is a mistake, Mr. Parpalaid. We have the self-appreciation that anybody else has, and although we don't like wasting our money, we don't hesitate to pay for what is necessary. You, Mr. Parpalaid, are a gentleman of the old times, who splits the coin in four and who would prefer to lose an eye or a leg rather than spending three francs on a medicine. Things have changed, thank God.[51]

Madame Rémy reauthors the story of her body and the collective body in light of the knowledge that the medical age has introduced. She imposes the dominant narrative on Parpalaid and seems ready to do so with anyone else she meets who has not yet embraced the new order. Knock has set in motion a system of peer surveillance, and now his authorial voice is reflected and amplified in the voices of others. Next, Knock chats with Mousquet, who has quintupled his business volume.[52]

It is only in act 3, scene 6, that Parpalaid meets with Knock. Knock, as if turning over a financial report, immediately shows him the figures. His graphs track the upward curve of visits and treatment, which have multiplied stunningly. He mentions people's incomes as a crucial part of the picture and of the planning, which confuses Parpalaid:

THE DOCTOR: What's this story of revenues?

KNOCK: ... I have four levels of treatment. The most modest, for incomes between twelve and twenty thousand, only entails one visit a week, and around fifty francs of pharmacy bills per month. At the other end, the deluxe treatment, for incomes over fifty thousand francs, calls for at least four visits per week and a three-hundred-franc expense for different items: X rays, radium, electric massages, diagnostic tests, ordinary medications, and so forth.

THE DOCTOR: But how do you know the income of your customers?

KNOCK: ... Not from the tax official, believe me. And to my advantage. While I identify 1,502 incomes over 12,000 francs, the tax official only counts 17. The highest income in his list is 20,000. The highest in my list is 120,000. We never agree. The fact that he works for the state makes me wonder.

THE DOCTOR: Where do you get your information?

KNOCK: It's a lot of work, on which I have spent almost the whole month of October. And I revise things constantly. Look at this: beautiful, isn't it?

THE DOCTOR: It looks like a map of the region. But what are all these red dots for?

KNOCK: This is the map of medical penetration. Every red point means the location of a regular patient. Only one month ago you would have seen an enormous gray pocket.... Today it has not disappeared, but it has been reduced, hasn't it? One barely sees it.

THE DOCTOR: ... I can't doubt your results. However, may I ask you a question of a higher order?

KNOCK: Please....

THE DOCTOR: Note that I am not pushing aside anything. I raise a very delicate point ... in your method, isn't the interest of the patient subordinated to the interest of the doctor?

KNOCK: Doctor Parpalaid, you forget an interest that is higher than both of them.

THE DOCTOR: Which one?

KNOCK: The interest of medicine. That's the only one I care for.

Silence. Parpalaid thinks.

THE DOCTOR: Yes, yes, yes.[53]

Finally, all barriers are blurred between medicine, marketing, and military invasion. The map of medical penetration, a highlight in the play, is

MEDICAL ENLIGHTENMENT IN THE EARLY 1920S

reminiscent of warfare maps: in 1923, France invaded the Ruhr Valley, and Romains may have also been familiar with military maps from the recently ended World War I, like the ones shown in figures 3.3 to 3.6. Knock's map of medical penetration could also be a reference to Saint François Régis, a seventeenth-century Jesuit priest who spent his life converting back the population of his region, the Languedoc, led astray by Protestantism, and

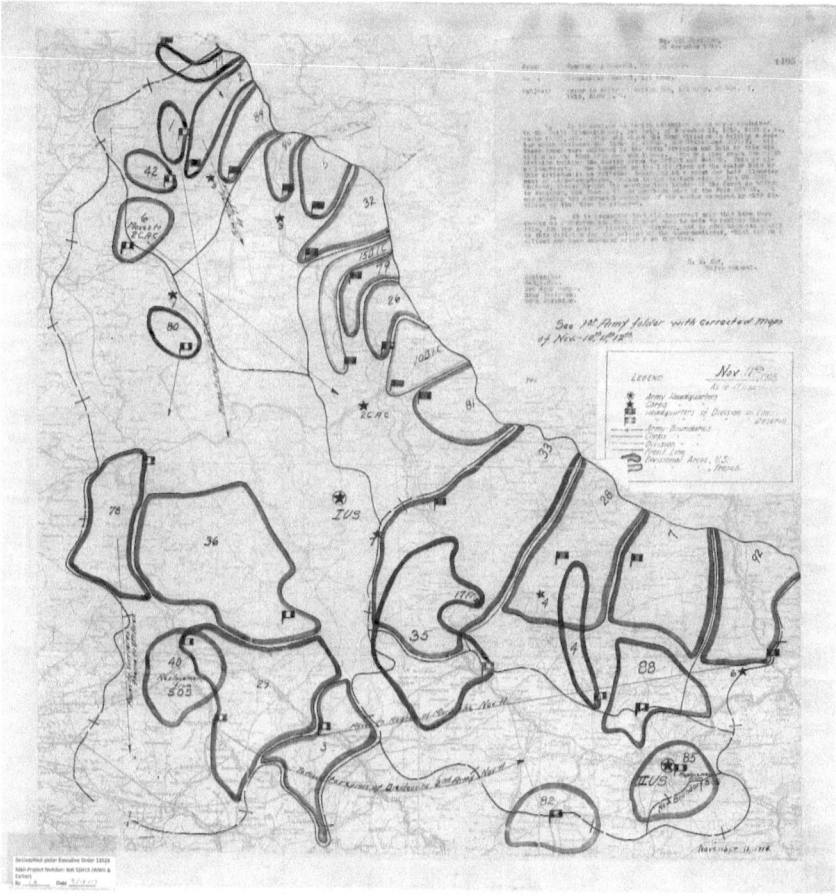

FIGURES 3.3–3.6. Situation maps produced by various military forces during World War I to display their daily activity on the front lines. 3.3: U.S. Army situation map of the French and American armies on November 11, 1918; 3.4: Italian map produced by the Military Geographic Institute (Istituto Geografico Militare) that shows information on the enemy on October 12, 1918; 3.5: Russian map detailing the enemy's positions on the southwestern front on April 20, 1916; 3.6: Russian map detailing the enemy's positions on the French front on August 26, 1916. *Sources*: Figures 3.3 and 3.4 are courtesy of the Cartographic Branch of the U.S. National Archive. Figures 3.5 and 3.6 are courtesy of the Russian National Library.

MEDICAL ENLIGHTENMENT IN THE EARLY 1920S

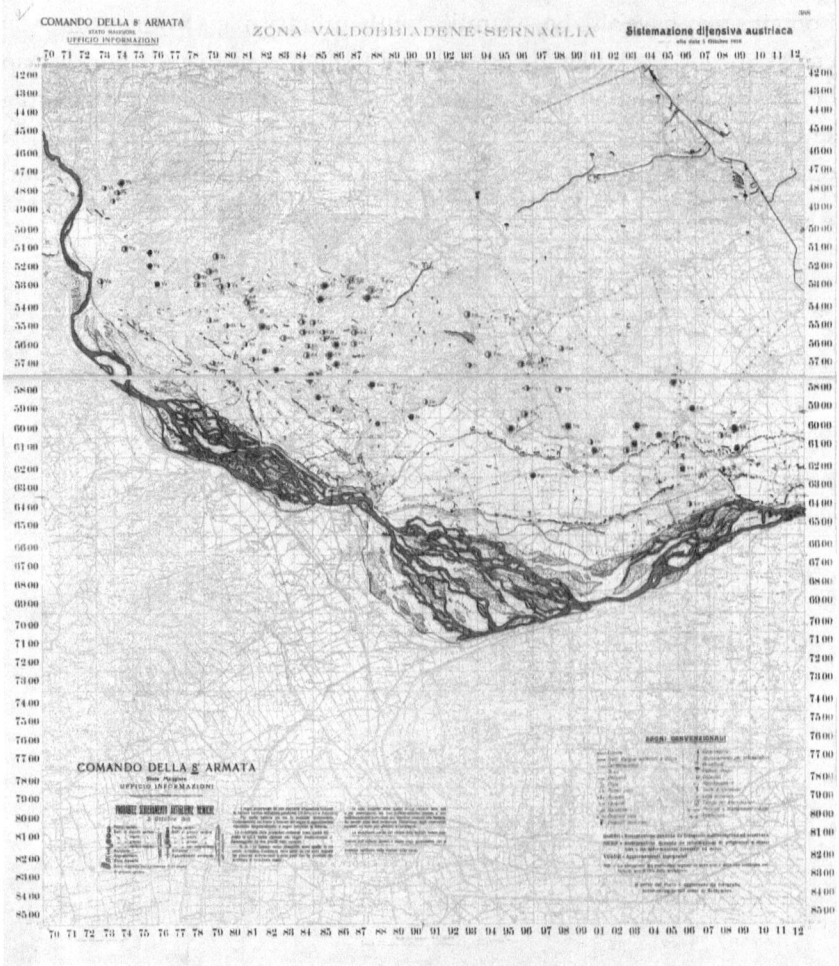

FIGURES 3.3–3.6. (continued)

died during one of his missions. Régis appears in the twenty-first volume (1942) of Romains's cycle of novels *Men of Good Will* (*Les hommes de bonne volonté*, 1932–1946). To some extent, Knock's enterprise has overtones of religious conversion, and so does the villagers' unconditional faith in medical progress, whereby medicine is almost a dogma. However, maps are also widely used to provide a snapshot assessment of a specific business in its geographical expansion,[54] which further creates overlap between

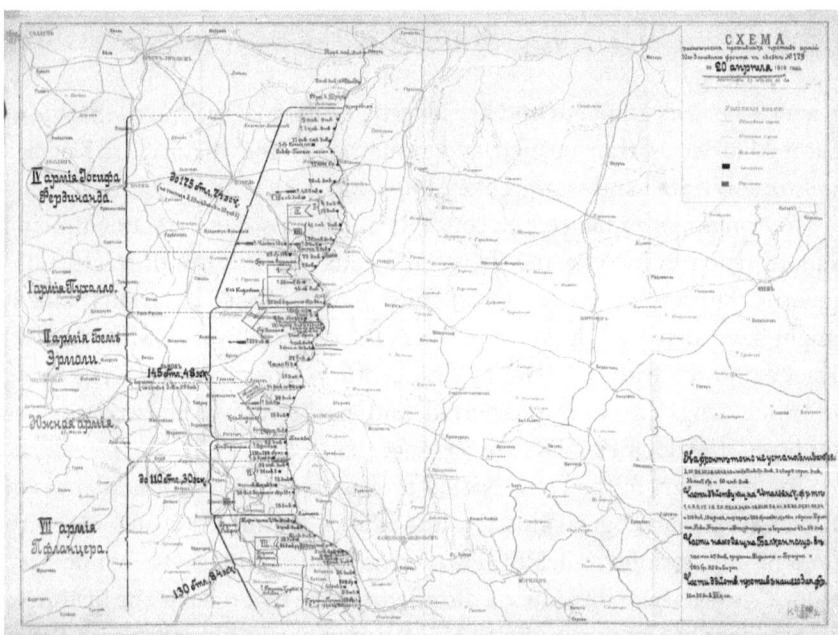

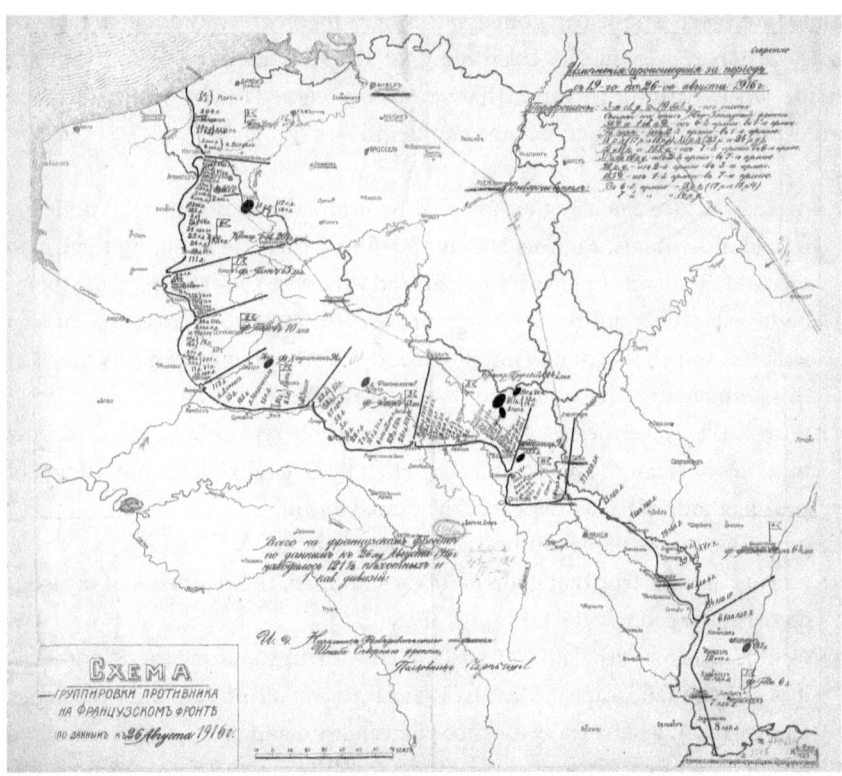

FIGURES 3.3–3.6. (continued)

Knock's health campaign and his advertising campaign. The *campagne* of Saint-Maurice is transformed and reshaped by the rhetoric of Knock's well-orchestrated and warfarelike *campagne*.

To Romains's audience, the concepts of diagnosis and treatment being subordinated to income and financial means ("four levels of treatments" [quatre échelons de traitements]) must have sounded hilarious, and it might have increased the comic effect of the piece. However, when we read Knock's words from our twenty-first-century, late-capitalist perspective, in which drugs are conceived, tested, and marketed by private companies for profit, the doctor's views are no longer so absurd.[55]

The final part of the conversation probes the most profound depths of Knock's epistemological mission and allows for more resonances with present-day notions of health. Furthermore, in an otherwise comic play, Knock's words here introduce a disquieting tone that reflects the historical circumstances and the anxieties of interwar Europe. Together with Parpalaid, we learn about the concepts *lumière médicale* and *existence médicale*, which represent the fulfillment of Knock's earlier pronouncement made while driving through that same *campagne* that he would reshape and transform: "the medical age can begin."

KNOCK: You give me a region peopled by a few thousand neutral, undetermined individuals. My role is that of defining them, of bringing them into medical existence. I put them in bed, and I see who they can become: somebody with tuberculosis, with a neurosis, with arteriosclerosis—what you will, but somebody, good God! Somebody! Nothing annoys me as much as this being neither meat nor fish that you call a healthy man.

THE DOCTOR: Nevertheless, you cannot put a whole region in bed!... You only think of medicine... Aren't you afraid that by generalizing the application of your methods social activities will be slowed down?

KNOCK: That's none of my business. I practice medicine.

THE DOCTOR: It is true that upon building a railroad, the engineer doesn't wonder what the country doctor thinks about it....

KNOCK: ... Doctor Parpalaid. You are familiar with the view from this window.... It is a rough landscape.... Today, I give it to you all imbued with medicine, animated and irradiated by the subterranean fire of our art.... In two hundred fifty of these houses ... there are two hundred fifty rooms where somebody testifies about medicine, two hundred thousand beds where a lying body confirms that life has a meaning, and thanks to me, a medical meaning. It is even more beautiful at night, because there are lights. And all the lights are mine. The nonpatients sleep in the darkness. They are suppressed.... The night clears the vision of everything that stays at the margins of medicine.... The region becomes a sort of firmament of which I am continuously the creator.[56]

Literary scholars have interpreted the scene of Knock's triumph through the lens of Romains's notion of *unanimisme*, which informs his poetics and is in dialogue with the psychology of groups and crowds. The idea of *les unanimes* or "collective beings"—which resonates strongly with what today we would define as "the social"—can be described as follows: "When a number of men meet, however chance that meeting may be, provided they remain together and begin to do something together, they tend to become 'something other than a certain number of men,' to become part of an individuality greater than their own, the individuality of the group.... Groups of people... have a soul distinct from, and usually superior to, individual souls."[57]

In *Knock*, Romains illustrates the creation of a collective state of mind, a process that constituted a very concrete anxiety in Europe in the 1920s. Unanimists highlight the relationship between Knock and Hitler, "both of whom turn the groups they control into collective beings at the mercy of their selfish designs," and wonder: "If a group will respond to a doctor in this way, what chances have the masses when confronted with a modern dictator?"[58] Interestingly, the Nazi regime banned productions of *Knock* in Germany.[59] The scene at the end of the third act, when all the patients accompany Doctor Parpalaid to his room, not only represents the apex of the play's comic effect but also constitutes the culmination of unanimism's most disquieting traits and potentials.[60]

However, I would like to suggest additional interpretations of Knock's tirade on the *lumière médicale* on the basis of the parallel I have drawn thus far between Romains's text and modern developments in medical epistemology and medical communication. The *lumière médicale* and the streetlights here signify the supposed enlightenment brought about by Knock's mission. Those who are not yet part of his medical kingdom are living in the dark and left on the margins of visibility and recognition. By employing language and imagery that are quite Foucauldian avant la lettre, Knock claims that undiagnosed and undefined people ("neither fish nor fowl" [ni chair ni poisson], as he refers to them) are awaiting a diagnosis, a definition, in order to be brought into existence ("My role is that of defining them, of bringing them into medical existence" [Mon rôle, c'est de les déterminer, de les amener à l'existence médicale]).

The stage directions for this scene read: "From this moment until the end of the play, the lighting of the scene takes on little by little the characteristics of Medical Enlightenment, which, as we know, is richer than simple Earthly Light in green and violet beams."[61] Notably, as soon as Knock lights the stage with the *lumière médicale*, he starts ushering Parpalaid gradually into medical existence. This final reification of the doctor is in part reminiscent of Chekhov's novella *Ward No. 6* (*Palata No. 6*, 1892), in which the physician Andrei Efimich Ragin, like Parpalaid, is confined in a clinic by the newcomer, the illiterate and ambitious Khobotov. Chekhov's narrative technique—especially the employment of perspective—develops the claim that Ragin, like Parpalaid, is not sick and gives him (and the reader) hints that gradually reveal the conspiracy enacted against him. As the title suggests, the reader is presented with the physical structure in which the institutionalization of medical care takes shape along with its discursive features. The same person uttering the same words and behaving in the same exact way either inside or outside the hospital will be considered, respectively, either mentally healthy or mentally ill. Ragin is pushed to a weak spot in the power dynamics at play, whose conventional nature he underlines by making reference to uniforms: "It's no matter. It does not matter whether it's a dress-coat or a uniform or this dressing gown."[62] He is now dressed exactly like the patient Ivan Dmitrich, with whom he had bonded intellectually, and has a bed in the same room, while the doctors wear a white uniform, which is just as conventional, and stay on the other side of the door. One's authority and credibility are not defined a priori on the basis of abstract common sense; instead, they depend largely on the community in which they originate, on its values and the power relationships among its members—that is, on one's position vis-à-vis the predominant institutional discourse in science and politics alike. This is something Ragin had known since his first conversations as a doctor with the patient Ivan Dmitrich: "When society protects itself from the criminal, mentally deranged, or otherwise inconvenient people, it is invincible.... So long as prisons and madhouses exist someone must be shut up in them. If not you, I. If not I, some third person. Wait till in the distant future prisons and madhouses no longer exist, and there will be neither bars on the windows nor hospital gowns. Of course, that time will come sooner or later."[63]

The poetics of borders, their arbitrariness and their negotiability, informs the novella and finds its most tangible embodiment in the hospital building and its wards. The crossing of boundaries and the exploration of their porosity, achieved in the text through the juxtaposition of the space inside the building and the space outside of it, anticipates the fluidity that will characterize modernist fiction on stylistic and aesthetic levels. It also anticipates a central concern of the history of medicine in later decades—namely, the social construction of truth, methods, and value judgments in the sciences. Therefore, in Chekhov's story the traditionally formal question of "narrative unreliability"[64] is tightly interwoven with major issues in the philosophy of medicine, such as the social constructedness of medical truth, the arbitrariness of the normal/pathological dichotomy, and the power dynamics associated with the medical gaze.[65]

In the scenes that lead to Parpalaid's entering the clinic in *Knock*, we see that medical enlightenment generates a new patient—educated, informed, aware, and free to make health choices and seek treatment actively, be it with the help of doctors or in spite of them. Parpalaid realizes that all the villagers have fallen prey to Knock's power of persuasion and have embraced his debatable diagnoses. In this respect, it is worth emphasizing that in the previous dialogue between Parpalaid and Knock, Romains calls Parpalaid "le docteur," while Knock is just "Knock." However, when Parpalaid calls Knock a charlatan,[66] he is met with the villagers' wrath, for they have been enlightened and empowered—or indoctrinated, when seen from the opposite perspective—by the concerted efforts of Knock, Bernard, and Mousquet. Parpalaid's exchange with Madame Rémy provides a remarkable demonstration of this conversion:

MADAME RÉMY: Mr. Parpalaid has always been a good man. And he did his job as well as anyone else would, to the extent that each of us could have been considered . . . a real physician.
THE DOCTOR: A real physician! What am I hearing! Wait until the next [world epidemic], and you'll see if Doctor Knock will turn out to be better than me.

MEDICAL ENLIGHTENMENT IN THE EARLY 1920S

MADAME RÉMY: ... I begin to understand what a patient is.... I can tell you that in a population where everybody is already in bed, we are well equipped to face your world epidemics.

MOUSQUET: I advise you against raising these sorts of controversies. The pharmaceutical-medical spirit floods the streets, notions abound, and anyone will be able to argue with you.[67]

Mousquet warns Parpalaid: now that the medical age has dawned in Saint-Maurice, everybody will be able to argue with him on his own terms. The villagers turned patients reveal a belligerent approach to those who disagree with their health system. These warlike tones echo in Madame Rémy's claim that a population where everybody is already in a hospital bed is better equipped to face world epidemics, an outlook that resonates with the call for countries to be preemptively prepared and constantly ready for war.

Indeed, Knock's *lumière médicale* has had a felicitous history, and in our times it manifests itself in the empowering and educational mission of pharmaceutical companies, carried out through their websites, advertorials, ads proper, campaigns to raise awareness about newly discovered syndromes, and online self-diagnostic tools. The recurring motto seems to be "Help your doctor help you."[68] All major pharmaceutical companies have on their websites a section on how to talk with your doctor about the disease they target with their drugs. The whole world of witnessing is interesting and pertinent to the present analysis because through these stories companies suggest to potential customers how they might speak to a doctor specifically to obtain a prescription.[69]

Just like the self-defined, empowered patients of our times, Madame Rémy knows how to talk back to Parpalaid from a position of enlightenment. She is a reliable narrator insofar as she is a knowledgeable and liberated patient who has been made aware of what health is and how to keep informed about and improve hers without waiting for a doctor to diagnose her. Medical enlightenment has brought about a new definition of physician, of patient, and of sickness in Saint-Maurice.

Jules Romains's play, a story that takes place in a French mountain village in the 1920s, seems to anticipate questions that would appeal to historians and philosophers of medicine several decades later. The "medical age" and "medical enlightenment" concepts appear to be the most prophetic, especially when we consider today's mass medicalization, self-diagnosis, and preemptive treatment. It is no surprise that *Knock* has enjoyed enduring fame, even to this day, and inspired other works of theater, among which is the Italian play *Pharmageddon: The Last Healthy Person on Earth* (*Farmageddon: L'ultimo uomo sano sulla terra*, 2016) by Patrizia Pasqui. By playing off of emergent medical discourse and taking its obsession with risk, prevention, responsibility, and peer surveillance to its extreme consequences—so absurd that it made the perfect subject for a successful comedy—Romains's play demonstrated that medicine, with its supposedly objective definitions, was just as much constructed through rhetoric and storytelling and just as much open to interpretation as any nonscientific domain. Unlike traditional quack doctors on the stage, Knock does not even have to disguise himself—as Despina does in *Così fan tutte*—or fear being unmasked as a fraud. Quite the contrary: the beginning of the medical era unfolds under a blinding light, with shining silver and transparent glass tools and no scarcity of information and education. Although Romains's comical figure certainly relates to Molière's and Mozart's, he also significantly departs from them. Profit, overprescription, power, and social control as Knock's main goals entail consequences of a greater magnitude. This is clear in the final scene, which freezes the comic effect and inserts disquieting elements into the play.

THE SOVIET BODY AND THE BODY SOVIET: PLOT BUILDING AS SOCIETY BUILDING IN PUBLIC-HEALTH CAMPAIGNS OF THE 1920S

Romains wrote his play in response to the changing language of medicine in early twentieth-century Europe, which developed within the context of emerging totalitarian regimes. All throughout the 1920s in Europe, corporeal and organismic metaphors came to shape and structure both knowledge of the societal body and techniques for its effective management and treatment. These metaphors promoted a productive blurring of the boundaries among the biological sciences, the social sciences, and nationalism and developed, along with that blurring, a continuum from the biological individual to the population as a whole, society, and the nation. The description of societies in terms of living organisms dates back to ancient Greek philosophers, who mentioned the "social body" and compared statesmen with doctors; organic metaphors were also employed in the Middle Ages to explain and justify the sovereignty of popes and kings, and they remained pervasive until the time of the Scientific Revolution, when they gave way to mechanistic metaphors.[70]

In the late nineteenth century, with the rise of physiology and the social sciences, body metaphors became a privileged way to conceptualize "social problems" and to articulate technical or "medical" solutions to those problems. David Horn points out how the "new organicism" that lay at the core of projects as disparate as Émile Durkheim's sociology and the German racial sciences proposed a new way to conceptualize the relationship between the society as a whole and its constitutive parts and provided the vocabulary to define social pathologies, while social hierarchies could be mapped onto the hierarchy of organic functions. Although modern organicists claimed to draw their principles from nature, they instead constructed both individual bodies and social organisms as sites of engineering, active management, and normalization.[71]

As a result, societies could be characterized medically as diseased or in good shape, and social bodies, like physiological bodies, could be cured, protected, and made objects of ongoing preemptive, prophylactic treatment. In the name of social defense and well-being, previously private behaviors were now targeted by permanent governmental management. The rise of the organic model to conceptualize society redrew the relationship between individuals and the population, whereby the individual was reduced to a cell in the social organism.

In *The Will to Knowledge* (formerly translated as *An Introduction*, 1976), the first volume of *The History of Sexuality*, Michel Foucault refers to biopower (*biopouvoir*) to describe how modern nation-states regulate their subjects "through an explosion of numerous and diverse techniques for achieving the subjugations of bodies and the control of populations."[72] Around the same time in the lecture series at the Collège de France titled "Society Must Be Defended" (1975–1976), Foucault addressed the concept of biopolitics as an extension of this state power over both the physical bodies of individuals and the political body of a population: "We are, then, in a power that has taken control of both the body and life or that has, if you like, taken control of life in general—with the body as one pole and the population as the other," and "what we are dealing with in this new technology of power is not exactly society (or at least not the social body, as defined by the jurists), nor is it the individual body. It is a new body, a multiple body, a body with so many heads that, while they might not be infinite in number, cannot necessarily be counted."[73] Within the frame of emerging totalitarian societies in interwar Europe, Foucault's concepts of biopower and biopolitics highlight medicine and medical discourse as instrumental in legitimizing the new political and social order.[74]

Although from our twenty-first-century perspective *Knock* speaks to these subtle rhetorical mechanisms quite clearly and pronouncedly, which likely led the Third Reich to ban the play, contemporaneous reviewers in Italy and Russia failed to detect those aspects in Romains's play or the author's warning to his readers in France and all over Europe against the alarming political developments he foresaw.

Jules Romains's oeuvre enjoyed remarkable success in Russia, where the author was praised by reviewers for both his narrative techniques—he was often compared to John Dos Passos[75]—and his views on society, groups, and collectives.[76] As early as 1925, at the peak of Romains's career, Academia started publishing a multivolume edition of his collected works in translation,[77] whose back cover quoted Anatolii Lunacharskii's remarks on Romains's unanimistic crowd as "the one that is most visible in our times" and on Romains himself as an "extremely serious and thoughtful, but at the same time brilliant and sharp-witted writer."[78] *Knock* was never staged in Russia but was published in 1926 and reviewed widely. Early Soviet commentators highlighted in the work the "transformation of a shapeless, amorphous crowd into an energetic and unified mass contaminated by unity of thoughts and passions"[79] and referred to the principles regarding the psychology and behavior of crowds that Romains had expressed elsewhere in dialogue with Gabriel Tarde (1843–1904) and Émile Durkheim (1858–1917).

Regarding the plot, Russian reviewers referenced the "curious and absurd [nelepaia i kur'ëznaia] idea that there are no healthy people but just ill ones" and praised Romains's "brilliant satire of modern medicine [when it is] placed in the hands of charlatans who practice it only for the sake of money,"[80] while inscribing *Knock* in the rich literary tradition that sees Molière's play *The Imaginary Invalid* as one of its most notable expressions. Instead of recognizing a warning against a threatening scenario that was closer to home than one might have thought, numerous Soviet authors emphasized the difference between Russia and the capitalistic West, a system defined by petit bourgeois values on the verge of implosion.[81] After all, not only were physicians in Russia state employed, but all pharmacies (formerly managed by the state, unofficial public organizations, and private institutions) were nationalized right after the October Revolution. Nikolai A. Semashko had claimed right after the Civil War that "the Soviet power regards the supply of medicines to the population as one of the most important functions of the State, serving to improve the health of the population, and it cannot allow this function to be handled privately, as a commercial enterprise,"[82] and such a message made Soviet readers of *Knock* feel immunized against the medical rhetoric that Knock, in cahoots with Mousquet, employs to his advantage. In the introduction to the Academia edition, Aleksandr Smirnov was able to move beyond all these predictable reactions. After mentioning the tradition of Molière, he gets one step closer to the play's aesthetics by foregrounding the "blurring of the boundaries between caricature and reality" in what he describes as a "masterpiece of deep and sophisticated acuteness" (shedevr glubokogo i iziashchnogo ostroumiia) that he hopes to see staged.[83] It is not surprising that Knock's most disquieting traits did not come across to Russian readers: by the 1920s, Chekhov's novella *Ward No. 6*, although written in prerevolutionary times—that is, before the rhetoric of state-centralized sanitary enlightenment—was the only text that through its staging of the conjuncture of medical discourse and institutional power had posed questions about biopower somewhat similar to Romains's.

The Italian public could both read the play, translated in 1925, and see it performed on stage in major cities by both Italian troupes in 1926 and 1928 and by Louis Jouvet's troupe in 1931. *Knock* achieved remarkable success in Italy, yet neither intellectuals nor physicians received its message as relevant to Italian society. Reviewers in major newspapers—*Corriere della sera*, *La Stampa*, *Il Messaggero*, and *La Gazzetta del popolo*—focused on comparing the play to Molière's, determining to what extent it could be inscribed in a longer tradition with its roots in classical antiquity, and examined the acting, the lighting, and components of the mise-en-scène. Similarly, in the pages of the medical journal *Hygiene and Life* (*L'igiene e la vita*), a physician-reviewer enthusiastically pointed out the "mighty comicality" (*possente comicità*) of Romains's work.

MEDICAL ENLIGHTENMENT IN THE EARLY 1920S

These reviewers of *Knock* in Russia and Italy, two societies that were transitioning to new forms of government and for which Knock's clinic and his mass manipulation on a scientific basis could have provided a mirror, failed to see precisely the deep connection that Romains suggests between scientific rhetoric and rhetoric legitimizing political power and state control. However, as we turn to early Soviet Russia, we will see a noteworthy exception to this trend.

Besides *Knock*, which appeared in the seventh volume (1926) of the Academia edition of Romains's collected works in Russian translation, another satirical work by Jules Romains, *Donogoo-Tonka, or The Miracles of Science*,[84] stages the allegedly objective field of science as prone to rhetorical manipulation to the extent that even arbitrary and inaccurate representations of reality, when supported by rhetorical techniques, can be superimposed on any and all previously shared knowledge and establish themselves as scientifically rigorous until they *become* reality. Written in 1920 but not staged until 1930, *Donogoo-Tonka* tells the story of a famous geographer who is denied membership in the Academy of Science after it is revealed that his most famous work contains a highly inaccurate map of South America—the map shows a city named Donogoo-Tonka, which is allegedly full of gold but in fact does not exist. At that point, a previously suicidal man, Lamendin, finds a new goal to sustain his life: to embark on a one-man expedition to South America to help the disgraced geographer regain his fame. Through a series of incidents and the employment of photographic falsification, he inadvertently helps establish an actual city in South America with that name, which becomes a thriving metropolis. The novel ends with the founding in the city of the Donogoo-Tonka Society, widely advertised on billboards all across town in an almost postmodern gesture; with the erection of a monument to scientific error, to which the city owes its existence; and with the geographer's final redemption—his reputation and the city are built in tandem, even though both of them have supposedly always already been there. Some of the anxieties that echo through both *Knock* and *Donogoo-Tonka* certainly have their root in normative and totalizing systems and sets of values that were replacing the old status quo in interwar Europe supported by pervasive and persuasive rhetoric. Totalitarian systems employed science as a legitimizing field and borrowed from it the rhetoric of self-evidence, (historical) necessity, and indisputability. It is not by chance that *Donogoo-Tonka*, which was translated into Russian right after its appearance, made a strong impression on formalist literary scholar Viktor Shklovskii (1893–1984), who went so far as to mention Romains's work in his supposed recantation of the formal method in 1930, which he titled "A Monument to a Scientific Error" ("Pamiatnik nauchnoi oshibke").[85] Although this text was long understood as a sign of capitulation,[86] some scholars have offered more intriguing interpretations. Among them, Richard Sheldon has pointed out that Shklovskii had a history of using the rhetoric of surrender itself as a formal device and of employing tropes to suggest that he was not in fact repudiating his beliefs. Far from being an admission of guilt, Shklovskii's text employs sophisticated rhetorical and stylistic tools to craft a ringing defense of artistic freedom in the face of a new state of affairs in politics and society.[87] Just like Romains, Shklovskii, who was *the* scholar of plot construction, could easily lay bare even the most sophisticated rhetorical devices underlying the most cogent and totalizing narratives, political and scientific alike. Even science, a domain apparently objective and impermeable to rhetoric, is prone to emplotment choices and authorial goals. Paradoxically, even a scientific error may turn into a tenet of science when appropriately presented, reframed, and legitimized. As institutions were reshaping the concepts of health, illness, and healing from the end of the Russian Civil War in 1922 and throughout the 1920s, the vast majority of Soviet citizens were not as incisive readers as Shklovskii, and they ended up participating in the massive reordering of public health that took place over the course of that decade, both as subjects and as protagonists, while the individual Soviet body became the smallest constitutive unit of a greater organism, the body Soviet.[88]

Despite the pronouncedly different political circumstances, economic systems, and goals of Jules Romains's work and of early Soviet public-health campaigns—we observe, on the one hand, a physician who wants to make money by convincing everyone in a village that they need his treatment and, on the other, a state-administered healthcare system that aims mostly to contain epidemics and that develops as part of an emergent totalitarian system—we can identify strikingly similar rhetorical patterns in the discourse on medicine and health that both articulate and that authorities in both (medical in *Knock*, political in the young Soviet state) employ to legitimize their power. A comparative rhetorical analysis in this vein illuminates the similarities.

The early Soviet authorities had to address abysmal health and social conditions among the population. Health Commissar Nikolai A. Semashko (1874–1949) wrote that in June 1918, when the Commissariat of Public Health (Narkomzdrav) was created, "the situation was unquestionably grave. During the years of the Civil War, the country was in the throes of epidemics."[89] The war years had created major disruptions in the economy, and the droughts of 1920–1921 had crippled agriculture. As urban dwellers fled to the countryside to find food and sustenance, Moscow saw its population decrease by half, while factory closures and shortages of food led to hunger, unemployment, and decay. In 1919–1923, severe epidemics of typhus, cholera, and Spanish influenza as well as famine killed millions; during the period in which the New Economic Policy (NEP) was in place (1922–1928), the authorities described a city filled with spaces that were dangerous to people's health, such as restaurants, drinking halls, and boulevards, where temptation led to so-called social diseases, such as venereal diseases.[90]

Semashko served as the people's commissar of health from 1918 to 1930. Lenin's comrade in arms, Semashko returned with him to Russia in April 1917 and became the first head of Narkomzdrav in July of the following year, possessing a long record of medical practice and political activism. The public-health agenda that Semashko set out in 1918 was based on the principle that healthcare should be directed as much at preventing diseases as at curing them. The same emphasis on the preemptive and prophylactic aspects of healthcare that Doctor Knock employs to serve his purposes in Romains's play was introduced in Russia after the October Revolution, and one may note how the language of public health clearly reflected such intentions: although the word *zdravookhranenie*, "health preservation," had existed already in the late nineteenth century, after the revolution and the Civil War, when epidemics and health emergencies were most prominent on the front, and when the new Soviet state was centralizing healthcare goals, administration, and resources, now in the hands of Narkomzdrav the meaning of the word shifted to "health *protection*." Besides the evident military connotation, common to all state-as-body rhetoric, *zdravookhranenie* as health protection (the word shares a root with *okhrana*, the word for "protection" and "guarding" in a military context and the equivalent of the English term *security*) rather than as health preservation gestured at a new concept of health, now seen not as a condition to take for granted but as something one has constantly to protect from insidious threats and maintain through work and effort. The emerging field of social hygiene (*sotsial'naia gigiena*) was paramount to such a view of medicine.[91] In a small brochure penned by Semashko in 1921, *Science of a Healthy Society: Social Hygiene* (*Nauka o zdorov'e obshchestva: Sotsial'naia gigiena*), social hygiene is defined in the very title as the science of the health of society. Social hygienists, "as much at home in sociology as in biology, as much interested in preventing illness as in curing it,"[92] argued that diseases were not to be understood merely by their biological causes but rather as social phenomena that were best addressed by studying the social conditions in which they originated. In support of his proposal, Semashko cited German pioneers in social medicine (Alfred Grotjahn, Benno Chajes, Alfons Fischer). In order to prevent disease and modify the lifestyle and habits of the society, he determined that Narkomzdrav would provide centralized and prophylactic care to all citizens. Just as in *Knock*, in the new Soviet state health came to be seen not as the absence of pathology but instead as the result of a set of preemptive measures and the active protection and maintenance of well-being.[93]

Semashko explained the utility of the new scholarly field of social hygiene by mentioning two pressing problems in postrevolutionary Russia: living space and nutrition. While general hygienists were interested in air quality and the location and suitability of homes, social hygienists studied the relationship between living space and social structure. Along the same lines, while general hygienists concentrated on the cleanliness and quality of food, it was the task of social hygienists to analyze how nutrition depended on class. It was precisely through the topics of hygiene and nutrition that public-health officials could articulate the continuity between individual Soviet bodies and the collective body Soviet.

Vladimir Lenin famously claimed that "either the lice will defeat socialism, or socialism will defeat the lice,"[94] whereby the louse signified the insect itself but also other types of parasites. In a famous poster by Viktor Deni titled *Comrade Lenin Cleans the Earth Globe of the Scum* (1920), Lenin is portrayed at work, wielding a broom and sweeping the planet clean of a priest, two kings, and a banker.[95] Indeed, the language of hygiene permeated

Soviet political discourse and aesthetics. Lenin labeled his enemies *vermin*, *filth*, and *pests* and described those of different political mindsets as suffering from illness. Revolutionary rhetoric employed such binary oppositions as pure/polluted and healthy/sick to articulate ideological judgments.[96] Dirt and germs in general became metaphors for the vestiges of capitalism and tsarism, and therefore the NEP allegedly introduced capitalist contagion.[97] Literature and the arts were not immune to the lures of the hygiene metaphor. Even before the revolution, in the futurist manifesto *A Slap in the Face of Public Taste* (*Poshchëchina obshchestvennomu vkusu*, 1912), David Burliuk, Nikolai Burliuk, Aleksei Kruchënykh, Vasilii Kandinskii, Benedikt Livshits, Vladimir Maiakovskii, and Velimir Khlebnikov instructed their readers to "wash [their] hands, which have touched the filthy slime of the books written by those countless Leonid Andreevs."[98] Remarkably, in those same years Italian futurism was embracing hygiene as one of its longest-lasting aesthetic categories, and national public-health campaigns in Italy warned the population against diseases carried by insects.[99] Later in the decade, Vladimir Maiakovskii reiterated the concept of capitalism as contagion in *The Bedbug* (1928).[100]

Soviet hygienists' obsession with nutrition can be explained with the massive concerted attempt by public-health authorities and the party to regiment work production and consequently the worker's body. Tables for a clock-ruled life displayed how an entire day should be rationally laid out. By employing the metaphor of the body-as-machine, which reflected their aspirational views of the new Soviet society and could also be easily understood by the masses, hygienists applied the language of factory production to their descriptions of the body and incorporated the rhythm of the industrial clock into recommendations for leisure, nutrition, and rest. The assembly-line production methods developed by Frederick Winslow Taylor, Frank and Lillian Gilbreth, and Henry Ford were at that point well established in the West, and Lenin adopted them enthusiastically.[101] With the rhythmic lines of his collection *Poetry of the Worker's Blow* (*Poeziia rabochego udara*, 1918), which Evgenii Zamiatin (1884–1937?) revisited in his dystopian novel *We* (*My*, 1921), the poet and theorist Aleksei Gastev (1882–1939) inspired a new way of organizing production. Gastev, whose concept of a mechanized body remained popular throughout the 1920s,[102] designed courses based on European biomechanics, a field brought about by the machine age that director Vsevolod Meyerhold (1874–1940), too, explored in his choreographies.

Such a harmonious relationship between the human body and industrial machinery, based not merely on analogy but on a felicitous and modular integration, stands in stark contrast to the reflections on health and the environment that Chekhov had expressed only twenty years earlier in the short story "A Doctor's Visit" ("Sluchai iz praktiki," 1898). In this prerevolutionary text, the young doctor Korolëv is called in from Moscow to visit the heir of a factory owner, Liza, who lives in the family house on the factory premises and suffers from anxiety and heart problems. After visiting the patient, Korolëv takes a nighttime walk around the house and is troubled by the disquieting noises coming from the factory building, with its windows lit up, which sound as if they were "produced by a monster with crimson eyes, the devil himself" (kak budto ... izdavalo eti zvuki samo chudovishche s bagrovymi glazami, sam d'iavol).[103] Only then does the doctor realize that the well-being of the woman has been hindered by the factory and its detrimental socioenvironmental impact. When Korolëv was still in the house, assessing Liza's health, an unsettling noise coming from the factory building had drawn his attention, as if to underscore how deeply the industrial machinery, production, and socioenvironmental impact had extended their influence into the woman's room and affected her body. Now, as Korolëv is taking a stroll, at one point he hears that same upsetting noise interrupting the quiet of the night. The adverb *suddenly* (*vdrug*), introducing the sentence in the text, conveys the epiphany that strikes Korolëv upon hearing the sound—that is, his quick realization of the clinical picture in the context and as the result of the surrounding social and natural environment. Earlier in the day, while approaching Liza's house, Korolëv had also noticed the workers' dire physical and living conditions. The legacy of Claude Bernard's theories about the body's internal (physiological) milieu being deeply connected with the external (social and natural) milieu was still prominent when Chekhov wrote this story.[104] This particular use of sounds, intra- and extradiegetic at once, allows for a portrayal of the human-made and the natural environment in strained coexistence, with the anthropomorphic figure of the devilish factory and its loud and haunting noises displacing the singing of frogs and nightingales, now barely audible from far away.[105]

Soviet aesthetics, in contrast, promoted a virtuous fluidity between the human body and industrial production and industrialization itself as indisputably good, with the "worker's blow" becoming a key source of inspiration for Gastev's poetry. Gastev's goal was to make labor more efficient, and by the mid-1920s hundreds of cells and several laboratories worked toward applying Taylor's concept of scientific management—which in Russia took the name "Scientific Organization of Labor" (Nauchnaia organizatsiia truda, NOT)—to all aspects of society. NOT theorists applied their principles and techniques not only to work but also to leisure.[106] The detailed schedules NOT produced to micromanage the worker's daily life included bathing, diet, and exercise recommendations and extended their normative mission beyond factory shifts. Workers' lifestyle outside the factory constituted a particular locus of concern because it could lead to unnecessary energy dispersion.[107] Physical education (*fizkul'tura*), which Semashko viewed as a panacea, was part of this detailed calculation as well. Within this picture of energy economics, quite reminiscent of thermodynamics, nutrition guidelines were paramount. In his collection *Youth, Go!* (*Iunost', idi!*, 1923), Gastev extended the machine metaphor to nutrition viewed as fueling the body and recommended a diet of black bread, onion, potatoes, nuts, dried apples in water, and water, all in modest quantities, to support mental labor, physical labor, walking, sleeping, domestic labor, and other unspecified activities.[108] Public-health authorities produced diet guidelines that underscored the importance of vitamins, which had been recently discovered, and, quite expectedly, of calories for achieving bodily efficiency and strength. However, revolutionaries barely ate, and Lenin was known to sustain himself almost exclusively on strong tea. Within the framework of what Eric Naiman calls "revolutionary anorexia," gastronomic (as well as sexual) consumption and pleasure were viewed as bourgeois.[109] The language employed by the official guidelines presented a military rhetoric—the body became the arena where battles between diseases and health, germs and vitamins, were fought. In *Social Illnesses and the Fight Against Them* (*Sotsial'nye bolezni i bor'ba s nimi*, 1926), Semashko defines the human organism as "literally, a fortress" (krepost', v priamom smysle etogo slova)[110] and describes public-health strategies by employing language that almost evokes military tactics, such as "line of intervention" (*liniia raboty*), while the word *fight* (*bor'ba*) appears very often in his writings—and not only in the title of this publication—in connection with epidemics, dirt, and prerevolutionary habits. As early as in his first pamphlet in 1921, *Science of a Healthy Society: Social Hygiene,* he had maintained that bacteria are *the* "enemies of humans" (*vragi cheloveka—bakterii*) and exhorted Russian citizens to strengthen their bodies' defenses ("zashchitel'nye sily organizma").[111]

We have encountered military metaphors in *Knock* as well, not only when Knock refers to fighting infections as the body's defense against the invasion of germs but also when he defines his home visits as part of his *campaign* to expand his influence and gain more patients. In the late nineteenth century, war and medicine became tightly connected, the former catalyzing the latter's developments and providing an extreme testing ground for surgical techniques and newly discovered medications for generations of European physicians. Bullet wounds in the Franco-Prussian War of 1870 offered the opportunity to prove Joseph Lister's (1827–1912) antisepsis as an effective treatment for infections. World War I, causing shrapnel wounds, highlighted the need to replace conservative treatment and Lister's medication with the amputation of necrotic tissues and continual irrigation with Dakin-Carrel's solution.[112] The chemical war on syphilis and other infectious diseases prompted the development of pharmaceutical companies that were branching out of chemical industries, first in Germany and then in the rest of Europe.[113] In interwar Europe, state authorities were often instrumental in marketing new remedies that the industry provided to address public-health emergencies such as the epidemics of infectious diseases—including the remedy for syphilis, Salvarsan, and, naturally, aspirin.[114] What today would be seen as a conflict of interest was common practice in the face of health crises. It is particularly noteworthy that in the early twentieth century the chemical industry was crucial to war, medicine, and agriculture, the same basic molecules sometimes being employed in all three fields. According to the historian Mary Schaeffer Conroy, "World War I was a wake-up call for Russia's need for a robust chemical/chemical-pharmaceutical industry and for domestic sources of iodine and opium. The chemical industry would supply fertilizers and weapons as well as medicines."[115] Besides offering one more interpretive layer for our analysis of the word *campagne*, this conjuncture shows that for any state with hegemonic ambitions, chemicals fueled two crucial missions at once—ensuring a strong and healthy population and preparing for war. Weapons and medications shared the same *roots*, the same constitutive components. Along similar lines, the visual rhetoric of Soviet public-health maps is comparable to that of military-strategy maps. In both types of maps, the country becomes a unified body to be protected

MEDICAL ENLIGHTENMENT IN THE EARLY 1920S

and defended from enemies who threaten it from within and without. Just as war maps display information about trench layouts, roads, situation assessment (static), direction of expansion (action over time), and enemy information, public-health maps (see figures 3.7–10) show the spread of epidemics (one or more "enemies" combined); the location of hospitals,

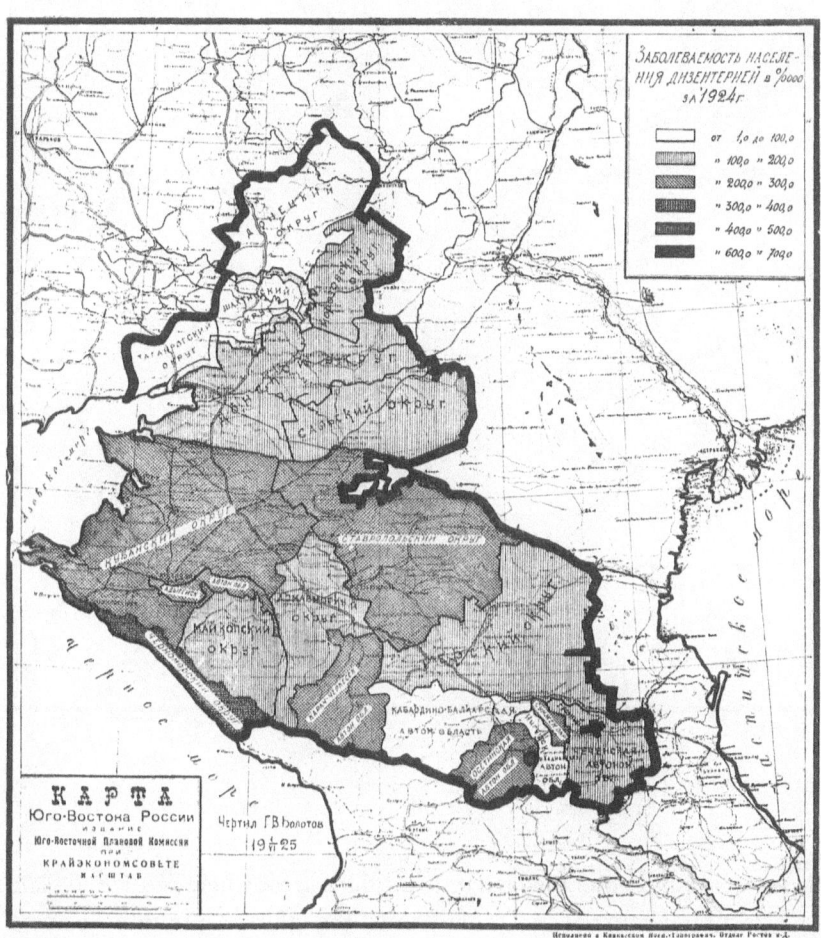

FIGURES 3.7–3.10. Russian public-health maps from the 1920s. 3.7: Snapshot assessment of the dysentery epidemic in the southwest of Russia (1924). 3.8: Map of the spread of malaria in the southwest of the Russian Federative Socialist Republic (RSFSR) in the years 1920–1922 (1922). 3.9: Map showing the areas where medicinal plants were grown in the northwest of the country (1920s). 3.10: Outline of medical facilities and logistic units in the area from Leningrad to Moscow on January 1, 1925. *Source*: Courtesy of the Russian National Library.

FIGURES 3.7–3.10. (continued)

dispensaries, and other medical units; and the areas where medicinal plants are grown and sourced—in other words, the efforts, munitions, achievements, and losses of a sort of medical army during its *campaigns*. Figure 3.10, in particular, illustrates a process that Doctor Knock would define as *pénétration médicale*. Like Knock's map of Saint-Maurice and the surrounding valley, showing all the houses that had been reached by medical enlightenment, this drawing accounts for the location of every medical

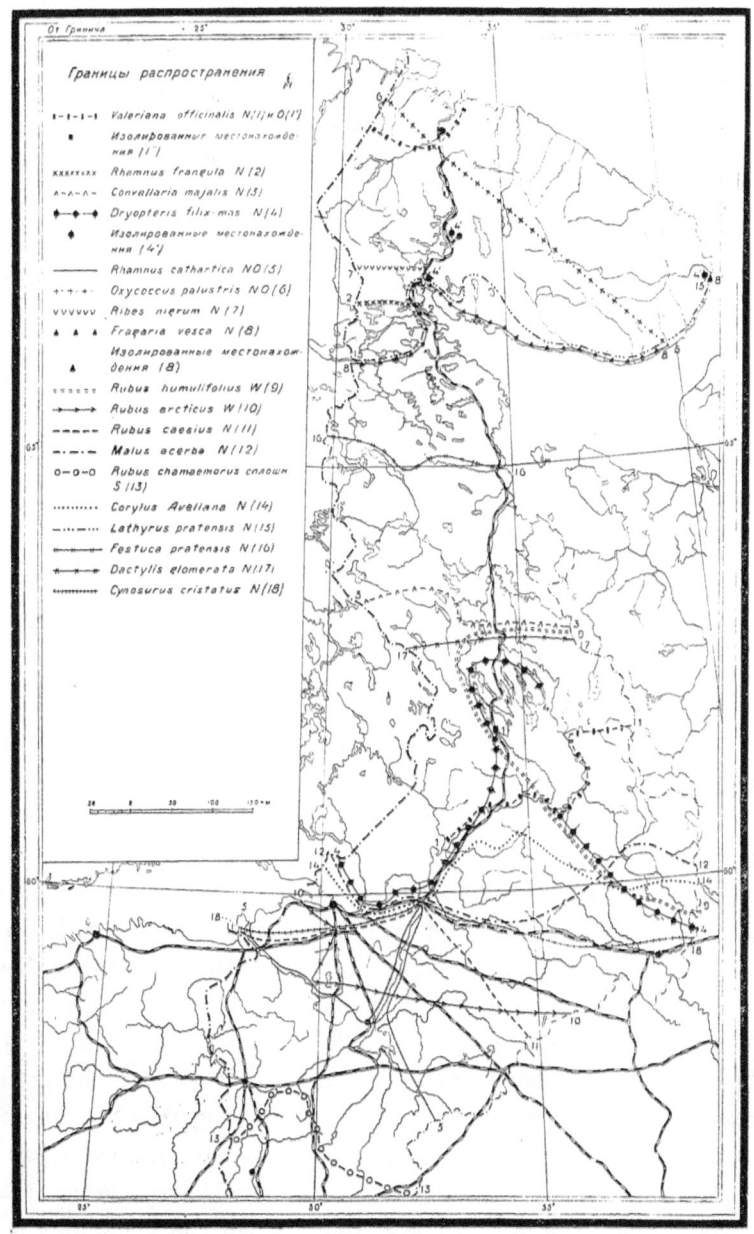

FIGURES 3.7–3.10. (continued)

FIGURES 3.7–3.10. (continued)

facility and industrial and logistic unit in the territory that extends from Leningrad to Moscow and west—hospitals and clinics, dispensaries, pediatric care centers, chemical laboratories, storage units, medical-vehicle parking lots.

Of course, steering away from hygienists' guidelines on nutrition and lifestyle would lead to the ruin of the citizen's body as well as of the Soviet society. Alcoholism, for instance, produced intoxication of the body and mind, which entailed reduced work productivity and losses for the national economy. In a poster from an anti-alcoholism campaign in 1929 (figure 3.11), an intoxicated man is pouring himself a glass of vodka and inadvertently spills some onto a factory drawn below him. The proportions in the image give a sense of the magnitude of the problem: the man's face and hands (we don't see any other part of his body) are enormous compared to the factory, which seems to suggest that the consequences of what looks like a harmless and insignificant habit are indeed huge and of interest to the collective. The slogan reads, "Let's Expel Drunkards from the Thicket of Workers!," while

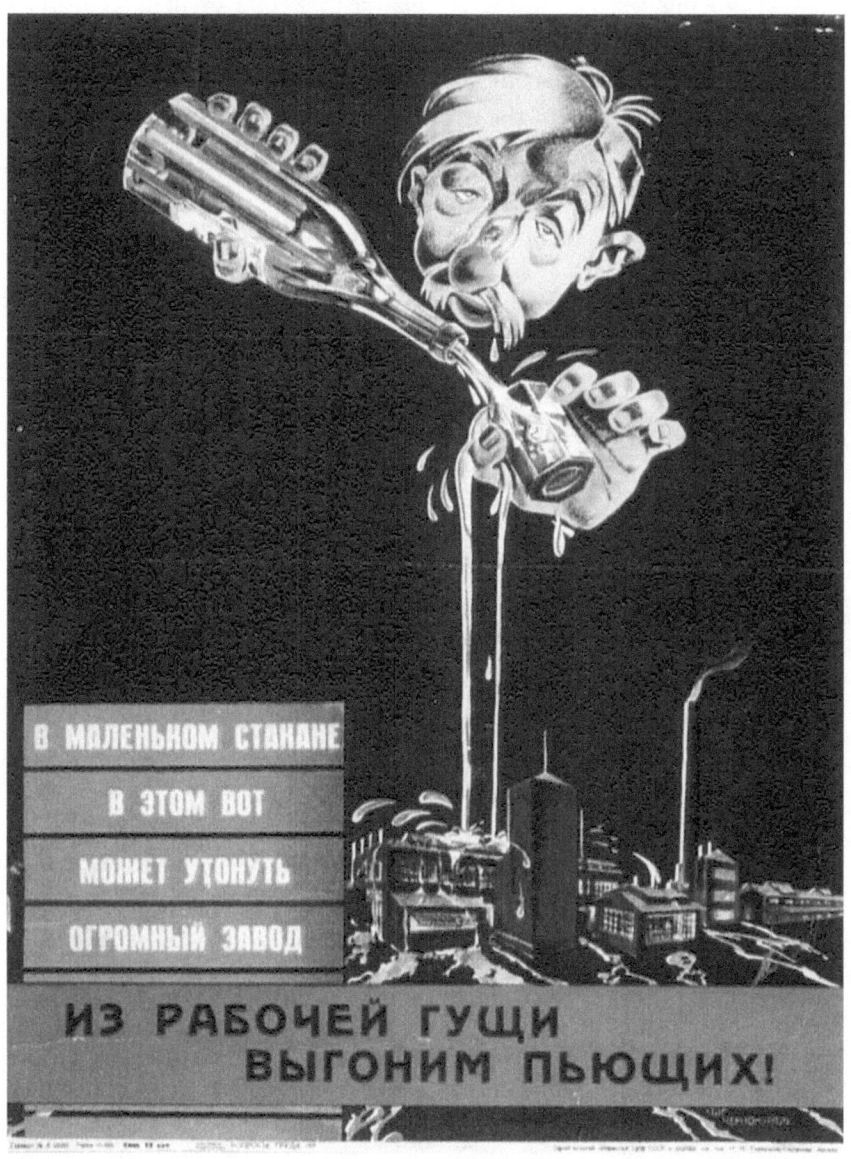

FIGURE 3.11. *Let's Expel Drunkards from the Thicket of Workers!* (poster, 1929). *Source:* Courtesy of the Russian State Library.

the text in white letters reminds the viewer that "in a small glass one can drown an enormous factory." The stream of vodka running down from the bottle also resembles the strings of a puppeteer, all the more so as we see only the hands and face of the drunkard, placed above the factory landscape. In other words, production, development, and the well-being of the society are in the hands of a drunk man whose eyes are half-closed, whose nose is red, and who is not even aware that he is spilling vodka while pouring it. Individual bad behavior harms the state-as-body.

Although seemingly cultural, hygienists' concerns were in fact political in motivation. Physical health and political well-being were considered tied to each other, and there were categories of people (disease carriers, the morally suspect) whose actions and very existence threatened the regime's health. Health policies were obviously part of an overarching political agenda. Prophylactic and preemptive medicine as well as the concept of health as something to promote and achieve actively sprang from broader directives for the new society, the ideals it should embody, and the goals it should pursue. Italian fascist authorities identified the betterment and correction of the state-as-body as their foremost goals, with rhetorical choices that privileged medical imagery. Benito Mussolini's Ascension Day Speech (May 26, 1927) constitutes a famous instance of medical discourse placed at the core of totalitarian rhetoric:

> Somebody in the past has claimed that the state should not be concerned with the physical health of the population.... Such a theory is suicidal. It is obvious that in a well-governed state care for the physical health of the population should come first. How are we doing on this front? What is the current picture? Is the Italian race, that is, Italian people in its physical expression, in a flourishing phase, or are there symptoms of decay?...
>
> Laws are like medical treatment: given to an organism that is still capable of some reaction, they are effective; given to an organism that is close to decomposing, they speed up its death with fatal congestions.
>
> Here I come to mafia, Gentlemen Members of the Parliament! In this respect, too, I will be clear: I do not mind the international press reporting my statistics. The international press, though, will have to admit that fascist surgery is indeed courageous and really prompt. Let's take a look. Because many of you are not aware of the size of that phenomenon, I am now

presenting it to you as if on the operating table: and the body is already cut by my scalpel....

Is this terror, gentlemen? No, not terror, and barely even rigor. And perhaps not even that—it is social hygiene, national prophylaxis. We remove these individuals from circulation as a doctor would an infected person.[116]

Mussolini's speech abounds in medical metaphors, which promotes the concept of governance as therapeutic intervention: the leader figures as the chief surgeon who operates on a societal body that is afflicted by fatal diseases and "unhealthy" behavior (note the "circulation" metaphor, among others). He prescribes medicines that either cure the patient or precipitate death, he does not fear employing his medical tools to remove social illnesses from a body that is lying on the surgical table, and he thus ensures the health of the state.[117] Just as Soviet authorities were regimenting human bodies at the same time that they were reshaping the landscape by rechanneling waterways through dams, building canals, and repurposing whole regions to yield specific crops, Mussolini as a leader-clinician was performing operations on the state-as-body both at the level of society and on the landscape. The purification of the social body was advertised in the same breath as the bonification of the swampland where malaria was widespread and its conversion into arable soil—and both were described as vast surgical operations.[118]

Schedules, regimentation, and discipline constituted the main therapeutic remedies of the new Soviet state. Hygienists presented regimentation as a cure-all for personal and societal illnesses. Yet reformers had greater goals than simply making citizens keep their homes clean and their bodies fit by engaging in *fizkul'tura* and maintaining a healthy lifestyle through proper behavior. Hygienists aimed for an overhaul of the citizens' lives through the manipulation of their everyday habits, whereby personal choices were presented as political ones. Such a scheme did not leave room for alternative choices in matters of health. Like the villagers in Romains's play, Soviet citizens were told that they could not trust their bodies. Pointed toward their organisms, the torch of enlightenment brought about by the synergy of state-of-the-art medical knowledge and state institutions could reveal what people were unaware of. A poster from the mid-1920s warns that even when we think that we are clean, we may be carrying bacteria—the sworn enemies of humankind, to paraphrase Semashko—as the tools of science show. In a wordplay on two terms, *zdorovo!* (hello!) and *zdorov* (healthy), which share an etymological root (the same as in the word *zdorov'e*, "health"), and in the style and size of the letters that form them, the merry-sounding and light-hearted exclamation *Zdorovo!*, accompanied by a large-size greeting hand, placed right in the middle of the poster, is soon undercut by the sinister doubt introduced by the question "But are you healthy?" (A zdorov li ty?). The color-coding is relevant as well. White letters are employed for words that describe the status quo, *ty* (you) and *zdorov* (healthy)—one assumes one to be healthy. The word that instills doubt, *li*, is instead colored red, thus introducing some alarm. Red is employed for expressions that are not emotionally neutral, whether in a positive or a disquieting sense—*li* and the question mark are written in red, but so is the greeting *zdorovo!*, with the exception of the final letter *o*, as if to highlight the wordplay with *zdorov* in the question, the former being red and the latter white.[119] Impressions are deceptive, and the citizens had better trust those who possess much more knowledge about their bodies than they ever could and who know how best to manage them and the nation. By abiding by public-health guidelines, Soviet citizens could march beyond the untidy social and political environment of the 1920s and advance directly to a utopian state. The economic, cultural, and political battle for a new state could be fought with the most meager resources. Any individual, by following the hygienists' rules, would not only become a healthier person but also embody the success of the Soviet experiment. The human organism became a privileged ground for the making and unmaking of the world.

Socialism would be achieved only if the entire population embraced and promoted the new model of public health and actively contributed to maintaining their individual health and to making sure that everybody else complied with the guidelines as well. Such a totalizing, choral approach recalls the final scenes in *Knock*, with the village of Saint-Maurice turned into a clinic whose patients/inhabitants are the most fervent promoters of medical enlightenment.

The newly achieved collective membership in the new body politic entailed collective responsibility for its well-being. Lenin claimed that "the fight for socialism is at the same time the fight for health,"[120] and one of the first goals the revolutionary government set when it came to power in

MEDICAL ENLIGHTENMENT IN THE EARLY 1920S

October 1917 was that of involving the whole population in campaigns against epidemics, both social and medical. As one might expect, similar claims can be made about early fascist Italy: according to Ruth Ben-Ghiat, "[Party leaders] had long argued that fascism's survival depended on its ability to have younger Italians identify their interests with those of the state[, whereby] the construct of 'youth' performed for the fascists in the same way that class and race had for the Bolsheviks and National Socialists—as a mobilizing and integrating national myth."[121]

In an article published in 1922, Al'fred Mol'kov (1870–1947), director of the State Institute for Social Hygiene (Gosudarstvennyi institut sotsial'noi gigieny) and former member of the Pirogov Society's educational wing, succinctly conveyed one of the main tenets of Soviet medicine by stating that "the health of the workers is the task of workers themselves" (zdorov'e trudiashchikhsia—delo samykh trudiashchikhsia).[122] A poster from the same year read, "The Workers of the USSR Do Not Have the Right to Poison Their Strength, Body, and Mind, Which Are Needed for the Collective Work of the Socialist Construction of the Proletarian State," and conveyed that same urgent responsibility. A shabby worker holding a bottle in his hands is portrayed at the center, as if at a crossroads of two completely different paths: the vignettes in the left column, introduced by a quotation from Lenin, "Alcoholism and socialism are incompatible," denote a deplorable lifestyle characterized by vices, dirt, and trouble—a lifestyle that the worker is currently leading; the vignettes in the right column, next to the slogan "Eliminate vodka from our lifestyle," celebrate instead a virtuous life of work, healthy interactions with family, friends, and coworkers, and *fizkul'tura*—a way of life that is not just easily attainable by the worker but that constitutes his duty. The opposition of the two lifestyles is emphasized by the symmetry of the shapes and frames as well as by the bold use of color, in stark contrast with the representation of negative elements hailing from the four corners—alcohol, prostitutes, criminal behavior, and death—which appear in washed-out dark hues and with undefined contours, as if cowardly sneaking from their hiding place in the shadows to lure the workers into making deplorable choices. The worker is placed at the center—with his feet directed toward virtue, but his head and torso turned back and facing vice—as the target of a moral reproach and at the same time as a citizen endowed with agency and responsibility for himself and the whole nation. Once more, the causal connection between one's careless, private behavior, seemingly unimportant for the collective and the fate of the country, is highlighted visually in such elements as the parallel lines of the streak of vodka ingested by the worker and the flames rising from a factory set on fire as a result of the worker's deplorable behavior.[123] In both Mol'kov's slogan and the poster, the underlying assumption was again that continuum between individual bodies and the social bodies that had already formed part of the European imaginary since Thomas Hobbes's *Leviathan* (1651); the body of the Soviet citizen belonged to the state, and the health problems caused by alcohol abuse and other deviant behavior were viewed as mutilations inflicted on the whole organism of society, the collective. This understanding of individuals as forming a larger entity, a collective being that transcends the sum of its component parts and displays one unified will, shares many traits with Romains's definition of *les unanimes* examined earlier. For this reason, the final scenes of *Knock*, featuring a crowd that celebrates medical enlightenment, conjure up visions of the dystopian One State as a perfectly functioning machine in which citizens are cogs that Zamiatin describes in *We* as a condemnation of the early Soviet social experiment.[124]

Education was considered the most effective measure to ensure that Soviet citizens would adopt proper everyday behavior and follow public-health guidelines. The Department of Sanitary Enlightenment (Sanprosvet) was a branch of Narkomzdrav whose mission was to spread health literacy (*sangramota*) and promote hygienists' principles of prophylactic medicine among the masses.[125] Whereas in Romains's play, Doctor Knock carries out his medical campaign on his own, Soviet sanitary enlightenment employed several media and genres to reach the general public—posters, pamphlets, plays, mock trials, lectures, railroad-car exhibitions, movies, magic-lantern shows, and campaigns devoted to sanitizing infected areas.[126]

The amount of health-related messages in Soviet propaganda was massive. Tricia Starks remarks that "between January 1919 and June 1922, during a period of relative austerity, hygienists published over 13 million pieces of public health literature and put out millions more pieces over the decade."[127] The penetration of Soviet health propaganda and its capillarity throughout the national territory reminds us at once of Doctor Knock's map of his medical expansion and of the historical maps we have encountered and compared: those compiled by Soviet public-health officials and by various armed forces during World War I, in both cases as tools of assessment and planning of operations and campaigns.

The loose Soviet equivalent of Knock's *âge médicale*, sanitary enlightenment was truly a product of the October Revolution and its mission; just like agitprop, it mobilized the masses against enemies that this time took the form of diseases, ignorance (*nevezhestvo*) of basic hygiene, as well as the socially deviant and carriers of diseases—prostitutes, drunkards, bootleggers. It is no surprise that analogous techniques of engineering and control over the state-as-body were employed in fascist Italy. As David Horn describes the situation in Italy, "At the same time that the bodies of criminals, workers, and women of reproductive age were made 'social bodies,' society was reimagined as a body to be defended against itself: an organism whose component parts posed predictable risks to the survival of the whole."[128]

Sanprosvet developed significantly during the fight against epidemics in 1918–1920. Education (*vospitanie*) was deemed vital to combat and prevent illness and thus to ensure the health of the population that would build a new society. Naturally, public-health officials considered schools and teachers to be precious allies: they would convey hygiene principles to younger citizens, who would in turn "educate" their parents and families. We have seen that Doctor Knock seeks that same close cooperation with Bernard, the village teacher, in order to further his plans for the population of Saint-Maurice.

Far from being passive recipients of hygienists' campaigns, citizens were instead the main actors in this mass mobilization. Through education, sanitary literacy, and enlightenment, they, just like Knock's villagers, became empowered. As the historian Frances Lee Bernstein remarks, in 1921 health education in Russia shifted from a "defensive" role to an "offensive" one.[129] Considerable efforts were directed toward prevention and toward training citizens to independently manage their own physical and psychological well-being. In return, the state would guarantee free, universal, and qualified medical assistance. Good health therefore became at the same time a communal duty and an individual duty. Most importantly, the collective mandate to make labor and lifestyle healthy entailed appointing each citizen to monitor the progress toward health of every other citizen. In order to be healthy, everyone had to ensure that those around them complied with the same guidelines for healthy conduct.[130] This element of mutual surveillance and diffused agency makes early Soviet society similar to Romains's fictional village of Saint-Maurice that Knock's medical enlightenment turns into a permanent clinic by means of the active promotion of the new order by the citizens turned patients.

Because before 1917 health education was defined as the "dissemination of hygienic knowledge" (rasprostranenie gigienicheskikh znanii),[131] the new label *sanitary enlightenment* implied an important shift—previously simply imparting factual information, health authorities were now moving to shape an entire worldview through the lens of health and the principles of science. We are looking at a total, large-scale, and unconditioned "triumph of medicine," as Romains's subtitle reads.

To combat "lifestyle" illnesses, Semashko and the physicians, workers, and volunteers of Narkomzdrav used new institutions as distribution points to provide care. The most prevalent were the dispensary, the consultation clinic, the sanatorium, and the House of Leisure (Dom otdykha), while chemical-pharmaceutical companies from prerevolutionary times were nationalized.[132] All of them combined education and treatment to improve public health. These Narkomzdrav programs brought health propaganda into the private life of the home and family. Dispensaries, in particular, monitored both the sick and the healthy, and given the combination of education, treatment, and surveillance they promoted and practiced, they were quite invasive in the life of the patient beyond medical care and illness prevention. This intrusion of healthcare propaganda into private life is reminiscent of Knock's visits as he goes from home to home to assess potential patients and expand his business. The active involvement of enlightened citizens as volunteers and promoters of hygiene guidelines inevitably entailed peer surveillance, just as it does in Saint-Maurice by the end of Romains's play.

In *Discipline and Punish* (1975), Foucault claims that "it is largely as a force of production that the body is invested with relations of power and domination; but, on the other hand, its constitution as labour power is possible only if it is caught up in a system of subjection (in which need is also a political instrument, meticulously prepared); the body becomes a useful force only if it is both a productive body and a subjected body."[133] As we have seen, medical enlightenment and state intervention in citizens' bodies in matters of public health were certainly not an exclusively Soviet phenomenon and had an already established tradition in western Europe. In his discussion of biopower in the first volume of *The History of Sexuality*, Foucault remarks that the need to ensure citizens' compliance in the way they used their bodies was as much a matter of return on investment as it was a political, military, and economic requirement, and it translated into increasingly invasive programs.[134] In early Soviet Russia, as in other European states, health did become a right, but for the state's benefit the people had the duty not to fall ill. Although the Soviets rejected capitalism, in their pursuit of the socialist dream they embraced Western population-control techniques, most notably the surveillance state and the medical gaze, which Romains masterfully staged in *Knock*. The hygienists produced plenty of propaganda, and health inspectors—medical professionals or citizen volunteers—served as their infantry squads in towns and villages. Although the use of health inspectors to control private lives in the early Soviet state mirrored similar programs already in place in Britain, France, and Germany, Soviet health programs were more thoroughly applied, more intense in their surveillance, and more radically conceived than anywhere else.[135] Italian public-health authorities viewed the Soviet state as an inspiring model. In 1919, when the creation of a ministry of public health was at the center of Italian political debate, in the pages of the medical journal *L'igiene e la vita* (Hygiene and life) physician Giulio Casalini mentioned the Soviet example and praised its Commissariat of Public Health (Narkomzdrav).[136] If the main model for the new ministry was the British National Health Insurance Act of 1911 by virtue of the universal healthcare, medical coverage, and supply of pharmaceutical and medical devices it granted to all citizens, at the National Congress of Medicine in 1921 Casalini also mentioned the Soviet decree of December 22, 1917–January 4, 1918, that approved health insurance for the whole population.[137]

Yuri Lotman has foregrounded and examined the "theatricality" of Russian culture in depth in his work on the early nineteenth century. In "The Theater and Theatricality as Components of Early Nineteenth-Century Culture," he argues that "in the process of becoming theatrical the world as a whole is reconstructed according to the laws of theatrical space in which things become the signs of things.... Specific forms of staginess move out from the theatrical stage and take command of life.... There are epochs when art intrudes imperiously upon everyday life, making its day-to-day course aesthetic in the process."[138] Theatricality was also a core component of early Soviet society, as historians of Soviet drama, culture, and ideology attest.[139] The first decade of the Bolshevik state witnessed a remarkable flourishing of theatrical and theatricalized activity, not only in the form of large, celebrated spectacles involving thousands of participant-spectators but also in the form of amateur theatrical circles, which Shklovskii interestingly described through public-health imagery as "propagating across the country like a cloud of microorganisms."[140] Scholars such as Katerina Clark and Boris Groys have revealed the avant-garde origins of the theatrical experimentation that by the end of the 1920s would crystalize in regimented rituals of state conformity.[141] The theater form, by virtue of its popularity, constituted one of the most successful media that health propaganda employed in early Soviet Russia.[142] Based on prerevolutionary peasant forms, the mock trial emerged shortly after the October Revolution to attack the enemies of the people. After the Civil War, the focus shifted from outside enemies to those within the society—the prostitute, the bootlegger, the drunkard. Mock trials (*agitatsionnye sudy*) began as a form of entertainment and education and became a genre that both doctors and public-health authorities started employing in 1921 in order to teach public sanitation and hygiene to the illiterate masses. Their goal was to "saturate the whole working class" with sanitation enlightenment.[143]

The accessible format, the moral topics, and the sometimes allegorical names made these performances almost an early twentieth-century equivalent of morality plays. Health administrators established special medical-sanitation theaters for the performances they penned; popular topics were alcoholism, venereal diseases, folk medicine, and prostitution. In 1921, Narkomzdrav created the Sanitation-Education Drama Studio (Teatr sanprosveta) in Moscow, and prominent theater personalities such as Anatolii Lunacharskii, Vsevolod Meyerhold, Aleksandr Iuzhin, Konstantin Stanislavskii, and Vladimir Nemirovich-Danchenko were invited to participate in a public debate on the studio's productions.[144] It is worth mentioning that Konstantin Stanislavskii had staged Molière's *Imaginary Invalid* at the Moscow Art Theater in 1913, yet with aesthetic and artistic goals that were different from those that would inform sanitation trials only a decade later. Other doctors that Russian audiences had seen on stage in relatively recent times were Chekhov's—L'vov in *Ivanov* (1887), Dorn in *The Seagull* (*Chaika*, 1895–1896), Astrov in *Uncle Vania* (*Diadia*

Vania, 1898), and Chebutykin in *The Three Sisters* (*Tri sestry*, 1900–1901). Those characters were clearly different in complexity from the new Sanprosvet physicians. However, one cannot ignore that medicine in Chekhov is often distinct from art in that it serves utilitarian ends (for instance, in "The Grasshopper" ["Poprygun'ia"], 1892); that specific literary tradition was of most obvious importance to early Soviet culture when the latter came to conceiving the bizarre, hybrid genre that was the sanitary play. Health Commissar Semashko himself, along with leading physicians and professional playwrights, penned a few of the first plays. By writing sanitation trials, Soviet doctors could see their prestige, authority, and power grow. Such a surge in their popularity had been unknown since the second half of the nineteenth century, when the management of epidemics and the establishment of germ theory cast light on the competence and importance of *zemstvo* doctors and led to representation and *korporativnost'*, as noted in chapter 2. In sanitary plays, the judge relies heavily on the expert witness, and the defendant's admission of guilt further celebrates the victory of science over ignorance.[145]

The first two sanitation trials, both staged in 1922, were *The Trial of a Prostitute* and *The Trial of Citizen Kisilëv Accused of Infecting His Wife with Gonorrhea Which Resulted in Her Suicide*, the latter possessing an almost Swiftian title. In 1924, efforts began to create the Central Sanitation Education Theater (Tsentral'nyi teatr sanitarnogo prosveshcheniia). All-Union Young Communist League (Komsomol) officials increasingly instructed sanitary-theater companies to perform agitational trials of real people, and performances were often publicized as if they were actual legal proceedings and not dramatizations. These practices blurred the distinctions between dramatized agitation trials and show trials and promoted a spectacularization of justice. Audience members were encouraged to serve on the jury in the dramatized trials, so verisimilitude was a key factor: if they could feel that they were truly participating and helping the judge make a decision, the educational and propagandistic goals were fully achieved. In her work on mock trials, Julie A. Cassiday even argues that "during the 1920s, both actual and mock trials fell under the rubric of the *pokazatel'nyi protsess* [show trial] and only the slenderest of lines divided the two types of trials in theory and practice. Although the defendants, judges, and sentences in the *agitsud* [propaganda trial] were entirely fictional, it attacked the same problems as actual show trials of the time. And in spite of the show trial's indisputable reality, actual court cases of the 1920s increasingly contained traits of Russia's avant-garde theater borrowed by the *agitsud*."[146]

Doctor P. D. Iushkov's *sanitarnaia komediia* in four acts, *When the Babka Treats the People, She Ruins Them* (*Babka lechit—narod kalechit*), premiered in the Perm Sanprosvet theater in February 1927 and was staged ten more times in workers' clubs and village venues. Almost twenty-five hundred people attended what M. A. Rozentul, a professor at Perm State University, describes in his enthusiastic introduction to the play as the first sanitary piece on the theme of traditional healing (*znakharstvo*) as quack medicine. Folk healers, especially the old lady, the *babka*, had been the target of Narkomzdrav for years, even if not through the medium of theater. A poster titled *Vasilii Goes to the Babka and Not to the Hospital* was produced continuously throughout the years 1921–1925. It portrays a man seeking treatment for his ailment from a *babka*, a Chinese healer, and a priest.

The main target of the campaign, the *babka* occupies the entire upper row of panels in the poster. She has a hunchback, her healing space is filthy and untidy (it features a stove, a cat, rags hanging on clotheslines), and she even has icons in the corner of her hut. In the first panel, she prepares a potion as a witch would; in the second panel, she instructs Vasilii to take it twice a day and to cross himself facing east; and in the third, she uses her nonscientific techniques to treat Vasilii. The Chinese healer, presented quite stereotypically as he tends to some mysterious remedy, and the priest, who claims to set Vasilii free of evil spirits, are also untrustworthy but are not characterized as negatively as the old lady. The sentence in the middle of the poster warns citizens not to seek treatment by these categories of people but to go to a doctor instead.[147] In Russian culture, there is a long tradition of the comic doctor, especially the quack who claims miraculous powers, in genres of popular entertainment—from New Year and spring fertility games to traditional puppet theater, the *vertep* and *Petrushka* widespread in the seventeenth century, and to the farcical *intermedii* (interludes) originally performed between the (serious) acts of plays at Academic theaters in the late seventeenth and eighteenth centuries, which by the late eighteenth century had become stand-alone performances.[148] Although the old lady in *Babka lechit* is undoubtedly a comic figure, ridiculed by the author and the audience at once, the institutional component and the pronouncedly educational goal of this play were absent from folklore and popular genres. Rozentul writes in his introduction: "Doctor Iushkov's piece achieves the goal of entertainment very effectively, which is crucial to the effect of Sanprosvet propaganda on the audience, by contrasting quackery and the results of medical practice accurately and harshly enough."[149] The more entertaining the show, the more the propaganda message would influence the audience.

Babka lechit is a mock trial, and, as such, it features a simple plot and few characters, all defined by their profession or their plights—the judge, the prosecutor, the doctor, the paramedic and first-aid man, peasants with different ailments (a sore leg, a sore belly, a sore eye, malaria, syphilis) who have seen their condition worsen severely (or even die) after receiving medical assistance by the main defendant, the *babka*. The stage directions are remarkably detailed and of utmost importance. They open by making it clear that the entirety of the action should revolve around a clash between two characters, the doctor and the *babka*: "The director should emphasize in every detail the impressive difference between the environment and tools of the *babka* and those in the doctor's cabinet." The *babka*'s healing methods should be "obviously and deliberately crude" (ochevidno i namerenno grubye).[150] Sure enough, in the first act, when the *babka* is healing a woman who suffers from eye pain, she directs her to perform irrational rituals: "Stand facing east / and rub this stone on your neck, / then apply it to your eye and throw it over your shoulder."[151] The first act takes place entirely in the *babka*'s hut, which is described in detail as a typical side domestic setting—from the burning stove to the rye loaf and the *kvas* mug on the table—messy and dirty, with an overlapping of living and healing space. In the second act, we move to the village dispensary, and we find a "table with bottles, thermometers, a tall glass cylinder, a stethoscope"—all scientific, professional pieces of equipment.[152] On the walls hang informative posters on malaria, which speaks to the dispensary as a place of learning and enlightenment for the patient. The tidiness of the dispensary is often emphasized in the literature of this era, even in children's books, as the illustrations in Sofiia Zak's *Boria at the Dispensary* (*Boria v ambulatorii*, 1928) show (figures 3.12–13).[153]

Instruments and medicines are kept in their places on the shelf, a standardized poster to measure sight is hanging on the wall, and the doctor, who is wearing a white overall, washes his hands before attending to Boria and employs medical equipment to do so. The play sets this tidy, scientifically

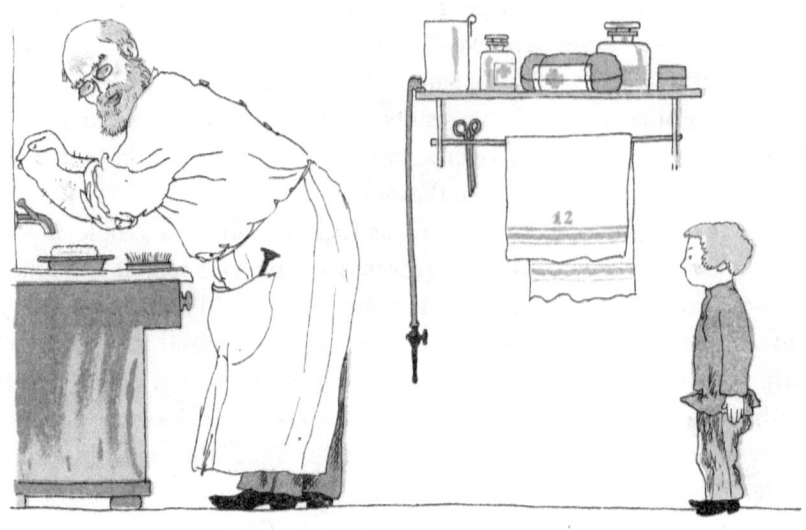

FIGURES 3.12–3.13. From Sofiia Zak, *Boria v ambulatorii*, with illustrations by Vladimir Konashevich (Moscow: Gosizdat, 1928), 5–6. *Source:* Courtesy of the Cotsen Children's Library, Department of Rare Books and Special Collections, Princeton University Library.

approved, and therefore reassuring environment and protocol procedure in stark contrast with the *babka*'s healing space and tools. Whereas the *babka* allegedly cures her patients at home and with incomprehensible techniques, medicine employs clear, measurable tools and scientific expertise, its authority as evident as the setting is tidy, as clear as the doctor's coverall is white. Across all genres and formats of Sanprosvet propaganda, from sanitation trials to posters to illustrated children's books, the physician is portrayed in a bright light and wearing an immaculate white smock, in contrast with nonmedical healers, whose darker hues signify ignorance, ill intentions, and backwardness. The poster *Only the Doctor Can Formulate an Exact Diagnosis and Determine the Right Course of Treatment"* (1921–1925) displayed this visual metaphor in a powerful chiaroscuro: the luminous doctor can offer an accurate diagnosis and determine an effective, scientifically informed treatment for the patient, with no shadows of doubt and no specks of uncertainty; he pushes the *babka*, whose methods are unclear, suspicious, and untrustworthy, back into the shadows.[154] In his reports on the achievements of Sanprosvet campaigns, Semashko celebrates "the eradication of those medieval sanitary conditions under which the Tsarist villages labored" and describes, among other case studies, the "Lightning" (Molniia) collective farm in Chuvashiia, "one of the most backward regions before November 1917, [whose members] removed from the bog in which the squires had driven them under the Tsarist regime to a healthy wooded situation, and built new houses and new buildings (cattle-sheds, barns, dairies, etc.)—they built a school, a public dining-room, a crèche, kindergarten and hostel."[155] Sanitary enlightenment (further emphasized by the Lightning collective in Semashko's report) has allegedly closed the urban–rural divide. We have seen how Madame Rémy explains a similar concept to a confused Doctor Parpalaid toward the end of *Knock*: "All is different now. Some think that in the countryside we are still in a wild state, that we don't have any care for ourselves, that we just wait until the time comes for us to die like animals, and that the remedies, the diets, the equipment, and all the progress is for big cities. This is a mistake, Mr. Parpalaid."[156] Interestingly, in fascist Italy the two areas—the city and the countryside—have the opposite connotations, with the latter providing a healthier lifestyle, air, water, and food as well as a higher fertility rate.[157] However, metaphors referencing light characterized the figure of the physician in fascist Italy as well: the medical professional was considered "a torch" and "a beacon" that cast light on society and brought knowledge and modernity.¹⁵⁸ The visual rhetoric in the description of the dispensary in *Babka lechit* strongly resonates with the description of Knock's clinic in the stage directions of act 3 of Romains's play. The Russian translation of *Knock* employs the same language and imagery, ubiquitous in Sanprosvet materials, that we find in *Babka lechit* and *Boria v ambulatorii*—silver objects (*nikelevye predmety*), the color white (*belaia kraska*), clean linen (*chistoe bel'ë*), antisepsis (*aseptika*). In the countryside dispensary depicted in *Babka lechit*, we find not only posters on malaria but also modern, state-of-the-art equipment, including a stethoscope (*stetoskop*) and a tall cylindrical glass container (*vysokii stekliannyi tsilindr*), both of which carry the same connotations of clarity and transparency as the décor in Knock's clinic. Both the stethoscope, its name literally meaning "to look inside the chest" (from the ancient Greek στῆθος, "chest,"and σκοπέω, "to look into, to examine"), and X rays, which were discovered by Wilhelm Röntgen in 1895 and had recently become common in Russian medical practice (where they were called *röntgen*), made human bodies transparent. Young Boria in *Boria v ambulatorii* also finds at the dispensary a friendly and competent doctor, dressed in a white smock (*v khalate belom*) and washing his hands, and sees on the table so many different shining things (*blestiashchie shtuki*), all types and sizes of surgery tools, that he is overwhelmed ("ne to nozhnitsy, ne to nozh,—ne razberësh'").¹⁵⁹ Boria's doctor, too, enabled by the light of medical knowledge and equipment, casts a clinical glance that cuts through the boy's chest and allows the doctor to examine his lungs and internal organs with a stethoscope and a medical hammer (*molotok*).¹⁶⁰

In the second act of *Babka lechit*, different areas within the dispensary are clearly separated, which stands in contrast to the *babka*'s home: there is a waiting room, a bandaging area, and the cabinet proper, where the physician and his aid are sitting at a table. The patient with a sore eye from act 1 has meanwhile lost her sight altogether. Another peasant, whose sore leg had been treated by the *babka*, has seen his condition worsen, too, and the physician wonders how the man has even remained alive after the quackery he has undergone ("Kak ty zhiv eshchë ostalsia?!"), thus effectively discrediting the *babka* with his tone and remarks and without lengthy explanations. Next comes another old man who has been misdiagnosed and turns out to have malaria. The friendly physician patiently explains to the old man the symptoms of his disease in a scientific yet clear fashion. Even when the ill man raises doubts and questions medicine ("This must be a joke, not science!"), the doctor cooperatively explains to him how malaria is contracted and what it does to the body. Next, a crying mother laments the death of her child, wrongly treated by the *babka*, at which the worried doctor exclaims: "Here is one more number by that *babka*!... She will harm the whole village!"[161] This line closes the second act on a strong, dramatic note. The character of the physician is quite clearly defined in the notes for the mise-en-scène: "His friendly, delicate approach to the patient, and his prolonged and attentive visit remind the viewer of the usual dispensary setting."[162]

The third act, set up by the preceding two, is the single most important part of the play. It provides a reflection on and a ready-made interpretation of what just took place, and it offers an edifying opportunity for enlightenment and empowerment to audience members, who at this point have been hooked by the comic parts and engaged by the story of the crippled peasants (onto whom they may well project themselves). On managing the audience's reactions and best preparing them to receiving the play's main message, the stage directions are again very clear: "If during the first episode the audience laughs,... if during the recess between acts they talk about the *babka*'s techniques, then the goal of this production will be achieved." The prosecutor's speech in the third act "should not bear the shadow of acting technique or pathos. It should be calm, as naturalistic as a photograph, and down-to-earth."[163] In *Knock*, too, first comes the comic effect built up visit after visit as we learn about the absurdity of Knock's diagnoses and plans. A disquieting effect overcomes laughter by the end, though, when Knock has imposed his reign, everybody complies with his rules, and he claims that he is the creator of the new world that has unfolded before everyone's eyes. Here, similarly, although the *babka*'s disasters are funny at the beginning, the tone becomes increasingly serious.

The third act of *Babka lechit* is devoted entirely to the trial of citizen Gruzdeva, the *babka*, and takes place in a courtroom. The scene opens with a speech by the prosecutor, who insists on the rhetoric of empowerment by remarking that the most effective weapons to eradicate quack medicine are enlightening the masses and raising their awareness ("put' prosveshcheniia, put' samosoznaniia"). Only when such weapons are not sufficient should trials be held. The prosecutor briefly reports the cases of harm caused by the *babka* and sharply contrasts medicine with quackery by employing the language of *vospitanie* and progress: "Quackery is absolutely ignorant and illiterate [*nevezhestvennaia, negramotnaia*], while a doctor, with the assets of his medical knowledge, preparations [*lekarstva*] and many years of experience will cure the ill.... Yet our dark [*tëmnaia*], credulous [*doverchivaia*] village has not understood this yet. People go to the *babka*, bring her their last coin, their last *pud* of flour, their last calf." The prosecutor's tirade hinges upon two corresponding dichotomies, light versus darkness and knowledge versus ignorance. Knowledge, enlightenment, and empowerment go hand in hand, their clarity reflected in the tidy, crystal-clear, and unquestioned world of medicine. The mother of the dead child, the family of those whom the *babka* has crippled, and the audience cannot but accept this compelling logic. Only the *babka* keeps yelling, swearing, spitting, and denying her crime. She is obviously found guilty, and just in case the play's message is still not clear, it is spelled out in the closing moral: "Citizen-judges [*grazhdane sud'i*], this trial has a strong demonstrative, social [*obshchestvennoe*] meaning. Here the people from our backward village [*otstalaia derevnia*] can see with their eyes that they can find a remedy for their ailments not at the ignorant *babka*, but at the hospital. At the hospital everyone will be met by reasonable, free medical assistance. When the *babka* cures the people, she cripples them!"[164] The punchline in the end coincides with the title. The curtains are drawn over the courtroom and reopen on the prison walls for act 4, which is a paragraph-long coda. The *babka* is sitting in jail, and a choir, accompanied by a musical instrument, sings "the sun rises and sets," and the curtains are drawn shortly after that.

Sanitary mock trials are artfully crafted according to detailed rhetorical choices. Everything is staged and fashioned in order to elicit certain reactions and judgments from the audience—laughter, trust, disgust. The authority and trustworthiness of physicians is conveyed not only by their attire and their environment but also by their tone and approach to the patient—all of which is presented in a contrasting light to quack medicine. The authority of medicine is self-evident and shines through in the white overalls, the gleaming pieces of equipment, the transparent glass bottles, the clear explanatory posters, and the standardized and measurable procedure doctors follow in approaching the patient. We have seen how the appeal to science, the tone and pace of speech, the gestures, and the use of modern equipment alone confer authority on Doctor Knock in Romains's play. However, the role of Soviet doctors in sanitary trials is distinct: they were undisputed experts who offered patients scientifically approved treatment and at the same time were representatives of the new enlightened Soviet order (the judge relied on the doctor's expert opinion when pronouncing a sentence). As such, they positioned themselves directly in between the body of the individual and the body of the state. Through sanitary theater, they had the power to elevate the patient and the participating audience from a state of ignorance and humiliation to a state of knowledge and active participation in a new healthy society.

The careful planning and predicting of how the villagers (and potential patients) will react to medical rhetoric is another characteristic that Soviet sanitary plays and *Knock* share. The collective participation in the mock trial and the consequent collective condemnation of behavior that health authorities disapproved of generated social pressure on the individual to comply. Moreover, the involvement of the audience in sanitary theater prefigures their enlightenment—their consequent alignment with the state rhetoric—thus encouraging peer surveillance. One may expect these villagers to leave the theater as the mouthpiece of state propaganda. Just like Madame Rémy in *Knock*, they will impose the official narrative on anyone not yet enlightened who comes their way. Originally the formulation of a few Sanprosvet authors, the story has now found many new narrators. Authorship is refracted and reflected: the message will be announced from multiple sources in all directions. It is through these same steps that the village of Saint-Maurice turns into a Foucauldian clinic in Romains's play. Specifically, the elements of the choir (*khor*) and the sun (*solntse*) in the epilogue to *Babka lechit* resonate with the illumination that comes with medical enlightenment and with the villagers coming together as one body and one voice under the aegis of the clinic in *Knock*. In the Russian translation of Romains's play, the stage directions for the moment in which Knock tells an astonished Parpalaid that he has built the clinic and inaugurated the medical era solely "in the interest of medicine" indicate that the Zemnoi Svet (Earthly Light) gives way to the green and violet Meditsinskii Svet (Medical Light). While cool colors can be associated with science and objectivity (unlike warm colors, which traditionally denote passions), the capitalized word *Svet* (Light) resonates with "Sanprosvet" (Health Education) and with the term *prosveshchenie* (enlightenment), *svet* (light) being the root of both. Even if the geographic setting of *Knock* (the French countryside), the healthcare system of its society, and the intent of the protagonist (to make money by transforming the villagers into medical subjects) were not perceived as familiar by an early Soviet reader—the words *klienty* and *klientura* are used throughout the Russian edition to identify patients as paying customers—the language employed in the Academia translation of 1926 interestingly coincides with that of contemporaneous Soviet public-health rhetoric. Just a matter of modifying Knock's words slightly, it is easy to picture a public-health official describing the detailed management and unprecedented control of people's bodies, home environment, and everyday behavior—in other words, the biopower that the early Soviet state and Doctor Knock share—as something to be pursued "in the interest of public health."

We have seen how in *Knock* Romains illustrates the creation of a collective state of mind, a process that is informed by interwar anxieties. The choir of citizens whose individual bodies come together as the state body in the sun of medical enlightenment at the end of *Babka lechit* resonates with the scene at the end of the third act in Knock, in which Parpalaid is led to his room by all the patients. The stage directions that regulate every single detail in *Babka lechit* in order to achieve the goals of sanitary propaganda constitute a mise en abyme of the Bolshevik Party's decision to found Sanprosvet and launch the age of sanitary enlightenment. The very act of setting in motion a massive public-health effort to control the citizens' bodies and the state body equates with Knock's famous line: "The medical age can begin!"

The attribution of agency and authority to statements about someone's normal or pathological condition has become slippery, while authorship and accountability have become diffused and multifaceted. Although public-health measures and pharmaceutical advertisement emerged before the time period examined here, the scale, sophistication, and pervasiveness of the health-related communication we see in the 1920s were unprecedented. The introduction of health-themed mass communication marked the transition to a new epoch of storytelling in medicine. As we have seen in the previous chapters, for most of the second half of the nineteenth century authorship still firmly resided in the person of the physician, but with the fin de siècle monolithic and all-encompassing focalization began to be questioned as much in medicine as it was in literature and the arts, the rise of psychoanalysis being one major catalyst of such a profound yet all-but-linear change. In the "medical age" brought about by medical-themed propaganda, authorship of and authority over matters of illness and health seemed to evaporate out of the hands of individual doctors and patients alone; what originated as the point of view of the few was echoed and refracted in the voice of the many until the message was uttered and reiterated by the collective voice of entire societies. State authorities, medical professionals, and for-profit enterprises all partook in redefining and negotiating illness narratives. Embracing scientific enlightenment and able to master the language of medicine, the new patients who emerge from this picture as narrators who are as reliable as a professional not only talk back but actively coauthor an illness narrative that, from a rhetorical perspective, is undistinguishable from the words of a physician.[165] The new citizens turned patients are able to counteremplot their doctor's narrative or become their own physician through self-diagnosis—in other words, they are now the subject and the object of their own medicalization, of their medical reification, of their "coming into medical existence." When staying healthy becomes a citizen's major duty and abiding by guidelines equates to serving the well-being of the nation, peer pressure and peer surveillance emerge. With the utmost compliance that results from a supposed empowerment, authorship circles back in unexpected ways, the message being replicated and reassembled on a large scale by self-appointed speakers. With the phenomenon of interpellation, the addressees quickly become the authors of their own stories of disease. As authorship gets diffused, multiplied, and refracted among the myriad actors who play a role in this storytelling process, it can no longer be traced to a specific voice or group. The choir celebrating the triumph of science over ignorance at the end of *Babka lechit* technically performs on stage but actually involves every audience member and even those who are not attending the performance. It reiterates the same message that is pushed, in different modulations, not only by propaganda posters and political leaders but also by the volunteers at the dispensary and by neighbors. In *Knock*, Parpalaid experiences something uncanny in hearing Madame Rémy's empowered speech, and so do, perhaps, our doctors today when their patients bring an ad to their office and comment, "That's me."[166] Romains's play adds a further interpretative narrative frame to this communication dynamic by staging the new system and warning his audience against it; the targets of Soviet public-health propaganda and of modern-day medical advertising and institutional campaigns are not necessarily provided with the tools that would grant them a salutary critical distance from the messages to which they are exposed. In narrative terms and functions, it is as if Doctor Knock corresponds to Rozentul and Iushkov, the inhabitants of Saint-Maurice to the audience of *Babka lechit*, but the equivalent of Romains's voice and function could be found virtually nowhere in Soviet sanitary enlightenment, except in Shklovskii's sharp yet soft tone in "Monument to a Scientific Error." Although one is fictional and the other real, and each was sparked by different concerns and in different contexts, informed by different values, and put to different uses, Knock's self-serving medical rhetoric and the Soviet state-run public-health campaigns of the 1920s examined here share major tropes and storytelling techniques, which we can still detect in modern direct-to-consumer advertising and state health campaigns. Most importantly, Soviet campaigns and Romains's play, both the fruit of European interwar aesthetics, foreground in similar ways the marriage of institutional control with the rhetoric of self-evidence and necessity characteristic of the sciences. A close analysis of the structure and style of these sources sheds light on the proliferation and plurality of voices involved in the diffused, vaporous, yet normative authorship of health and illness that characterizes our times.

Chapter Four

TIME, AGENCY, AND BODILY GLANDS
Metabolic Storytelling in Italo Svevo and Mikhail Bulgakov

Over the past twenty years, the challenge to agency, authorship, and authority posed by alien entities within the body has emerged quite insistently in medicine as prosthetic components and human-made devices—such as hearing aids, pacemakers, artificial limbs—have increasingly become parts of our organisms. In her contribution to the edited volume *The Inner History of Devices* (2008), the medical anthropologist Anne Pollock reports her interviews with cardiac surgery patients who had internal cardiac defibrillators (ICDs) implanted in their chests. The ICD is a device that intervenes when the heartbeat falters and restarts it with an electric discharge. From a narratological perspective, when the patient's life story is about to end, the device comes in and grants it an epilogue or a few extra chapters. The device has saved millions of lives, and all the patients in Pollock's study are immensely grateful for it. However, their descriptions of the experience are not devoid of unsettling overtones, as the following passage shows:

> A 42-year-old worker from the Rust Belt, Stan received his ICD when he passed out while running. Now he considers that the death he almost had would have been an "easy death." "Like blacking out on the road, dying like that would be nothing. There would be no pain

whatsoever...." The ICD spared him that "easy death."... Stan feels that the ICD has allowed him to make a trade-off. He gets, and is grateful for, the extra time: "I don't want to die tomorrow." But he has lost the easy death. His greatest fear is that he will receive multiple shocks from his ICD and then die.[1]

Regardless of the subject's will or powers, the ICD becomes a deus ex machina that activates and determines that the story is not over yet and should instead continue. However, the transition to this newly acquired phase of one's life is not seamless: cardiac surgery patients experience a caesura and a shock that they describe as painful, frightening, and uncanny. Having an ICD, "a foreign thing" in one's body, as other patients interviewed by Pollock define it, brings death, or the ending, into new focus: while a sense of closure still informs the general teleology of one's life trajectory, the time horizon becomes an uncomfortably flickering concept.

The negotiation of agency between humans and nonhuman entities has been the focus of object-oriented ontology and thing theory for at least two decades.[2] Specifically, questions of identity, subjectivity, and agency that arise from the hybridization of humans and machines have been addressed most eloquently by Donna Haraway. In her discussion of the cyborg, "a hybrid of machine and organism," she claims that "late twentieth-century machines have made thoroughly ambiguous the difference between natural and artificial, mind and body, self-developing and externally designed, and many other distinctions that used to apply to organisms and machines. Our machines are disturbingly lively, and we ourselves frighteningly inert."[3] Moreover, in *When Species Meet* (2007), by addressing the entanglements, cross-species interaction, and diffused agency among humans, animals, and machines, Haraway further complicates the definition of "human organism." In what is partly a manifesto and partly an introduction to the book, Haraway points out:

> Human genomes can be found in only about 10 percent of all the cells that occupy the mundane space I call my body; the other 90 percent of the cells are filled with the genomes of bacteria, fungi, protists, and such, some of which play in a symphony necessary to my being alive at all, and some

of which are hitching a ride and doing the rest of me, of us, no harm. I am vastly outnumbered by my tiny companions; better put, I become an adult human being in company with these tiny messmates. To be one is always to *become with* many. Some of these personal microscopic biota are dangerous to the me who is writing this sentence; they are held in check for now by the measures of the coordinated symphony of all the others, human cells and not, that make the conscious me possible.... [W]e are in a knot of species coshaping one another in layers of reciprocating complexity all the way down.[4]

The discussion of an entity that resides within a body and seems to function independently of its host, sometimes even against the host's will, has recently emerged in academic conversations about agency and subjectivity as well as in popular culture.[5] The renewed attention that Haraway and others place on the biome as a microcosm of independent organisms (yeasts and other microscopic beings) that are necessary to the human body's successful functioning points in that direction. The scientific scrutiny of endocrine glands and of their hormonal production in particular (paramount to sleep studies, nutrition, gender studies, and several other disciplines) has seeped into popular culture as well. The everyday expressions derived from that research, such as "chemical imbalance" and "sugar blues," highlight a tension between the will of the subject and the functions of the subject's inner organs or molecules, thus adding modern nuances to the mind–body split of Cartesian dualism. When an additional, competing source of authority resides within, and it is not a machine, then the subject's experience of negotiating or delegating agency becomes uncanny, raising questions on subjectivity and on whether the self is coextensive with the body (a major concern of disability studies).

This chapter is devoted to the endocrine system and its associated hormones. In it, I examine how bodily glands, specifically the thyroid and the hypophysis (or pituitary), and their activities complicate our established notions of narrative time and agency. I do so by analyzing two texts from the early twentieth century—Italo Svevo's short story "Doctor Menghi's Drug" ("Lo specifico del dottor Menghi," ca. 1904) and Mikhail Bulgakov's novella *The Heart of a Dog* (*Sobach'e serdtse*, 1925)—and by taking into account the history of early twentieth-century endocrinology, narrative theory, and recent works of object-oriented ontology.

Since Greco-Roman antiquity, when diviners revealed how the future would unfold by examining the entrails of animals, bodily organs and storytelling have been closely connected. The tradition of personifying body parts and endowing them with agency in their fierce competition for supremacy over the state-as-body is quite long and rich, too, as one can see in allegorical texts of political philosophy from antiquity through the Middle Ages and the Renaissance.[6] Metabolism and the notion of time have been tied together for centuries as well—the ancient Greek god Chronos was believed to have eaten his children, which seems to suggest that living in time entails being eaten, digested, and expelled by it in a metabolic fashion.

Natural philosophers recognized the function of glands in the human body as crucial well before the time when the literary texts examined here were produced—René Descartes (1596–1650) famously designated the pineal gland as the seat of the soul as early as his *Treatise of Man* (*Traité de l'homme*, 1633) and *Passions of the Soul* (*Les passions de l'âme*, 1649). However, the decades from the late nineteenth century to the early twentieth century were marked by major medical discoveries that drew unprecedented scholarly attention to the endocrine system, and in the early 1900s the field of endocrinology was founded.[7] At the turn of the century, researchers found that some glands—including the thyroid, the hypophysis, the suprarenal glands, and the gonads—do not yield their secretions into other organs through a duct but instead release their chemical messengers directly into the blood. Such glands were named *endocrine glands*, a twentieth-century neologism formed by the ancient Greek prefix ἐνδο-, "inside" (versus ἔξω, "outer") and the verb κρίνειν, "to separate," "to distinguish";[8] the word *hormone* itself was coined in 1905 by Ernest Starling (1866–1927), who modeled it on another ancient Greek term, ὁρμή, "impetus," "onrush," to emphasize the essential role of these chemical secretions in all life functions. By the 1900s, the medical community recognized the complex regulatory mechanism within the glandular system, and by the 1930s the metaphor of an "endocrine orchestra" emerged in medical literature.

As we turn specifically to the thyroid and the hypophysis, it is worth mentioning that in the 1840s and 1850s two surgeons, Carl Adolph von Basedow (1799–1854) in Germany and Robert James Graves (1797–1853) in Ireland, independently discovered that a thyroid that produces an excessive amount of secretions can cause destruction, consumption, and excessive metabolic activity. The most common symptoms of this syndrome, called Basedow-Graves disease or hyperthyroidism, are an increased heart rate, bulging eyes, and goiter. Conversely, insufficient thyroid activity (hypothyroidism) results in slow movements and slow reactions to stimuli. Basedow and Graves's theories seeped into popular culture by the turn of the twentieth century, when other major discoveries in the field were made.[9]

The role of the hypophysis was also reassessed around the same time as its functions became clearer. Until the beginning of the twentieth century, this gland, located at the base of the brain, was regarded as little more than a vestigial relic, but over the course of twenty years it became known as the smallest but most important endocrine gland. Through the secretion of numerous hormones, it regulates the endocrine and metabolic activity of the whole organism. Harvey William Cushing (1869–1939), a renowned American endocrinologist and surgeon in the 1910s and 1920s, was the first to describe the gland as the conductor of the endocrine orchestra in the explanation of the condition that bears his name (Cushing's disease, a hyperactivity of the hypophysis).[10] Over the following century, it was proved that the brain partially expresses itself through the hormonal synthesis of the hypophysis.[11]

At the turn of the twentieth century, endocrinology was in an active stage of development, as if influenced by a growth hormone. It received valuable help from organic chemists, who were elucidating the structure and synthesis of hormones (adrenaline and testosterone were isolated right around that time). The first three decades of the twentieth century arguably represent a golden age in endocrinology for yet another reason: the flowering of experimental surgery. In the early 1890s, physiologist Charles-Édouard Brown-Séquard (1817–1894) had begun grafting animal glands and tissue and injecting animal organ extracts (especially thyroids from monkeys) into humans for therapeutic purposes. Brown-Séquard paved the way for the work of two surgeons who were pioneers in the use of organ therapy for rejuvenation—Sergei (Serge) Voronoff (1866–1951), a

French surgeon of Russian descent, on whom Bulgakov likely modeled his character Professor Filipp Filippovich Preobrazhenskii in *The Heart of a Dog*,[12] and Eugen Steinach (1861–1944), an Austrian physiologist. By the 1920s, the two surgeons became by far the most famous and the most sought after in Europe: they would implant glands sourced from chimpanzees and guinea pigs—mostly testicles but not exclusively—under the skin of humans with the goal of obtaining mental and physical rejuvenation through an overproduction of testosterone.[13] A popular educational documentary of the period, *Der Steinach-Film* (1922), showed these operations and promoted Steinach's technique. In a way, to late nineteenth-century "degeneration" as both a biological and a literary-aesthetic concept, early twentieth-century culture responded with "regeneration"—surgeons were claiming to rewind the body's biological clock. Such operations were very popular, and even William Butler Yeats underwent one of them in 1933.[14] Of course, this trend generated a plethora of satirical articles in the press (see figures 4.1 and 4.2).

The Triestine writer Italo Svevo (a pseudonym of Aron Hector Schmitz, 1861–1928) was fascinated by the recent findings in the field of endocrinology, even as he looked at rejuvenation operations and their popularity with skepticism and amusement, and wrote several short satirical articles on the topic in local newspapers.[15] Aside from the fad of using animal glands for rejuvenation, a topic that Svevo would touch upon in his play *Regeneration* (*La rigenerazione*, probably written in 1926) and in his unfinished novel *Continuations* (*Continuazioni*, 1928), what fascinated him immensely was Basedow's discovery that the thyroid was a mitigating organ that influenced the individual's inner pace and rhythm, promptness and vitality. Svevo incorporated this principle in his writings on the stylistic and rhetorical levels. In his best-known novel, *Zeno's Conscience* (*La coscienza di Zeno*, 1923), written as a memoir narrated by the main character, Zeno Cosini, for his psychoanalyst, Doctor S., we find several references to Basedow's discoveries about the thyroid's cycles. One of the characters, Ada, for whom Zeno harbors an unrequited love and whose sister Augusta he has married instead, is diagnosed with hyperthyroidism. This allows Zeno to postulate that the thyroid not only regulates individuals' strictly physiological rhythms, their perceptions of time, speed of action, and general vivacity, but also dictates the course and pace of history's turns and the trajectories of nations.

FIGURE 4.1. Cover page of the *Illustrated Tribune* (*La Tribuna illustrata*) from August 7, 1932. According to the caption, the image shows a chimp who has just escaped from the operating room of a hospital in Prague, where surgeons wanted to remove his glands for the second time, and has found refuge on the roof. He takes revenge over the city by throwing roofing tiles at terrified people on the street, but he is captured after two hours. *Source:* Courtesy of Archivio Storico del Corriere della Sera.

FIGURE 4.2. Monkey riot (*obez'ianii bunt*) on a page of *Crocodile* (*Krokodil*, no. 34 [1923]: 1044). The caption reads: "Professor Voronoff has invented a method of transplantation of monkey glands to rejuvenate humans." The monkey with a rifle says: "Enough is enough. You've been sucking our blood long enough."

Basedow's is a great, significant disease!... But only I lived on Basedow! It seemed to me that he had shed light on the roots of life, which is made thus: All organisms extend along a line. At one end is Basedow's disease, which implies the generous, mad consumption of vital force at a precipitous pace, the pounding of an uncurbed heart. At the other end are the organisms depressed through organic avarice, destined to die of a disease that would appear to be exhaustion but which is, on the contrary, sloth. The golden mean between the two diseases is found in the center and is improperly defined as health, which is only a way station.... Society proceeds because the Basedowians push it, and it doesn't crash because the others hold it back. I am convinced that anyone wishing to construct a society could do so more simply, but this is the way it's been made, with goiter at one end and edema at the other, and there's no help for it. In the middle are those who have either incipient goiter or incipient edema, and along the entire line, in all mankind, absolute health is missing.[16]

Although Ada is diagnosed with hyperthyroidism, it is Zeno himself who behaves as if his thyroid were engaged in an overproduction of hormones. He is constantly running—to his father's deathbed, only to receive a slap in the face from him; to the rescue of his brother-in-law's business and across the city to arrive at his brother-in-law's funeral in time. He mostly fails to achieve his goals and is constantly attempting to escape from what he calls "the poisons of life," which come from both inside and outside of his body: "You have to keep moving. Life has poisons, but also some other poisons that serve as antidotes. Only by running can you elude the former and take advantage of the latter."[17] Zeno acknowledges that his life's rhythms can be explained by Basedow's laws. He is running on a metabolic wave in order to expel toxins and excess hormones and to stay alive, but with only fluctuating success.

Svevo scholars have extensively explored the tension in this novel between health and sickness within the frame of psychoanalytic literary theory.[18] What interests me here instead is the role of the thyroid as *agent*. If we look at Svevo's literary production, glands and hormones feature most prominently in a much earlier text,[19] a short story written in his "periodo del silenzio," a long gap between his second novel, *As a Man Grows Old* (*Senilità*, 1898) and the third one, *Zeno's Conscience*, and that precedes the latter by twenty years. The story is entitled "Doctor Menghi's Drug"

("Lo specifico del dottor Menghi"); it was probably written in 1904, but it was only published posthumously, in 1954, with other archival materials.[20] In "Doctor Menghi's Drug," Svevo articulates in greater detail precisely that aesthetic question around time, agency, and thyroid hormones that he would formulate in a more distilled fashion two decades later in his masterpiece. The protagonist is Menghi, an experimental endocrinologist, and the story is his first-person account of his pharmacological discoveries and experiments, a text that is read posthumously, per his will, during a meeting of the Medical Society.

Menghi extracts a hormone produced by the gland of a mysterious animal, the longest living on earth, and he interestingly defines that gland a "mitigating organ," an attribute often used to describe the thyroid in medical literature.[21] First, he implants the gland in a rabbit and then extracts a serum that is ready for use in humans. Menghi calls this newly produced hormone "Annina"—he names it after his mother, Anna—and it is not by chance that "Annina" rhymes with the names of major thyroid hormones that had recently been discovered, *tiroxina* (thyroxine) and *tri-iodotironina* (triiodothyronine), which today we call T3 and T4. Menghi's goal is to create a hormone-based drug that will enrich the human thyroid and influence metabolic rhythms as well as the subject's perception of time and consequently people's vitality and their promptness to action. He is convinced that an excess of vivacity and emotions should be avoided because it makes people burn out fast, besides creating problems in society and in history—irrational decisions, wars—and that an additional agent is needed to mitigate the relationship between the individual and the world. This mitigating agent will prolong people's lives and allow for a gradual and controlled dispersion of one's energies over the years, without sudden emotional peaks or intensity of feelings. Menghi defines the condition he aspires to create as "economy of life" (*economia vitale*). Fascinated by Napoleon, "whose heart beat in sync with the clock," Menghi aims for that perfect rate with his serum. Unlike fashionable operations, this newly created drug will not rejuvenate people, an effect Menghi had tried to pursue with a former mixture he had created, the "Menghi alcohol" (*alcole Menghi*). Instead, Annina will slow down bodily functions and metabolic rhythms.

Once the drug that will change the world is ready, Menghi tests it on himself; in his account we read how the experiment unfolds and learn about his findings. The doctor does not write his notes for an audience, and it is only upon dying that he decides to share them with the scientific community in order to warn them against such a direction in endocrinology. As Menghi describes how his body reacts to the introduction of a new hormone, he is both the author and the hero of his text, which is read aloud both for the audience in the story and for us readers by the doctors of the Medical Society.

> June 2nd, 10:15 a.m.—The injection has been made. An absolute calm reigns in my organism. My pulse is 84, clearly ... [t]he serum is being absorbed slowly ...
> 10:35 a.m. Underneath the skin there is no residual serum left. My temperature is 98.9. ... I can measure the heartbeat with my ear pressed against the pillow and I end up determining that it is in sync with the pulse.[22]

During the first forty-five minutes after giving himself the injection, Menghi offers a meticulous commentary of what is happening to him, but we soon learn that he is not feeling well. The following entry is from the next morning, when he relates the violent fever he had during the night as the Annina was taking effect. The style of these new entries suggests that something has changed in the doctor's body as well as in his writing, which Menghi acknowledges and reports. Although on the previous day he could keep the reins of the narrative firmly in hand, serving as both the observer and the observed, both the narrator and the main character, by the morning his heart rate, breathing, and bodily functions slow down, and so does the rhythm of his narration: "June 3rd, 9 a.m. The pulse ... is now 66—18 fewer pulsations than last night. ... The room appeared to me totally dark; only a little yellow square was hitting my retina, the gas flame ... cold and little, my only contact with the external world. ... Over there my legs, that appeared far away, well beyond the bed, felt enormously heavy. ... I did not hear my breathing, nor did I feel my heart beating."[23] For the sake of comparison, here is Basedow's description of a hypothyroidean patient: "The whole expression of the face remarkably placid, tissues softened, pronunciation as if the tongue were too large for the mouth ... it is the weakest of all existing living beings ... this is no more the animated countenance, the proud eye, which reflects its will; it is a dumb face, similar to those old pieces of coin, where continuous use has erased the imprint of the coin-face."[24] In Menghi's notes, the account of a few minutes takes six pages. Formal measurements and observations disappear from the doctor's report, and he suddenly realizes that "the brain was less affected by Annina than any other organ." Indeed, Menghi is alert and lucid, acknowledging the manipulation of time and vitality that Annina is performing in his body: "It was with a great effort that I could touch my naked feet with my hand."[25] However, he cannot set himself into motion.

> I thought: I should note down my observations immediately. I was certain I could spring from my bed and run to write up my notes. But I did not move. My mind was set on the notes and I lingered thinking about what I would write, were I to write something. . . . It would have been enough for me to lift my head above the table to see the clock that night but I did not make that effort. I kept lying on my back, glad to see that one of the hopes I had put on Annina was confirmed: I was not rushing to action unbecomingly. . . . Without the slightest intention of grabbing a pencil with my hand, I analyzed my senses.[26]

While Menghi is gladly observing the effect of the hormone, the reader realizes that in fact a whole day has passed with no other action than Menghi's slow pondering and considering. Trapped in a numb, alienated body, Menghi is frozen in time—his brain is functional and registers what is happening, but his vital energy and his grip on his body have eerily disappeared. Because he is not able to continue writing his chronicle of the experiment, we learn about that day's events from his recollections ex post facto.

The sun sets once more, and in this quiet nocturnal scene something happens that surprises Menghi and does not depend on his will. Up to that moment, he still considers himself the principal chronicler, the sole narrator of the events, the repository of his will, and somebody potentially able to make his body move (although much more slowly than usual). Suddenly it becomes clear to him that an additional narrative voice is emerging from within his body in spite of him. Menghi vacillates on the threshold between being the narrator and the narratee (as defined by Gerald Prince).[27] He sits back and becomes the audience of Annina's *pièce*, whose main characters are the doctor, a flame, and a wardrobe.

TIME, AGENCY, AND BODILY GLANDS

The fact that Menghi gives up his note writing is an additional sign of the denial or interruption of his authorship. As his inner time slows, Menghi slips back from authorship, and Annina takes control: the hormone is now circulating at full steam in his body and taking over the management of the narrative frame.

> The effort caused by perceiving an object was largely rewarded by the acuteness of vision. I could analyze the slightest color nuance.... Now I could see... within the flame the most varied gradations of those color tones. *That flame was speaking!* I lifted my neck a bit and stared into the darkness, while I tried to make out the wardrobe, which was supposed to stand beside the mirror. I did not perceive it right away, but as if *per my will*, my sight became more intense, and therefore the object—*as if I had called it*—came out of the dark.[28]

"The flame is speaking," and the doctor finally lifts his neck, the first actual movement in twenty-four hours and six pages, as a spectator's response to a show that appeals to his attention and curiosity. Menghi seems to acknowledge a second narrator, housed in his body and directing the action through his perceptions, which are much more acute than usual. Soon follows the description of the wardrobe as it stands out on stage in the gas flame's spotlight:

> The wardrobe had an old, sturdy, baroque frame, a bad-quality antique. Its lacquer was worn and on its side there were two pretentious little columns from which grapes were hanging. I had never seen it like that, and since it was an object I had had at home since my childhood, I was appalled to find it so surprisingly strange.... I was surprised by the precision and fineness of my eye.... [A]round this present vision coalesced all the visions I had had of that wardrobe since my youth. And I saw it again, always dark and menacing, when it stood in a dimly lit room in our first house in Venice.... The enormous wardrobe that guarded with utmost seriousness my first tiny clothes. Inside it there was a strong scent of lavender, which Mother liked much.... I saw it in the outdoors... looking rougher than usual, with several grapes broken... yellow wood wounds appeared almost bleeding against the rest of the wardrobe.[29]

In this passage, Menghi experiences yet another manipulation of narrative time, a collapsing of distinct moments—past and recent perceptions of that same object are evoked and crystalize in the present experience of observing the wardrobe as characterized by the hormone Annina. He sees it and contemporarily also resees it ("lo rividi"). The emphasis on vision gestures to the experience of a spectacle, of a performance. Objects interact with one another independently of Menghi: under the direction of Annina, the flame animates and illuminates the wardrobe, which in turn takes on a life that is a projection of the doctor's past and present perceptions. In *Reassembling the Social: An Introduction to Actor-Network Theory*, Bruno Latour argues that the "social" is best understood as an impure and ever-shifting assemblage of humans and nonhumans.[30] In this scene, the flame is almost a Latourian quasi-object or quasi-subject in its weaving of a network among different things or actants—Menghi and the wardrobe, most notably—whereby their reciprocal status as subjects and objects is defined contingently on the basis of their momentary relationships, which must be traced before they can be understood.

Another voice within the field of object-oriented ontology that may illuminate this passage is Donna Haraway's. Although the thyroid's hormones are not machines, the claim Haraway makes about cyborgs, alien objects within the human body, and their agency ("Our machines are disturbingly lively, and we ourselves frighteningly inert") applies fruitfully to the passage of Menghi's account just reported.[31]

When the sun rises again, it is presented as an additional character in Annina's story: "Meanwhile the sun was rising. The window of the wall that was the farthest from me came alive and showed up, at first discrete, as if knocking to be allowed in. Soon it became the most prominent thing in the room." The sunrise serves the purpose of a stage light that indicates the transition to a different scene. Indeed, Annina's story at this point features its own change of register and focus with a metagesture. Menghi cannot sleep, and his brain keeps working and creating, but what does it create? "Future experiments that I have to carry out. First I had to see whether Annina would accumulate within the human organism. . . . Then I had to investigate if and how our organism could develop tolerance or addiction to Annina."[32] One could read this passage as Annina's attempt to divine her own fate within the scientific field and the pharmaceutical market. Is she going to become a star drug and widely employed? Is she going to be discarded? She is pushing Menghi to find answers to these questions.

By manipulating Menghi's bodily functions and disrupting his hormonal balance, Annina steps up to the role of co-narrator of the doctor's notes. However, this peculiar role of the Annina hormone is not limited to a few episodes but rather affects the general plot of the text. As the effect of the drug wanes, Menghi learns that while he was lying in bed motionless and slowed down by Annina, his colleagues were trying to contact him to tell him that his mother had had a heart attack. Menghi's perceptions were then so strictly channeled and his energies so carefully economized that he did not notice his friends' attempts and failed to run to his mother's rescue.

Now the old lady has little hope of surviving, and Menghi decides to administer Annina to her, too—he is worried that an excess of vitality may further harm her feeble heart. While his mother is on Annina, Menghi can witness from an external perspective the same stages he has gone through. She, too, freezes and does not seem to react to people's words or stimuli. In the meantime, the effect of Annina on Menghi has completely worn off, and in reaction his body experiences an excess of vivacity, which concerns the doctor—his mother, too, will experience this belated exuberance, and her heart will not be able to bear it. Sure enough, when the old woman wakes up from the semihibernation that Annina caused, she confirms having had a similar experience to her son's, and she reports it with unusual animation: "How could you conceive such a horrible thing? You buried me alive, you!. . . I wanted, I wanted to move, to scream, yet I could not and everything was dead inside of me but the desire to live, scream, move . . . buried alive. . . . You thought you were serving everybody's wellbeing; instead your invention is nothing but a new plague. Oh! Poor thing! How are you going to console yourself now that you are losing your mother and years of work at the same time?"[33]

The reduced vitality caused by Annina slows narrative time, as we have seen in Menghi's experiment notes. Conversely, an excess of vitality translates into impassioned utterances and a faster-paced account of events. Under this countereffect to Annina, the character's bodily functions and speech speed up, as do the prose rhythm and the plot: within half a page, the old mother wakes up, in shock describes to Menghi her experience, has him promise that he will discard Annina, and dies.

Menghi is confronted with the shortcomings of his newly fashioned hormone. Not only does he notice that when its effect is over, the exuberance so long withheld explodes at once and may be lethal, but he also realizes that a surplus of vitality in one's body is necessary to defeat infections or to recover from illness. Such resilience would be annihilated by the effect of Annina.

Annina's additional narrative voice throughout the text is also reminiscent of narratives of the split self in the personified dialectics or inner dialogism that we call schizophrenia. However, whereas diseases and their demons are often intangible and not clearly localized, here this alien presence inside the subject is real; it occupies physical space and bears a name: we are talking about the biological functions of the thyroid or its fictional equivalent, the specific mixture of hormones it produces and their dosage.

A newly acquired mastery of time, nature, and the human body was among the most pompously celebrated achievements of the Bolshevik Revolution. Throughout the 1920s, Soviet authorities teamed up with scientists in different fields—biology, physics, medicine, engineering—in order to forge the new society envisioned by the revolution. As seen extensively in chapter 3, pervasive and prescriptive public-health propaganda, Taylorism, and the goal of efficiency in industrial production regimented the human body; just as "the body Soviet" as a monolithic entity had individual organisms as its constitutive units, citizens' bodies became the first testing ground of the revolution and a stage for meaning making. Among the most notable biomedical experiments, blood transfusions and gland transplants would make humans younger, stronger, and more resilient, while anabiosis, or body freezing, promised to defeat death (a technique at some point considered to preserve Lenin's body, too).[34] Lenin's heart may not have been beating in sync with the clock, unlike Napoleon's, but Dziga Vertov's film *Three Songs About Lenin* (*Tri pesni o Lenine*, 1934) suggests a close association between the body of the leader and the unfolding of history. By using montage and the Kuleshov effect, the second part of the film articulates how Lenin's death in January 1924 caused the immediate interruption of all industrial production, transportation, and agricultural work. When the leader's life functions stop, so does history—everything is suddenly still, crystallized in frozen shots in a masterful exploration of temporality within and without the human body. The field of endocrinology was on the rise in early Soviet Russia as well: the authorities understood its potentials, and Lenin's wife, Nadezhda Krupskaia, suffered from hyperthyroidism, which contributed to making gland research a priority. The documentary *Der Steinach-Film* was screened in Petrograd, Moscow, and other major cities in 1922, and in 1923 Iakov Tobolkin and Vasilii Shervinskii founded the Institute for Organotherapeutic Preparations (Institut organoterapevticheskikh preparatov) at their experimental goat farm on the outskirts of Moscow. Needless to say, characters with endocrine malfunctions soon made their appearance in Russian literature. Among them is Dvoira Krik, the king's sister in Isaac Babel's *Odessa Tales* (*Odesskie rasskazy*, 1921–1924), who suffers from Basedow's disease and whose swollen goiter and bulging eyes make her a poor candidate for marriage.

Mikhail Bulgakov (1891–1940) had a more detailed knowledge of endocrinology than Svevo (or Babel'), and his novella *The Heart of a Dog* (*Sobach'e serdtse*, 1925) challenges the view of time and agency that characterized early Soviet aesthetics. After graduating from Kiev Medical School, Bulgakov was a practicing physician for several years, including service as a war doctor, before becoming a full-time writer.[35] *The Heart of a Dog* takes place in Moscow and captures the atmosphere of NEP-era Russia (1921–1928). Characterized by a satirical take on the new political order and the society, the novella circulated exclusively in underground circuits between the late 1930s and 1968, when the first Russian-language edition was published in Germany (in *Grani* 9:3–85). It did not appear officially in the Soviet Union until 1987 (in *Znamia* 6: 76–135).

In the story, Professor Filipp Filippovich Preobrazhenskii belongs to the high Moscow bourgeoisie. He lives in a sumptuous apartment embellished with expensive furniture, indulges in excellent food, wine, and cigars, and enjoys opera. He is a world authority on surgery and performs rejuvenating operations in his apartment on bored and rich people of dubious morals. The humorous sketches of his exchanges with patients convey well the spirit of the rejuvenation craze and the fascination with reproductive-gland transplants characteristic of that time, which scholars such as Mark Adams and Eric Naiman have analyzed in depth.[36] Toward the end of his career, Preobrazhenskii decides to engage in a challenging operation, the first of its sort in Europe: he intends to replace a dog's hypophysis and reproductive glands with those of a twenty-eight-year-old alcoholic and thief, Klim Chugunkin, who dies four hours and four minutes before the operation: "Aim of the operation: the mounting of an experiment by Preobrazhenskii of a combined transplant of the hypophysis and the testes to explore the acceptability of hypophysis transplant and its potential for the rejuvenation of the human organism."[37]

Rejuvenation is only one of the long-term goals in the surgeon's agenda—the emphasis is in fact on "acceptability" (*prizhivaemost'*). If this transplant proves successful, the next step will be a human-to-human operation to create a new type of human, the New Soviet Person (*novyi sovetskii chelovek*). In the 1920s, party authorities and Soviet scientists together envisioned a new citizen who could fit and thrive in an entirely new society, informed by communism and the slogan "Everything anew" (Vsë zanovo), which appeared on the revolutionary flag.[38] In *Literature and Revolution* (*Literatura i revoliutsiia*, 1923), Leon Trotsky described the New Soviet Person thus: "He [the New Man] will make it his business to achieve beauty by giving the movement of his own limbs the utmost precision, purposefulness and economy in his work, his walk and his play. He will try to master first the semiconscious and then the subconscious processes in his own organism, such as breathing, the circulation of the blood, digestion, reproduction, and, within necessary limits, he will try to subordinate them to the control of reason and will."[39]

Bulgakov may have been familiar with the writings of Nikolai Kol'tsov (1872–1940), one of the founders of the Russian Eugenics Society (Russkoe evgenicheskoe obshchestvo). Kol'tsov was the author of "The Amelioration of Humankind" ("Uluchshenie chelovecheskoi porody," 1921), the lead article for the first issue of the society's journal, and the editor of the volume *Rejuvenation* (*Omolozhenie*, 1923). Bulgakov was certainly acquainted with Moscow scientists of Kol'tsov's circle and with their social milieu.[40] Dogs were commonly employed in experimental surgery and, in general, as laboratory animals, Ivan Pavlov's (1849–1936) experiments probably being the most renowned examples of this practice.

In our text, Preobrazhenskii finds a stray dog named Sharik, takes it home, feeds it well, brings it to optimal shape, and then performs the operation. Up until the operation scene, the story is told in the third-person singular, but from Sharik's focalization, with passages of free indirect discourse that read as his inner monologues, including the opening one that is four pages long. Sharik's gaze is estranging, and so the reader must match elements from his monologues with those that follow. For instance, Sharik bites the professor's assistant, Bormental, whom it describes as a "person of male gender in a smock"[41] and for this reason keeps referring to him as "the bitten man" (*tiapnutyi*). It is only later in the text, when after the operation the narration is conducted in the third-person singular with no specific focalization, that we see Bormental bearing the marks of the dog's bite, and we understand that he is the same person. In the first part, the dog's estranging gaze also serves the purpose of conveying to the reader the atmosphere of decay in NEP-era Moscow.[42]

From the moment Sharik wakes up from the anesthesia, something begins hijacking Professor Preobrazhenskii's plans for how the experiment should end and disrupting his expectations for the innovations it should introduce into medicine. An external agent challenges his authority over how events should unfold, and this agent is the hypophysis.

Doctor Bormental, the surgeon's assistant, records the very first results of the operation in his notes. The most strikingly unexpected trait that the dog shows is his use of language. His barking slowly turns into intelligible utterances: first he pronounces a word, "Abyrvalg," which turns out to be the word on the fishmonger's sign, "Glavryba" (from *ryba*, "fish"), read in reverse; then he continues with slang expressions, such as "a couple more" and more phrases such as "Cabby," "There's no seats," "Evening paper," and all the swearwords in the Russian lexicon.[43] Political vocabulary and phrases, such as "bourgeois" and "the recognition of America" are soon added to the pool, although constantly interspersed with curses and requests for alcohol and cigarettes. Soon the dog speaks, reads, interacts, engages in conversations, and sings. The new individual even chooses for himself the name "Sharikov" in homage to his previous name, "Sharik."

In the wake of this surprise, Bormental's tentative explanation of what might be happening inside the dog's body acknowledges the agency and creative powers of the hypophysis:

> What I suggest happened is this: *the hypophysis*, having been accepted by the organism after the operation, *opened up the speech-centres* in the dog's brain, and words came flooding out in a rush. In my opinion, we are

dealing with a revived and developing, not with a newly created brain.... Another hypothesis: Sharik's brain, during his period as a dog, collected a mass of information. All the words with which he first began to operate are street words, he had heard them and they had been conserved in his mind. Now as I walk along the street I look with secret horror upon every dog I meet. God knows what is stored away in their brains.[44]

The language valve is opened by the hypophysis (note the active form used in the text), and now preexisting as well as new thoughts and knowledge can be conveyed verbally. Here we are not dealing with Madgie and Fidèle, the two dogs who speak and write letters to each other in Poprishchin's head in Gogol's "Diary of a Madman" ("Zapiski sumasshedshego," 1835). Here the dog's language skills are real. He is a dog-man.

What we know from reading the first part of the novella but the doctors do not is that the dog Sharik used to have articulated thoughts, although it had no language to express them:

> You think I judge by the coat? Nonsense.... It's by the eyes you can tell—from afar and close up. Oh, eyes are very important. Something like a barometer. You can see everything—who has a great drought in his soul, who is likely to put the toe of his boot to your ribs for no good reason, who is himself afraid of everyone and everything. It's the ankles of the last type one really enjoys taking a snap at. You're afraid—take that. If you're afraid—you deserve... gr-r-r... gruff... wuff...[45]

What is audible to people on the streets is only the last part, the barking, as a sort of preverbal (or nonverbal) expression. All of Sharik's other thoughts are potential words that are forced to remain unintelligible. Only readers are aware of Sharik's remarks before the operation scene: in the first part of the novella, when Preobrazhenskii tries to reassure his regular patients that the dog doesn't bite, Sharik in his head reacts with surprise: "—I don't bite?—the dog was taken aback."[46]

After the operation, Sharikov's utterances do not match the tone of Sharik's earlier thoughts, though they do convey pieces of Sharik's sensorial experiences. Now that the hypophysis has endowed Sharik with language skills, he can read aloud what his auditory and visual memory had stored on the streets: from the first part of the novella, we know that Sharik had learned to recognize the fish-market sign because he would often find leftover food there, but he used to look at the word from the last letter backward because a policeman was always standing by the first letter with a threatening expression—this is why Sharik pronounces the word *glavryba* backward.[47] Now he can say his name, "Sharik," aloud and eventually upgrade it to "Sharikov." However, these utterances are colonized by the voice and intonation of Klim, the gland's original owner. A ventriloquism of sorts results from the operation or, rather, an inner, encompassed heteroglossia in Bakhtinian terminology: an intertwining of two verbal worlds results in the dog-man's discourse, and this mixture is unstable and transitory as it constantly evolves together with the creature.

As quickly as the dog gains language skills, he also sheds his hair and looks more and more like a human being. In his notes about the operation's outcomes, Bormental at one point writes "hind paws," but he is immediately prompted to correct it with "feet." By secreting its hormones, the hypophysis gives its input to the story faster than the surgeons can describe, thus dictating the pace of storytelling in addition to influencing the rhythm of the plot's unfolding. Rather than reversing biological time, the effect that animal sexual glands had on previous patients, here our gland engages more strictly with diegetic time, the time of the story.

Over the two months Sharikov spends in the apartment, he teams up with the building's accommodation cooperative, constituted by a few young people who quote Marx and Engels without really understanding them and who have been trying to force Preobrazhenskii to give up a portion of his apartment and redistribute it to other citizens. Basically the new individual, Sharikov, starts behaving like the former owner of his glands—the deceased thief Klim.

Professor Preobrazhenskii is shocked from the first day. Things are not unfolding according to his emplotting plans, and he immediately acknowledges his own mistake: "Late this evening the diagnosis was made.... [T]he transplant of the hypophysis gives not rejuvenation but total humanisation (underlined three times)."[48] Questions of agency are raised at this point. The hypophysis seems to have a clear agenda—to transform the dog into Klim—and it carries out this program in spite of the doctor's plans and with undisputed power over the body that hosts it. In the text, the body parts of other animals appear, especially through the inviting vapors that come to Sharik's nose from the kitchen but also as whole bodies stuffed or mounted as decorations. Against this foil of harmless body parts, Sharikov's hypophysis and its activities emerge in vivid contrast. Special emphasis on individual organs or discrete parts being independent of the body once they are properly operated by machines was common in the experimental biology of that time. In 1925, a young medical researcher, Sergei Briukhonenko, succeeded in reviving the severed head of a dog using a special apparatus he had devised to keep the head alive. Only a few months earlier, Aleksandr Beliaev (1884–1942) had written "Professor Dowell's Head" ("Golova Professora Douelia," 1925), a science fiction story that staged the adventures of a severed human head living in a laboratory, supported by special machinery.

After enabling language, the gland proceeds to rewrite the story, recasting the professor's draft plan on its own terms until it performs an overall transformation—by secreting hormones, not only does it bend to its purposes all the other organs in the body, but it also dictates Sharikov's thoughts and desires (the word *heart* in the title refers generally to emotions and humanity, not to the specific organ). There is no adaptation or modulation to the dog's organism: Sharik's body is only a new medium through which the hypophysis intends to retell and reproduce a previous life story, that of the body to which it used to belong. The progression of Sharikov's evolutionary stages from dog to man is like the different acts of the hypophysis's "show," presented to the flabbergasted doctors, to those who live in the apartment building, and to the whole city of Moscow.

The hypophysis determines the turn of the plot as well: the process of transforming Sharik's organism into Klim's translates into a series of problems and misadventures in the plotline. Sharikov steals money and precious objects from home, breaks pieces of furniture, floods the bathroom, attacks and offends people, makes obscene proposals to the cook, and for the accommodation cooperative serves as a Trojan horse in the professor's apartment.

The compelling power of the hypophysis and its control of the events is finally recognized by the professor, who is the material "author," the creator of the new individual: he ultimately acknowledges that his operation was useless. "'But who is he? Klim!' cried the professor. 'Klim Chugunkin.[49] . . . In a word, the hypophysis is a closed chamber which contains the blueprint for the individual human personality. The individual personality!... and not just general human traits. It is a miniature of the brain itself... These hormones in the hypophysis, oh Lord... Doctor, all I see before me is dull despair and, I must confess, I have lost my way.'" There is no need to wait to find out how things will develop. At this point, Preobrazhenskii can predict how the story will end but cannot change the course of the events that the hypophysis has set in motion or interfere with them. He knows that Sharik will eventually be transformed into Klim. "The hypophysis is not suspended in thin air. It is attached to the brain of a dog, after all. Give it time to adapt. At this stage Sharikov is exhibiting only residuary canine behavioural traits and, understand this, chasing cats is quite the best thing he does. You have to realise that the whole horror of the thing is that he already has not the heart of a dog but the heart of a man. And one of the most rotten in nature!"[50]

The professor surrenders before the gland and its hormones. From the point of view of narrative agency, this moment of recognition and surrender constitutes the climax of a titanic battle between Preobrazhenskii and the gland over authorship and authority in the storyworld that the professor has created. Up until the operation, he was the author of the masterplan. After the operation, a new power hierarchy emerges gradually but clearly, with the hypophysis taking the lead of Sharikov's body and, from its location below the dog's brain, extending its influence to the whole fictional world of the story that Preobrazhenskii had in mind. Sharikov constitutes little more than a disputed territory between the authorial will of the gland and that of the surgeon.

It should not be neglected, though, that on a narratological level Sharikov, too, is endowed with some agency. He is a source of stories and a narrator in his own right—he makes up excuses to justify the damage he causes; he crafts artful lies for the girl he seduces; he conspires to confiscate Preobrazhenskii's rooms for the cooperative—and these colorful stories within the story occupy the innermost narrative frame.

Toward the end of the story, Sharikov shows the professor a document from the accommodation cooperative that assigns him, Sharikov, thirteen square yards in the professor's apartment, and he appears ready to kill the two doctors when they reject his request.[51] This dramatic climax of the story seems to have been foreshadowed in medical terms in the first pages of the doctors' log, when Bormental declares that the operation aimed "to explore the acceptability [*prizhivaemost'*] of hypophysis transplant and its potential for the rejuvenation of the human organism."⁵² Although referring specifically to the gland transplant into the dog's body, the word *prizhivaemost'*, which also translates as "adaptability," seems to foreshadow several chief nodes in the novella by way of analogy—the theme of a challenging cohabitation points to the redistribution of portions of Preobrazhenskii's apartment to other citizens, promoted by the accommodation cooperative; to the reemerging of the seemingly settled question of class differences in NEP-era Russia; but also to the negotiation of agency and authorship between human and nonhuman entities.

Since the nineteenth century, metabolic processes had served as a privileged analogy to discuss the place of humankind within nature and any possible *prizhivaemost'*. As John Bellamy Foster contends, Karl Marx became fascinated with metabolic activities at a time when scientists were elucidating them, and he employed metabolism (*Stoffwechsel*) as an extended metaphor to address the earth and nonhuman agency. Foster points out that in *Capital* Marx defines labor as "a process between man and nature, a process by which man, through his own actions, mediates, regulates and controls the metabolism between himself and nature." Yet capitalism has caused a "metabolic rift" by alienating the earth from the peasants in order to obtain more resources from it than it can metabolically provide.⁵³ As noted in chapter 3, at a time when authorities reshaped the landscape by inverting the direction of rivers and rechanneling waterways by building dams and canals, the making of the Soviet body was inextricably linked with the making of the Soviet ecology.⁵⁴ Bulgakov's concept of *prizhivaemost'* can therefore serve as an extended analogy in that it allows us to argue that in the Soviet project—addressed by chapter 3 in more depth—the metabolic rift, a phenomenon proper to Earth's system as a result of human intervention, is mirrored by the metabolic storytelling that originates in Sharikov's body and has to be reconciled with Preobrazhenskii's master plot as well as by the difficult "accommodation" of the class divide within the body Soviet.⁵⁵

As seen before in literary history, Preobrazhenskii realizes that he has lost control of his creature and must amend his mistake. He therefore forces Sharikov into the operating room and undoes the procedure, replacing Klim's hypophysis with the dog's original gland. This way he is able to rewind time and see the half-human turn back into a dog. The gland, therefore, becomes the gravitational center of a troubled and multifaceted attempt at accommodation—a process, initially biological, that originates in the dog-man's body but that has repercussions on the life in Preobrazhenskii's apartment and on the NEP-era class struggle and that also resonates with early Soviet ecology. The hypophysis casts new configurations around it and sets plots in motion. As early as 1929, just a few years after Bulgakov completed his novella but several decades before Latour's actor-network theory, the Soviet constructivist writer Sergei Tret'iakov (1892–1937), too, showed interest in the relational function of things. In his essay "The Biography of the Object" ("Biografiia veshchi," 1929), which predates by several decades such collected volumes as *The Social Life of Things* (edited by Arjun Appadurai, 1986), *Biographies of Scientific Objects* (edited by Lorraine Daston, 2000), and *The Inner History of Devices* (edited Sherry Turkle, 2008),[56] Tret'iakov suggested that writers shift away from a "Ptolemaic system" in which human characters are the aesthetic and structural pivots of literary texts and that they turn instead to things:

> The compositional structure of the "biography of the object" is a conveyer belt along which a unit of raw material is moved and transformed into a useful product through human effort.... The biography of the object has an extraordinary capacity to incorporate human material. People approach the object at a cross section of the conveyer belt. Every segment introduces a new group of people. Quantitatively, it can track the development of a large number of people without disrupting the narrative's proportions. They come into contact with the object through their social aspects and production skills.... This longitudinal section of the human masses is one that cuts across classes.... In the biography of the object we can view class struggle synoptically at all stages of the production process.... Thus: not the individual person moving through a system of objects, but the object proceeding through a system of people.... [O]nce we run a human along the narrative conveyer belt like an object, he will appear before us in a new light and in his full worth. But that can happen only after we have reoriented the reception practices of readers raised on belles lettres toward a literature structured according to the method of the "biography of the object."[57]

Tret'iakov here seems to revisit a classic formalist concept, Viktor Shklovskii's threading device (*nanizyvanie*), and to turn it inside out by replacing the hero with the object. If we wish to follow Tret'iakov's astronomical analogy ("The Onegins, Rudins, Karamazovs... are the suns of independent planetary systems around which characters, ideas, objects, and historical processes orbit submissively... in a Ptolemaic system of literature"),[58] then we can claim that he is suggesting a Copernican revolution in the structure and configuration of the literary text. Whereas the scrutiny of the relationship between bodies and things had been paramount to Aleksei Gastev's Scientific Organization of Labor—an early Soviet adaptation of Taylorism explored here in chapter 3 along with the state's intervention in citizens' bodies and other questions of biopolitics in the 1920s—both Tret'iakov and Bulgakov take such a relationship a step further by introducing nonhuman entities as plot aggregators, thus highlighting questions of distributed agency as necessarily intertwined with questions of narrative structure.

As was the case in Svevo's text, in *The Heart of a Dog* we encounter an alien being that dwells within an organism and temporarily takes control of bodily functions as well as of the plot. Haraway's theories of the cyborg certainly apply to our reading of the dog-man Sharikov as fruitfully as to our analysis of Menghi's frozen state vis-à-vis Annina in Svevo's short story. Moreover, the entanglements, cross-species interaction, and diffused agency among humans, animals, and machines that Haraway addresses in *When Species Meet* appear, in nuce, in these texts. Haraway's theories complicate the very definition of human, which was, of course, a pressing question and a major concern in Bulgakov's times.

In both Svevo's short story and Bulgakov's novella, an issue of parenthood emerges, which is little more than peripheral in the former but a main aesthetic thread in the latter. Menghi's drug is his one brainchild, and it is not by chance that he names it "Annina" according to an old Italian tradition of naming one's children after one's parents. Moreover, Menghi's being a doctor in itself makes him even more a paternal figure as it confers upon him special authority even over his own parent, on whose life or death he has the final word when he decides what treatment she should receive. Menghi's story being told as instructed in his will certainly adds to this poetic of lineage and heritage, two concepts that in the story ought to be considered in their biological meaning as well as in terms of scholarly progeny.

In *The Heart of a Dog*, parenthood suggests godlike powers to give birth to one's own creatures and sketch one's miniature storyworld. In this novella, the act of naming becomes crucial: although Preobrazhenskii is Sharikov's father, who gives him life, buys him clothes, and tries in vain to teach him manners and values, the dog-man chooses for himself a last name that acknowledges a different predecessor, Sharik the dog. Moreover, the name and patronymic that Sharikov decides to adopt are "Poligraf Poligrafich." Besides reminding the reader of a whole lineage of meaningless names in Russian literature (such as "Akakii Akakievich" in Gogol's "The Overcoat" ["Shinel'," 1842]) and also mocking the absurd names in vogue in the early Soviet Union (such as "Elektrifikatsia," Electricity, or "Mel" for "Marx, Engels, Lenin" and "Kim" for "Kommunisticheskii internatsional molodëzhi" [International Communist Youth]), "Poligraf Poligrafich" is remarkably a name that Sharikov picks from the calendar according to a traditional, pre-Soviet Russian habit of naming newborns after saints. Of course, "Poligraf" is not the name of a saint but rather corresponds to the word *press*, which Sharikov has found at the bottom or on the side of the calendar in small print. Sharikov's clumsy adoption of old traditions resonates with the meaning of the last name "Preobrazhenskii," "Transfiguration" (from *obraz*, "image"), which was once popular among priests and here confers religious overtones to the character of a surgeon who plays God. Bulgakov here seems to address the origins, heritage, and evolutionary trajectory of a nation, a pressing and complex question in the 1920s. While authorities and scientists plan to fashion the New Soviet Person and discard the old world and its vestiges, the operating-room creature follows the old rule of choosing a name from the calendar, thus rejecting with this gesture the slogan "all anew" and his own laboratory origins and claiming instead continuity with the past, a continuity that is affirmed by the activity of his hypophysis, against all the plans that Preobrazhenskii and the Soviet authorities have in store for him and for the whole population. Moreover, the word *poligraf* also gestures to the polygraph, a duplicating device that consists of a series of pantographs assembled together and allows for the production of several copies of a text simultaneously while only one is actually being written. Sharikov's chosen name may therefore be interpreted as a further hint at the complex question of authorship.

By pushing metabolic activity to the foreground, with bodily functions informing their style and structure, Svevo's story "Doctor Menghi's Drug" and Bulgakov's novella *The Heart of a Dog* prompt us to rethink our established notions of narrative time and agency. In both works, glands and their secretions propel the plot and therefore operate on a structural level as if they were fully developed characters in competition with the person who is supposed to be the protagonist of the storyworld at the onset (Annina versus Menghi; the hypophysis versus Preobrazhenskii). However, in accomplishing this goal, the two authors make very different stylistic choices. In "Doctor Menghi's Drug," Annina's coauthorship of the doctor's notes operates at a structural level (it determines how the story unfolds, and it manipulates narrative time) as well as at a stylistic level: the hormone inhabits Menghi's narration and modulates the narration to its will, which generates a ventriloquism of sorts. On a textual level, Annina competes with another intradiegetic narrator, Menghi himself. Moreover, as we have learned from both the doctor's and his mother's experience with Annina, the rhythm of the prose gets slower or faster depending on whether hormone levels are increasing or decreasing.

In Bulgakov's novella, however, the gland's competition with the surgeon takes place on structural and aesthetic levels—it informs the development of the plot and raises questions of language and authorship as parenthood—but it is not reflected in any way in the style. From a strictly formal point of view, this competition is not reflected as strongly in Bulgakov's employment of perspective, and although the narrative focalization changes after the operation scene, the whole story is told in the third-person singular by an omniscient narrator. The clash of authority between the hypophysis and Preobrazhenskii takes place within the borders of a thought experiment, a miniature storyworld that the surgeon is trying to create as a demiurge, but this clash stays steadily within a solid narrative frame that is never questioned. In other words, although the gland is the source of Sharikov's utterances, it never becomes a narrator from whose perspective the events are presented to the general reading audience of the text or to an audience within the text. Finally, the relationships and networks among things that are independent of human will and the issues of agency and nonhuman intervention in narrative time that these texts raise are best observed through the lens of object-oriented ontology and the posthuman theories that have emerged in the past twenty years.

Two major characteristics of modernism and the historical avant-garde are their emphasis on movement and rhythm and their questioning of narrative authority by a sophisticated employment of perspectives. The analysis of Svevo's and Bulgakov's texts here reveals that metabolism and bodily rhythms should be centered in this picture. The body in the early twentieth century became exposed to more sensory stimuli than ever before because of technology, warfare, and a faster-paced routine. Therefore, bodily functions and bodily rhythms necessarily played a leading role in how stories were told, both as a response to and as a consequence of such an environment. Far from promoting a biodeterministic view of storytelling and from asserting that by the end of the 1920s authorship and agency were completely taken over by nonhuman entities, this reading of two literary sources from the early twentieth century illuminates modern debates on hormonal agency and on the biological redefinition of the human vis-à-vis machines and nonhuman entities, within and without our bodies. Finally, the investigation of the aesthetics and poetics of metabolism offers an additional interpretive lens through which to examine a dense period in literature and the arts that, no matter how extensively scholars have analyzed it, seems to keep lending itself continuously to further exploration.

AFTERWORD

The COVID-19 pandemic that has swept through our societies and caught us unawares this past year has highlighted the need, individual and collective, to create stories that can confer meaning upon what unfolds around us—precisely that crucial operation, described in chapter 1, of making sense of otherwise scattered events and phenomena by ordering them into causal-temporal chains and into configurations. Because we humans are mortal, we experience a pressing need for intelligible ends and the urge to assess our present from an imagined vantage point in the future, as observed in chapter 2: "We project ourselves . . . past the End, so as to see the structure whole, a thing we cannot do from our spot of time in the middle," Frank Kermode remarks.[1] However, because the health crisis is still ongoing, we can only count on provisional, estimated endings and do not have the option to appeal to an omniscient narrator who can provide the big picture or offer a final word. We rather find ourselves in a situation similar to that of readers of serialized stories or patients undergoing long-term treatment with an uncertain, potentially frightening outcome. Even if those who have been guiding us through this crisis are extremely knowledgeable and rigorous, they are navigating it in the present, as we are, and not speaking to us from that position of certainty that omniscient narrators enjoy. The U.S. Centers for Disease Control and Prevention and the World Health Organization constantly update their recommendations as scientists are presented with more evidence, patterns, and data that allow them to formulate more accurate predictions, epidemiological claims, and guidelines. Accordingly, public-health policies are prone to frequent changes and amendments. Just like the oncologists and the authors of novels written in installments encountered in chapter 2, our scientific institutes and legislative bodies are as steeped in contingency as we are, even though they may stand a few steps ahead by virtue of their knowledge and expertise. As we live through the pandemic suspended in unpredictability, tentative planning has become our best option, while nobody can state with absolute certainty when and whether this global crisis will subside, especially now that experts have pointed to the threat of other species—most recently the mink—as carriers of more viruses, potentially as lethal as COVID-19, that may afflict our societies in the near future. Of course, the tradition of the good death, also examined in chapter 2 in the discussion of Tolstoy's *The Death of Ivan Ilych*, has been largely foregone, with social distancing and the threat of contagion making hospital visits to terminal COVID-19 patients as well as traditional funerals impracticable.

The global dimension of the pandemic has created the conditions for the occasional overlapping of public-health concerns with geopolitical relations. In some notable cases, such as Boris Johnson's and Donald J. Trump's illnesses, narratives about the nature, spread, management, and consequences of the pandemic have been intertwined with the body of the leader. Just as with the making of the New Soviet Person in the early twentieth century, examined in chapter 3, the human body has become once more a stage for meaning making, its functions and well-being epitomizing social, political, and economic stability or the lack thereof. The tendency to pathologize otherness and praise compliance when it blends with conformity—all elements that often run through public-health campaigns, as discussed in chapter 3—has been historically embedded in the ways societies have explained the spread of deadly diseases. Scapegoating was infamously common during the AIDS epidemic in the 1980s, as it was during the seventeenth-century bubonic plague in Europe, described in Alessandro Manzoni's historical novel *The Betrothed* (*I promessi sposi*, 1840–1842), wherein the disease was allegedly caused by *untori* (greasers), people sent by the devil to grease doorframes with the infection. With COVID-19, we have witnessed the urge to pathologize a place along with its population and culture every time the disease, despite its global scale, has been

AFTERWORD

referred to as "the Chinese virus" or "the Wuhan flu." This nationalistic tendency in pathologizing otherness is nothing new. Suffice it to mention the Italian Renaissance author Girolamo Fracastoro's definition of syphilis as "the French disease" and the mysterious "Asian plague" that threatens Europe at the end of *Crime and Punishment*. In chapter 3, we also saw how in the 1920s "patient empowerment" and "sanitary enlightenment" were mobilized in propaganda to increase political consensus and exploited by private companies to increase their profits. These already slippery notions are further complicated in our times by the phenomenon of fake news, which misleads the public and causes it to become miseducated and misinformed, while prompting it to reject even the most basic and widely shared tenets of science. The complexity and mechanisms of storytelling in the era of fake news and a world-scale pandemic certainly deserve further exploration.

The phenomenon of viruses jumping species and moving across that human–nonhuman divide that we have taken for granted for centuries inscribes itself in the debate on complex human–nonhuman configurations examined in chapter 4. The enmeshment of human activity and our evolutionary trajectory with the environment is the object of study of the medical humanities where they intersect with the burgeoning field of environmental studies. Just as the discrete bodily organs take on a life of their own in chapter 4, the body in parts still takes center stage today in practices such as organ harvesting and pregnancy surrogacy that are occurring in a global market. Moreover, the interaction and coevolution of humans with nonhuman entities—be they organisms or machines—postulated by literary authors at the beginning of the twentieth century and widely addressed today in discussions of microbiota and prosthetics, appear more entangled than ever in current circumstances. In formulating their strategies and predictions, public-health experts consider the deep enmeshment of human life with the environment understood in the broadest sense—not only Earth's strata, water, and atmosphere but also economic systems, planetary-level logistics, and the global circulation of goods and values. It is worth noting that in early twentieth-century Russian prose, such entanglement and fluidity were explored not only by Mikhail Bulgakov but also by another physician-writer, Aleksandr Bogdanov (1873–1928), especially in his system thinking (the discipline he founded, tektology—*tektologiia* in Russian—is considered the ancestor of cybernetics) and in his philosophical reflections on blood transfusion and other exchanges between the human species and nonhuman forms of life (consider his novel *Red Star* [*Krasnaia zvezda*, 1908]). Aleksandr Beliaev's science fiction stories (among others, "Professor Dowell's Head" ["Golova professora Douelia," 1925] and "Neither Life, nor Death" ["Ni zhizn', ni smert'," 1926]) explored those themes as insightfully. In terms of bodies, networks, and technology, the COVID-19 pandemic has seen the explosive growth of recently established arenas, real and virtual, in which the health of individual bodies and collectives is assessed, in addition to the arenas to which we were already accustomed. Among them are telemedicine, computer-made diagnoses, self-assessment websites and apps, the digital tracking of compliance, and online chats with increasingly "intelligent" bots, whose facial features and voices are adapted to consumers' biases and thus make them seem reliable and reassuring in unsettling times like these. All existing considerations on the origin and spread of the COVID-19 virus and on viable strategies to fight it have been based on the acknowledgment of this indissoluble enmeshment of human bodies and human health with the environment as a whole.

In fascinating ways, this pandemic has also acted as a signifier; that is, it has teased out the deep-seated values and fears of the societies it has afflicted. Just by way of example, in South Korea the virus offered the opportunity to employ technology for population surveillance at an even higher degree than before; in Italy, the first Western country affected during the pandemic's first wave, the public-health crisis has highlighted the proverbial disorganization of the country's centralized institutions and at the same time the strong sense of community of its people, who engaged in admirable collective efforts to face the emergency in spite of the belated institutional response; in the United States, the COVID-19 pandemic has made evident that individual freedom and economic growth may be valued more than collective well-being and public-health concerns. Certainly, over the past year, scientists, politicians, interest groups, and common people alike have created several, often clashing plots to explain such a devastating and widespread public-health crisis; those stories cover the full spectrum, with conspiracy theorists on one end and staunch advocates for more decisive public-health measures and for the rights of "essential workers" on the other.[2]

This study has employed a medical-themed point of entry into canonical works of literature to unveil elements of their aesthetics previously

AFTERWORD

understudied or entirely overlooked by literary scholars. By the same token, the literary works analyzed here, although conceived in historical and cultural milieus quite distant from ours, have been shown to illuminate medical and public-health debates and circumstances that are still current and pressing, most notably by scrutinizing the tight and multifaceted relationship between agency and storytelling. The authors and texts examined in each of the chapters stage a crisis of agency, which is challenged by official and constraining narratives that seek to generalize about human bodies and lives, supported by claims of supposed objectivity. Yet in each instance that crisis is turned into an opportunity for storytelling, which becomes a highly powerful response and the most effective way out of the crisis. At the level of individual experience, when someone is vulnerable—literally "prone to being wounded" (from the Latin *vulnus*, "wound")—their wound is generative and produces stories, as we know not only from Tiresias in the *Odyssey* and Jacob in the Book of Genesis but also from Dostoevsky's Underground Man, who is "sick [*bol'noi*], malicious [*zloi*], unattractive [*neprivlekatel'nyi*]" and whose "liver is diseased" (*bolit pechen'*), as the incipit of his notes, written in first person, reads (part 1, chapter 1).[3] At the level of public health and the establishment of health standards, emplotment emerges as an effective and sophisticated tool that both authors and their characters employ to expose and warn against otherwise hard-to-detect power dynamics and arbitrary measures that limit individuals' rights in order to serve the agenda of the few. We have seen how the act of storytelling, mediated through the body, allows the protagonists, real and fictional, described in each chapter to gain ownership of existential and philosophical claims about mortality, health, and society that are silenced or put in jeopardy by seemingly unassailable biomedical truths and to turn those constraining narratives on their heads by showing their limitations and risks. The same holds true for us today, outside of and beyond the current pandemic. Great art poses fundamental questions, and although offering ready-made answers is not its goal, those questions remain relevant over time, even in such a rapidly evolving field as medicine. In times of health crises, be they local or global, individual or collective, the art of skillful and insightful storytelling emerges as the single most powerful antidote.

Boston, November 2020

NOTES

INTRODUCTION

1. Rita Charon's book *Narrative Medicine: Honoring the Stories of Illness* (New York: Oxford University Press, 2006) was preceded chronologically by other foundational studies in the medical humanities that employed approaches from literary theory and theories of narrative. They include Cheryl Mattingly and Linda Garro, eds., *Narrative and the Cultural Construction of Illness and Healing* (Berkeley: University of California Press, 2000); and Byron Good, *Medicine, Rationality, and Experience: An Anthropological Perspective* (Cambridge, MA: Harvard University Press, 1993), which engages with Mikhail Bakhtin's theories and semiotics. The journal *Literature and Medicine* offers work that charts and examines medicine stylistically and structurally rather than merely thematically, and the annual "Narrative" conference consistently features multiple panels on topics related to sickness and health across media (literature, film, comic books, video games), genres, and national traditions. In December 2016, the journal of philosophy and literary theory *Enthymema* published a special issue on narrative theory and medicine that assessed the field twenty years after the founding of the narrative-medicine program at Columbia University and outlined research avenues for the years to come. The issue included contributions from the founders of the field—Rita Charon, James Phelan, Catherine Belling, Arthur Frank—as well as by younger scholars. See Elena Fratto, ed., "Narrative and Medicine," special issue of *Enthymema* 16 (2016).
2. In *Storytelling and the Sciences of Mind* (Cambridge, MA: MIT Press, 2013), David Herman sets theories of narrative and the sciences of mind in dialogue by defining two complementary activities, which he defines as "worlding the story" and "storying the world." My book engages with the latter activity, characterizing the mind–narrative nexus, a process by which, according to Herman, "narrative . . .

constitutes a primary resource for configuring circumstances and events into (more or less) coherent scenarios involving the experience of persons." In other words, Herman argues, "narrative afford[s] scaffolding for making sense of experience, via the process that I have termed *storying the world*" (xi, 227). Hence, my choice for this book's title.

3. Paul Ricoeur, *Hermeneutics and the Human Sciences* (Cambridge: Cambridge University Press, 1981), 278.

4. The very first Nobel Prize recipients, in 1901, were Wilhelm Conrad Röntgen, who discovered X rays, and Emil von Behring, who invented a serum therapy for diphtheria. New technology and new clinical methods afforded unprecedented precision in diagnosis and success in treatment, and hygiene principles would be applied to public health, thus delivering the promise of healthier populations, until the First World War disrupted that optimistic pattern, introduced new priorities, and pointed to new directions for medicine and healthcare—which included battlefield surgery, shell shock, and new sociopolitical configurations and prospects.

5. This is true of Russian writers and artists in general and not only of physician-writers of that era, such as Anton Chekhov, Vikentii Veresaev, and Mikhail Bulgakov. Remarkably, the tradition of Russian physician-writers runs all the way to contemporary author and cardiologist Maxim Osipov (1963–), whose short stories vividly depict Russian provincial medical practice today and have recently appeared in English translation in the collection *Rock, Paper, Scissors and Other Stories*, trans. Boris Dralyuk, Alex Fleming, and Anne Marie Jackson (New York: New York Review of Books, 2019).

6. The concept of the human body as the testing ground for the Soviet experiment and the utopia it promised is articulated in detail by the historian of science Nikolai Krementsov in Krementsov, *Revolutionary Experiments: The Quest for Immortality in Bolshevik Science and Fiction* (Oxford: Oxford University Press, 2013), and by the literary scholar Eric Naiman in Naiman, *Sex in Public: The Incarnation of Early Soviet Ideology* (Princeton, NJ: Princeton University Press, 1997).

7. Wayne C. Booth, *The Rhetoric of Fiction* (1961; reprint, Chicago: University of Chicago Press, 1983). For the distinction between fallible and untrustworthy narrators, see Greta Olson, "Reconsidering Unreliability: Fallible and Untrustworthy Narrators," *Narrative* 11 (2003): 93–109. For a refined definition of Booth's concept, see James Phelan, "Estranging Unreliability, Bonding Unreliability, and the Ethics of *Lolita*," *Narrative* 15 (2007): 222–38.

8. Mark Haddon, *The Curious Incident of the Dog in the Night-Time* (London: Jonathan Cape, 2003).

9. Angela Brintlinger and Ilya Vinitsky, eds., *Madness and the Mad in Russian Culture* (Toronto: University of Toronto Press, 2007); Harriet Murav, *Holy Foolishness: Dostoevsky's Novels and the Poetics of Cultural Critique* (Stanford, CA: Stanford University Press, 1992); Cathy Popkin, "Hysterical Episodes: Case Histories and Silent Subjects," in *Self and Story in Russian History*, ed. Laura Engelstein and Stephanie Sandler (Ithaca, NY: Cornell University Press, 2000), 189–216; and Rebecca Reich, *State of Madness: Psychiatry, Literature, and Dissent After Stalin* (DeKalb: Northern Illinois University Press, 2018). Beyond the territory of mental health, it is important to point to disability studies in general as a growing field within Russian literary and cultural studies. Following the collapse of the

INTRODUCTION

Soviet Union, the disabled population in Russia became increasingly visible and vocal in demanding legal rights and adequate representation. Over the past two decades, research by José Alaniz, Frances Lee Bernstein, Cassandra Hartblay, Anastasia Kayiatos, Sarah D. Phillips, Claire L. Shaw, and others has brought attention to the cultural dimension of disability and the representation of disabled people in literature, media, and the arts both in the Soviet Union and in post-Soviet Russia. See José Alaniz, "'People Endure': The Function of Autism in *Anton's Right Here* (2012)," in *Cultures of Representation: Disability in World Cinema Contexts*, ed. Benjamin Fraser (London: Wallflower, 2016), 110–25; Frances Lee Bernstein, "Prosthetic Manhood in the Soviet Union at the End of World War II," *Osiris* 30, no. 1 (2015): 113–33; Cassandra Hartblay, "After Marginalization: Pixelization, Disability, and Social Difference in Digital Russia," *South Atlantic Quarterly* 118, no. 3 (2019): 543–72; Anastasia Kayiatos, "'Sooner Speaking Than Silent, Sooner Silent Than Mute': Soviet Deaf Theatre and Pantomime After Stalin," *Theatre Survey* 51, no. 1 (2010): 5–31; Sarah D. Phillips, "'There Are No Invalids in the USSR!': A Missing Soviet Chapter in the New Disability History," *Disability Studies Quarterly* 29, no. 3 (2009), https://dsq-sds.org/article/view/936; and Claire L. Shaw, *Deaf in the USSR: Marginality, Community, and Soviet Identity, 1917–1991* (Ithaca, NY: Cornell University Press, 2017).

Moreover, Lilya Kaganovsky's investigation of the mutilated male body in Stalin-era literature and film, *How the Soviet Man Was Unmade* (Pittsburgh, PA: University of Pittsburgh Press, 2008), has prompted us to reconsider masculinity in that epoch.

10. The pioneer of Russian psychoanalysis, the psychiatrist Nikolai Osipov (1877–1934), studied in Vienna with Sigmund Freud in 1908 and published his first case study the following year. In the early 1910s, a small group of Russian adherents to Freud's theories, who referred their patients to him (the Wolf Man being the most famous in medical literature), was planning a professional group modeled on the Psychoanalytic Society in Vienna, but the outbreak of World War I halted the momentum. The medical profession joined the effort to defend the country, and the two main proponents of Freudian psychoanalysis in Russia were lost: Osipov left for Europe, and the psychiatrist Tat'iana Rosenthal (1885–1921) committed suicide. It was only in 1922 that the Russian Psychoanalytic Society (Russkoe psikhoanaliticheskoe obshchestvo) was formed. See Martin A. Miller, *Freud and the Bolsheviks: Psychoanalysis in Imperial Russia and the Soviet Union* (New Haven, CT: Yale University Press, 1998), 24–60. See also Alexander Etkind, *Eros of the Impossible: The History of Psychoanalysis in Russia* (Boulder, CO: Westview, 1997).

11. Established scholarly works in the field of Russian literary studies have addressed the intersections of Russian literature, medicine, technology, and the body in their cultural, historical, stylistic, and aesthetic valences. Among them are Murav, *Holy Foolishness*; Naiman, *Sex in Public*; Michael Finke, *Seeing Chekhov: Life and Art* (Ithaca, NY: Cornell University Press, 2005); Rikkardo Nikolozi, Konstantin Bogdanov, and Iurii Murashov, eds., *Russkaia literatura i meditsina: Telo, predpisaniia, sotsial'naia praktika* (Moscow: Novoe izdatel'stvo, 2005); Brintlinger and Vinitsky, eds., *Madness and the Mad*; Valeria Sobol, *Febris Erotica: Lovesickness and the Russian Literary Imagination* (Seattle: University of Washington Press, 2009);

INTRODUCTION

Julia Vaingurt, *Wonderlands of the Avant-Garde: Technology and the Arts in Russia of the 1920s* (Chicago: Northwestern University Press, 2013); Riccardo Nicolosi, *Degeneration Erzählen: Literatur und Psychiatrie im Russland der 1880er und 1890er Jahre* (Paderborn, Germany: Wilhelm Fink, 2017); and Elena Trubetskova, *"Novoe zrenie": Bolezn' kak priëm ostraneniia v russkoi literature XX veka* (Moscow: Novoe literaturnoe obozrenie, 2019). My book is rooted in that tradition and shares with it the goal of enriching established readings of Russian literary texts and cultural manifestations by putting them in dialogue with contemporaneous medical sources, practices, and trends. However, approaches to Russian literature and medicine have tended not to engage in notable depth with current North American debates in the medical humanities, nor do they mobilize concepts and devices from theories of narrative in substantial and systematic ways. This study demonstrates the importance of transhistorical and interdisciplinary connections that are articulated and made visible by placing emphasis on storytelling devices.

12. Viktor Shklovsky, *Theory of Prose*, trans. Benjamin Sher (Elmwood Park, IL: Dalkey Archive, 1990), 1–14.
13. Mikhail Bakhtin, "Response to a Question from the *Novyi Mir* Editorial Staff (1970)," in *Speech Genres and Other Late Essays*, ed. Caryl Emerson and Michael Holquist (Austin: University of Texas Press, 1986), 7, emphasis in original.
14. Among others, Philippe Ariès draws on Tolstoy's literary production, especially *The Death of Ivan Ilych*, to analyze the tradition of the "good death" in Ariès, *The Hour of Our Death: The Classic History of Western Attitudes Toward Death Over the Last One Thousand Years*, trans. Helen Weaver (New York: Random House, 1981), chapter 12, "Death Denied." In the introduction to his recent best-selling book about the condition of mortality, *Being Mortal: Medicine and What Matters in the End* (London: Picador, 2014), the surgeon-writer and public-health researcher Atul Gawande discusses caregiving by examining the relationship between the character of Ivan Ilych and that of Gerasim, the butler's young assistant in Ilych's household (99–100, 144).
15. Oliver Sacks considered himself indebted to the Soviet neuropsychologist Alexander Luria (1902–1977) and his case studies. During the last years of Luria's life, the two corresponded about the genre and style of their writings, and Luria became Sacks's mentor. Sacks also wrote the foreword to *The Man with a Shattered World: The History of a Brain Wound* (Cambridge, MA: Harvard University Press, 1987), the translation of Luria's description of a case in 1971. However, in his "clinical tales," Sacks turned to Dostoevsky's descriptions of epileptic fits in order to celebrate neurodiversity and to strengthen his definition of neurological conditions "as 'portals' to the beyond or the unknown" (Sacks, *The Man Who Mistook His Wife for a Hat and Other Clinical Tales* [1985; reprint, New York: Simon and Schuster, 1998], 130). In this respect, popular-culture depictions of people with Asperger's syndrome as savants can be fruitfully placed in dialogue with Dostoevsky's characterization of Prince Myshkin in *The Idiot* and the Russian tradition of the Holy Fool. See, for instance, the protagonist of Barry Levinson's film *Rain Man* (1988) or, to some extent, Sacks's own representation of Temple Grandin in *An Anthropologist on Mars: Seven Paradoxical Tales* (New York: Random House, 1995), 244–96.

16. The U.S. physician-poet par excellence William Carlos Williams understood language as constitutive of medical practice and the foundation upon which it rests as well as words as the building blocks of a world that is made and unmade at each bedside encounter. He admired Chekhov's careful use of language, structural elegance, and masterful economy of words, especially in his short stories detailing the lives of physicians. To a medical student seeking his advice, Williams said: "Read Chekhov, read story after story of his. . . . I turn to him all the time; stories like 'Anyuta' and 'Enemies' remind me of the danger around the corner in this doctoring life: smugness, and one of the consequences, callousness, and then the decline into being a big shot, full of oneself (the occupational hazard of our trade)—Chekhov knew of all that, saw it in others, and thereby saw himself in danger" (quoted in Robert Coles, foreword to Anton Chekhov, *Chekhov's Doctors: A Collection of Chekhov's Medical Tales*, ed. Jack Coulehan [Kent, OH: Kent State University Press, 2003], xii).

1. THE GRAND FINALE: DEATH AS THE REVELATORY ENDING

1. Boris Eikhenbaum, *O. Henry and the Theory of the Short Story*, trans. I. R. Titunik (Ann Arbor: University of Michigan Press, 1968), 4, 21–22.
2. This scene is described by Eikhenbaum's daughter, Ol'ga Eikhenbaum, in "Iz vospominanii O. B. Eikhenbaum," in Boris Eikhenbaum, *Moi vremennik: Khudozhestvennaia proza i izbrannye stat'i 20-30kh godov* (Saint Petersburg: Inapress, 2001), 642; by Viktor Shklovskii in "Boris Eikhenbaum," in *Tetiva: O neskhodstve skhodnogo* (Moscow: Sovetskii Pisatel', 1970), 45 and passim; and by Roman Jakobson in "Boris Mikhailovich Eikhenbaum," *International Journal of Slavic Linguistics and Poetics* 6 (1963): 160–67. The two formalist scholars, however, did not witness that tragic event. The most comprehensive account on Eikhenbaum's life and scholarly trajectory, including his later, postformalist production, is Carol J. Any, *Boris Eikhenbaum: Voices of a Russian Formalist* (Stanford, CA: Stanford University Press, 1994).
3. Aage Hansen-Löve, "Le formalisme russe," in *Le XXe siècle: La révolution et les années vingt*, vol. 3 of *Histoire de la littérature russe*, ed. Efim Etkind, Georges Nivat, Ilya Serman, and Vittorio Strada (Paris: Fayard, 1988), 646. Unless otherwise noted, all translations of non-English text quoted in the chapter and its notes are my own.
4. Hansen-Löve, "Le formalisme russe," 637.
5. Hayden White's seminal work *Metahistory: The Historical Imagination in Nineteenth-Century Europe* (Baltimore, MD: Johns Hopkins University Press, 1973) was the birthplace of the term *emplotment*, defined as "the way by which a sequence of events fashioned into a story is gradually revealed to be a story of a particular kind" and as the process of building "a structure of relationships by which the events contained in the account are endowed with a meaning by being identified as part of a whole" (7). See also Hayden White, "The Value of Narrativity in the Representation of Reality," in *On Narrative*, ed. W. J. T. Mitchell (Chicago: University of Chicago Press, 1981), 9.

1. THE GRAND FINALE

6. See Cheryl Mattingly, "Emergent Narratives," in *Narrative and the Cultural Construction of Illness and Healing*, ed. Cheryl Mattingly and Linda Garro (Berkeley: University of California Press, 2000), 181–211.
7. See "Direktor instituta RAN predlozhil nadelit' pravom golosa pogibshikh vo vremia Velikoi Otechestvennoi voiny," newsru.com, May 20, 2016, http://www.newsru.com/russia/20may2016/elections.html.
8. See Mikhail Epstein, post, LiveJournal (webpage), May 22, 2016, http://mikhail-epstein.livejournal.com/193456.html.
9. Arthur Kleinman, *The Illness Narratives: Suffering, Healing, and the Human Condition* (New York: Basic, 1988), 157.
10. For more on the problem of defining death, see Margaret Lock, "Inventing a New Death and Making It Believable," *Anthropology and Medicine* 9 (2002): 97–115.
11. Darshak Sanghavi, "When Does Death Start?," *New York Times Magazine*, December 20, 2009.
12. Paul Ricoeur, *Hermeneutics and the Human Sciences* (Cambridge: Cambridge University Press, 1981), 278.
13. Peter Brooks, *Reading for the Plot: Design and Intention in Narrative* (Cambridge, MA: Harvard University Press, 1984), xi.
14. Ricoeur, *Hermeneutics and the Human Sciences*, 277–80. See also Paul Ricoeur, *Time and Narrative*, vol. 1 (Chicago: University of Chicago Press, 1984).
15. This spatial aspect of medical emplotment took on particular importance in Renaissance Europe: alongside Vesalius's anatomical method, characterized by an inherent temporality, a cartographic approach to the study of the body's interiority and its discrete parts, viewed in constant correspondence with the outside world, established itself, with the first anatomical atlases as its most tangible results. A few excellent studies have been produced on this topic, including Jonathan Sawday, *The Body Emblazoned: Dissection and the Human Body in Renaissance Culture* (London: Routledge, 1995).
16. Thomas W. Laqueur, "Bodies, Detail, and the Humanitarian Narrative," in *The New Cultural History*, ed. Lynn Hunt (Berkeley: University of California Press, 1989), 176–205.
17. Carlo Ginzburg, "Clues: Roots of an Evidential Paradigm" (orig. "Spie: Radici di un paradigma indiziario," 1986), in *Clues, Myths, and the Historical Method*, trans. John Tedeschi and Anne C. Tedeschi (Baltimore, MD: Johns Hopkins University Press, 1989), 96–125. Arthur Conan Doyle, a physician and detective-story writer, is mentioned in the opening of Ginzburg's essay, alongside Sigmund Freud and Giovanni Morelli in a threefold analogy. On inductive reasoning in medical practice, see also Kathryn Montgomery, *Doctors' Stories: The Narrative Structure of Medical Knowledge* (Princeton, NJ: Princeton University Press, 1991).
18. Case 9431, *New England Journal of Medicine* 189, no. 17 (1923): 595, and Case 11-2014, *New England Journal of Medicine* 370, no. 15 (2014): 1441, respectively. See the online archives of the *New England Journal of Medicine* for more, http://www.nejm.org/medical-index. For a fuller discussion of Yuri Lotman's definitions of event and eventfulness, see chapter 2.
19. Respectively, Case 9433, *New England Journal of Medicine* 189 (1923): 602, and Case 32-2006, *New England Journal of Medicine* 355 (2006): 1593.

1. THE GRAND FINALE

20. In instances where the patient is still alive and there is no autopsy report, an "Addendum" at the end of the case report summarizes the subsequent clinical course, and the narrative voice is the same omniscient and unspecified one that presented the case at the beginning.
21. *New England Journal of Medicine* 189 (1923): 79.
22. Henry Fielding, *The History of Tom Jones, a Foundling* (1749; reprint, London: Dent & Sons and Dutton, 1922), 122.
23. Michel Foucault, *The Birth of the Clinic: An Archaeology of Medical Perception*, trans. A. M. Sheridan-Smith (New York: Pantheon, 1973), xix.
24. Foucault, *The Birth of the Clinic*, 196.
25. Anne Harrington, "Kurt Goldstein's Neurology of Healing and Wholeness: A Weimar Story," in *Greater Than the Parts: Holism in Biomedicine, 1920–1950*, ed. Christopher Lawrence and George Weisz (New York: Oxford University Press, 1998), 26.
26. Paul Broca, "Remarks on the Seat of the Faculty of Articulated Language, Following an Observation of Aphemia (Loss of Speech)," trans. Christopher D. Green, *Bulletin de la société anatomique* 6 (1861): 330–57; Carl Wernicke, "The Symptom Complex of Aphasia: A Psychological Study on an Anatomical Basis" (1874), English translation in *Boston Studies in the Philosophy of Science: Proceedings of the Boston Colloquium for the Philosophy of Science*, vol. 4, ed. R. S. Cohen and M. W. Wartowfsky (Dortrecht, Netherlands: Reidel, 1966–1968), 34–97.
27. Barbara Tizard (1959), quoted in Anne Harrington, "Beyond Phrenology: Localization Theory in the Modern Era," in *The Enchanted Loom: Chapters in the History of Neuroscience*, ed. Pietro Corsi (New York: Oxford University Press, 1991), 208.
28. L. S. Jacyna, *Lost Words: Narratives of Language and the Brain, 1825–1926* (Princeton, NJ: Princeton University Press, 2000), 119.
29. In M. Allen Starr's study on aphasia in the late 1880s, for instance, patients' cases are introduced only by progressive numbers, with no mention of names or other individual characteristics. See Starr, "The Pathology of Sensory Aphasia, with an Analysis of Fifty Cases in Which Broca's Centre Was Not Diseased," *Brain* 12 (July 1889): 82–99. Moreover, in the 1860s at the Hôtel-Dieu in Paris, patients were offered as "gifts" by colleagues for the sake of the advancement of science (see "The Discourse of Aphasia," in Jacyna, *Lost Words*, 85).
30. Harrington, "Kurt Goldstein's Neurology," 27.
31. Broca, "Remarks," 343.
32. Broca, "Remarks," 347–48.
33. Broca, "Remarks," 348.
34. Broca, "Remarks," 355.
35. Broca's approach is quite paradigmatic of his era. Another example one could mention is E. A. Shaw, who while presenting his cases in "The Sensory Side of Aphasia" keeps emphasizing the importance and decisiveness of the postmortem examination to formulate a final diagnosis, which would confirm or amend the provisional, premortem one. See Shaw, "The Sensory Side of Aphasia," *Brain* 16, no. 4 (January 1, 1893): 492–514.
36. See Cesare Lombroso, "Anthropometry and Physiognomy of 832 Criminals," chapter 2 in *Criminal Man*, trans. and with a new introduction by Mary Gibson

and Nicole Hahn Rafter (Durham, NC: Duke University Press, 2006), 50–57. For the analysis in the text, I use the fifth and last edition of the book (1897), which has not been translated into English but has been reprinted. See Cesare Lombroso, *L'uomo delinquente*, 5th ed. (Turin, 1897) (Milan: Bompiani, 2013).

37. Lombroso, *L'uomo delinquente*, 13–15.
38. To these topics Lombroso devoted *The Palimpsests of Prison*: Cesare Lombroso, *Palinsesti del carcere* (Turin: Bocca, 1888).
39. Cesare Lombroso, "Discours d'ouverture au VI Congrès d'anthropologie criminelle," in *Comptes rendus du VI Congrès international d'anthropologie criminelle. Turin, 28 April–3 May, 1906* (Turin: Fratelli Bocca, 1908), xxxii.
40. Cesare Lombroso Museum of Criminal Anthropology, *Visitor's Guide* (Turin: Museo di Antropologia Criminale Cesare Lombroso, 2008), 39.
41. For a history of craniology, phrenological measurements, and biological determinism, see Stephen Jay Gould, *The Mismeasure of Man* (New York: Norton, 1981).
42. See Cesare Lombroso, "Atavism and Evolution," *Contemporary Review* 68 (1895): 42–49.
43. Cesare Lombroso, *Genio e follia* (Milan: Giuseppe Chiusi, 1864). For more on arrested development in evolution, see also Lombroso, "Atavism and Evolution."
44. Cesare Lombroso, *L'uomo di genio in rapporto alla psichiatria, alla storia ed all'estetica* (Turin: Bocca, 1888), 7.
45. Cesare Lombroso, "*La bête humaine* e l'antropologia criminale," *Fanfulla della domenica*, June 15, 1890. An English translation of this essay is published as "'La Bête Humaine' and Criminal Anthropology," in *The Criminal Anthropological Writings of Cesare Lombroso Published in the English Language Periodical Literature during the Late 19th and Early 20th Centuries*, ed. David M. Horton and Katherine E. Rich (Lewiston, NY: Edwin Mellen Press, 2004), 1–25. Lombroso further comments on Zola in *Più recenti scoperte ed applicazioni della psichiatria ed antropologia criminale* (Turin: Bocca, 1893), 354–60.
46. Jacyna, *Lost Words*, 118–19. This wedding of criminal anthropology and literature took fascinating forms all over Europe. One could mention among the most interesting examples August Goll (1866–1936), lawyer and chief of police in Copenhagen. He investigated the ways in which crime evolves in the individual against the background of literary portraits. For instance, he considered Macbeth an example of the occasional criminal who chooses to do wrong. See Goll, *Criminal Types in Shakespeare*, trans. C. Hagee (Groningen, Netherlands: Wolters, 1908).
47. Lombroso, *L'uomo delinquente*, 610–611.
48. Lombroso, *Più recenti scoperte*, 344.
49. Lombroso, *L'uomo delinquente*, 507, 511, 530.
50. Lombroso, *Più recenti scoperte*, 349–52.
51. Lombroso, *L'uomo delinquente*, 549 n. 2.
52. Lombroso, *L'uomo delinquente*, 539–41.
53. Lombroso, *L'uomo delinquente*, 539.
54. Lombroso, *L'uomo delinquente*, 539.
55. Lombroso, *L'uomo delinquente*, 541.
56. James L. Rice, *Dostoevsky and the Healing Art: An Essay in Literary and Medical History* (Ann Arbor, MI: Ardis, 1985).

1. THE GRAND FINALE

57. Stepan D. Ianovskii, "Vospominaniia o Dostoevskom," in *Dostoevskii v vospominaniiakh sovremennikov*, 2 vols., ed. Konstantin Tiun'kin (Moscow: Khudozhestvennaia literatura, 1990), 1:239.
58. Konstantin Barsht, *Risunki v rukopisiakh Dostoevskogo* (Saint Petersburg: Formika, 1996).
59. Fëdor Dostoevskii, *Prestuplenie i nakazanie*, vol. 6 of *Polnoe sobranie sochinenii*, ed. V. G. Bazanov (Leningrad: Nauka, 1973), 315, emphasis in the original.
60. Fëdor Dostoevskii, *Idiot*, vol. 8 of *Polnoe sobranie sochinenii*, ed. V. G. Bazanov (Leningrad: Nauka, 1973), 195.
61. Fyodor Dostoevsky, *The Idiot*, trans. David McDuff, with an introduction by William Mills Todd III (London: Penguin, 2004), 77–78.
62. The French physician Claude Bernard first revealed the correspondences between bodily functions (the inner milieu, or *milieu intérieur*) and the surrounding social and natural environment (the external milieu, or *milieu extérieur*) in the 1850s and kept refining his theory until his death in 1878. In *Lectures on the Phenomena Common to Animals and Plants*, he maintained that "the constancy of the environment presupposes a perfection of the organism such that external variations are at every instant compensated and brought into balance. In consequence, far from being indifferent to the external world, the higher animal is on the contrary in a close and wise relation with it, so that its equilibrium results from a continuous and delicate compensation established as if the most sensitive of balances" (*Lectures on the Phenomena Common to Animals and Plants*, trans. H. E. Hoff, R. Guillemin, and L. Guillemin [Springfield, IL: Charles C. Thomas, 1974], 19).
63. Émile Hennequin, *Études de critique scientifique: Écrivains francisés: Dickens, Heine, Tourguénef, Poe, Dostoïewski, Tolstoï* (Paris: Perrin et Cie, 1889), 181–82.
64. Dostoevskii, *Prestuplenie i nakazanie*, 419–20.
65. Fyodor Dostoevsky, *Crime and Punishment*, trans. Jessie Coulson, ed. George Gibian (New York: Norton, 1964), 523–24.
66. Fyodor Dostoevsky, *The Brothers Karamazov*, 2nd ed., ed. Susan McReynolds Oddo, trans. Constance Garnett, revised by Ralph E. Matlaw (New York: Norton, 2011), 565.
67. Dostoevsky, *The Brothers Karamazov*, 566.
68. Dostoevsky, *The Brothers Karamazov*, 566–67.
69. Cesare Lombroso, "Mein Besuch bei Tolstoi," *Das freie Wort* 1 (1902): 393.
70. Lombroso, "Mein Besuch bei Tolstoi," 394.
71. Lombroso, "Mein Besuch bei Tolstoi," 396.
72. Lombroso, "Mein Besuch bei Tolstoi," 396.
73. Lev Tolstoi, *Dnevniki i zapisnye knizhki, 1895–1899*, vol. 53 of *Polnoe sobranie sochinenii*, ed. V. G. Chertkov (Moscow: Khudozhestvennaia literatura, 1953), 150, journal entry for August 15, 1897. The term *ogranichennyi*, "limited," bears both a literal meaning, "little," and a figurative one, "parochial," "obtuse." It is quite telling that Tolstoy's library in Iasnaia Poliana contains most of the books by Lombroso with the pages still uncut.
74. Lev Tolstoi, *Dnevniki, zapisnye knizhki i otdel'nye zapiski, 1901–1903*, vol. 54 of *Polnoe sobranie sochinenii*, ed. V. G. Chertkov (Moscow: Khudozhestvennaia literatura, 1935), 7, journal entry for January 8, 1900.

1. THE GRAND FINALE

75. Leo Tolstoy, *Resurrection*, trans. Louise Maude (Oxford: Oxford University Press, 1999), 79. For the original, see Lev Tolstoi, *Voskresenie*, vol. 32 of *Polnoe sobranie sochinenii*, ed. V. G. Chertkov (Moscow: Khudozhestvennaia literatura, 1936), 72.
76. Tolstoy, *Resurrection*, 82.
77. Tolstoy, *Resurrection*, 340–41.
78. Lombroso, "Mein Besuch bei Tolstoi," 396.
79. "We have to agree with Lombroso, who claims that Gogol' revealed his pathological setup by writing about the most disparate topics in an extremely shallow fashion"; also: "Lombroso is absolutely correct in pointing out that most exceptional people who suffered from mental disorder possessed a psychopathic structure" (Vladimir Fëdorovich Chizh, "Bolezn' Gogolia," in *Bolezn' Gogolia: Zapiski psikhiatra*, ed. N. T. Unaniants [Moscow: Respublika, 2001], 124, 202). Riccardo Nicolosi has investigated the poetics and aesthetics of "degeneration" (*vyrozhdenie*) in late nineteenth-century Russian culture at the intersection of literature and psychiatry. See Nicolosi, *Degeneration Erzählen: Literatur und Psychiatrie im Russland der 1880er und 1890er Jahre* (Paderborn, Germany: Wilhelm Fink, 2017).
80. See Irina Sirotkina, *Diagnosing Literary Genius: A Cultural History of Psychiatry in Russia, 1880–1930* (Baltimore, MD: Johns Hopkins University Press, 2002), 25. Sirotkina also remarks that another fervent supporter of Lombroso's work in Russia was the literary critic and linguist Dmitrii Ovsianiko-Kulikovskii (1853–1920). Ovsianiko-Kulikovskii reported that Lombroso "immediately had a tremendous appeal to me.... The existence of a criminal type (at least a psychic one) which reproduced atavistically the psyche and 'morals' of the primitive man was for me not to be doubted" (quoted in Sirotkina, *Diagnosing Literary Genius*, 24).
81. In "I. S. Turgenev as a Psychopathologist," Chizh explains that "Lombroso and his followers devoted scholarly attention to a poorly understood characteristic of degenerate people, 'invulnerability'"—that is, an inborn high tolerance to pain. He then finds it "remarkable [*zamechatel'no*]" that in Turgenev's short story "A Desperate Character" (1882), the protagonist, Misha, is portrayed by the author as "invulnerable." As Lombroso has shown, Chizh contends, most criminals are cowards and desperate at the same time, like Misha. Although their "invulnerability" makes them fear nothing, when their life is in danger, they succumb to fear (Vladimir Fëdorovich Chizh, "I. S. Turgenev kak psikhopatolog," in Chizh, *Bolezn' Gogolia*, 220–21).
82. Vladimir Fëdorovich Chizh, "Dostoevskii kak psikhopatolog i kriminolog," in Chizh, *Bolezn' Gogolia*, 292.

2. END OF STORY: TEMPORALITY AND THE PROSPECT OF THE ENDING IN *IVAN ILYCH, ANNA KARENINA*, AND (POTENTIAL) CANCER PATIENTS

1. Philippe Ariès, *The Hour of Our Death: The Classic History of Western Attitudes Toward Death Over the Last One Thousand Years*, trans. Helen Weaver (New York: Random House, 1981), 559–60.
2. Ariès, *The Hour of Our Death*, 196.

2. END OF STORY

3. Drew Gilpin Faust, *This Republic of Suffering: Death and the American Civil War* (New York: Knopf, 2008), 3–31. Faust's first chapter, "Dying," and Ariès's work are my main sources for the discussion of the *ars moriendi* tradition.
4. See Nancy Frieden, *Russian Physicians in an Era of Reform and Revolution* (Princeton, NJ: Princeton University Press, 1981), chaps. 1, 3, and 4; Alexander Vucinich, *Science in Russian Culture, 1861–1917* (Stanford, CA: Stanford University Press, 1970), chaps. 2 and 3.
5. See Frieden, *Russian Physicians*, 5–11, 53–75, 105–20.
6. Scholars have commented extensively on Tolstoy's obsession with death. See, among others, Kathleen Parthé, "Death Masks in Tolstoy," *Slavic Review* 2, no. 41 (Summer 1982): 297–305, and "The Metamorphosis of Death in Tolstoy," *Language and Style* 18 (1985): 205–14; Liza Knapp, "Language and Death in Tolstoy's *Childhood* and *Boyhood*: Rousseau and the Holy Fool," *Tolstoy Studies Journal* 10 (1998): 50–62, and "'Tue-la! Tue-le!': Death Sentences, Words, and Inner Monologue in Tolstoy's *Anna Karenina* and 'Three More Deaths,'" *Tolstoy Studies Journal* 11 (January 1, 1999): 1–19; Hugh McLean, *In Quest of Tolstoy* (Boston: Academic Studies, 2008), the chapter "Truth in Dying," 30–52. In "The Tolstoy Connection in Bakhtin," in *Rethinking Bakhtin: Extensions and Challenges*, ed. Gary Saul Morson and Caryl Emerson (Evanston, IL: Northwestern University Press, 1989), Caryl Emerson remarks on how Bakhtin looked at Tolstoy as "the poet of death" (151).
7. Determining whether Tolstoy's death scenes are realistic is not the point, according to Eikhenbaum ("the only witnesses and judges could obviously be only the dead"); rather, one should examine the linguistic and literary devices that Tolstoy employed in his descriptions of death and dying to understand how he achieved that quite unparalleled effect (Boris Eikhenbaum, *Molodoi Tolstoi* [Petrograd: Grzhebin, 1922], 129). Unless otherwise noted, all translations of non-English text quoted in the chapter and its notes are my own.
8. On Tolstoy's diaries as the translation of life into an open book, see Irina Paperno, "'Who, What Is I?': Tolstoy in His Diaries," *Tolstoy Studies Journal* 11 (January 1, 1999): 32–54. We will return to Tolstoy's diaries in the second part of this chapter.
9. Both statements are reported in Irina Sirotkina, *Diagnosing Literary Genius: A Cultural History of Psychiatry in Russia, 1880–1930* (Baltimore, MD: Johns Hopkins University Press, 2002), 85–86.
10. Within the scholarship devoted specifically to *The Death of Ivan Ilych*, which has fascinated generations of readers, critics, and physicians, it is worth mentioning Gary R. Jahn, *"The Death of Ivan Ilich": An Interpretation* (New York: Twayne, 1993); Gary R. Jahn, ed., *Tolstoy's "The Death of Ivan Il'ich": A Critical Companion* (Evanston, IL: Northwestern University Press, 1999); Robert Louis Jackson, "Text and Subtext in the Opening and Closing Lines of *The Death of Ivan Ilych*, or Phonetic Orchestration in the Semantic Development of the Story," *Tolstoy Studies Journal* 9 (1997): 11–25; and the chapter on *Ivan Ilych* in Inessa Medzhibovskaya, *Tolstoy and the Religious Culture of His Time: A Biography of a Long Conversion, 1845–1887* (Lanham, MD: Lexington, 2008), 295–333.
11. Ariès, *The Hour of Our Death*, 563–67, 573–75; Atul Gawande, *Being Mortal: Illness, Medicine, and What Matters in the End* (London: Picador, 2014), introduction, 99–100, 144.

2. END OF STORY

12. See Elena Fratto, "Meditsinskaia praktika kak siuzhetoslozhenie: Interpretatsiia bolezni Ivana Il'icha," in *Lev Tolstoi i mirovaia literatura: Materialy IX mezhdunarodnoi nauchnoi konferentsii, prokhodivshei v Iasnoi Poliane v 10–15 avgusta 2014 g.*, ed. Galina Alekseeva (Tula, Russia: Muzei-Usad'ba L. N. Tolstogo "Iasnaia Poliana," 2016), 207–15.
13. Leo Tolstoy, *The Death of Ivan Ilych*, in *Tolstoy's Short Fiction*, ed. and with revised translations by Michael R. Katz, 2nd Norton Critical Edition (New York: Norton, 2008), 89. Inessa Medzhibovskaya points out that the character Ivan Ilych had appeared already in "The Noble Family" and "Man of Affairs," two dramatic satirical works that Tolstoy began writing in 1856, as well as in his tragicomic autobiographical dialogue titled *Interlocutors from 1877*. See Medzhibovskaya, *Tolstoy and the Religious Culture of His Time*, 296.
14. Yuri Lotman, *The Structure of the Artistic Text*, trans. Gail Lenhof and Ronald Vroon (Ann Arbor: University of Michigan Press, 1977), 232–33, my emphasis.
15. Tolstoy, *The Death of Ivan Ilych*, 101, 108.
16. Tolstoy, *The Death of Ivan Ilych*, 105.
17. Besides the characters of the novella, generations of physician-readers have diagnosed Ivan Ilych since the text was published; over the decades, they have come to agree that the protagonist suffered from pancreatic cancer.
18. Because medical practice is in many respects an exercise in storytelling, this juxtaposition of contrasting perspectives on Ivan Ilych's illness, which distances our character from doctors, his family, and his acquaintances, lends itself to fruitful narratological exploration, as I have shown in Fratto, "Meditsinskaia praktika."
19. Tolstoy, *The Death of Ivan Ilych*, 102–3. In this passage, Tolstoy uses the word *spor*, which is better translated as "quarrel" than as "question": "spor mezhdu bluzhdaiushchei pochkoi i slepoi kishkoi" (a quarrel between a floating kidney and the appendix) (Lev Tolstoi, *Smert' Ivana Il'icha*, in *Proizvedeniia 1895–1899 gg.*, vol. 26 of *Polnoe sobranie sochinenii*, ed. V. G. Chertkov [Moscow: Khudozhestvennaia literatura, 1936], 84). Bodily organs seem to have agency and emplotment privileges: they can determine how the illness will proceed and, consequently, how the plot will unfold. The narrative agency of body parts is the focus of chapter 4.
20. "Total pain" has been the subject of three meetings in 2017 and 2018 of the working group Palliative Care and Classical Antiquity, of which I have been a member. Based in New York City, the working group comprises physicians from leading U.S. research hospitals, bioethics experts, and literary scholars, and its research focus is terminal-illness pain in its biomedical, philosophical, and existential facets.
21. Arthur Kleinman, *The Illness Narratives: Suffering, Healing, and the Human Condition* (New York: Basic, 1988), 3–5.
22. Tolstoy, *The Death of Ivan Ilych*, 102–3, first ellipsis in the original.
23. Tolstoy, *The Death of Ivan Ilych*, 102–3.
24. Michel Foucault, *The Order of Things: An Archaeology of Human Sciences* (New York: Pantheon, 1971); *The Birth of the Clinic: An Archaeology of Medical Perception*, trans. A. M. Sheridan-Smith (New York: Pantheon, 1973); *Discipline and Punish: The Birth of the Prison*, trans. Alan Sheridan (New York: Vintage, 1979).
25. Charles Rosenberg, "The Tyranny of Diagnosis: Specific Entities and Individual Experience," *Milbank Quarterly* 80, no. 2 (June 2002): 237–60.

2. END OF STORY

26. Tolstoy, *The Death of Ivan Ilych*, 110.
27. A cornerstone of narratology, the definition of "unreliable narrator" was first formulated by Wayne C. Booth in *The Rhetoric of Fiction* as a rhetorical device intentionally encoded in the text by the author with the intent of obtaining a specific reaction from the implied reader. A narrator is "reliable when he speaks for or acts in accordance with the norms of the work, . . . unreliable when he does not" (*The Rhetoric of Fiction* [1961; reprint, Chicago: University of Chicago Press, 1983], 158–59). When unreliability is employed, the reader will experience a distance between the author and the narrator, which creates a bond between the author and the reader behind the narrator's back. Lawrence Sterne's novel *Tristram Shandy* (1759) provides the most famous and most cited example to illustrate this technique. With Foucault's reflections on language and power dynamics, the category has taken on new nuances, and the assessment of the narrator's reliability takes into account discursive checks, as is the case in my reading of Ivan Ilych as "unreliable" in the eyes of his doctors.
28. Tolstoy, *The Death of Ivan Ilych*, 105, 107.
29. Elaine Scarry, *The Body in Pain: The Making and Unmaking of the World* (New York: Oxford University Press, 1985), 4, 6. In addition to Scarry's claims, one could argue that pain itself constitutes a sort of "language" that our body employs to communicate with us and inform us that something is not proceeding as it should or, through shifts in pain intensity, to convey to us how quickly the body is healing from an injury or ailment.
30. Present-day science fiction sketches out scenarios in which this gap is completely bridged. In 2017, the British dystopian sci-fi television series *Black Mirror* devoted one episode to a doctor who could feel exactly his patient's pain after getting an experimental neurological implant (Colm McCarthy, dir., "Black Museum," episode 6 of *Black Mirror*, season 4, Channel 4, U.K., aired December 29, 2017). In his mid-twentieth-century writings, the U.S. physician-writer par excellence William Carlos Williams maintained that words and language come into being through physician–patient interactions at the bedside: "The physician enjoys a wonderful opportunity actually to witness the words being born. Their actual colors and shapes are laid before him carrying their tiny burdens which he is privileged to take into his care with their unspoiled newness. . . . No one else is present but the speaker and ourselves, we have been the words' very parents. Nothing is more moving. . . . Under that language to which we have been listening all our lives a new, a more profound language, underlying all the dialectics offers itself. It is what they call poetry. That is the final phase" (William Carlos Williams, *The Doctor Stories* [New York: New Directions, 1984], 125).
31. Tolstoy, *The Death of Ivan Ilych*, 108; Tolstoi, *Smert' Ivana Il'icha*, 91, third ellipsis in the original.
32. Tolstoy, *The Death of Ivan Ilych*, 111, emphasis in original; Tolstoi, *Smert' Ivana Il'icha*, 94.
33. In *Tolstoy's Major Fiction* (Chicago: University of Chicago Press, 1978), Edward Wasiolek has noted that *ona* refers to both pain and death (176). Kathleen Parthé has analyzed the shift in meaning of that pronoun, which midsentence comes to denote something larger and more ineffable than pain ("The Metamorphosis," 207–10).

2. END OF STORY

34. Susan Sontag, *Illness as Metaphor; and AIDS and Its Metaphors* (1990; reprint, New York: Doubleday, 2001). Not only are diseases personified, as is the case in this novella, but they also take on distinguishing attributes and a whole aesthetics, as is the case with tuberculosis, traditionally attributed to airy people with an enhanced sensitivity or powerful ideas (for example, Ippolit Terent'ev in Dostoevsky's *The Idiot*).
35. Lev Tolstoi, *Dnevniki i zapisnye knizhki, 1891–94*, vol. 52 of *Polnoe sobranie sochinenii*, ed. V. G. Chertkov (Moscow: Khudozhestvennaia literatura, 1952), 110, diary entry for January 24, 1894.
36. Lev Tolstoi, *Dnevnik 1847–1854*, vol. 46 of *Polnoe sobranie sochinenii*, ed. V. G. Chertkov (Moscow: Khudozhestvennaia literatura, 1937), 128, diary entry for June 29, 1852. Hugh McLean analyzes Tolstoy's concept of double-ended immortality in the chapter "Rousseau's God and Tolstoy's God" in his book *In Quest of Tolstoy*, 152–54.
37. Tolstoy, *The Death of Ivan Ilych*, 109.
38. Gerasim is the one caregiver who is "present" both physically and emotionally to Ivan Ilych, as Arthur Kleinman would put it. Kleinman claims that the most crucial attributes of an effective caregiver are empathy and "presence," physical and emotional, in all interactions with the ill ("Caregiving as Moral Experience," *Lancet* 380, no. 9853 [November 3, 2012]: 1550–551).
39. Tolstoy, *The Death of Ivan Ilych*, 126–27; Tolstoi, *Smert' Ivana Il'icha*, 110–11.
40. Tolstoy, *The Death of Ivan Ilych*, 114.
41. Tolstoy, *The Death of Ivan Ilych*, 117.
42. Tolstoy, *The Death of Ivan Ilych*, 117–18.
43. Tolstoi, *Smert' Ivana Il'icha*, 113.
44. Sophocles, *Philoctetes*, in *Greek Drama (Tragedy)*, vol. 2 of *Works: English and Greek*, 3 vols., ed. and trans. Hugh Lloyd-Jones (Cambridge, MA: Harvard University Press, 1994), 325, 327, ll. 732–50.
45. Sophocles, *Philoctetes*, 328, ll. 745–46.
46. Tolstoi, *Smert' Ivana Il'icha*, 112.
47. Jahn, "The Death of Ivan Ilych," 82.
48. Tolstoy, *The Death of Ivan Ilych*, 85.
49. Paul Ricoeur, *Hermeneutics and the Human Sciences* (Cambridge: Cambridge University Press, 1981), 278. See also my discussion of plot tenets in chapter 1.
50. This management of patients' focus resonates with Ivan Ilych's dreamy state in which he concentrates his attention on the task of grabbing his organs and moving them around as if to make the feared prospect of death dissolve.
51. Quoted in Mary-Jo DelVecchio Good, Tseunetsugu Munakata, Yasuki Kobayashi, Cheryl Mattingly, and Byron J. Good, "Oncology and Narrative Time," *Social Science and Medicine* 38, no. 6 (1994): 857.
52. Paul Kalanithi, *When Breath Becomes Air* (New York: Random House, 2016), 123.
53. Good et al., "Oncology and Narrative Time," 857.
54. Kalanithi, *When Breath Becomes Air*, 127, 180.
55. Wolfgang Iser, *The Implied Reader: Patterns of Communication in Prose from Bunyan to Beckett* (Baltimore, MD: Johns Hopkins University Press, 1978); Roman Ingarden, *The Literary Work of Art* (Evanston, IL: Northwestern University Press, 1973); Umberto Eco, *The Role of the Reader: Explorations in the*

2. END OF STORY

Semiotics of Texts (Bloomington: Indiana University Press, 1979); Stanley Fish, *Is There a Text in This Class?* (Cambridge, MA: Harvard University Press, 1980). On reading as a meaning-making activity, see also Tzvetan Todorov, "Reading as Construction," in *The Reader in the Text: Essays on Audience and Interpretation*, ed. Susan Suleiman and Inge Crosman (Princeton, NJ: Princeton University Press, 1980), 67–82.

56. Iser, *The Implied Reader*, 279.
57. The most prominent collection to address serial narratives is Frank Kelleter, ed., *Media of Serial Narrative* (Columbus: Ohio University Press, 2017). Kelleter is the director of the Popular Seriality Research Unit at Freie Universität in Berlin, which has produced leading publications on the aesthetic and practice of popular seriality.
58. William Mills Todd III, "The Responsibilities of (Co-)Authorship: Notes on Revising the Serialized Version of *Anna Karenina*," in *Freedom and Responsibility in Russian Literature: Essays in Honor of Robert Louis Jackson*, ed. Elizabeth Cheresh Allen and Gary Saul Morson (Evanston, IL: Northwestern University Press, 1995), 163.
59. Prince Vladimir Mikhailovich Golitsyn, diary, translated and quoted in William Mills Todd III, "V. M. Golitsyn Reads *Anna Karenina*: How One of Karenin's Colleagues Responded to the Novel," in *Reading in Russia: Practices of Reading and Literary Communication, 1760–1930*, ed. Damiano Rebecchini and Raffaella Vassena (Milan: Ledizioni, 2014), 194.
60. Golitsyn, diary, quoted in Todd, "V. M. Golitsyn," 194.
61. "As in life, a sequence of relative closures *is all we ever get*" (Gary Saul Morson, "Anna Karenina's Omens," in *Freedom and Responsibility in Russian Literature*, ed. Allen and Morson, 137, emphasis in the original).
62. Tolstoy, *The Death of Ivan Ilych*, 128.
63. Hugh McLean shows how the death of Nikolai Levin bears echoes of the death of Tolstoy's brother Dmitrii by pointing out parallels between the description of the former in *Anna Karenina* and passages about the latter in Tolstoy's diary entries (*In Quest of Tolstoy*, 45–46).
64. Parallels between the descriptions of Frou-Frou and Anna were first pointed out in D. S. Merezhkovskii, "L. Tolstoi i Dostoevskii: Zhizn', tvorchestvo, i religiia" (1912), translated as "Tolstoy's Physical Descriptions," trans. Zoreslava Kushner, in Leo Tolstoy, *Anna Karenina*, ed. George Gibian, trans. Louise Maude and Aylmer Maude, 2nd Norton Critical Edition (New York: Norton, 1995), 774.
65. Eikhenbaum points out that "Froufrou" was the name of the titular tragic heroine in a popular French play by Henri Meilhac and Ludovic Halévy, *Froufrou*, which came onto the Russian stage in the early 1870s and became very popular. In the play, Froufrou is a light-minded girl who gets married and soon deserts her husband and son and goes off with her lover. In the tragic denouement, the husband kills the lover in a duel, and Froufrou returns home and dies. See Boris Eikhenbaum, *Lev Tolstoi: Semidesiatye gody* (Leningrad: Sovetskii pisatel', 1960), 224.
66. Eikhenbaum, *Lev Tolstoi: Semidesiatye gody*, 204.
67. Tolstoy, *Anna Karenina*, ed. Gibian, trans. Maude and Maude, 377; all of the quotations in English are from this edition. All of the quotations in the original

2. END OF STORY

Russian are from Lev Tolstoi, *Anna Karenina*, vols. 18–19 of *Polnoe sobranie sochinenii* (abbreviated *PSS* in citations to this Russian edition), ed. V. G. Chertkov (Moscow: Khudozhestvennaia literatura, 1934–1935), 18:435.

68. Tolstoy, *Anna Karenina*, 690, 691.
69. Tolstoy, *Anna Karenina*, 637.
70. Knapp, "'Tue-la! Tue-le,'" 8. In discussing how Anna remains "incommunicada," in linguistic isolation from the rest of the world, Justin Weir observes that "the relation of modernism to the disjunction of language and consciousness is part of Anna's story, for it is she, rather than Levin, who experiences the full force of Tolstoy's criticism of realist aesthetics" (*Leo Tolstoy and the Alibi of Narrative* [New Haven, CT: Yale University Press, 2011], 144). We have seen earlier in this chapter how Tolstoy anticipates modernist motifs in his description of Ivan Ilych's dreamy vision while on morphine; indeed, in many ways modernism shows stylistic continuity with the portrayal of dreamy states in the psychological realism of the preceding literary epoch.
71. Tolstoy, *The Death of Ivan Ilych*, 102. We encounter trains as instruments of fate not only in *Anna Karenina*, in which a train brings Anna into the storyworld and another train violently effaces her from it, but also in *Kreutzer Sonata* (1889). Tolstoy himself died at the wayside station of Astapovo, albeit not killed by a train.
72. Morson, "Anna Karenina's Omens," 146–48.
73. Morson, "Anna Karenina's Omens," 145.
74. Tolstoy, *Anna Karenina*, 328, 639.
75. Tolstoy, *Anna Karenina*, 578.
76. Tolstoy, *Anna Karenina*, 680.
77. This is also Anna's revenge on Vronsky; it is in part her vengefulness that leads her to see her future tragic death as inescapable.
78. Tolstoy, *Anna Karenina*, 580.
79. Tolstoy, *Anna Karenina*, 694.
80. Tolstoi, *Anna Karenina*, *PSS*, 19:348.
81. Vladimir Alexandrov, *Limits to Interpretation: The Meanings of Anna Karenina* (Madison: University of Wisconsin Press, 2004), 113–14. See also Robert Louis Jackson, "Chance and Design in *Anna Karenina*," in *The Disciplines of Criticism*, ed. Peter Demetz, Thomas Greene, and Lowry Nelson Jr. (New Haven, CT: Yale University Press, 1968), 315–29. Gary Saul Morson remarks that "more often than not, readers have interpreted *Anna Karenina* as if it, and not its eponymous heroine, relied on omens and foreshadowing" ("Anna Karenina's Omens," 151).
82. Tolstoy, *Anna Karenina*, 60, 272; Tolstoi, *Anna Karenina*, *PSS*, 18:70. David Sloane holds that Anna "fashions her own life into a tragedy with all the semblance of fateful inevitability that this genre requires" ("Pushkin's Legacy in *Anna Karenina*," *Tolstoy Studies Journal* 4 [1991]: 15). In other words, it is as though Anna's fatality were the result of her deliberate choice, as though she had chosen to make her tragic ending predetermined and inescapable.
83. Tolstoy, *Anna Karenina*, 560, 569.
84. Donna Tussing Orwin, *Tolstoy's Art and Thought, 1847–1880* (Princeton, NJ: Princeton University Press, 1993), 179; Tolstoy, *Anna Karenina*, 67.
85. Tolstoy *Anna Karenina*, 271; Tolstoi, *Anna Karenina*, *PSS*, 18:314. Here the published English translation has "for a novel," which suggests she may be a good

2. END OF STORY

candidate to have her life described in a novel. I contend that "from a novel" or "out of a novel" are more faithful to the Russian original, "geroina romana," and convey the message more effectively.

86. Amy Mandelker, *Framing Anna Karenina: Tolstoy, the Woman Question, and the Victorian Novel* (Columbus: Ohio University Press, 1993), 60.
87. Tolstoy *Anna Karenina*, 695.
88. Lotman, *The Structure of the Artistic Text*, 72, 195.
89. Frank Kermode, *The Sense of an Ending: Studies in the Theory of Fiction* (Oxford: Oxford University Press, 1967), 4.
90. Kermode, *The Sense of an Ending*, 8.
91. Amanda Ewart Toland, Andrea Forman, Fergus J. Couch, Julie O. Culver, Diana M. Eccles, William D. Foulkes, Frans B. L. Hogervorst, Claude Houdayer, Ephrat Levy-Lahad, Alvaro N. Monteiro, et al., "Clinical Testing of BRCA1 and BRCA2: A Worldwide Snapshot of Technological Practices," *npj Genomic Medicine* 3 (February 15, 2018): 1–8. This study reveals how widely testing protocols and standards differ across countries.
92. Among them is Jeremy Greene, *Prescribing by Numbers* (Baltimore, MD: Johns Hopkins University Press, 2007). The concept of "risk" is further explored here in chapter 3.
93. In chapter 2 of *Illness as Narrative* (Pittsburgh, PA: University of Pittsburgh Press, 2012), Ann Jurecic examines how illness narratives in the United States are influenced by growing awareness of statistical risk.
94. In June 2020, Masha Gessen announced a preference for the plural pronouns *they, them*, and *theirs* in reference to themselves (see https://twitter.com/mashagessen/status/1275529665466302466?lang=en). Because the blog posts examined here were produced in 2004, when Gessen still used *she, her, hers*, and in them Gessen addresses deep bioethical questions surrounding the female body while often inscribing reflections and thoughts within a collective women's narrative (especially in the book that later collected all the blog postings, *Blood Matters*), and because Gessen's posts are steeped in their present time—both in terms of the state of breast and ovarian cancer research and diagnostics and in the way the readers followed Gessen's serialized process of decision-making installment after installment, post after post—I have maintained here the singular feminine pronouns that were commonly used during that period to refer to Gessen.
95. When Gessen collected her posts into a book, she offered a comprehensive bibliography of studies on these matters. See, most prominently, the sources listed for the chapter "A Decision at Any Cost," in *Blood Matters: From Inherited Illness to Designer Babies, How the World and I Found Ourselves in the Future of the Gene* (New York: Harcourt, 2008), 294–97.
96. See Gessen's post on *Slate* from June 13, 2004, "In Which I Find out that I Am Genetically Mutant," https://slate.com/technology/2004/06/in-which-i-find-out-that-i-am-genetically-mutant.html. For subsequent quotations from Gessen's posts on *Slate* in this period, her page on the *Slate* website lists all of the posts ordered from the most recent to the oldest, including the ones I analyze in this chapter: https://slate.com/author/masha-gessen.
97. Gessen, *Blood Matters*, 116.

2. END OF STORY

98. Eikhenbaum, *Molodoi Tolstoi*, 13; Boris Eikhenbaum, *Lev Tolstoi: Piatidesiatye gody* (Leningrad: Priboi, 1928), 34–35; Viktor Shklovskii, *Lev Tolstoi*, 2nd ed. (Moscow: Khudozhestvennaia literatura, 1967), 77–78; Paperno, "'Who, What Is I?'"
99. Tolstoi, *Dnevnik 1847–1854*, 245–61.
100. Lev Tolstoi, *Dnevniki i zapisnye knizhki, 1904–1906*, vol. 55 of *Polnoe sobranie sochinenii*, ed. V. G. Chertkov (Moscow: Khudozhestvennaia literatura, 1937); *Dnevniki, zapisnye knizhki i otdel'nye zapiski, 1907–1908*, vol. 56 of *Polnoe sobranie sochinenii*, ed. V. G. Chertkov (Moscow: Khudozhestvennaia literatura, 1937); *Dnevniki i zapisnye knizhki, 1909*, vol. 57 of *Polnoe sobranie sochinenii*, ed. V. G. Chertkov (Moscow: Khudozhestvennaia literatura, 1952); *Dnevniki i zapisnye knizhki, 1910*, vol. 58 of *Polnoe sobranie sochinenii*, ed. V. G. Chertkov (Moscow: Khudozhestvennaia literatura, 1934).
101. Lev Tolstoi to N. N. Strakhov, April 23, 1876, in Lev Tolstoi, *Pis'ma 1873–1879*, vol. 62 of *Polnoe sobranie sochinenii*, ed. V. G. Chertkov (Moscow: Khudozhestvennaia literatura, 1953), 269.
102. In the finale of an earlier draft of *Crime and Punishment*, "Raskolnikov goes to shoot himself." See Fyodor Dostoevsky, *The Notebooks for "Crime and Punishment,"* ed. and trans. Edward Wasiolek (Chicago: University of Chicago Press, 1967), 243.
103. Merezhkovskii analyzes the description of Anna's body in "Tolstoy's Physical Descriptions," 776–77.
104. Reported in Andrew Kaufman, *Understanding Tolstoy* (Columbus: Ohio University Press, 2011), 175. Kaufman also points out that an early draft of part 8 includes Levin's vision of Anna's dead body, which prompts his reflections on life.
105. Sof'ia Andreevna's description of Pirogova's corpse resonates with the descriptions of Anna's body in the novel: "Then there was a post mortem. Lev Nikolaevich attended, and saw her [Pirogova] lying there at the Yasenki barracks, her skull smashed in and her naked body beautifully mutilated. It had the most terrible effect on him. Anna Stepanova was a tall, plump woman with a typically Russian temperament and appearance. She had dark hair and grey eyes, and although she wasn't beautiful she was very pleasant-looking" (Sophia Tolstoy, *The Diaries of Sophia Tolstoy*, trans. Cathy Porter [New York: Random House, 1985], 855).
106. As George Steiner puts it, Tolstoy can be compared to Heraclitus in that he offers not "a skein which is unraveled and rewound, but... a river, incessantly in motion and flowing beyond our sight" (*Tolstoy or Dostoevsky: An Essay in the Old Criticism* [New York: Knopf, 1959], 102).

3. MEDICAL ENLIGHTENMENT IN THE EARLY 1920S: RHETORIC AND DIFFUSED AUTHORSHIP IN JULES ROMAINS'S *KNOCK* AND SOVIET PUBLIC-HEALTH CAMPAIGNS

1. Clifton K. Meador, "The Last Well Person," *New England Journal of Medicine* 330, no. 6 (February 10, 1994): 440.
2. Meador, "The Last Well Person," 440.

3. Meador, "The Last Well Person," 440, my emphasis.
4. Meador, "The Last Well Person," 440.
5. Meador, "The Last Well Person," 440–41.
6. Meador, "The Last Well Person," 441.
7. Joseph Dumit, *Drugs for Life: How Pharmaceutical Companies Define Our Health* (Durham, NC: Duke University Press, 2012).
8. In *Prescribing by Numbers* (Baltimore, MD: Johns Hopkins University Press, 2007), Jeremy Greene analyzes three case studies of pharmaceuticals whose popularity over the years has been tightly interwoven with the rise of the notion of "risk" and with the progressive lowering of the numerical parameters that define whether a person is in need of treatment.
9. Robert Aronowitz, *Making Sense of Illness: Science, Society, and Disease* (Cambridge: Cambridge University Press, 1998).
10. Georges Canguilhem, *The Normal and the Pathological*, trans. Carolyn Fawcett, with an introduction by Michel Foucault (Dordrecht, Netherlands: D. Reidel, 1978).
11. Annie Angremy, preface to Jules Romains, *Knock, ou Le triomphe de la médecine* (Paris: Gallimard, 1993), 8. Jouvet's troupe toured major Italian cities with *Knock* in 1931, although the play had already been translated into Italian and staged by local troupes in 1926 and 1928.
12. Interviewed on the choice of the name "Knock," all Romains said was that "to knock, in English, means *frapper*. It's not a title, it's a noise, an onomatopoeia. It is, in the art of boxing, the decisive blow, the knockout. *The Triumph of Medicine* is just a subtitle for the Bibliothèque rose [publisher of children's literature]" (quoted in the editors' "Notice," in Romains, *Knock*, 145; unless otherwise noted, all translations of non-English text quoted in the chapter and its notes are my own). In any event, *Nosferatu* was successful to the extent that it is nearly impossible not to assume some level of intertextuality.
13. Aristotle, *Rhetoric*, in *The Rhetoric and the Poetics of Aristotle*, trans. W. Rhys Roberts and Ingram Bywater (New York: Modern Library, 1954), 24.
14. There is a long-standing tradition that Mozart enjoyed posing as a quack doctor. According to Edward Holmes, Mozart "acquitted himself in prescriptions to his numerous patients with great address and promptness of wit" (*The Life of Mozart, Including His Correspondence* [New York: Harper, 1854], 311). The quack doctor in Russian popular and folk theater is discussed later in this chapter.
15. By contrast, Tolstoy, particularly in *Anna Karenina* and *The Death of Ivan Ilych*, took a similarly skeptical attitude toward medical practitioners, often portraying them as frauds and manipulators.
16. Jules Romains, "Pourquoi j'ai écrit *Donogoo*," *Revue de Paris*, November 1951, 3–4, translated and quoted in Denis Boak, *Jules Romains* (New York: Twayne, 1974), 73.
17. Romains, *Knock*, 1.1.39–40.
18. Romains, *Knock*, 1.1.42–43.
19. Romains, *Knock*, 1.1.43.
20. Romains, *Knock*, 1.1.45.
21. Romains, *Knock*, 1.1.38.
22. Romains, *Knock*, 1.1.55.

3. MEDICAL ENLIGHTENMENT IN THE EARLY 1920S

23. Romains, *Knock*, 2.1.62.
24. Michel Foucault, *The Order of Things: An Archaeology of Human Sciences* (New York: Pantheon, 1971).
25. Romains, *Knock*, 2.1.62.
26. Romains, *Knock*, 2.1.64.
27. Robin Landa, *Designing Brand Experiences* (New York: Thomson Delmar, 2006), xx.
28. Romains, *Knock*, 2.1.63–64.
29. Romains, *Knock*, 2.1.66–68.
30. Romains, *Knock*, 2.2.70.
31. Romains, *Knock*, 2.2.72–74, with all but the first and fifth ellipses in the original.
32. Canguilhem, *The Normal and the Pathological*, 138.
33. Dumit, *Drugs for Life*, 15.
34. As Dumit puts it, "Neither health nor illnesses are states of being: they are states of knowledge, they are epistemic" (*Drugs for Life*, 13). Sometimes just the fact of being a certain age and gender or belonging to a specific social group causes people to be considered at risk for developing diseases and to be put on preemptive-treatment plans. Jeremy Green investigates the whole notion of risk and of the parameters set to determine where to draw the lines among normal, at risk, and pathological in his book *Prescribing by Numbers*, where he focuses on the historical and sociological trajectory of three best-selling drugs and of the conditions they treat—Diuril for hypertension, Orinase for diabetes, and Mevacor for high cholesterol. Building on Canguilhem's reflections to describe a major change in medical epistemology in the second half of the twentieth century, Greene shows how the distinction between the normal and the pathological has become a matter of numerical abstraction.
35. Louis Althusser, "Ideology and State Apparatuses" (1970), in *Lenin and Philosophy and Other Essays*, trans. Ben Brewster (New York: Monthly Review Press, 1971), 170, 174–75.
36. Joseph Dumit has coined the term *inter-pill-ation*, which he defines as "the process of calling into being biomedical subjects as having been always-already in need of treatment" ("Inter-pill-ation and the Instrumentalization of Compliance," *Anthropology and Medicine* 17, no. 2 [2010]: 246). Although most people do not even register that "call," for pharmaceutical companies it is enough that a few feel interpellated so that the companies can get a small additional percentage of people to consider that they might be depressed, have high cholesterol, or suffer from a newly discovered syndrome. That small percentage will justify the cost of the drug campaign. See Dumit, *Drugs for Life*, 56.
37. Romains, *Knock*, 2.3.75.
38. Romains, *Knock*, 2.3.76.
39. Romains, *Knock*, 2.3.78–79.
40. Canguilhem, *The Normal and the Pathological*, 36.
41. Modern ways to refer to overmedicalization in North America depict drugs as being coterminous with the country (e.g., "Prozac nation").
42. Romains, *Knock*, 1.1.50.
43. "There is always room for another ... treatment, perhaps until we can't take any more treatment because of side effects, costs, or effort" (Dumit, *Drugs for Life*, 95).

3. MEDICAL ENLIGHTENMENT IN THE EARLY 1920S

44. Romains, *Knock*, 2.1.64.
45. Romains, *Knock*, 2.5.86–88, second ellipsis (after "Hmm") in the original.
46. In a more constructive tone, Chekhov, in a letter to his editor, Alexei Suvorin, in 1890, celebrated the scientific discoveries, such as germ theory, that contributed to the rise in status and prestige of Russian physicians: "I believe in both [Robert] Koch and spermine and I praise God for it. All that—that is the kochines, spermines, and so on—seem to the public a kind of miracle . . . but people who have a closer acquaintance with the facts know that they are only the natural sequel of what has been done during the last twenty years. A great deal has been done, my dear fellow. Surgery alone has done so much that one is fairly dumbfounded at it. To one who is studying medicine now, the time before twenty years ago seems simply pitiable" (Anton Chekhov, *Letters of Anton Chekhov to His Family and Friends with Biographical Sketch*, trans. Constance Garnett [New York: Macmillan, 1920], 245).
47. Joseph Dumit, "Prescription Maximization and the Accumulation of Surplus Health in the Pharmaceutical Industry: The _BioMarx_ Experiment," in *Lively Capital: Biotechnologies, Ethics, and Governance in Global Markets*, ed. Kaushik Sunder Rajan (Durham, NC: Duke University Press, 2012), 63.
48. Romains, *Knock*, 2.5.89, 2.4.81, 2.1.67.
49. Yuri Lotman, *The Structure of the Artistic Text*, trans. Gail Lenhof and Ronald Vroon (Ann Arbor: University of Michigan Press, 1977). I discuss Lotman's definition of what constitutes an "event" in chapter 2.
50. See Dumit's analysis of a Prozac commercial in "Prescription Maximization," 58. See also, in this respect, the concept "cancer previvors" as opposed to "cancer survivors" discussed in chapter 2.
51. Romains, *Knock*, 3.4.105.
52. Romains, *Knock*, 3.4.108.
53. Romains, *Knock*, 3.6.112–14.
54. See, for instance, the map *The World of Coffee* (Oxford: Oxford Cartographers, 1998).
55. Dumit remarks that the reasoning behind the marketing choices made by pharmaceutical companies proceeds in the opposite direction one would expect: instead of developing drugs targeted to public-health priorities, thus serving the interest of the people, the companies instead study the market to determine which clinical trials it makes sense to carry out and which drugs to develop and patent in order to recoup their research and production costs. In other words, clinical studies that are important to conduct from a scientific or medical perspective are not necessarily as important to conduct from a drug-development perspective (Dumit, *Drugs for Life*, 66, 91).
56. Romains, *Knock*, 3.6.114–16.
57. Peter J. Norrish, *Drama of the Group: A Study of Unanimism in the Plays of Jules Romains* (Cambridge: Cambridge University Press, 1958), 4–5.
58. Norrish, *Drama of the Group*, 143, 89.
59. Norrish, *Drama of the Group*, 77.
60. On unanimism in *Knock*, see also Boak, *Jules Romains*, 174.
61. Romains, *Knock*, 3.6.114.
62. Anton Chekhov, *Ward No. 6*, in Anton Chekhov, *Chekhov's Doctors: A Collection of Chekhov's Medical Tales*, ed. John L. Coulehan, with a foreword by Robert

Coles (Kent, OH: Kent State University Press, 2003), 130. Literature, famously defined by Chekhov as his "mistress," as opposed to medicine, his "lawful wife" (Anton Chekhov to Alexei Suvorin, September 11, 1892, in *Letters of Anton Chekhov*, 99), allowed him to show physicians to be far from invincible. Vulnerable and human, they are assailed by doubt, fear, and uncertainty and, just like their patients, fall prey to passions, vices, and despair. In *Seeing Chekhov: Life and Art* (Ithaca, NY: Cornell University Press, 2005), Michael Finke reveals and scrutinizes previously unconsidered seams between Chekhov's literary style and his medical practice.

63. Chekhov, *Ward No. 6*, 110.
64. The trope of the mentally ill individual as an unreliable narrator who, precisely by virtue of his or her impairment and estranging gaze upon society, is able to attain and reveal deeper truths runs through the Russian cultural tradition. One can trace its origins back to the figure of the Holy Fool and proceed all the way to the nineteenth-century character Poprishchin in Gogol's "Diary of a Madman" (1835), Dostoevsky's Underground Man in *Notes from Underground* (1864) and Prince Myshkin in *The Idiot* (1869) (see Harriet Murav, *Holy Foolishness: Dostoevsky's Novels and the Poetics of Cultural Critique* [Stanford, CA: Stanford University Press, 1993]), and the protagonist of Vsevolod Garshin's story "Red Flower" (1883). The case of Ragin, however, is different. His unreliability is not as obvious to the reader as Poprishchin's (nor does it, for that matter, spring from a clash of paradigms, as in Ivan Ilych's experience). Ragin is a doctor and knows his medicine, but he falls prey to the power dynamics of a coercive institutionalized system of which he himself has been part and which he has helped to create. Unlike Gogol', who employs first-person narration and can show his character's unreliability only through estrangement and the grotesque, Chekhov communicates his opinions on Ragin to the reader very explicitly. Nothing is left to interpretation: through the voice of an omniscient narrator, Chekhov shows that despite Ragin's idleness and his unethical conduct, his reasoning is sound and that, in fact, he is the most knowledgeable and acute among the hospital authorities.
65. Medical sociologists today would claim that Ragin, like his fictional colleagues Preobrazhenskii and Persikov in Mikhail Bulgakov's science fiction a couple of decades later, lacks "structural competency"—that is, "the trained ability to discern how a host of issues defined clinically as symptoms, attitudes, or diseases . . . also represent the downstream implications of a number of upstream decisions about such matters as health care and food delivery systems, . . . urban and rural infrastructures, medicalization, or even about the very definitions of illness and health. . . . And structure connotes assumptions embedded in language and attitude that serve as rhetorical social conduits for some groups of persons, and as barriers to others" (Jonathan Metzl and Helena Hansen, "Structural Competency: Theorizing a New Medical Engagement with Stigma and Inequality," *Social Science and Medicine* 103 (February 2014): 128.
66. Romains, *Knock*, 3.8.121.
67. Romains, *Knock*, 3.8.122–23.
68. These very words appear, for instance, on the website Parkinson's Health, where Teva Pharmaceuticals, which produces a drug for Parkinson's, gives information on the syndrome. Sometimes in order to make patients feel empowered,

3. MEDICAL ENLIGHTENMENT IN THE EARLY 1920S

pharmaceutical advertising borrows language and imagery from civil right campaigns of the 1960s and 1970s (such as the concept "democratization of knowledge"). Nathan Greenslit examines this phenomenon in "Depression and Consumption: Psychopharmaceuticals, Branding, and New Identity Practices," *Culture, Medicine, and Psychiatry* 29 (2005): 477–501. Up until the 1960s, Greenslit reminds us, all pills were round and white (480). The phenomenon of branding has increased the importance of those attributes of drugs such as the color of the pills or the commercial name that Jean Baudrillard would define as "inessential": "The inessential is no longer left to the whims of individual demand and manufacture, but instead picked up and systematized by the production process, which today defines its aims by reference to what is inessential" (*The System of Objects*, trans. James Benedict [New York: Verso, 1968], 9).

69. The website of the drug Myrbetriq, which is prescribed in case of an overactive bladder, not only has testimonial videos, which alone provide examples of how to speak about the syndrome, but also an interactive questionnaire that has you answer multiple-choice questions about your symptoms and comes up with a number of "conversation starters," which include the following: "It's embarrassing having to constantly run to the bathroom," or "I'm doing what I can to manage my bladder problems, but it's not enough. What are my other options?" (https://www.myrbetriq.com/oab-treatment-stories/). Other websites offer entire stories that one can draw upon or even repeat verbatim during a doctor's visit. In other words, these tools turn patients into reliable narrators in the eyes of physicians.

70. As explained in David Horn, *Social Bodies* (Princeton, NJ: Princeton University Press, 1994), 19.

71. Horn, *Social Bodies*, 20.

72. Michel Foucault, *An Introduction*, vol. 1 of *The History of Sexuality*, trans. Robert Hurley (New York: Vintage, 1980), 140.

73. Michel Foucault, *Society Must Be Defended: Lectures at the Collège de France*, trans. David Macey (New York: Picador, 2003), 252–53, 245.

74. Debates on biopower have only multiplied since Foucault's formulation of the concept. A recent debate followed the release of the first U.S. Food and Drug Administration–approved "digital pill," a medication for schizophrenia, in November 2017. The patient swallows a tracking device that collects and transmits data about compliance to the physician through Bluetooth technology and the patient's smartphone.

75. See, among others, S. Margolin, "Zhiul' Romen," *Novyi mir* 9 (1927): 186–93; Ia. Frid, "Chetyre tomika epopei," *Literaturnyi kritik* 2 (1933): 176–79; K. Zelinskii, "Novyi manifest Zhiulia Romena," *Literaturnyi kritik* 5 (1933): 135–39; V. Pertsov, "Potolok lichnosti," *Krasnaia nov'* 1 (1934): 170–80.

76. By the late 1930s, Jules Romains had earned an entry in the *Literaturnaia entsiklopediia*. See E. Gal'perina, "Zhiul' Romen," in *Literaturnaia entsiklopediia*, vol. 10 (Moscow: Khudozhestvennaia literatura, 1937), 41–44.

77. Russian translations of individual works by Romains had appeared before the Academia edition, and two of them, the novel *Les Copains* (1913) and the piece *Cromedeyre-le-Vieil* (1920), were translated by Osip Mandel'shtam as *Obormoty* (Leningrad: Gosizdat, 1925) and *Kromdeier-Staryi* (Leningrad-Moscow:

Gosizdat, 1925), respectively. Mandel'shtam also wrote the introduction to *Kromdeier-Staryi*.
78. Zhiul' Romen, *Knok, ili Torzhestvo meditsiny*, vol. 7 of *Sobranie sochinenii* (Leningrad: Academia, 1926), back cover.
79. Margolin, "Zhiul' Romen," 187.
80. Nikolai Vol'kov, "Zhiul' Romen: *Sobranie sochinenii*, Izd. Academia, 1926 g.," *Izvestiia* 178 (August 5, 1926): 5.
81. V. Barvin, "Zhiul' Romen: *Knok, ili Torzhestvo meditsiny*," *Pravda* 161 (July 16, 1926): 6.
82. Nikolai A. Semashko, *Health Protection in the USSR* (London: Gollancz, 1934), 33–34.
83. Aleksandr Smirnov, "Predislovie," in Romen, *Knock, ili Torzhestvo meditsiny*, 5, 6.
84. Jules Romains, *Donogoo-Tonka, ou Les Miracles de la science* (Paris: Nouvelle revue française, 1920).
85. "In Jules Romains's novel *Donogoo-Tonka*, a city built as a result of a scientist's error erects a monument to a scientific error. I had no desire to stand as a monument to my own error" (Viktor Shklovskii, "Pamiatnik nauchnoi oshibke," *Literaturnaia gazeta*, no. 4 [January 27, 1930]: 1).
86. In *Russian Formalism: History, Doctrine* (The Hague: Mouton, 1955), Victor Erlich describes Shklovskii's gesture as an "externally induced capitulation" (136).
87. See Richard Sheldon, "Viktor Shklovsky and the Device of Ostensible Surrender," *Slavic Review* 34, no. 1 (March 1975): 86–108.
88. In *The Body Soviet: Propaganda, Hygiene, and the Revolutionary State* (Madison: University of Wisconsin Press, 2008), Tricia Stark examines precisely how this continuity is determined and articulated through the public-health agenda of the early Soviet state.
89. Semashko, *Health Protection in the USSR*, 37. This retrospective report was compiled at the end of the first five-year plan and in view of the second.
90. Among the major historical sources on early Soviet public health produced in recent years are Susan Gross Solomon and John F. Hutchinson, eds., *Health and Society in Revolutionary Russia* (Bloomington: Indiana University Press, 1990), as well as Frances Lee Bernstein, Christopher Burton, and Dan Healey, eds., *Soviet Medicine: Culture, Practice, and Science* (DeKalb: Northern Illinois University Press, 2010).
91. The State Museum of Social Hygiene was founded in Moscow in 1919.
92. Nikolai A. Semashko, "Sotsial'naia gigiena, eë sushchnost', metod i znachenie," *Sotsial'naia gigiena* 1 (1922): 8.
93. See Susan Gross Solomon, "Social Hygiene and Soviet Public Health, 1921–1930," in *Health and Society in Revolutionary Russia*, ed. Solomon and Hutchinson, 175. There was a history of social hygiene in Russia dating back to Nikolai Pirogov, but Semashko took the discipline out of the circumscribed medical field and made it the chief guiding principle for the political and institutional reorganization of the Russian society.
94. Vladimir Lenin, *Report of the All-Russia Central Executive Committee and the Council of People's Commissar*, December 5, 1919, in *Collected Works*, vol. 30: *September 1919–April 1920*, 4th English ed. (Moscow: Progress, 1961), 228. Lenin's statement ("Ili vshi pobediat sotsializm, ili sotsializm pobedit vshei") was

3. MEDICAL ENLIGHTENMENT IN THE EARLY 1920S

dutifully mentioned by Health Commissar Nikolai A. Semashko in his article that celebrated the first ten years of Narkomzdrav: "Politika v dele zdravookhraneniia za desiat' let," in *Desiat' let oktiabria i sovetskoe zdorov'e* (Moscow: Izdatel'stvo Narkomzdrava, 1927), 5.

95. For a picture of this poster, see the entry "Viktor Deni" on the website for the Comiclopedia of Lambiek, the world's oldest comic shop and sequential art gallery, third poster from the top, https://www.lambiek.net/artists/d/deni_viktor.htm. Numerous studies have been devoted to the intersection of revolutionary ideas, lifestyle, and artistic expression: Katerina Clark traces the prerevolutionary roots of Stalinist aesthetics in *Petersburg, Crucible of Cultural Revolution* (Cambridge, MA: Harvard University Press, 1995); Richard Stites examines revolutionary utopias in *Revolutionary Dreams: Utopian Visions and Experimental Life in the Russian Revolution* (Oxford: Oxford University Press, 1991); Eric Naiman shows how largely utopian ideals rested upon a disciplined and male body in *Sex in Public: The Incarnation of Early Soviet Ideology* (Princeton, NJ: Princeton University Press, 1997); Catriona Kelly addresses early revolutionary Soviet culture and, in particular, hygiene as a major, normative component in *Refining Russia: Advice Literature, Polite Culture, and Gender from Catherine to Yeltsin* (New York: Oxford University Press, 2001) and in Catriona Kelly and David Shepherd, eds., *Constructing Russian Culture in the Age of Revolution, 1881–1940* (Oxford: Oxford University Press, 1998); Svetlana Boym examines everyday life in *Common Places: Mythologies of Everyday Life* (Cambridge, MA: Harvard University Press, 1994); Frances Lee Bernstein discusses sexuality, power, and control in *The Dictatorship of Sex: Lifestyle Advice for the Soviet Masses* (DeKalb: Northern Illinois University Press, 2007).

96. In her discussion of "romantic anticapitalism" in the Russian intelligentsia, Katerina Clark addresses the origins of these binary oppositions (*Petersburg*, 16–17).

97. In this regard, Naiman remarks that the NEP was "a type of vaccination on an unprecedented economic and ideological scale" (*Sex in Public*, 263).

98. David Burliuk, Nikolai Burliuk, Aleksei Kruchënykh, Vasilii Kandinskii, Benedikt Livshits, Vladimir Maiakovskii, and Velimir Khlebnikov, *Poshchëchina obshchestvennomu vkusu* (Moscow: G. L. Kuz'min, 1912), 1.

99. Filippo Tommaso Marinetti's (1876–1944) infamous manifesto "War, the Only Hygiene of the World" ("Guerra, sola igiene del mondo," 1911) exhorted Italians to embrace arms against all enemies of the new order, the status quo, and hypocritical pacifism. For public-health campaigns on hygiene in Italy, including the war on flies, viewed as carriers of lethal diseases, see Horn, *Social Bodies*.

100. Daniel Beer's large-scale study *Renovating Russia: The Human Sciences and the Fate of Liberal Modernity, 1880–1930* (Ithaca, NY: Cornell University Press, 2000) provides an extensive exploration of this metaphor. Children's literature was informed by hygiene as well, as attested to in Kornei Chukovskii's book *Washuntilthereareholes* (*Moidodyr*, 1923). For more on this trend, see Evgeny Steiner, *Stories for Little Comrades: Revolutionary Artists and the Making of Early Soviet Children's Books* (Seattle: University of Washington Press, 1999), 98–99. However, Tricia Starks comments that "not everyone was convinced of the evils of dirt, and some even saw revolution in the presence of filth" (*The Body Soviet*, 14). In general, avant-garde artists participated in both real and satirical celebrations of the

"medical age." One of Vladimir Maiakovskii's ROSTA (Russian Telegraph Agency) Windows from 1921 described the symptoms of cholera (vomiting, cramps, diarrhea) and informed the public of how to avoid contracting the disease and prevent its spread in everyday situations (at home, at the factory, while fishing, eating, and drinking) and what to do in case of an epidemic; and the Russian edition of Romains's *Knock* (Academia, 1926) was illustrated by the experimental artist Nikolai Akimov (1901–1968).

101. See Toby Clark, "The 'New Man's' Body: A Motif in Early Soviet Culture," in *Art of the Soviets: Painting, Sculpture, and Architecture in a One-Party State, 1917–1922*, ed. Matthew Cullerne Brown and Brandon Taylor (Manchester, U.K.: Manchester University Press, 1993), 36.

102. See Slava Gerovitch, "Love–Hate for Man–Machine Metaphors in Soviet Physiology: From Pavlov to 'Physiological Cybernetics,'" *Science in Context* 15 (2002): 344. On the fusion between technology and aesthetics in the postrevolutionary decade, see Julia Vaingurt, *Wonderlands of the Avant-Garde: Technology and the Arts in Russia of the 1920s* (Chicago: Northwestern University Press, 2013).

103. Anton Chekhov, "Sluchai iz praktiki" (1898), in *Rasskazy: Povesti, 1898–1903*, vol. 10 of *Sochineniia*, 18 vols. of *Polnoe sobranie sochinenii i pisem*, ed. N. F. Bel'chikov (Moscow: Nauka, 1977), 81.

104. On Claude Bernard's theory of the inner milieu, see note 62, chapter 1.

105. One could also note that Chekhov's epidemiological survey of Sakhalin Island, conducted in 1890, published in parts between 1891 and 1893, and comprising elements as disparate as statistics, journalistic sketches, personal reflections, and geographic observations, differed sharply in genre, methodology, and goals from early Soviet public-health surveys, even though it was conceived and compiled only thirty years earlier.

106. Children were not spared this rational organization of the day, and Pioneers were expected to follow a specific regimen. Catriona Kelly argues that the goal of such *rezhim* was not only to discipline the body and its functions but also "[to] inculcat[e] in the young ... a sense of exact time and punctuality" ("Shaping the 'Future Race': Regulating the Daily Life of Children in Early Soviet Russia," in *Everyday Life in Early Soviet Russia: Taking the Revolution Inside*, ed. Christina Kiaer and Eric Naiman [Bloomington: Indiana University Press, 2005], 261).

107. Frances Lee Bernstein addresses masturbation as energy dispersion in early Soviet Russia in "Conserving Soviet Power: Thermodynamics and the Sins of Youth," chapter 5 of *The Dictatorship of Sex*, 129–58.

108. Aleksei Gastev, *Iunost', idi!* (Moscow: VTsSPS, 1923), 55.

109. Naiman, *Sex in Public*, 209.

110. Nikolai A. Semashko, *Sotsial'nye bolezni i bor'ba s nimi* (Moscow: Voprosy truda, 1926), 4, 15.

111. Nikolai A. Semashko, *Nauka o zdorov'e obshchestva: Sotsial'naia gigiena*, 2nd ed. (Moscow: Izdatel'stvo Narkomzdrava, 1926), 8, 11.

112. Giorgio Cosmacini, *Storia della medicina e della sanità in Italia dalla peste nera ai giorni nostri* (Bari, Italy: Laterza, 2005), 366.

113. See Vittorio A. Sironi, "La nascita dell'industria farmaceutica," in *Il farmaco nei tempi: Dal laboratorio all'industria*, ed. Attilio Zanca (Milan: Farmitalia Carlo

3. MEDICAL ENLIGHTENMENT IN THE EARLY 1920S

Erba, 1989), 175–77; Mary Schaeffer Conroy, *The Soviet Pharmaceutical Business During the First Two Decades (1917–1937)* (New York: Peter Lang, 2006).
114. Cosmacini, *Storia della medicina*, 383. In Russia, Salvarsan was produced by chemist Ivan I. Ostromyslenskii (1880–1939) and called Arsol. See Mary Schaeffer Conroy, *In Health and Sickness: Pharmacy, Pharmacists, and the Pharmaceutical Industry in Late Imperial, Early Soviet Russia* (Boulder, CO: East European Monographs, 1994), 340.
115. Conroy, *The Soviet Pharmaceutical Business*, 29.
116. Benito Mussolini, "Discorso dell'Ascensione" (May 26, 1927), in *Opera omnia di Benito Mussolini*, vol. 2, ed. Edoardo Susmel and Duilio Susmel (Florence: La Fenice, 1957), 360–90.
117. In fact, in interwar Italy the art of government would increasingly be defined by Mussolini and others as a "medical" art. On other occasions, Mussolini likened Italian society to a cancer-ridden body and himself to an uncompromising surgeon (see Horn, *Social Bodies*, 23, 131 n. 10). David Horn points out that Mussolini's use of medical metaphors dates to his involvement with socialism before World War II, and he compares Mussolini's rhetorical choices with Émile Durkheim's equating the modern statesman with the doctor.
118. Another excellent source that examines organic metaphors applied by Mussolini to the Italian society and landscape is Ruth Ben-Ghiat, *Fascist Modernities: Italy 1922–1945* (Berkeley: University of California Press, 2001), especially the introduction and chapter 1.
119. An image of this poster can be found on the website of the Russian Federal Service for Surveillance on Consumer Rights Protection and Human Well-Being (Rospotrebnadzor), third poster from the top, http://cgon.rospotrebnadzor.ru/content/33/4528.
120. Vladimir Lenin, quoted in I. A. Slonimskaia, "V. I. Lenin ob okhrane zdorov'ia naroda," translated and quoted in Starks, *The Body Soviet*, 3.
121. Ben-Ghiat, *Fascist Modernities*, 29–30.
122. Semashko reports this famous slogan in *Nauka o zdorov'e obshchestva*, 49.
123. An image of the poster can be found in Starks, *The Body Soviet*, plate 6.
124. As a model of modernity and mass society, Soviet Russia generated the most curiosity in Italians. In the late 1920s, more than fifty books appeared in Italy on the country that one writer (Gaetano Ciocca) described as "the grandest laboratory of social experience in existence" (quoted in Ben-Ghiat, *Fascist Modernities*, 38).
125. The Narkomzdrav logo, shaped like a light bulb containing a torch, celebrated sanitary enlightenment and appeared on all public-health posters.
126. In 1923, the medical-scientific section of the State Publishing House (Gosizdat) took charge of medical publications.
127. Starks, *The Body Soviet*, 5.
128. Horn, *Social Bodies*, 18. Foucault argues that corporeal metaphors were prominent because the healthy/morbid dichotomy could be easily applied to the discussion of societies (*The Birth of the Clinic: An Archaeology of Medical Perception*, trans. A. M. Sheridan-Smith [New York: Pantheon, 1973], 35–36). In the late nineteenth century, besides Lombroso, the major proponents of degeneration theories who had employed bodily metaphors in their diagnoses of societies were Henry Maudsley (1835–1918) in England and Bénédict Morel (1809–1873) in France.

3. MEDICAL ENLIGHTENMENT IN THE EARLY 1920S

129. Bernstein, *The Dictatorship of Sex*, 104.
130. See Al'fred Mol'kov, "Sanitarnoe prosveshchenie, ego zadachi i metody," *Sotsial'naia gigiena* 1 (1922): 42; Semashko, *Health Protection in the USSR*, 17.
131. Quoted in Bernstein, *The Dictatorship of Sex*, 103.
132. The most established chemical-pharmaceutical companies in Soviet Russia at the outbreak of World War I were Shtol' and Schmidt, Tentelevskii, Ferrein, and Keler. On the history of the pharmaceutical industry in early Soviet Russia, see Conroy, *The Soviet Pharmaceutical Business*. Trips to spas soon became another asset of Soviet public health. Diane P. Koenker's *Club Red: Vacation Travel and the Soviet Dream* (Ithaca, NY: Cornell University Press, 2013) is devoted to this topic.
133. Michel Foucault, *Discipline and Punish: The Birth of the Prison*, trans. Alan Sheridan (New York: Vintage, 1979), 26.
134. Foucault, *An Introduction*, 144–45. For Foucault in a Soviet context, see Stephen Kotkin, *Magnetic Mountain: Stalinism as a Civilization* (Berkeley: University of California Press, 1997), 157–237.
135. Peter Holquist maintains that Soviet control and surveillance techniques were the same as the ones employed by other states and that only the driving ideology was different. See Holquist, *Making War, Forging Revolution: Russia's Continuum of Crisis, 1914–1921* (Cambridge, MA: Harvard University Press, 2002), 6–8; and Holquist, "'Information Is the Alpha and Omega of Our Work': Bolshevik Surveillance in Its Pan-European Context," *Journal of Modern History* 69, no. 3 (1997): 427–28.
136. Giulio Casalini, "Un ministero per la salute pubblica?," *L'igiene e la vita* 2, no. 9 (1919): 258.
137. Giulio Casalini, "Sia richiesta l'assicurazione contro le malattie," *L'igiene e la vita* 4, no. 11 (1921): 322.
138. Yuri Lotman, "The Theater and Theatricality as Components of Early Nineteenth-Century Culture," in Yuri Lotman and Boris Uspenskii, *The Semiotics of Russian Culture*, ed. Ann Shukman (Ann Arbor: University of Michigan Press, 1984), 141, 147, 159. As Lotman moves specifically to the nineteenth century, he defines it as "a period [that] ran its course under the sign of the incursion of art—and first and foremost the theater—into Russian life" (160).
139. See Stites, *Revolutionary Dreams*; and Konstantin Rudnitsky, *Russian and Soviet Theater: Tradition and the Avant-Garde* (London: Thames and Hudson, 1988).
140. "Deistvitel'no, nikto ne znaet chto delat' s dramaticheskimi kruzhkami; oni plodiatsia kak infusorii" (Viktor Shklovskii, *Khod Konia: Sbornik statei* [Moscow: Gelikon, 1923], 59).
141. Clark, *Petersburg*; Boris Groys, *The Total Art of Stalinism: Avant-Garde, Aesthetic Dictatorship, and Beyond* (Princeton, NJ: Princeton University Press, 1992). See also Julie A. Cassiday's work on Soviet show trials (*pokazatel'nye sudy*), *The Enemy on Trial: Early Soviet Courts on Stage and Screen* (DeKalb: Northern Illinois University Press, 2000).
142. Film was another popular form. Sanitation films such as *Fight for Life* (on malaria), *Life's Truths* (on syphilis), and *Abortion* were shown in clubs and factories. On the use of the film medium in Soviet propaganda of the 1920s, see John MacKay's monumental work on Dziga Vertov over the course of several articles

3. MEDICAL ENLIGHTENMENT IN THE EARLY 1920S

and most notably in *Dziga Vertov: Life and Work*, vol. 1: *1896–1921* (Boston: Academic Studies, 2018), recently released as the first of a trilogy.

143. This quote from the proceedings of the first national meeting of sanitation education doctors in March 1921 is translated in Elizabeth A. Wood, *Performing Justice: Agitation Trials in Early Soviet Russia* (Ithaca, NY: Cornell University Press, 2005), 106.

144. Wood, *Performing Justice*, 111.

145. Interestingly, as Horn points out in *Social Bodies*, in Italy the state would often delegitimize physicians as not sufficiently concerned with state guidelines on hygiene and disease prevention, whereas in the early Soviet state they were seen instead as organic arms of the public-health machine.

146. Julie A. Cassiday, "Marble Columns and Jupiter Lights: Theatrical and Cinematic Modeling of Soviet Show Trials in the 1920s," *Slavic and East European Journal* 42, no. 4 (1998): 642; see also Cassiday, *The Enemy on Trial*, 51–80.

147. A picture of this poster can be found in Starks, *The Body Soviet*, 153, fig. 5.6.

148. See Elizabeth Warner, "The Quack Doctor in Russian Folk and Popular Theater," *Folklore* 93, no. 2 (1982): 166–75.

149. M. A. Rozentul, introduction to P. D. Iushkov, *Babka lechit—narod kalechit: Sanitarnaia komediia v 4-kh epizodakh* (Perm, Russia: Permskii Sanprosvet, 1927), 2.

150. Iushkov, *Babka lechit*, 4.

151. Iushkov, *Babka lechit*, 12.

152. Iushkov, *Babka lechit*, 23.

153. Sofiia Zak, *Boria v ambulatorii*, with illustrations by Vladimir Konashevich (Moscow: Gosizdat, 1928).

154. An image of this poster can be found in the online version of Frances Lee Bernstein, "Predstavleniia o zdorov'e v revoliutsionnoi Rossii: Gendernaia politika v plakatakh po polovomu prosvesheniiu v 1920-e gody," in *Vizual'naia antropologiia: Rezhimy vidimosti pri sotsializme*, ed. Elena Iarskaia-Smirnova and Pavel Romanov (Moscow: Variant, 2009), 237, https://docplayer.ru/87162672-Rezhimy-vidimosti-pri-socialisme.html.

155. Semashko, *Health Protection in the USSR*, 121–22.

156. Romains, *Knock*, 3.3.105.

157. Horn, *Social Bodies*, 100.

158. Cosmacini, *Storia della medicina*, 429.

159. Zak, *Boria v ambulatorii*, 5.

160. Zak, *Boria v ambulatorii*, 6.

161. Iushkov, *Babka lechit*, 25, 27, 29, 33.

162. Iushkov, *Babka lechit*, 4.

163. Iushkov, *Babka lechit*, 4.

164. Iushkov, *Babka lechit*, 34, 36, 39.

165. Russian literature features ill characters talking back if not directly to a specific doctor, then to the society's parameters of what constitutes healthy behavior—most notably, Dostoevsky's Underground Man and Raskol'nikov. However, the psychoanalytic tradition did not penetrate the Russian literary tradition at the turn of the twentieth century as it did in the rest of Europe (Italo Svevo's *Zeno's Conscience* [*La coscienza di Zeno*, 1923], among other prominent cases, is influenced by Freud's theories and presents a first-person narrative of a patient who is

writing to his psychoanalyst and talking back). This is not surprising if we consider that Freud's theories did not become popular in Russia until after the revolution.
166. Dumit, *Drugs for Life*, 55.

4. TIME, AGENCY, AND BODILY GLANDS: METABOLIC STORYTELLING IN ITALO SVEVO AND MIKHAIL BULGAKOV

1. Anne Pollock, "The Internal Cardiac Defibrillator," in *The Inner History of Devices*, ed. Sherry Turkle (Cambridge, MA: MIT Press, 2008), 101.
2. Originated in Graham Harman's rereading of Heidegger's concept of *Zuhandenheit* (readiness-to-hand) and further developed by Levi Bryant and Ian Bogost, object-oriented ontology offers a critique of anthropocentrism and of all philosophical currents that undermine objects. See Graham Harman, *Tool-Being: Heidegger and the Metaphysics of Objects* (Peru, IL: Open Court, 2002); Levi Bryant, *The Democracy of Objects* (London: Open Humanities, 2011); Ian Bogost, *Alien Phenomenology, or What It's Like to Be a Thing* (Minneapolis: University of Minnesota Press, 2012). Thing theory is instead more markedly a branch of literary and cultural theory, although it is still indebted to Heidegger, specifically to his distinction between *object* (*die Sache*) and *thing* (*das Ding*), as spelled out in the essay *The Thing* (1950). Thing theory was founded by Bill Brown, who edited a special issue of *Critical Inquiry* in 2001 ("Things," special issue of *Critical Inquiry* 28, no. 1 [2001]) and devoted two monographs to it, *A Sense of Things: The Object Matter of American Literature* (Chicago: University of Chicago Press, 2003) and *Other Things* (Chicago: University of Chicago Press, 2015). For discussions of the posthuman in Russia, see Julia Vaingurt and Colleen McQuillen, eds., *The Human Reimagined: Posthumanism in Russia* (Boston: Academic Studies, 2018).
3. Donna J. Haraway, "A Cyborg Manifesto: Science, Technology, and Socialist-Feminism in the Late Twentieth Century," in *Simians, Cyborgs, and Women: The Reinvention of Nature* (New York: Routledge, 1991), 149, 152.
4. Donna J. Haraway, *When Species Meet* (Minneapolis: University of Minnesota Press, 2007), 3–4, 42, emphasis in original.
5. Among others, two recent books attest to the renewed attention that both science and popular culture direct at the human gut, which is elevated from a lower-order organ to a regulatory system comparable to the brain: Giulia Enders, *Gut: The Inside Story of Our Body's Most Underrated Organ* (Vancouver: Greystone Books, 2015); and Emeran Mayer, *The Mind–Gut Connection: How the Inner Conversation Within Our Bodies Impacts Our Mood, Our Choices, and Our Overall Health* (New York: Harper Wave, 2016).
6. A passage from Livy's *History of Rome* (*Ab urbe condita*, 27–29 BCE) reads as follows: "They therefore decided to send as an ambassador to the commons Menenius Agrippa, an eloquent man and dear to the plebeians as being one of themselves by birth. On being admitted to the camp he is said merely to have related the following apologue, in the quaint and uncouth style of that age: In the days when man's members did not all agree amongst themselves, as is now the case,

4. TIME, AGENCY, AND BODILY GLANDS

but had each its own ideas and a voice of its own, the other parts thought it unfair that they should have the worry and the trouble and the labour of providing everything for the belly, while the belly remained quietly in their midst with nothing to do but to enjoy the good things which they bestowed upon it; they therefore conspired together that the hands should carry no food to the mouth, nor the mouth accept anything that was given it, nor the teeth grind up what they received. While they sought in this angry spirit to starve the belly into submission, the members themselves and the whole body were reduced to the utmost weakness. Hence it had become clear that even the belly had no idle task to perform, and was no more nourished than it nourished the rest, by giving out to all parts of the body that by which we live and thrive, when it has been divided equally amongst the veins and is enriched with digested food—that is, the blood. Drawing a parallel from this to show how like was the internal dissension of the bodily members to the anger of the plebs against the Fathers [the senatorial class], he prevailed upon the minds of his hearers" (Livy, *History of Rome*, vol. 1., ed. and trans. B. O. Foster [Cambridge, MA: Harvard University Press, 1919], book 2, chap. 32). Along the same lines, Renaissance anatomist and natural philosopher Bernardino Montaña de Monserrate (c. 1480–1588) explains the degenerative process of the state-as-body as the result of discrete parts or subsystems interrupting their cooperation for the well-being of the community: "The fortification was well founded, but aged with the passing of time, and in that manner, it began to incline a little, and the stove lost its heat, and the stoker could not produce enough heat for the chambers, and everybody in the fortification died; because of the cold the scullions quitted their place and the cook did everything wrong. The chef lost his sense of smell and the servant stopped serving: and finally, everybody in the whole fortification died of starvation, the watchtower lost its sense of touch and the mayor lost all judgment, the butlers became thin and could not open the door, so the fortification was bound to be ruined" (*Libro de la anathomia del hombre* [1551], fol. 78, translated and quoted in Josep Lluís Barona, "The Body Republic: Social Order and Human Body in Renaissance Medical Thought," *History and Philosophy of the Life Sciences* 15, no. 2 (1993): 172.

7. My sources for this excursus are: Victor Cornelius Medvei, *A History of Endocrinology* (Lancaster, U.K.: MTP Press, 1982), and Thomas Schlich, *The Origins of Organ Transplantation: Surgery and Laboratory Science 1880–1930* (Rochester, NY: University of Rochester Press, 2010).

8. At that time, physicians knew that some bodily glands have a double function: they excrete chemical substances through special ducts leading into other organs (as the pancreas does into the intestine), and at the same time they have islands or groups of different cells that produce special chemical messengers such as insulin, which is discharged directly into the blood and regulates sugar metabolism. Back in 1855, Claude Bernard first used the expression "internal secretion" in a lecture and mentioned that the liver yields an external secretion in the form of bile and an internal one of sugar, which passes directly into the general circulation.

9. Among others, the German chemist Eugen Baumann (1846–1896) was able to prove that thyroxine and iodine were active components in the thyroid gland. Today we know that thyroid hormones regulate kidney activity, cardiac function,

4. TIME, AGENCY, AND BODILY GLANDS

ventilation, as well as the breakdown of fats, proteins, and carbohydrates; they also influence thermoregulation.

10. This role of the hypophysis was somehow redimensioned to that of a concert master when the functions of the hypothalamus were revealed.
11. The names of these two glands are related to their shape or function. The term *thyroid* comes from the Greek θυρεοειδής, meaning "shieldlike" or "shield shaped." In the Galenic corpus, the pituitary gland is called simply "gland" (ἀδήν) and is described as part of a complex secretory system for the expulsion of nasal mucus. For this reason, in the sixteenth century Vesalius translated ἀδήν as *glandula pituitaria*, whereby *glandula* means "small gland" and *pituitaria* comes from *pituita*, "slime." *Hypophysis*, however, is a much more recent word: it appeared in the nineteenth century and is composed of ὑπό (under) and φύειν (to grow). For more etymological information, see Joseph Hyrtl, ed., *Onomatologia Anatomica: Geschichte und Kritik der anatomischen Sprache der Gegenwart* (Vienna: Wilhelm Braumüller und Universitätsbuchhändler, 1880).
12. As Jörgen Nordenström suggests in *The Hunt for the Parathyroids* (Oxford: Wiley-Blackwell 2013), 61, Voronoff also likely inspired Arthur Conan Doyle's short story "The Adventure of the Creeping Man" (1923). Epistolary correspondence between the surgeon and the Italian writer Gabriele D'Annunzio (1863–1938) is found in the latter's archive, as reported in Elda Garetto, "Da Bazarov a Lysenko: Medici e biologi nella letteratura russa tra ottocento e novecento," in *Formula e metafora: Figure di scienziati nelle letterature e culture contemporanee*, ed. Marco Castellari (Milan: Ledizioni, 2014), 33–40.
13. It was only after the 1930s that synthetized hormones replaced transplants of whole glands (such as the spleen and, of course, the thyroid and the pituitary) for therapeutic purposes.
14. For the technical details of Yeats's operation, see Dirk Schultheiss, Joachim Denil, and Uwe Jonas, "Rejuvenation in the Early Twentieth Century," *Andrologia* 29, no. 6 (November–December 1997): 351–55.
15. On Svevo's self-positioning vis-à-vis these new techniques, see Riccardo Cepach, *Guarire dalla cura: Italo Svevo e i medici* (Trieste: Comune di Trieste, Museo Sveviano, 2008), 156.
16. Italo Svevo, *Zeno's Conscience*, trans. W. Weaver (New York: Vintage Books, 2003), 316.
17. Svevo, *Zeno's Conscience*, 317.
18. Among the most prominent studies within this trend, see Mario Lavagetto, *L'impiegato Schmitz e altri saggi su Svevo* (Turin: Einaudi, 1986) and his introduction to the prestigious Meridiani edition of Svevo's work, "Il romanzo oltre la fine del mondo," in Italo Svevo, *Romanzi e "Continuazioni,"* vol. 1 of *Tutte le opere*, ed. Mario Lavagetto (Milan: Mondadori Meridiani, 2004), xiv–xc; Teresa de Lauretis, *La sintassi del desiderio: Struttura e forme del romanzo sveviano* (Ravenna: Longo, 1976); and Mario Fusco, *Italo Svevo: Conscience et réalité* (Paris: Gallimard, 1973).
19. In considerations of the role of the thyroid in Svevo's literary production, the question arises whether and to what extent the Triestine writer and James Joyce ever discussed the poetics of bodily organs. In Joyce's informal description of the chapters of *Ulysses*, he would have each of them governed by a bodily organ (for instance, the kidneys inform the first chapter). Joyce and Svevo famously met in

4. TIME, AGENCY, AND BODILY GLANDS

Trieste in 1907, when the former became the latter's English teacher and helped him promote his literary works in European intellectual circles. We know from Svevo's letters that Joyce was familiar with a few of the short stories that he wrote during his "periodo del silenzio," including "Ombre notturne / Vino generoso," which Joyce read in 1914, according to a letter Svevo wrote to Benjamin Crémieux on March 15, 1927. See Svevo, *Carteggio con James Joyce, Eugenio Montale, Valery Larbaud, Benjamin Crémieux, Marie Anne Comnène, Valerio Jahier*, ed. B. Maier (Milan: Dall'Oglio, 1965), 85. However, it is not clear whether Joyce read "Doctor Menghi's Drug" as well.
20. "Lo specifico del dottor Menghi" appeared in print for the first time in Italo Svevo, *Saggi e pagine sparse*, ed. Umbro Apollonio (Milan: Mondadori, 1954). The autograph is located in the Svevo Museum by the Hortis Library in Trieste.
21. See Medvei, *A History of Endocrinology*, 219.
22. Italo Svevo, "Lo specifico del dottor Menghi," in *Due racconti* (Milan: All'insegna del pesce d'oro, 1967), 44–45. Unless otherwise noted, all translations of non-English material quoted in the chapter and its notes are my own.
23. Svevo, "Lo specifico del dottor Menghi," 46–47.
24. Carl Adolph von Basedow, translated and quoted in Medvei, *A History of Endocrinology*, 245, 251.
25. Svevo, "Lo specifico del dottor Menghi," 47, 48.
26. Svevo, "Lo specifico del dottor Menghi," 48–49.
27. Gerald Prince coined the term *narratee* by modeling it on Roland Barthes's term *narrataire*: "All narration," Prince explains, "whether it is oral or written, whether it recounts real or mythical events, whether it tells a story or relates a simple sequence of actions in time, presupposes not only (at least) one narrator, but also (at least) one narratee, the narratee being someone whom the narrator addresses.... [N]arratees are distinct from real, virtual, or ideal readers.... The narratee can exercise an entire series of functions in a narrative: he constitutes a relay between the narrator and the reader, he helps establish the narrative framework, he serves to characterize the narrator, he emphasizes certain themes, he contributes to the development of the plot, he becomes the spokesman for the moral of the work" ("Notes Toward a Characterization of Fictional Narratees," *Genre* 4 [1971]: 100, 105).
28. Svevo, "Lo specifico del dottor Menghi," 50, my emphasis except in the case of "*per my will.*"
29. Svevo, "Lo specifico del dottor Menghi," 51–52.
30. Bruno Latour, *Reassembling the Social: An Introduction to Actor-Network Theory* (Oxford: Oxford University Press, 2005), 1–17.
31. Haraway, "A Cyborg Manifesto," 152.
32. Svevo, "Lo specifico del dottor Menghi," 42, 53.
33. Svevo, "Lo specifico del dottor Menghi," 73.
34. On the Bolshevik Revolution and biomedical experimentation, see Nikolai Krementsov, *Revolutionary Experiments: The Quest for Immortality in Bolshevik Science and Fiction* (Oxford: Oxford University Press, 2013).
35. Bulgakov's work *A Young Doctor's Notes* (*Zapiski iunogo vracha*, written in the 1920s and first published in a volume in 1963), based on his experience as a newly graduated doctor in a small village hospital in the Smolensk Governorate in

4. TIME, AGENCY, AND BODILY GLANDS

1916–1918, inspired the recent television series *A Young Doctor's Notebook & Other Stories* (released in the United Kingdom in English, 2012–2013). The success of the series attests to the continuing relevance of the physician-writer's observations today in highbrow and lowbrow culture alike.

36. See Mark Adams, "The Soviet Nature–Nurture Debate," in *Science and the Soviet Social Order*, ed. Loren Graham (Cambridge, MA: Harvard University Press, 1990), 94–138. Eric Naiman has emphasized the connection between popular scientific discourse and the social agenda in the 1920s, pointing out that in some cases "hormones emerge as a kind of corporeal proletariat that has thrown off the domination of the brain" (*Sex in Public: The Incarnation of Early Soviet Ideology* [Princeton, NJ: Princeton University Press, 1997], 143), a metaphor that seems to inscribe itself within the century-long tradition of personified organs mentioned in the opening of this chapter. For a discussion of the emergence of modernity in fin-de-siècle Russia through educated people's discourse on sex, see Laura Engelstein, *The Keys to Happiness: Sex and the Search for Modernity in Fin-de-Siècle Russia* (Ithaca, NY: Cornell University Press, 1992).
37. Mikhail Bulgakov, *The Heart of a Dog*, in *The Heart of a Dog and Other Stories*, trans. Kathleen Cook-Horujy and Avril Pyman (Moscow: Raduga, 1990), 432.
38. See Andrei Siniavskii, *Soviet Civilization: A Cultural History* (New York: Arcade, 1990), 114.
39. Leon Trotsky, *Literature and Revolution*, trans. Rose Strunsky (1925; reprint, New York: Russell and Russell, 1957), 254. The making of a "new person" was also part of the fascist project in Italy (as well as of the Nazi agenda in Germany). According to Mussolini, the new fascist man would be a soldier-citizen, "serious, intrepid, tenacious" and characterized by self-discipline and specific physical attributes, which included being slim and in excellent shape. As we have seen in chapter 3 with respect to early Soviet public-health guidelines and the pronounced intervention on citizens' bodies in order to build a stronger state, in Mussolini's Italy, too, the molding of a new fascist Italian and a new fascist lifestyle would lead to the forging of a stronger and long-lasting fascist Italy. Just like in the early Soviet state, everyone in Italy was responsible for reaching this collective goal, and Mussolini called for the unconditional participation of all persons. See Simonetta Falasca-Zamponi, *Fascist Spectacle: Aesthetics of Power in Mussolini's Italy* (Berkeley: University of California Press, 1997), 26, 100–118.
40. For a reading of Bulgakov's work within the context of eugenics, see Yvonne Howell, "Eugenics, Rejuvenation, and Bulgakov's Journey Into the Heart of Dogness," *Slavic Review* 65, no. 3 (August 2006): 544–62.
41. Bulgakov, *The Heart of a Dog*, 365.
42. Traditional readings of Bulgakov's novella tend to follow two major avenues—one emphasizes the anti-Soviet satire embedded in the text (this is especially true for Cold War literary criticism), while the other inscribes Preobrazhenskii within the rich genealogy of scientists who are punished for their hubris (from Dr. Frankenstein on) that literary history offers. See, among others, Ellendea Proffer, *Bulgakov: Life and Work* (Ann Arbor, MI: Ardis, 1984), and Colin Wright, *Mikhail Bulgakov: Life and Interpretation* (Toronto: University of Toronto Press, 1978). Although I am indebted to this body of scholarship, my reading of Bulgakov's novella aims to release additional meanings from the text and the literary epoch

4. TIME, AGENCY, AND BODILY GLANDS

in which it was produced. The foremost scholar of Bulgakov in Russia is Marietta Chudakova, who conducted extensive research in Bulgakov's archives, reconstructed from the author's notebooks parts of the manuscript of *Master and Margarita* that had been lost or damaged, re-created Bulgakov's reading library, and authored the commanding biography *Zhizneopisanie Mikhaila Bulgakova* (Moscow: Kniga, 1988). For a detailed and comprehensive account of Bulgakov's life and literary production, see Boris Sokolov, *Bulgakovskaia entsiklopediia* (Moscow: Lokid, 1996).

43. Bulgakov, *The Heart of a Dog*, 435, 437.
44. Bulgakov, *The Heart of a Dog*, 444–45, my emphasis.
45. Bulgakov, *The Heart of a Dog*, 349–50, ellipses in last sentence in the original.
46. Bulgakov, *The Heart of a Dog*, 372.
47. Bulgakov, *The Heart of a Dog*, 359–60.
48. Bulgakov, *The Heart of a Dog*, 439.
49. Here the translation erroneously has "Chugunov," which I have changed to "Chugunkin," as given elsewhere throughout Bulgakov's text.
50. Bulgakov, *The Heart of a Dog*, 510–11, 513, last ellipsis in the original.
51. Sharikov makes this request by employing an official, bureaucratic expression, one that Preobrazhenskii and Bormental have never heard before from him: "blagovolite," which the translators, Kathleen Cook-Horujy and Avril Pyman, render as "with your kind permission" (Bulgakov, *The Heart of a Dog*, 498) but that is a closer equivalent to "please oblige." In *Language and Society* (*Iazyk i obshchestvo*), the linguist Nikolai Marr (1864–1934) claimed that language, like any other superstructure, mirrors class consciousness (*Iazyk i obshchestvo*, vol. 3 of *Izbrannye raboty* [Leningrad: GAIMK, 1934]). In Bulgakov's text, Preobrazhenskii is extremely articulate and well read, whereas the accommodation committee members speak a dry language that is a mix of bureaucratic jargon and quotes from canonical works of socialism, and Sharikov constantly curses but uses bureaucratic lexicon when he wants to sound authoritative. Mikhail Bakhtin showed instead how language, inherently dialogic, can be subversive in its reversing of social hierarchies, and the phenomenon of the dog-man speaking the language of bureaucrats only in specific situations could be read in this light.
52. Bulgakov, *The Heart of a Dog*, 432.
53. John Bellamy Foster, *Marx's Ecology: Materialism and Nature* (New York: Monthly Review Press, 2000), 141, quoting Karl Marx, *Capital*, vol. 1, trans. Ben Fowkes (New York: Vintage, 1976), 283, and *Capital*, vol. 3, trans. David Fernbach (New York: Vintage, 1981), 949–50, 959. See also John Bellamy Foster, Brett Clark, and Richard York, *Ecological Rift: Capitalism's War on the Earth* (New York: Monthly Review Press, 2010), 159. It was specifically Justus von Liebig's book *Chemistry in Its Application to Agriculture and Physiology* (*Die organische Chemie in ihrer Anwendung auf Agricultur und Physiologie*, 1840) that provided Marx with the notion that the soil could be "depleted."
54. Marx's argument regarding an "earthly metabolism" and a "metabolic rift" has entered recent debates on the Anthropocene—the name that Paul J. Crutzen and Eugene F. Stoermer have assigned to the current geological epoch, which is characterized by "the central role of mankind in geology and ecology" ("The 'Anthropocene,'" *IGPB Newsletter* 41 [2000]: 17). Will Steffen's question on whether

Earth's system can metabolize the carbon dioxide in the atmosphere draws on this "ecological" side of Marx's *Capital* ("An Integrated Approach to Understanding Earth's Metabolism," *IGPB Newsletter* 41 [2000]: 9–10). McKenzie Wark's rereading of Alexander Bogdanov and Andrei Platonov in *Molecular Red: A Theory for the Anthropocene* (New York: Verso, 2015) brings together the social and the ecological strands of Marx's work effectively and within a unified theoretical frame.

55. The concept of nature as a blind force, an organism characterized by processes that resemble our own but are independent of human will, has deep roots in Russian culture. Among others, Nikolai Fëdorov (1829–1903) investigated natural catastrophes and severe weather in his reflections on humankind and agency in the second half of the nineteenth century. On environmental studies in the field of Russian literature, see Alec Brookes and Elena Fratto, eds., "Anthropocene and Russian Literature," special issue of *Russian Literature* 114–15 (June–July 2020).

56. Arjun Appadurai, ed., *The Social Life of Things* (Cambridge: Cambridge University Press, 1986); Lorraine Daston, ed., *Biographies of Scientific Objects* (Chicago: University of Chicago Press, 2000); Turkle, *The Inner History of Devices*.

57. Sergei Tret'iakov, "The Biography of the Object," *October* 118 (Fall 2006): 61–62, originally published as "Biografiia veshchi," in *Literatura fakta*, ed. Nikolai Chuzhak (Moscow: Federatsiia, 1929), 66–70.

58. Tret'iakov, "The Biography of the Object," 59.

AFTERWORD

1. Frank Kermode, *The Sense of an Ending: Studies in the Theory of Fiction* (Oxford: Oxford University Press, 1967), 8.

2. Historians of medicine have pointed to collective authorship as a distinguishing trait of epidemics. Among them, Charles Rosenberg compares the construction of epidemic narratives to dramaturgy when he states: "Thus, as a social phenomenon, an epidemic has a dramaturgic form. Epidemics start at a moment in time, proceed on a stage limited in space and duration, follow a plot line of increasing and revelatory tension, move to a crisis of individual and collective character, then drift toward closure. . . . For the social scientist, . . . [e]pidemics constitute a transverse section through society, reflecting in that cross-sectional perspective a particular configuration of institutional forms and cultural assumptions. Just as a playwright chooses a theme and manages plot development, so a particular society constructs its characteristic response to an epidemic" ("What Is an Epidemic? AIDS in Historical Perspective," *Daedalus* 118, no. 2 [Spring 1989]: 2). Moreover, in his extensive study on epidemics, the historian of medicine Frank Snowden argues that "epidemic diseases are not random events that afflict societies capriciously and without warning. On the contrary, every society produces its own specific vulnerabilities. To study them is to understand that society's structure, its standard of living, and its political priorities" (*Epidemics and Societies: From the Black Death to the Present* [New Haven, CT: Yale University Press, 2019], 7). Literary history certainly abounds in depictions of epidemics that have been deemed relevant to the current times, from Giovanni Boccaccio's *Decameron*

AFTERWORD

(1353) to Daniel Defoe's *Journal of the Plague Year* (1722) to Albert Camus's *The Plague* (*La peste*, 1947). A novel that has had particular resonance during the COVID-19 pandemic is Thomas Mann's *Death in Venice* (*Der Tod in Venedig*, 1912), in which the authorities deny and hide the outbreak of a cholera epidemic.

3. Fëdor Dostoevskii, *Zapiski iz podpol'ia*, in *Povesti i rasskazy, 1862–66; Igrok: Roman*, vol. 5 of *Polnoe sobranie sochinenii*, ed. V. G. Bazanov (Leningrad: Nauka, 1973), 99. The formalist critic Yuri Tynianov maintained that, along with childhood, illness is "the most convenient springboard to catapult yourself right to the object [*veshch'*] and awaken it" (Iurii Tynianov, "Promezhutok" [1924], in *Poetika. Istoriia literatury. Kino* [Moscow: Nauka, 1977], 184). That concept resonates with Viktor Shklovskii's definition of *ostranenie* as the process through which art neutralizes the automatism of perception and makes us see things anew.

BIBLIOGRAPHY

Adams, Mark B. "The Soviet Nature-Nurture Debate." In *Science and the Soviet Social Order*, ed. Loren R. Graham, 94–138. Cambridge, MA: Harvard University Press, 1990.
Alaniz, José. "'People Endure': The Function of Autism in *Anton's Right Here* (2012)." In *Cultures of Representation: Disability in World Cinema Contexts*, ed. Benjamin Fraser, 110–25. London: Wallflower, 2016.
Alexandrov, Vladimir. *Limits to Interpretation: The Meanings of Anna Karenina*. Madison: University of Wisconsin Press, 2004.
Allen, Elizabeth Cheresh, and Gary Saul Morson, eds. *Freedom and Responsibility in Russian Literature: Essays in Honor of Robert Louis Jackson*. Evanston, IL: Northwestern University Press, 1995.
Althusser, Louis. "Ideology and State Apparatuses" (1970). In *Lenin and Philosophy and Other Essays*, trans. Ben Brewster, 127–86. New York: Monthly Review Press, 1971.
Angremy, Annie. Preface to Jules Romains, *Knock, ou Le triomphe de la médecine*, 7–28. Paris: Gallimard, 1993.
Any, Carol J. *Boris Eikhenbaum: Voices of a Russian Formalist*. Stanford, CA: Stanford University Press, 1994.
Appadurai, Arjun, ed. *The Social Life of Things*. Cambridge: Cambridge University Press, 1986.
Ariès, Philippe. *The Hour of Our Death: The Classic History of Western Attitudes Toward Death Over the Last One Thousand Years*. Trans. Helen Weaver. New York: Random House, 1981.
Aristotle. *Rhetoric*. In *The Rhetoric and the Poetics of Aristotle*, trans. W. Rhys Roberts and Ingram Bywater, 19–218. New York: Modern Library, 1954.

BIBLIOGRAPHY

Aronowitz, Robert. *Making Sense of Illness: Science, Society, and Disease.* Cambridge: Cambridge University Press, 1998.
Bakhtin, Mikhail. *The Dialogic Imagination: Four Essays.* Ed. Michael Holquist. Trans. Caryl Emerson and Michael Holquist. Austin: University of Texas Press, 1981.
——. "Response to a Question from the *Novyi Mir* Editorial Staff (1970)." In *Speech Genres and Other Late Essays,* ed. Caryl Emerson and Michael Holquist, 1–7. Austin: University of Texas Press, 1986.
Barona, Josep Lluís. "The Body Republic: Social Order and Human Body in Renaissance Medical Thought." *History and Philosophy of the Life Sciences* 15, no. 2 (1993): 165–80.
Barsht, Konstantin. *Risunki v rukopisiakh Dostoevskogo.* Saint Petersburg: Formika, 1996.
Barvin, V. "Zhiul' Romen: *Knok, ili Torzhestvo meditsiny.*" *Pravda* 161 (July 16, 1926): 6.
Baudrillard, Jean. *The System of Objects.* Trans. James Benedict. New York: Verso, 1968.
Beer, Daniel. *Renovating Russia: The Human Sciences and the Fate of Liberal Modernity, 1880–1930.* Ithaca, NY: Cornell University Press, 2000.
Ben-Ghiat, Ruth. *Fascist Modernities: Italy 1922–1945.* Berkeley: University of California Press, 2001.
Bernard, Claude. *Lectures on the Phenomena Common to Animals and Plants.* Trans. H. E. Hoff, R. Guillemin, and L. Guillemin. Springfield, IL: Charles C. Thomas, 1974.
Bernstein, Frances Lee. *The Dictatorship of Sex: Lifestyle Advice for the Soviet Masses.* DeKalb: Northern Illinois University Press, 2007.
——. "Predstavleniia o zdorov'e v revoliutsionnoi Rossii: Gendernaia politika v plakatakh po polovomu prosveshsheniiu v 1920-e gody." In *Vizual'naia antropologiia: Rezhimy vidimosti pri sotsializme,* ed. Elena Iarskaia-Smirnova and Pavel Romanov, 215–44. Moscow: Variant, 2009.
——. "Prosthetic Manhood in the Soviet Union at the End of World War II." *Osiris* vol. 30, no. 1 (2015): 113–33.
Bernstein, Frances Lee, Christopher Burton, and Dan Healey, eds. *Soviet Medicine: Culture, Practice, and Science.* DeKalb: Northern Illinois University Press, 2010.
Boak, Denis. *Jules Romains.* New York: Twayne, 1974.
Bogost, Ian. *Alien Phenomenology, or What It's Like to Be a Thing.* Minneapolis: University of Minnesota Press, 2012.
Booth, Wayne C. *The Rhetoric of Fiction.* 1961. Reprint. Chicago: University of Chicago Press, 1983.
Boym, Svetlana. *Common Places: Mythologies of Everyday Life.* Cambridge, MA: Harvard University Press, 1994.
Brintlinger, Angela, and Ilya Vinitsky, eds. *Madness and the Mad in Russian Culture.* Toronto: University of Toronto Press, 2007.
Broca, Paul. "Remarks on the Seat of the Faculty of Articulated Language, Following an Observation of Aphemia (Loss of Speech)." Trans. Christopher D. Green. *Bulletin de la société anatomique* 6 (1861): 330–57.
Brookes, Alec, and Elena Fratto, eds. "Anthropocene and Russian Literature." Special issue of *Russian Literature* 114–15 (June–July 2020).
Brooks, Peter. *Reading for the Plot: Design and Intention in Narrative.* Cambridge, MA: Harvard University Press, 1984.

BIBLIOGRAPHY

Brown, Bill. *Other Things*. Chicago: University of Chicago Press, 2015.
——. *A Sense of Things: The Object Matter of American Literature*. Chicago: University of Chicago Press, 2003.
——, ed. "Things." Special issue of *Critical Inquiry* 28, no. 1 (2001).
Bryant, Levi. *The Democracy of Objects*. London: Open Humanities, 2011.
Bulgakov, Mikhail. *The Heart of a Dog*. In *The Heart of a Dog and Other Stories*, trans. Kathleen Cook-Horujy and Avril Pyman, 343–541. Moscow: Raduga, 1990.
——. *Povesti*. Vol. 3 of *Sobranie sochinenii*. Ed. Ellendea Proffer. Ann Arbor, MI: Ardis, 1983.
Burliuk, David, Nikolai Burliuk, Aleksei Kruchënykh, Vasilii Kandinskii, Benedikt Livshits, Vladimir Maiakovskii, and Velimir Khlebnikov. *Poshchëchina obshchestvennomu vkusu*. Moscow: G. L. Kuz'min, 1912.
Canguilhem, Georges. *The Normal and the Pathological*. Trans. Carolyn Fawcett. With an introduction by Michel Foucault. Dordrecht, Netherlands: D. Reidel, 1978.
Casalini, Giulio. "Un ministero per la salute pubblica?" *L'igiene e la vita* 2, no. 9 (1919): 258.
——. "Sia richiesta l'assicurazione contro le malattie." *L'igiene e la vita* 4, no. 11 (1921): 322.
Cassiday, Julie A. *The Enemy on Trial: Early Soviet Courts on Stage and Screen*. DeKalb: Northern Illinois University Press, 2000.
——. "Marble Columns and Jupiter Lights: Theatrical and Cinematic Modeling of Soviet Show Trials in the 1920s." *Slavic and East European Journal* 42, no. 4 (1998): 640–60.
Cepach, Riccardo, ed. *Guarire dalla cura: Italo Svevo e i medici*. Trieste: Comune di Trieste, Museo Sveviano, 2008.
Cesare Lombroso Museum of Criminal Anthropology. *Visitor's Guide*. Turin: Museo di Antropologia Criminale Cesare Lombroso, 2008.
Charon, Rita. *Narrative Medicine: Honoring the Stories of Illness*. Oxford: Oxford University Press, 2006.
Chekhov, Anton. *Letters of Anton Chekhov to His Family and Friends with Biographical Sketch*. Trans. Constance Garnett. New York: Macmillan, 1920.
——. "Sluchai iz praktiki." In *Rasskazy: Povesti, 1898–1903*, vol. 10 of *Sochineniia*, 18 vols. of *Polnoe sobranie sochinenii i pisem*, ed. N. F. Bel'chikov, 75–85. Moscow: Nauka, 1977.
——. *Sochineniia*. 18 vols. of *Polnoe sobranie sochinenii i pisem*. Ed. N. F. Bel'chikov. Moscow: Nauka, 1974–1982.
——. *Ward No. 6*. In *Chekhov's Doctors: A Collection of Chekhov's Medical Tales*, ed. John L. Coulehan, with a foreword by Robert Coles, 91–134. Kent, OH: Kent State University Press, 2003.
Chizh, Vladimir Fëdorovich. *Bolezn' Gogolia: Zapiski psikhiatra*. Ed. N. T. Unaniants. Moscow: Respublika, 2001.
Chudakova, Marietta. *Zhizneopisanie Mikhaila Bulgakova*. Moscow: Kniga, 1988.
Clark, Katerina. *Petersburg, Crucible of Cultural Revolution*. Cambridge, MA: Harvard University Press, 1995.
Clark, Toby. "The 'New Man's' Body: A Motif in Early Soviet Culture." In *Art of the Soviets: Painting, Sculpture, and Architecture in a One-Party State, 1917–1922*, ed.

Matthew Cullerne Brown and Brandon Taylor, 33–50. Manchester, U.K.: Manchester University Press, 1993.

Coles, Robert. Foreword to Anton Chekhov, *Chekhov's Doctors: A Collection of Chekhov's Medical Tales*, ed. Jack Coulehan, ix–xii. Kent, OH: Kent State University Press, 2003.

Conan Doyle, Arthur. "The Adventures of a Scandal in Bohemia." In *The Adventures of Sherlock Holmes*, 1–29. London: George Newnes, 1901.

Conroy, Mary Schaeffer. *In Health and Sickness: Pharmacy, Pharmacists, and the Pharmaceutical Industry in Late Imperial, Early Soviet Russia*. Boulder, CO: East European Monographs, 1994.

———. *The Soviet Pharmaceutical Business During the First Two Decades (1917–1937)*. New York: Peter Lang, 2006.

Cosmacini, Giorgio. *Storia della medicina e della sanità in Italia dalla peste nera ai giorni nostri*. Bari, Italy: Laterza, 2005.

Crutzen, Paul J., and Eugene F. Stoermer. "The 'Anthropocene.'" *IGPB Newsletter* 41 (2000): 17–18.

Daston, Lorraine, ed. *Biographies of Scientific Objects*. Chicago: University of Chicago Press, 2000.

De Lauretis, Teresa. *La sintassi del desiderio: Struttura e forme del romanzo sveviano*. Ravenna: Longo, 1976.

Dilthey, Wilhelm. *Introduction to the Human Sciences*. Princeton, NJ: Princeton University Press, 1991.

Dostoevskii, Fëdor. *Brat'ia Karamazovy*. Vols. 14–15 of *Polnoe sobranie sochinenii*. Ed. V. G. Bazanov. Leningrad: Nauka, 1975–1976.

———. *Idiot*. Vol. 8 of *Polnoe sobranie sochinenii*. Edited by V. G. Bazanov. Leningrad: Nauka, 1973.

———. *Polnoe sobranie sochinenii*. 30 vols. Edited by V. G. Bazanov. Leningrad: Nauka, 1972–1990.

———. *Prestuplenie i nakazanie*. Vol. 6 of *Polnoe sobranie sochinenii*. Edited by V. G. Bazanov. Leningrad: Nauka, 1973.

———. *Zapiski iz podpol'ia*. In *Povesti i rasskazy, 1862–66; Igrok: Roman*, vol. 5 of *Polnoe sobranie sochinenii*, ed. V. G. Bazanov, 99–179. Leningrad: Nauka, 1973

Dostoevsky, Fyodor. *The Brothers Karamazov*. 2nd ed. Ed. Susan McReynolds Oddo. Trans. Constance Garnett, revised by Ralph E. Matlaw. New York: Norton, 2011.

———. *Crime and Punishment*. Trans. Jessie Coulson. Ed. George Gibian. New York: Norton, 1964.

———. *The Idiot*. Trans. David McDuff. With an introduction by William Mills Todd III. London: Penguin, 2004.

———. *The Notebooks for "Crime and Punishment."* Ed. and trans. Edward Wasiolek. Chicago: University of Chicago Press, 1967.

———. *Notes from Underground*. 2nd Norton Critical Edition. Ed. and trans. Michael R. Katz. New York: Norton, 2000.

Dumit, Joseph. *Drugs for Life: How Pharmaceutical Companies Define Our Health*. Durham, NC: Duke University Press, 2012.

———. "Inter-pill-ation and the Instrumentalization of Compliance." *Anthropology and Medicine* 17, no. 2 (2010): 245–47.

———. "Prescription Maximization and the Accumulation of Surplus Health in the Pharmaceutical Industry: The _BioMarx_ Experiment." In *Lively Capital: Biotechnologies, Ethics, and Governance in Global Markets*, ed. Kaushik Sunder Rajan, 45–92. Durham, NC: Duke University Press, 2012.

Eco, Umberto. *The Role of the Reader: Explorations in the Semiotics of Texts*. Bloomington: Indiana University Press, 1979.

Eikhenbaum, Boris. *Lev Tolstoi: Piatidesiatye gody*. Leningrad: Priboi, 1928.

———. *Lev Tolstoi: Semidesiatye gody*. Leningrad: Sovetskii pisatel', 1960.

———. *Literatura: Teoriia, kritika, polemika*. Leningrad: Priboi, 1927.

———. *Moi vremennik: Khudozhestvennaia proza i izbrannye stat'i 20–30kh godov*. Saint Petersburg: Inapress, 2001.

———. *Molodoi Tolstoi*. Petrograd: Grzhebin, 1922.

———. *O. Henry and the Theory of the Short Story*. Trans. I. R. Titunik. Ann Arbor: University of Michigan Press, 1968.

Eikhenbaum, Ol'ga. "Iz vospominanii O. B. Eikhenbaum." In Boris Eikhenbaum, *Moi vremennik: Khudozhestvennaia proza i izbrannye stat'i 20–30kh godov*, 618–45. Saint Petersburg: Inapress, 2001.

Emerson, Caryl. "The Tolstoy Connection in Bakhtin." In *Rethinking Bakhtin: Extensions and Challenges*, ed. Gary Saul Morson and Caryl Emerson, 149–72. Evanston, IL: Northwestern University Press, 1989.

Enders, Giulia. *Gut: The Inside Story of Our Body's Most Underrated Organ*. Vancouver: Greystone Books, 2015.

Engelstein, Laura. *The Keys to Happiness: Sex and the Search for Modernity in Fin-de-Siècle Russia*. Ithaca, NY: Cornell University Press, 1992.

Erlich, Victor. *Russian Formalism: History, Doctrine*. The Hague: Mouton, 1955.

Etkind, Alexander. *Eros of the Impossible: The History of Psychoanalysis in Russia*. Boulder, CO: Westview, 1997.

Falasca-Zamponi, Simonetta. *Fascist Spectacle: Aesthetics of Power in Mussolini's Italy*. Berkeley: University of California Press, 1997.

Faust, Drew Gilpin. *This Republic of Suffering: Death and the American Civil War*. New York: Knopf, 2008.

Fielding, Henry. *The History of Tom Jones, a Foundling*. 1749. Reprint. London: Dent & Sons and Dutton, 1922.

Finke, Michael. *Seeing Chekhov: Life and Art*. Ithaca, NY: Cornell University Press, 2005.

Fish, Stanley. *Is There a Text in This Class?* Cambridge, MA: Harvard University Press, 1980.

Foster, John Bellamy. *Marx's Ecology: Materialism and Nature*. New York: Monthly Review Press, 2000.

Foster, John Bellamy, Brett Clark, and Richard York. *Ecological Rift: Capitalism's War on the Earth*. New York: Monthly Review Press, 2010.

Foucault, Michel. *The Birth of the Clinic: An Archaeology of Medical Perception*. Trans. A. M. Sheridan-Smith. New York: Pantheon, 1973.

———. *Discipline and Punish: The Birth of the Prison*. Trans. Alan Sheridan. New York: Vintage, 1979.

———. *An Introduction*. Vol. 1 of *The History of Sexuality*. Trans. Robert Hurley. New York: Vintage, 1980.

———. *The Order of Things: An Archaeology of Human Sciences.* New York: Pantheon, 1971.
———. *Society Must Be Defended: Lectures at the Collège de France.* Trans. David Macey. New York: Picador, 2003.
Fratto, Elena. "Meditsinskaia praktika kak siuzhetoslozhenie: Interpretatsiia bolezni Ivana Il'icha." In *Lev Tolstoi i mirovaia literatura: Materialy IX mezhdunarodnoi nauchnoi konferentsii, prokhodivshei v Iasnoi Poliane v 10–15 avgusta 2014 g.*, ed. Galina Alekseeva, 207–15. Tula, Russia: Muzei-Usad'ba L. N. Tolstogo "Iasnaia Poliana," 2016.
———, ed. "Narrative and Medicine." Special issue of *Enthymema* 16 (2016).
Frid, Ia. "Chetyre tomika epopei." *Literaturnyi kritik* 2 (1933): 176–79.
Frieden, Nancy. *Russian Physicians in an Era of Reform and Revolution.* Princeton, NJ: Princeton University Press, 1981.
Fusco, Mario. *Italo Svevo: Conscience et réalité.* Paris: Gallimard, 1973.
Gal'perina, E. "Zhiul' Romen." In *Literaturnaia entsiklopediia*, vol. 10, 41–44. Moscow: Khudozhestvennaia literatura, 1937.
Garetto, Elda. "Da Bazarov a Lysenko: Medici e biologi nella letteratura russa tra ottocento e novecento." In *Formula e metafora: Figure di scienziati nelle letterature e culture contemporanee*, ed. Marco Castellari, 33–40. Milan: Ledizioni, 2014.
Gastev, Aleksei. *Iunost', idi!* Moscow: VTsSPS, 1923.
Gawande, Atul. *Being Mortal: Illness, Medicine, and What Matters in the End.* London: Picador, 2014.
Genette, Gérard. *Palimpsestes: La littérature au second degré.* Paris: Seuil, 1982.
Gerovitch, Slava. "Love-Hate for Man-Machine Metaphors in Soviet Physiology: From Pavlov to 'Physiological Cybernetics.'" *Science in Context* 15 (2002): 339–74.
Gessen, Masha. *Blood Matters: From Inherited Illness to Designer Babies, How the World and I Found Ourselves in the Future of the Gene.* New York: Harcourt, 2008.
Ginzburg, Carlo. "Clues: Roots of an Evidential Paradigm." In *Clues, Myths, and the Historical Method*, trans. John Tedeschi and Anne C. Tedeschi, 96–125. Baltimore, MD: Johns Hopkins University Press, 1989.
Goll, August. *Criminals Types in Shakespeare.* Trans. C. Hagee. Groningen, Netherlands: Wolters, 1908.
Good, Byron. *Medicine, Rationality, and Experience: An Anthropological Perspective.* Cambridge, MA: Harvard University Press, 1993.
Good, Mary-Jo DelVecchio, Tseunetsugu Munakata, Yasuki Kobayashi, Cheryl Mattingly, and Byron J. Good. "Oncology and Narrative Time." *Social Science and Medicine* 38, no. 6 (1994): 855–62.
Gould, Stephen Jay. *The Mismeasure of Man.* New York: Norton, 1981.
Graham, Loren, ed. *Science and the Soviet Social Order.* Cambridge, MA: Harvard University Press, 1990.
Greene, Jeremy A. *Prescribing by Numbers.* Baltimore, MD: Johns Hopkins University Press, 2007.
Greenslit, Nathan. "Depression and Consumption: Psychopharmaceuticals, Branding, and New Identity Practices." *Culture, Medicine, and Psychiatry* 29 (2005): 477–501.
Groys, Boris. *The Total Art of Stalinism: Avant-Garde, Aesthetic Dictatorship, and Beyond.* Princeton, NJ: Princeton University Press, 1992.

BIBLIOGRAPHY

Haddon, Mark. *The Curious Incident of the Dog in the Night-Time*. London: Jonathan Cape, 2003.
Hansen-Löve, Aage. "Le formalisme russe." In *Le XXe siècle: La révolution et les années vingt*, vol. 3 of *Histoire de la littérature russe*, ed. Efim Etkind, Georges Nivat, Ilya Serman, and Vittorio Strada, 618–55. Paris: Fayard, 1988.
Haraway, Donna. "A Cyborg Manifesto: Science, Technology, and Socialist-Feminism in the Late Twentieth Century." In *Simians, Cyborgs, and Women: The Reinvention of Nature*, 149–81. New York: Routledge, 1991.
———. *When Species Meet*. Minneapolis: University of Minnesota Press, 2007.
Harman, Graham. *Tool-Being: Heidegger and the Metaphysics of Objects*. Peru, IL: Open Court, 2002.
Harrington, Anne. "Beyond Phrenology: Localization Theory in the Modern Era." In *The Enchanted Loom: Chapters in the History of Neuroscience*, ed. Pietro Corsi, 207–39. New York: Oxford University Press, 1991.
———. "Kurt Goldstein's Neurology of Healing and Wholeness: A Weimar Story." In *Greater Than the Parts: Holism in Biomedicine, 1920–1950*, ed. Christopher Lawrence and George Weisz, 25–45. New York: Oxford University Press, 1998.
Hartblay, Cassandra. "After Marginalization: Pixelization, Disability, and Social Difference in Digital Russia." *South Atlantic Quarterly* 118, no. 3 (2019): 543–72.
Hennequin, Émile. *Études de critique scientifique: Écrivains francisés: Dickens, Heine, Tourguénef, Poe, Dostoïewski, Tolstoï*. Paris: Perrin et Cie, 1889.
Herman, David. *Storytelling and the Sciences of Mind*. Cambridge, MA: MIT Press, 2013.
Holmes, Edward. *The Life of Mozart, Including His Correspondence*. New York: Harper, 1854.
Holquist, Peter. "'Information Is the Alpha and Omega of Our Work': Bolshevik Surveillance in Its Pan-European Context." *Journal of Modern History* 69, no. 3 (1997): 415–50.
———. *Making War, Forging Revolution: Russia's Continuum of Crisis, 1914–1921*. Cambridge, MA: Harvard University Press, 2002.
Horn, David. *Social Bodies*. Princeton, NJ: Princeton University Press, 1994.
Howell, Yvonne. "Eugenics, Rejuvenation, and Bulgakov's Journey Into the Heart of Dogness." *Slavic Review* 65, no. 3 (August 2006): 544–62.
Hyrtl, Joseph, ed. *Onomatologia Anatomica: Geschichte und Kritik der anatomischen Sprache der Gegenwart*. Vienna: Wilhelm Braumüller und Universitätsbuchhändler, 1880.
Ianovskii, Stepan D. "Vospominaniia o Dostoevskom." In *Dostoevskii v vospominaniiakh sovremennikov*, 2 vols., ed. Konstantin Tiun'kin, 230–51. Moscow: Khudozhestvennaia literatura, 1990.
Iarskaia-Smirnova, Elena, and Pavel Romanov, eds. *Vizual'naia antropologiia: Rezhimy vidimosti pri sotsializme*. Moscow: Variant, 2009.
Ingarden, Roman. *The Literary Work of Art*. Evanston, IL: Northwestern University Press, 1973.
Iser, Wolfgang. *The Implied Reader: Patterns of Communication in Prose from Bunyan to Beckett*. Baltimore, MD: Johns Hopkins University Press, 1978.
Iushkov, P. D. *Babka lechit—narod kalechit: Sanitarnaia komediia v 4-kh epizodakh*. Perm, Russia: Permskii Sanprosvet, 1927.

Jackson, Robert Louis. "Chance and Design in *Anna Karenina*." In *The Disciplines of Criticism*, ed. Peter Demetz, Thomas Greene, and Lowry Nelson Jr., 315–29. New Haven, CT: Yale University Press, 1968.
———. "Text and Subtext in the Opening and Closing Lines of *The Death of Ivan Ilych*, or Phonetic Orchestration in the Semantic Development of the Story." *Tolstoy Studies Journal* 9 (1997): 11–25.
Jacyna, L. S. *Lost Words: Narratives of Language and the Brain, 1825–1926*. Princeton, NJ: Princeton University Press, 2000.
Jahn, Gary R. *"The Death of Ivan Ilich": An Interpretation*. New York: Twayne, 1993.
———, ed. *Tolstoy's "Death of Ivan Il'ich": A Critical Companion*. Evanston, IL: Northwestern University Press, 1999.
Jakobson, Roman. "Boris Mikhailovich Eikhenbaum." *International Journal of Slavic Linguistics and Poetics* 6 (1963): 160–67.
Jurecic, Ann. *Illness as Narrative*. Pittsburgh, PA: University of Pittsburgh Press, 2012.
Kaganovsky, Lilya. *How the Soviet Man Was Unmade*. Pittsburgh, PA: University of Pittsburgh Press, 2008.
Kalanithi, Paul. *When Breath Becomes Air*. New York: Random House, 2016.
Kaufman, Andrew. *Understanding Tolstoy*. Columbus: Ohio University Press, 2011.
Kayiatos, Anastasia. "'Sooner Speaking Than Silent, Sooner Silent Than Mute': Soviet Deaf Theatre and Pantomime After Stalin." *Theatre Survey* 51, no. 1 (2010): 5–31.
Kelleter, Frank, ed. *Media of Serial Narrative*. Columbus: Ohio University Press, 2017.
Kelly, Catriona. *Refining Russia: Advice Literature, Polite Culture, and Gender from Catherine to Yeltsin*. New York: Oxford University Press, 2001.
———. "Shaping the 'Future Race': Regulating the Daily Life of Children in Early Soviet Russia." In *Everyday Life in Early Soviet Russia: Taking the Revolution Inside*, ed. Christina Kiaer and Eric Naiman, 256–81. Bloomington: Indiana University Press, 2005.
Kelly, Catriona, and David Shepherd, eds. *Constructing Russian Culture in the Age of Revolution, 1881–1940*. Oxford: Oxford University Press, 1998.
Kermode, Frank. *The Sense of an Ending: Studies in the Theory of Fiction*. Oxford: Oxford University Press, 1967.
Kleinman, Arthur. "Caregiving as Moral Experience." *Lancet* 380, no. 9853 (November 3, 2012): 1550–551.
———. *The Illness Narratives: Suffering, Healing, and the Human Condition*. New York: Basic, 1988.
Knapp, Liza. "Language and Death in Tolstoy's *Childhood* and *Boyhood*: Rousseau and the Holy Fool." *Tolstoy Studies Journal* 10 (1998): 50–62.
———. "'Tue-la! Tue-le!': Death Sentences, Words, and Inner Monologue in Tolstoy's *Anna Karenina* and 'Three More Deaths.'" *Tolstoy Studies Journal* 11 (January 1, 1999): 1–19.
Koenker, Diane P. *Club Red: Vacation Travel and the Soviet Dream*. Ithaca, NY: Cornell University Press, 2013.
Kotkin, Stephen. *Magnetic Mountain: Stalinism as a Civilization*. Berkeley: University of California Press, 1997.
Krementsov, Nikolai. *Revolutionary Experiments: The Quest for Immortality in Bolshevik Science and Fiction*. Oxford: Oxford University Press, 2013.
Landa, Robin. *Designing Brand Experiences*. New York: Thomson Delmar, 2006.

BIBLIOGRAPHY

Laqueur, Thomas W. "Bodies, Detail, and the Humanitarian Narrative." In *The New Cultural History*, ed. Lynn Hunt, 176–205. Berkeley: University of California Press, 1989.
Latour, Bruno. *Reassembling the Social: An Introduction to Actor-Network Theory*. Oxford: Oxford University Press, 2005.
Lavagetto, Mario. *L'impiegato Schmitz e altri saggi su Svevo*. Turin: Einaudi, 1986.
———. "Il romanzo oltre la fine del mondo." In Italo Svevo, *Romanzi e "Continuazioni,"* vol. 1 of *Tutte le opere*, ed. Mario Lavagetto, xiv–xc. Milan: Mondadori Meridiani, 2004.
Lenin, Vladimir. *Collected Works*. Vol. 30: *September 1919–April 1920*. 4th English ed. Moscow: Progress, 1961.
Livy. *History of Rome*. Vol. 1. Ed. and trans. B. O. Foster. Cambridge, MA: Harvard University Press, 1919.
Lock, Margaret. "Inventing a New Death and Making It Believable." *Anthropology and Medicine* 9 (2002): 97–115.
Lombroso, Cesare. "Atavism and Evolution." *Contemporary Review* 68 (1895): 42–49.
———. "'La Bête Humaine' and Criminal Anthropology." In *The Criminal Anthropological Writings of Cesare Lombroso Published in the English Language Periodical Literature During the Late 19th and Early 20th Centuries*, ed. David M. Horton and Katherine E. Rich, 1–25. Lewiston, NY: Edwin Mellen Press, 2004.
———. "La bête humaine e l'antropologia criminale." *Fanfulla della domenica*, June 15, 1890.
———. *Criminal Man*. Trans. and with a new introduction by Mary Gibson and Nicole Hahn Rafter. Durham, NC: Duke University Press, 2006.
———. "Discours d'ouverture au VI Congrès d'anthropologie criminelle." In *Comptes rendus du VI Congrès international d'anthropologie criminelle. Turin, 28 April–3 May, 1906*, xxxi–xxxvi. Turin: Fratelli Bocca, 1908.
———. *Genio e follia*. Milan: Giuseppe Chiusi, 1864.
———. "Mein Besuch bei Tolstoi." *Das freie Wort* 1 (1902): 391–97.
———. *Palinsesti del carcere*. Turin: Bocca, 1888.
———. *Più recenti scoperte ed applicazioni della psichiatria ed antropologia criminale*. Turin: Bocca, 1893.
———. *L'uomo delinquente*. 5th ed. 1897. Reprint. Milan: Bompiani, 2013.
———. *L'uomo di genio in rapporto alla psichiatria, alla storia ed all'estetica*. Turin: Bocca, 1888.
Lotman, Yuri. *The Structure of the Artistic Text*. Trans. Gail Lenhof and Ronald Vroon. Ann Arbor: University of Michigan Press, 1977.
———. "The Theater and Theatricality as Components of Early Nineteenth-Century Culture." In Yuri Lotman and Boris Uspenskii, *The Semiotics of Russian Culture*, ed. Ann Shukman. 141–64. Ann Arbor: University of Michigan Press, 1984.
Luria, Alexander. *The Man with a Shattered World: The History of a Brain Wound*. With a foreword by Oliver Sacks. Cambridge, MA: Harvard University Press, 1987.
MacKay, John. *Dziga Vertov: Life and Work*. Vol. 1: *1896–1921*. Boston: Academic Studies, 2018.
Mandelker, Amy. *Framing "Anna Karenina": Tolstoy, the Woman Question, and the Victorian Novel*. Columbus: Ohio University Press, 1993.
Margolin, S. "Zhiul' Romen." *Novyi Mir* 9 (1927): 186–93.

Marr, Nikolai. *Iazyk i obshchestvo*. Vol. 3 of *Izbrannye raboty*. Leningrad: GAIMK, 1934.
Marx, Karl. *Capital*. Vol. 1. Trans. Ben Fowkes. New York: Vintage, 1977.
——. *Capital*. Vol. 3. Trans. David Fernbach. New York: Vintage, 1981.
Mattingly, Cheryl. "Emergent Narratives." In *Narrative and the Cultural Construction of Illness and Healing*, ed. Cheryl Mattingly and Linda Garro, 181–211. Berkeley: University of California Press, 2000.
Mattingly, Cheryl, and Linda Garro, eds. *Narrative and the Cultural Construction of Illness and Healing*. Berkeley: University of California Press, 2000.
Mayer, Emeran. *The Mind–Gut Connection: How the Inner Conversation Within Our Bodies Impacts Our Mood, Our Choices, and Our Overall Health*. New York: Harper Wave, 2016.
McLean, Hugh. *In Quest of Tolstoy*. Boston: Academic Studies, 2008.
Meador, Clifton K. "The Last Well Person." *New England Journal of Medicine* 330, no. 6 (February 10, 1994): 440–41.
Medvei, Victor Cornelius. *A History of Endocrinology*. Lancaster, U.K.: MTP Press, 1982.
Medzhibovskaya, Inessa. *Tolstoy and the Religious Culture of His Time: A Biography of a Long Conversion, 1845–1887*. Lanham, MD: Lexington, 2008.
Merezhkovskii, D. S. "Tolstoy's Physical Descriptions." Trans. Zoreslava Kushner. In Leo Tolstoy, *Anna Karenina*, ed. George Gibian, trans. Louise Maude and Aylmer Maude, 2nd Norton Critical Edition, 769–77. New York: Norton, 1995.
Metzl, Jonathan, and Helena Hansen. "Structural Competency: Theorizing a New Medical Engagement with Stigma and Inequality." *Social Science and Medicine* 103 (February 2014): 126–33.
Miller, Martin A. *Freud and the Bolsheviks: Psychoanalysis in Imperial Russia and the Soviet Union*. New Haven, CT: Yale University Press, 1998.
Mol'kov, Al'fred. "Sanitarnoe prosveshchenie, ego zadachi i metody." *Sotsial'naia gigiena* 1 (1922): 40–42.
Montgomery, Kathryn. *Doctors' Stories: The Narrative Structure of Medical Knowledge*. Princeton, NJ: Princeton University Press, 1991.
Morson, Gary Saul. "Anna Karenina's Omens." In *Freedom and Responsibility in Russian Literature: Essays in Honor of Robert Louis Jackson*, ed. Elizabeth Cheresh Allen and Gary Saul Morson, 134–52. Evanston, IL: Northwestern University Press, 1995.
Murav, Harriet. *Holy Foolishness: Dostoevsky's Novels and the Poetics of Cultural Critique*. Stanford, CA: Stanford University Press, 1992.
Mussolini, Benito. "Discorso dell'Ascensione" (May 26, 1927). In *Opera omnia di Benito Mussolini*, vol. 2, ed. Edoardo Susmel and Duilio Susmel, 360–90. Florence: La Fenice, 1957.
Naiman, Eric. *Sex in Public: The Incarnation of Early Soviet Ideology*. Princeton, NJ: Princeton University Press, 1997.
Nicolosi, Riccardo. *Degeneration Erzählen: Literatur und Psychiatrie im Russland der 1880er und 1890er Jahre*. Paderborn, Germany: Wilhelm Fink, 2017.
Nikolozi, Rikkardo, Konstantin Bogdanov, and Iurii Murashov, eds. *Russkaia literatura i meditsina: Telo, predpisaniia, sotsial'naia praktika*. Moscow: Novoe izdatel'stvo, 2005.
Nordenström, Jörgen. *The Hunt for the Parathyroids*. Oxford: Wiley-Blackwell, 2013.

BIBLIOGRAPHY

Norrish, Peter J. *Drama of the Group: A Study of Unanimism in the Plays of Jules Romains*. Cambridge: Cambridge University Press, 1958.
Olson, Greta. "Reconsidering Unreliability: Fallible and Untrustworthy Narrators." *Narrative* 11 (2003): 93–109.
Orwin, Donna Tussing. *Tolstoy's Art and Thought, 1847–1880*. Princeton, NJ: Princeton University Press, 1993.
Osipov, Maxim. *Rock, Paper, Scissors and Other Stories*. Trans. Boris Dralyuk, Alex Fleming, and Anne Marie Jackson. New York: New York Review of Books, 2019.
Paperno, Irina. "'Who, What Is I?': Tolstoy in His Diaries." *Tolstoy Studies Journal* 11 (January 1, 1999): 32–54.
Parthé, Kathleen. "Death Masks in Tolstoy." *Slavic Review* 2, no. 41 (Summer 1982): 297–305.
———. "The Metamorphosis of Death in Tolstoy." *Language and Style* 18 (1985): 205–14.
Pertsov, V. "Potolok lichnosti." *Krasnaia nov'* 1 (1934): 170–80.
Phelan, James. "Estranging Unreliability, Bonding Unreliability, and the Ethics of *Lolita*." *Narrative* 15 (2007): 222–38.
Phillips, Sarah D. "'There Are No Invalids in the USSR!': A Missing Soviet Chapter in the New Disability History." *Disability Studies Quarterly* 29, no. 3 (2009). https://dsq-sds.org/article/view/936.
Pollock, Anne. "The Internal Cardiac Defibrillator." In *The Inner History of Devices*, ed. Sherry Turkle, 98–111. Cambridge, MA: MIT Press, 2008.
Popkin, Cathy. "Hysterical Episodes: Case Histories and Silent Subjects." In *Self and Story in Russian History*, ed. Laura Engelstein and Stephanie Sandler, 189–216. Ithaca, NY: Cornell University Press, 2000.
Prince, Gerald. "Notes Toward a Characterization of Fictional Narratees." *Genre* 4 (1971): 100–105.
Proffer, Ellendea. *Bulgakov: Life and Work*. Ann Arbor, MI: Ardis, 1984.
Reich, Rebecca. *State of Madness: Psychiatry, Literature, and Dissent After Stalin*. DeKalb: Northern Illinois University Press, 2018.
Rice, James L. *Dostoevsky and the Healing Art: An Essay in Literary and Medical History*. Ann Arbor, MI: Ardis, 1985.
Ricoeur, Paul. *Hermeneutics and the Human Sciences*. Cambridge: Cambridge University Press, 1981.
———. *Time and Narrative*. Vol. 1. Chicago: University of Chicago Press, 1984.
Romains, Jules. *Donogoo-Tonka, ou Les miracles de la science*. Paris: Nouvelle revue française, 1920.
———. *Knock, ou Le triomphe de la médecine*. Paris: Gallimard, 1993.
———. "Pourquoi j'ai écrit *Donogoo*." *Revue de Paris*, November 1951, 3–4.
Romen, Zhiul'. *Knok, ili Torzhestvo meditsiny*. Vol. 7 of *Sobranie sochinenii*. Leningrad: Academia, 1926.
Rosenberg, Charles. "The Tyranny of Diagnosis: Specific Entities and Individual Experience." *Milbank Quarterly* 80, no. 2 (June 2002): 237–60.
———. "What Is an Epidemic? AIDS in Historical Perspective." *Daedalus* 118, no. 2 (Spring 1989): 1–17.
Rudnitsky, Konstantin. *Russian and Soviet Theater: Tradition and the Avant-Garde*. London: Thames and Hudson, 1988.

Ryan, Marie-Laure. *Possible Worlds, Artificial Intelligence, and Narrative Theory.* Bloomington: University of Indiana Press, 1991.
Sacks, Oliver. *An Anthropologist on Mars: Seven Paradoxical Tales.* New York: Random House, 1995.
———. *The Man Who Mistook His Wife for a Hat and Other Clinical Tales.* 1985. Reprint. New York: Simon and Schuster, 1998.
Sanghavi, Darshak. "When Does Death Start?" *New York Times Magazine*, December 20, 2009.
Sawday, Jonathan. *The Body Emblazoned: Dissection and the Human Body in Renaissance Culture.* London: Routledge, 1995.
Scarry, Elaine. *The Body in Pain: The Making and Unmaking of the World.* Oxford: Oxford University Press, 1985.
Schlich, Thomas. *The Origins of Organ Transplantation: Surgery and Laboratory Science 1880–1930.* Rochester, NY: University of Rochester Press, 2010.
Schultheiss, Dirk, Joachim Denil, and Uwe Jonas. "Rejuvenation in the Early Twentieth Century." *Andrologia* 29, no. 6 (November–December 1997): 351–55.
Semashko, Nikolai A. *Health Protection in the USSR.* London: Gollancz, 1934.
———. *Nauka o zdorov'e obshchestva: Sotsial'naia gigiena.* 2nd ed. Moscow: Izdatel'stvo Narkomzdrava, 1926.
———. "Politika v dele zdravookhraneniia za desiat' let." In *Desiat' let oktiabria i sovetskoe zdorov'e*, 3–30. Moscow: Izdatel'stvo Narkomzdrava, 1927.
———. "Sotsial'naia gigiena, eë sushchnost', metod i znachenie." *Sotsial'naia gigiena* 1 (1922): 5–11.
———. *Sotsial'nye bolezni i bor'ba s nimi.* Moscow: Voprosy truda, 1926.
Shaw, Claire L. *Deaf in the USSR: Marginality, Community, and Soviet Identity, 1917–1991.* Ithaca, NY: Cornell University Press, 2017.
Shaw, E. A. "The Sensory Side of Aphasia." *Brain* 16, no. 4 (January 1, 1893): 492–514.
Sheldon, Richard. "Viktor Shklovsky and the Device of Ostensible Surrender." *Slavic Review* 34, no. 1 (March 1975): 86–108.
Shklovskii, Viktor. *Khod Konia: Sbornik statei.* Moscow: Gelikon, 1923.
———. *Lev Tolstoi.* 2nd ed. Moscow: Khudozhestvennaia literatura, 1967.
———. "Pamiatnik nauchnoi oshibke." *Literaturnaia gazeta*, no. 4 (January 27, 1930): 1.
———. *Tetiva: O neskhodstve skhodnogo.* Moscow: Sovetskii Pisatel', 1970.
——— [Shklovsky]. *Theory of Prose.* Trans. Benjamin Sher. Elmwood Park, IL: Dalkey Archive, 1990.
Siniavskii, Andrei. *Soviet Civilization: A Cultural History.* New York: Arcade, 1990.
Sironi, Vittorio A. "La nascita dell'industria farmaceutica." In *Il farmaco nei tempi: Dal laboratorio all'industria*, ed. Attilio Zanca, 153–203. Milan: Farmitalia Carlo Erba, 1989.
Sirotkina, Irina. *Diagnosing Literary Genius: A Cultural History of Psychiatry in Russia, 1880–1930.* Baltimore, MD: Johns Hopkins University Press, 2002.
Sloane, David. "Pushkin's Legacy in *Anna Karenina*." *Tolstoy Studies Journal* 4 (1991): 1–23.
Smirnov, Aleksandr. "Predislovie." In Zhiul' Romen, *Knock, ili Torzhestvo meditsiny*, vol. 7 of *Sobranie sochinenii*, 5–6. Leningrad: Academia, 1926.
Snowden, Frank. *Epidemics and Societies: From the Black Death to the Present.* New Haven, CT: Yale University Press, 2019.

BIBLIOGRAPHY

Sobol, Valeria. *Febris Erotica: Lovesickness and the Russian Literary Imagination.* Seattle: University of Washington Press, 2009.
Sokolov, Boris. *Bulgakovskaia entsiklopediia.* Moscow: Lokid, 1996.
Solomon, Susan Gross. "Social Hygiene and Soviet Public Health, 1921–1930." In *Health and Society in Revolutionary Russia,* ed. Susan Gross Solomon and John F. Hutchinson, 175–99. Bloomington: Indiana University Press, 1990.
Solomon, Susan Gross, and John F. Hutchinson, eds. *Health and Society in Revolutionary Russia.* Bloomington: Indiana University Press, 1990.
Sontag, Susan. *Illness as Metaphor; and AIDS and Its Metaphors.* 1990. Reprint. New York: Picador, 2001.
Sophocles. *Philoctetes.* In *Greek Drama (Tragedy),* vol. 2 of *Works: English and Greek,* ed. and trans. Hugh Lloyd-Jones, 253–408. Cambridge, MA: Harvard University Press 1994.
Starks, Tricia. *The Body Soviet: Propaganda, Hygiene, and the Revolutionary State.* Madison: University of Wisconsin Press, 2008.
Starr, M. Allen. "The Pathology of Sensory Aphasia, with an Analysis of Fifty Cases in Which Broca's Centre Was Not Diseased." *Brain* 12 (July 1889): 82–99.
Steffen, Will. "An Integrated Approach to Understanding Earth's Metabolism." *IGPB Newsletter* 41 (2000): 9–10.
Steiner, Evgeny. *Stories for Little Comrades: Revolutionary Artists and the Making of Early Soviet Children's Books.* Seattle: University of Washington Press, 1999.
Steiner, George. *Tolstoy or Dostoevsky: An Essay in the Old Criticism.* New York: Knopf, 1959.
Stites, Richard. *Revolutionary Dreams: Utopian Visions and Experimental Life in the Russian Revolution.* Oxford: Oxford University Press, 1991.
Svevo, Italo. *Carteggio con James Joyce, Eugenio Montale, Valery Larbaud, Benjamin Crémieux, Marie Anne Comnène, Valerio Jahier.* Ed. B. Maier. Milan: Dall'Oglio, 1965.
——. *Romanzi e "Continuazioni."* Vol. 1 of *Tutte le opere.* Ed. Mario Lavagetto. Milan: Mondadori Meridiani, 2004.
——. *Saggi e pagine sparse.* Ed. Umbro Apollonio. Milan: Mondadori, 1954.
——. "Lo specifico del dottor Menghi." In *Due racconti,* 21–77. Milan: All'insegna del pesce d'oro, 1967.
——. *Zeno's Conscience.* Trans. W. Weaver. New York: Vintage Books, 2003.
Tiun'kin, Konstantin, ed. *Dostoevskii v vospominaniiakh sovremennikov.* 2 vols. Moscow: Khudozhestvennaia literatura, 1990.
Todd, William Mills, III. "The Responsibilities of (Co-)Authorship: Notes on Revising the Serialized Version of *Anna Karenina.*" In *Freedom and Responsibility in Russian Literature: Essays in Honor of Robert Louis Jackson,* ed. Elizabeth Cheresh Allen and Gary Saul Morson, 159–69. Evanston, IL: Northwestern University Press, 1995.
——. "V. M. Golitsyn Reads *Anna Karenina*: How One of Karenin's Colleagues Responded to the Novel." In *Reading in Russia: Practices of Reading and Literary Communication, 1760–1930,* ed. Damiano Rebecchini and Raffaella Vassena, 189–200. Milan: Ledizioni, 2014.
Todorov, Tzvetan. "Reading as Construction." In *The Reader in the Text: Essays on Audience and Interpretation,* ed. Susan Suleiman and Inge Crosman, 67–82. Princeton, NJ: Princeton University Press, 1980.

BIBLIOGRAPHY

Toland, Amanda Ewart, Andrea Forman, Fergus J. Couch, Julie O. Culver, Diana M. Eccles, William D. Foulkes, Frans B. L. Hogervorst, Claude Houdayer, Ephrat Levy-Lahad, Alvaro N. Monteiro, et al. "Clinical Testing of BRCA1 and BRCA2: A Worldwide Snapshot of Technological Practices." *npj Genomic Medicine* 3 (February 15, 2018): 1–8.

Tolstoi, Lev. *Anna Karenina*. Vols. 18–19 of *Polnoe sobranie sochinenii*. Ed. V. G. Chertkov. Moscow: Khudozhestvennaia literatura, 1934–1935.

——. *Dnevnik 1847–1854*. Vol. 46 of *Polnoe sobranie sochinenii*. Ed. V. G. Chertkov. Moscow: Khudozhestvennaia literatura, 1937.

——. *Dnevniki i zapisnye knizhki, 1891–94*. Vol. 52 of *Polnoe sobranie sochinenii*. Ed. V. G. Chertkov. Moscow: Khudozhestvennaia literatura, 1952.

——. *Dnevniki i zapisnye knizhki, 1895–1899*. Vol. 53 of *Polnoe sobranie sochinenii*. Ed. V. G. Chertkov. Moscow: Khudozhestvennaia literatura, 1953.

——. *Dnevniki i zapisnye knizhki, 1904–1906*. Vol. 55 of *Polnoe sobranie sochinenii*. Ed. V. G. Chertkov. Moscow: Khudozhestvennaia literatura, 1937.

——. *Dnevniki i zapisnye knizhki, 1909*. Vol. 57 of *Polnoe sobranie sochinenii*. Ed. V. G. Chertkov. Moscow: Khudozhestvennaia literatura, 1952.

——. *Dnevniki i zapisnye knizhki, 1910*. Vol. 58 of *Polnoe sobranie sochinenii*. Ed. V. G. Chertkov. Moscow: Khudozhestvennaia literatura, 1934.

——. *Dnevniki, zapisnye knizhki i otdel'nye zapiski, 1901–1903*. Vol. 54 of *Polnoe sobranie sochinenii*. Ed. V. G. Chertkov. Moscow: Khudozhestvennaia literatura, 1935.

——. *Dnevniki, zapisnye knizhki i otdel'nye zapiski, 1907–1908*. Vol. 56 of *Polnoe sobranie sochinenii*. Ed. V. G. Chertkov. Moscow: Khudozhestvennaia literatura, 1937.

——. *Pis'ma 1873–1879*. Vol. 62 of *Polnoe sobranie sochinenii*. Ed. V. G. Chertkov. Moscow: Khudozhestvennaia literatura, 1953.

——. *Polnoe sobranie sochinenii*. 90 vols. Ed. V. G. Chertkov. Moscow: Khudozhestvennaia literatura, 1928–1958.

——. *Smert' Ivana Il'icha*. In *Proizvedeniia 1895–1899 gg.*, vol. 26 of *Polnoe sobranie sochinenii*, ed. V. G. Chertkov, 60–113. Moscow: Khudozhestvennaia literatura, 1936.

——. *Voskresenie*. Vol. 32 of *Polnoe sobranie sochinenii*. Ed. V. G. Chertkov. Moscow: Khudozhestvennaia literatura, 1936.

Tolstoy, Leo. *Anna Karenina*. Ed. George Gibian. Trans. Louise Maude and Aylmer Maude. 2nd Norton Critical Edition. New York: Norton, 1995.

——. *The Death of Ivan Ilych*. In *Tolstoy's Short Fiction*, ed. and with revised translations by Michael R. Katz, 83–128. 2nd Norton Critical Edition. New York: Norton, 2008.

——. *Resurrection*. Trans. Louise Maude. Oxford: Oxford University Press, 1999.

Tolstoy, Sophia. *The Diaries of Sophia Tolstoy*. Trans. Cathy Porter. New York: Random House, 1985.

Tret'iakov, Sergei. "The Biography of the Object." *October* 118 (Fall 2006): 57–62. Originally published as "Biografiia veshchi," in *Literatura fakta*, ed. Nikolai Chuzhak, 66–70. Moscow: Federatsiia, 1929.

Trotsky, Leon. *Literature and Revolution*. Trans. Rose Strunsky. 1925. Reprint. New York: Russell and Russell, 1957.

Trubetskova, Elena. *"Novoe zrenie": Bolezn' kak priëm ostraneniia v russkoi literature XX veka*. Moscow: Novoe Literaturnoe Obozrenie, 2019.

BIBLIOGRAPHY

Turkle, Sherry, ed. *The Inner History of Devices*. Cambridge, MA: MIT Press, 2008.
Tynianov, Iurii. "Promezhutok" (1924). In *Poetika. Istoriia literatury. Kino*, 168–95. Moscow: Nauka, 1977.
Vaingurt, Julia. *Wonderlands of the Avant-Garde: Technology and the Arts in Russia of the 1920s*. Chicago: Northwestern University Press, 2013.
Vaingurt, Julia, and Colleen McQuillen, eds. *The Human Reimagined: Posthumanism in Russia*. Boston: Academic Studies, 2018.
Vol'kov, Nikolai. "Zhiul' Romen: *Sobranie sochinenii*, Izd. Academia, 1926 g." *Izvestiia* 178 (August 5, 1926): 5.
Vucinich, Alexander. *Science in Russian Culture, 1861–1917*. Stanford, CA: Stanford University Press, 1970.
Wark, McKenzie. *Molecular Red: A Theory for the Anthropocene*. New York: Verso, 2015.
Warner, Elizabeth. "The Quack Doctor in Russian Folk and Popular Theater." *Folklore* 93, no. 2 (1982): 166–75.
Wasiolek, Edward. *Tolstoy's Major Fiction*. Chicago: University of Chicago Press, 1978.
Weir, Justin. *Leo Tolstoy and the Alibi of Narrative*. New Haven, CT: Yale University Press, 2011.
Wernicke, Carl. "The Symptom Complex of Aphasia: A Psychological Study on an Anatomical Basis" (1874). English translation in *Boston Studies in the Philosophy of Science: Proceedings of the Boston Colloquium for the Philosophy of Science*, vol. 4, ed. R. S. Cohen and M. W. Wartowfsky, 34–97. Dortrecht, Netherlands: Reidel, 1966–1968.
White, Hayden. *Metahistory: The Historical Imagination in Nineteenth-Century Europe*. Baltimore, MD: Johns Hopkins University Press, 1973.
——. "The Value of Narrativity in the Representation of Reality." In *On Narrative*, ed. W. J. T. Mitchell, 1–27. Chicago: University of Chicago Press, 1981.
Williams, William Carlos. *The Doctor Stories*. New York: New Directions, 1984.
Wood, Elizabeth A. *Performing Justice: Agitation Trials in Early Soviet Russia*. Ithaca, NY: Cornell University Press, 2005.
The World of Coffee. Oxford: Oxford Cartographers, 1998.
Wright, Colin. *Mikhail Bulgakov: Life and Interpretation*. Toronto: University of Toronto Press, 1978.
Zak, Sofiia. *Boria v ambulatorii*. With illustrations by Vladimir Konashevich. Moscow: Gosizdat, 1928.
Zelinskii, K. "Novyi manifest Zhiulia Romena." *Literaturnyi kritik* 5 (1933): 135–39.

INDEX

adaptability (*prizhivaemost'*), 181–82
advancements, medical, 7, 47
advertising: medical, 93, 158; pharmaceutical, 93, 103, 109, 215n50, 217n69
aesthetics, Soviet, 129, 130, 175
Ageev, Aleksandr, 17
agency, 3–4, 156, 161, 186; hormonal, 171, 177, 187–89; nonhuman, 5, 160–61, 182; storytelling and, 9, 193
alcoholism, 136, *137*, 138; socialism and, 141–42, 171, 177–80
Alexandrov, Vladimir, 76
Althusser, Louis, 103, 104
anatomical specimens, 28, 30
anatomy, 47–48, 200n15, 226n11; pathological, 22, 23, 25
Andrei Efimich Ragin (fictional character), 118, 216n65
Anna Karenina (fictional character), 65, 68–80, 82, 83–85, 210n70, 210n82
Anna Karenina (Tolstoy), 44, 47, 63–87, 209n63, 210n82
Annina (fictional hormone), 168–74, 184, 186
Anthropocene, 229n54

anthropocentrism, 224n2
anthropology, criminal, 31–34, 38, 41–43, 202n46
anti-alcoholism campaigns, 136, *137*, 138
anxieties (triggered by the prospect of death): existential, 88; health, 101, 107
aphasia, 201n29, 201n35
Ariès, Philippe, 23, 45–46, 50
Aristotle, 3, 94
Aronowitz, Robert, 92
ars moriendi (good death), 45–46, 69, 71
art of dying. *See ars moriendi*
Ascension Day Speech (Mussolini), 138–39
asymptomatic body, 100–101, 109
atavism, theory of, 29, 30, 31, 41
Austen, Jane, 77
authors, 66, 85; patients as, 1–2, 53, 58–59, 66–67, 71; physicians as, 22, 43–44
authorship, 3, 8, 88, 92, 93, 156; epidemics and, 230n2; of illness, 16
autopsy, 23, 26–27, 201n20
avant-garde, and medicine, 219–20n100

INDEX

Babel, Isaac, 175
babka (fictional character), 149, 151–53, 154
Babka lechit. See When the Babka Treats the People, She Ruins Them
bacteria, 131–32, 140
Bakhtin, Mikhail, 10, 179, 205n6, 229n51
Barsht, Konstantin, 35
Basedow-Graves disease, 163, 167, 175
Baumann, Eugen, 225n9
Bedbug, The (Maiakovskii), 129
Beer, Daniel, 219n100
Behring, Emil von, 196n4
Bellocchio, Marco, 16
Ben-Ghiat, Ruth, 141
Bernard, Claude, 130, 203n62, 225n8
Bernheim, Hippolyte-Marie, 39–40
Bernstein, Frances Lee, 143, 220n107
bête humaine, La (Zola), 32–33
biome, 161
biomedical experimentation, 227n34
biopolitics, 4, 6, 123
biopower, 122–23, 145, 217n74
birth, 58
Birth of the Clinic, The (Foucault), 16, 25, 47, 54
Black Death plague, 45
body, 111, 122–23; asymptomatic, 101; colonization of, 2; as dataset, 2; disconnection from, 101; perception of, 25; state as, 10, 88, 127, 138, 221nn117–18, 224n6; as unreliable narrator, 101
body-as-machine, 129–31
Body in Pain, The (Scarry), 55, 207n29
body parts: mechanical, 5; as narrative agents, 162–63
Bogdanov, Aleksandr, 191–92
bol'. *See* pain
Bolsheviks, 4, 146, 174
Booth, Wayne C., 8, 196n7
Boria at the Dispensary (Zak), 149, *150*, 151
Bormental (fictional character), 177, 181–82
breast cancer, 80, 81, 82
British National Health Insurance Act (1911), 145

Briukhonenko, Sergei, 180
Broca, Paul, 19, 26, 27–28, 201n35
Brooks, Peter, 18
Brothers Karamazov, The (Dostoevsky), 38–39, 43
Brown-Séquard, Charles-Édouard, 163
Bulgakov, Mikhail, 4, 5, 10, 175–86, 228n42
business, medicine as, 111–12

Cabot, Richard, 20–21
campaigns: anti-alcoholism, 136, *137*, 138; direct-to-consumer, 109, 110; public-health, 7, 93, 101, *102*, 104, 107, 121–58, 219n98
cancer, 64, 79, 211n94; breast, 80, 81, 82; colorectal, 101, *102*; ovarian, 82; previvors of, 81; survivors of, 81
Canguilhem, Georges, 92, 100–101, 105
capitalism, 98; anti-, 219n96; as contagious, 129; Soviets and, 145
caregiving, 208n38
Cartesian split, 17, 161
"Case Records of the Massachusetts General Hospital" (Cabot), 20–22
case report as genre, 20
Cassiday, Julie, 147
cerebral localization theory, 26
Cesare Lombroso Museum of Criminal Anthropology, 28–29
Charon, Rita, 3, 195n1
Chekhov, Anton, 146–47, 199n16, 215n46; "A Doctor's Visit," 130; epidemiology and, 220n105; *Ward No. 6*, 118–19, 124
Chernyshevskii, Nikolai, 36
Childhood (Tolstoy), 49
children, Soviet, 220n105
children's literature, hygiene and, 219n100
Chizh, Vladimir Fëdorovich, 42–43
cholesterol, 110
choreographed death, 18
chronic illness, 64
Chudakova, Marietta, 228n42
Civil War, Russian, 126, 127
Civil War, United States, 46
Clark, Katerina, 219n96

INDEX

clinical diagnosis, 22
clinical-pathological conference (CPC), 20–24
clinical trials, 92, 215n55
clinical writing, 19–20
clinicians, 19, 22, 90
closure, 18, 19, 68, 75–76, 160
"Clues" (Ginzburg), 20, 200n17
cognition (narrative as cognitive necessity), 1, 3, 6, 63, 78
collective beings (*unanimes*), 117
collective state of mind, 156
colonization, of body, 2
colorectal cancer, 101, *102*
comas, 17
comic doctor, 148–49
commerce, and medicine, 96–97
Commissariat of Public Health (Narkomzdrav), 127, 144
communication, medical, 117
compliance, patient, 108, 109, 110
Comrade Lenin Cleans the Earth Globe of the Scum (poster), 128–29
configuration narrative, 19, 25–28, 44
Congress of Criminal Anthropology, 43
Conroy, Mary Schaeffer, 132
consciousness, 59–60, 72
contingency, 78
Continuations (Svevo), 164
COVID-19 pandemic, 189–93
CPC. *See* clinical-pathological conference
craniology, 30, 32, 202n41
Crime and Punishment (Dostoevsky), 34, 35, 37–38, 86–87, 212n102
crime and punishment theories, 31
criminal anthropology, 31–34, 38, 41–43, 202n46
criminality, 28, 29–34, 43
Criminal Man (Lombroso), 29, 31, 33
criminals: facial features of, 29, 30; traits of, 29–30, 31
criminology, 28–29, 32, 40
criticism, literary (of the late 19th century), 36–37
Curious Incident of the Dog in the Night-Time, The (Haddon), 8

Cushing, Harvey William, 163–64
customers, patients as, 96, 104, 106, 109, 112, 120, 156

Darwin, Charles, 30
DCD. *See* donation after cardiac death
death (*smert'*), 22, 25, 31, 43, 61–62; in *Anna Karenina*, 70, 75; of Anna Karenina, 68, 70–71; *ars moriendi*, 45–46, 69, 71; choreographed, 18; configuration and, 27; of Eikhenbaum, 14–15; as ending, 87, 210n82; fear of, 49, 87; plot and, 15–16, 17, 23, 44; Tolstoy on, 205nn6–7
deathbed speech, 16, 46
Death of Ivan Ilych, The (Tolstoy), 44, 46–63, 49–63, 68–69, 190, 206n13, 206nn17–20
death scene, 73, 83–84
death sentence, 40, 80, 81
defamiliarization (*ostranenie*), 10, 231n3
degeneration, 32, 204n79, 224n6; theory of, 43, 221n128
Degeneration (Nordau), 32
Demons (Dostoevsky), 34, 37
dernier jour d'un condamné, Le (Hugo), 85–86
Descartes, René, 162
devices: human-made, 159; mechanical, 5
diagnoses, 2, 20, 24, 27, 53–54, 90, 101; clinical, 22; neurological, 28; as plot, 1, 22–24; treatment and, 116
diagrams, 26, 27
diaries, 85–86, 87, 205n8
"Diary of a Madman" (Gogol), 178
Diary of an Old Doctor (Pirogov), 48
diffused authorship, 88, 92
digital pill, 217n74
direct-to-consumer campaigns, 109, 110
disability, 161, 196n9
Discipline and Punish (Foucault), 54, 144
disconnection, from body, 101
disease, 47, 91, 105; absence of, 90; illness and, 52, 53; infectious, 132; of Ivan Ilych, 51–52; personification of, 208n34; prevention of, 80

INDEX

dispensary, 149, 152
Dobroliubov, Nikolai, 36
Doctor Knock, or The Triumph of Medicine (Romains), 93–100, 103–11, 116–25, 152, 157–58, 213nn12–13; Russian edition of, 155–56
"Doctor Menghi's Drug" (Svevo), 4, 167–74, 184–85, 186
Doctor Parpalaid (fictional character), 94, 95–96, 97, 111–12, 116–20
doctors, 100; comic, 148–49; performance by, 60–61; quack, 95, 121, 213n14; on stage, 94–95; *zemstvo*, 47. *See also* physicians
"Doctor's Visit, A" (Chekhov), 130
donation after cardiac death (DCD), 18
Donogoo-Tonka, or The Miracles of Science (Romains), 95, 125–26, 218n85
Dostoevsky, Fyodor, 32; *The Brothers Karamazov*, 38–39, 43; *Crime and Punishment*, 34, 35, 37–38, 86–87, 212n102; *Demons*, 34, 37; *The Idiot*, 35–36, 80–81; *Memoirs from the House of the Dead*, 33, 43
double-ended immortality concept, 58, 58, 61, 63
Doyle, Arthur Conan, 19, 226n12
drugs, 120, 172–73, 214n41, 215n55
Drugs for Life (Dumit), 91–92
Dumit, Joseph, 91–92, 106, 110, 214n34, 214n36, 215n50
Durkheim, Émile, 122, 123

education: health, 99, 142, 144; physical, 131; sanitation, 223n143
Eikhenbaum, Boris, 13–15, 19, 46, 49, 85, 199n2, 209n65
Emerson, Caryl, 198n13
emplotment, 17, 78, 193; in *The Death of Ivan Ilych*, 49–63; medical, 1, 22–24, 200n15; therapeutic, 86
empowerment, 157; patient, 2, 6, 120, 216n68; women, 83
endings, 65, 78, 79, 80, 82–84; death as, 87, 210n82; fear of, 87; of story, 14–15
endocrine system, 161, 162

endocrinology, 163–64, 168–69, 175
end of life, 4; protocols, 6, 17–18. *See also* death
enlightenment: medical, 117–21, 155; sanitary, 124, 142–43, 144, 151, 221n125; scientific, 157
environment, health and, 36, 94, 130, 191, 192
epidemics, 48; authorship and, 230n2; narratives of, 230n2
epidemiology, Chekhov and, 220n105
epistemology, 3, 25, 50, 117
Epstein, Mikhail, 17
Erklären (explanation), 3
Erlich, Victor, 86
estrangement (*ostranenie*), 53, 216n54
Eugene Onegin (Pushkin), 77
event, Lotman on, 51
evidential paradigm, 20
examination, postmortem, 23, 27, 29, 30, 44, 87
existential isolation, 56
experimentation: biomedical, 227n34; Soviet, 196n6
explanation (*Erklären*), 3
explanation, medical, 53

faces, 35–37
facial features, of criminals, 29, 30
factory workers, and health, 131
fake news, 191
fascism, in Italy, 141, 143, 151–52
Fathers and Children (Turgenev), 37
Faust, Drew Gilpin, 46
fear, 110; of death, 49, 87; of endings, 87; of illness, 108
Fëdorov, Nikolai, 230n55
Ferri, Enrico, 31, 32
Feuillet, Octave, 67–68
Fielding, Henry, 24–25
Filipp Filippovich Preobrazhenskii (fictional character), 175–81, 182–83, 185, 186, 228n42
films, sanitation, 222n142
folk healers, 148, 151–53, 154
"forgive me" (*prosti*), 61–62
formal behavior, 15

INDEX

formalism. *See* Russian Formalism
Foster, John Bellamy, 182
Foucault, Michel: *The Birth of the Clinic*, 16, 25, 47, 54; *Discipline and Punish*, 54, 144; *The History of Sexuality*, 145; "Society Must Be Defended," 122–23; *The Will to Knowledge*, 122
Frankenstein theme, 4, 228n42
Freud, Sigmund, 197n10
future self, 83
futurism, and hygiene, 129

Gall, Franz Joseph, 30, 34–35
Gastev, Aleksei, 129, 131
Gawande, Atul, 50
genetic testing, 79–80, 81–83
Genius and Insanity (Lombroso), 32, 43
genius and madman, 32
geopolitics, and public health, 190
Gerasim (fictional character), 59
germs, 100, 103–4, 129, 132
germ theory, 7, 47, 215n46
Gessen, Masha, 81, 82–85, 87, 211nn94–96
Ginzburg, Carlo, 20, 200n17
goals, public-health, 2, 106
God, 58, 72
Gogol', Nikolai, 42–43, 178, 204n79
Golitsyn, Vladimir Mikhailovich, 67
Goll, August, 202n46
Good, Mary-Jo DelVecchio, 64
good death (*ars moriendi*), 45–46, 69, 71
Greene, Jeremy, 211n92, 213n8, 214n34
Greenslit, Nathan, 216n68
gut health, 224n5

Haddon, Mark, 8
Hansen-Löve, Aage, 15
Haraway, Donna, 160–61, 172
Harrington, Anne, 26
healers, folk, 148
health, 11, 89–92, 97, 105, 140; anxieties around, 101, 107; environment and, 36, 94, 130, 191, 192; gut, 224n5; language of, 57; power and, 111; state control over, 93, 124. *See also* public health

healthcare, 3, 11; early Soviet, 145; finances from, 106
healthcare propaganda, early Soviet, 126–27, 144
healthcare system, Soviet, 126–27, 144
health education, 144
health protection, 127–28
Heart of a Dog, The (Bulgakov), 4, 10, 175–86, 229n51
Hennequin, Émile, 36
heredity, 41–42, 43
Herman, David, 195n2
hermeneutic circle, 55
heteroglossia (Bakhtin), 179
Hippocrates, 20
History of Rome (Livy), 224n6
History of Sexuality, The (Foucault), 145
Hitler, Adolf, 117
Hobbes, Thomas, 142
hormonal agency, 171, 173, 177–81, 187
hormones, 161, 162, 224n13, 228n36
Horn, David, 122, 223n145
Hour of Our Death, The (Ariès), 45
Hugo, Victor, 85–86
humanitarian narrative, 20
humanities, medical, 3, 5, 10, 12, 195n1
human-made devices, 159
hygiene, 136, 140, 196n4; children's literature and, 219n100; metaphors for, 129; politics and, 138; social, 128–29, 218n93
hyperthyroidism, 163, 164, 167, 169–70, 175
hypophysis, 163, 176, 177–82, 183, 186, 226nn10–11
hypothalamus, 226n10
hypothyroidism, 163

ICDs. *See* internal cardiac defibrillators
"Ideology and State Apparatuses" (Althusser), 103
Idiot, The (Dostoevsky), 35–36, 80–81
illness, 51, 59, 91–92, 231n3; authorship of, 16; chronic, 64; disease and, 52, 53; fear of, 108; meaning of, 5; mental, 8–9, 196n9, 216n64; narratives of, 23, 211n93

INDEX

Illness as Metaphor (Sontag), 57
Illness Narratives, The (Kleinman), 17
Illustrated Tribune, The (cover page), 165
Imaginary Invalid, The (Molière), 123, 146
immortality, 58, *58*, 61, 63
income, treatment and, 112
induction coil, 28
industrialization, and the body, 130–31
INES RAN. *See* Russian Institute of Economic Strategy
infectious diseases, 132
Inner History of Devices, The (Pollock), 159–60
Institute for Organotherapeutic Preparations, 175
internal cardiac defibrillators (ICDs), 159–60
interpellation, 103
inter-pill-ation, 214n36
interwar medicine and public health, 92–93, 123, 132, 158
invulnerability, 204n81
isolation, existential, 56
Italy, 124–25, 221n124, 223n145; fascism in, 141, 143, 151–52; futurism and hygiene in, 129; public-health campaigns in, 219n98
Iushkov, P. D., 148
Ivan Dmitrich (fictional character), 118
Ivan Ilych (fictional character), 50–55, 56–61, 63, 72, 206nn17–20, 208n50

Johnson, Boris, 190
Jolie, Angelina, 80
journals. *See* diaries
Jouvet, Louis, 93
Joyce, James, 226n19
Judicial Reform (1864), 47

Kalanithi, Paul, 64–65, 67
Kaufman, Andrew, 212n104
Kelleter, Frank, 209n57
Kelly, Catriona, 220n106
Kermode, Frank, 79, 189
Kitty (fictional character), 68, 70, 77
Kleinman, Arthur, 17, 52

Klim Chugunkin (fictional character), 176, 179–81, 182–83
Knapp, Liza, 72
Knock (fictional character), 93–100, 103–12, 116–21, 123, 143
Kol'tsov, Nikolai, 176
Korolëv (fictional character), 130
Korsakov, Sergei, 40–41, 49
Krementsov, Nikolai, 227n34
Krupskaia, Nadezhda, 175

language, 26, 73, 199n16, 229n51; of criminals, 29; of health, 57; hypophysis and, 178, 179, 180; of medicine, 93, 121; pain and, 55–56, 207n29; of public health, 127
Laqueur, Thomas W., 20
"Last Well Person, The" (Meador), 89–90
Latour, Bruno, 172
Lavater, Johann Kaspar, 30
Lebrogne "Tan" (patient), 27–28
Lenin, Vladimir, 128–29, 131, 140–41, 174–75
Let's Expel Drunkards from the Thicket of Workers! (poster), 136, *137*, 138
Leviathan (Hobbes), 142
Levin, Nikolai (fictional character), 69, 209n63
light, as metaphor for sanitary education, 151–52
literary criticism, late 19th century, 36–37
literary theory. *See* narrative theory; Russian formalism
Livy, 224n6
Lombroso, Cesare, 19, 28–34, 39–43, 204n79, 204nn80–81
long-course treatment, 4, 6, 63, 73
long-term patients, 107–9
Lotman, Yuri, 78, 145, 215n49
Luria, Alexander, 198n15

machine, 160, 192; body as, 129–31; state as, 142
Madame Rémy (fictional character), 111, 119–20
madman, genius and, 32

INDEX

Magnan, Valentin, 43
Maiakovskii, Vladimir, 129
Making Sense of Illness (Aronowitz), 92
Mandelker, Amy, 77
manipulation, 125
Man of Genius, The (Tolstoy), 40
maps: military-strategy, 113, *113–14*, *115*; public-health, *133*, *134*, *135–36*
Marx, Karl, 182, 229n54
Maslova (fictional character), 42
Massachusetts General Hospital, 20–22
mastectomy, 84
Mattingly, Cheryl, 16
McLean, Hugh, 58
Meador, Clifton K., 89–91, 92
mechanical body parts, 5
mechanical devices, 5
medical age, new, 94, 97, 111, 120–21
medical institutions, Russian, 48
medicine, 26; as business, 111–12; commerce and, 96–97; language of, 93, 121; new medical age, 94, 97; quack, 148, 153–55; Russian, 7–8, 48; social, 128; war and, 132
Medzhibovskaya, Inessa, 201n13
Memoirs from the House of the Dead (Dostoevsky), 33, 43
Menghi (fictional character), 168–74, 184–85, 186
Men of Good Will (Romains), 114
mental health, 91, 196n9
mental illness, 8–9, 196n9, 216n64
metabolic storytelling, 182, 186
metabolism, 182, 187
Metahistory (White), 24
metaphors, 228n36; medical to describe a nation, 139, 221nn117–18; military, 57, 131, 132
milieu, 36, 130, 176, 203n62
military metaphors, 57, 131, 132, 221nn117–18
military-strategy maps, 113, *113–14*, *115*
Mitia Karamazov (fictional character), 38–39
mock trials, 146; sanitation, 147–48, 154–55
modernism, 187, 210n70, 221n124

Molière, 106, 123, 146
Mol'kov, Al'fred, 141
money, 104, 106–7, 109, 126
Monkey riot (illustration), *166*
Monserrate, Bernardino Montaña de, 224n6
"Monument to a Scientific Error, A" (Shklovskii), 126
Morel, Bénédict, 221n128
Morson, Gary Saul, 73, 74
mortality, 3, 5, 54–55
Mozart, 213n14
Mussolini, Benito, 138–39, 221n117, 228n39
Myshkin (Prince, fictional character), 35, 80–81, 198n15

Naiman, Eric, 228nm36
Narkomzdrav (Commissariat of Public Health), 127, 144, 221n125
narrative agency, 3–5, 160–61, 171, 177–80
narrative as cognitive necessity, 1, 3, 6, 63, 78
narrative authority, clash of, 181, 186, 187
narrative configuration, 19, 25–28, 44
Narrative Medicine (Charon), 195n1
narrative reliability, 8, 101, 207n27; mental illness and, 8, 216n64
narrative succession, 19–25, 43–44, 64–65; on COVID-19, 190; in *The Death of Ivan Ilych*, 50; epidemic, 230n2; humanitarian, 20; illness, 23, 211n93; manipulation of, 172, 173–74; in medicine, 1; narratives, 3–4, 8, 187, 193, 227n27; public-health, 97; serialized, 66–67, 69, 209n57; Tolstoy and, 84–85; of women, 211n94
narrative theory, 3, 18–19, 64–65, 80, 84, 195nn1–2, 196n7, 207n55
narrative time, 50, 73, 173, 186–87; death and, 46; manipulation of, 172; mastery of, 6, 9
narrative truth, 18–19
narrator, 76, 170, 196n7; body as, 101; patient as, 1–2, 53, 58–59, 66–67, 71; physician as, 22, 24–25, 43–44; as sick, 8–9; unreliable, 8, 101, 207n27, 216n64

nature, as blind force, 230n55
Nazi regime, 8, 117
necrocracy (*nekrokratiia*), 17
Nekhliudov (fictional character), 41–42, 49
nekrokratiia (necrocracy), 17
NEP. *See* New Economic Policy
neurodiversity, 8, 12, 198n15
neurology, 32; diagnosis of, 28; history of, 26–27
New Economic Policy (NEP), 4, 127
New England Journal of Medicine, 20–23, 89
news, fake, 191
New Soviet Person, 176, 185, 190, 228n39
New York Times Magazine, 18
Nicolosi, Riccardo, 204n79
nihilism, 37
Nikolai Levin (fictional character), 69–70, 209n63, 212n104
nonhuman agency, 5, 160–61, 177–80, 184
nonhuman entities, 4, 10, 160, 172, 187, 191
Nordau, Max, 32
normal, pathological and, 6, 25, 100–101, 106, 119, 165
Normal and the Pathological, The (Canguilhem), 92, 100–101, 105
Nosferatu the Vampire (film), 94
NOT. *See* "Scientific Organization of Labor"
nutrition, 128, 136

object-oriented ontology, 160
observation, visual, 28
October Revolution, 143, 146
Odessa Tales (Babel), 175
O. Henry and the Theory of the Short Story (Eikhenbaum), 13–14, 19
ona word, 56–57, 207n33
oncology, and narrative time, 64
onomatopoeia, and pain, 62–63
ontology, object-oriented, 160
operations, rejuvenation, 164
Order of Things, The (Foucault), 54, 97
Origin of Species, The (Darwin), 30
Orwin, Donna, 77
ostranenie (defamiliarization), 10, 231n3

outsideness (*vnenakhodimost'*), 10
ovarian cancer, 82
overmedicalization, 214n41
Ovsianiko-Kulikovskii, Dmitrii, 204n80

pain (*bol'*), 59, 62–63, 207n33; language and, 55–56, 62–63, 207n29; numerical value of, 56; total pain concept, 53, 206n20
palliative-care physicians, 53
pandemic, COVID-19, 189–93
Paperno, Irina, 85
paradigm, evidential, 20
Pasqui, Patrizia, 121
pathological: normal and, 6, 25, 100–101, 106, 119, 165; physiological and, 106
pathological anatomy, 25
pathology, 22, 26, 27
patients, 105, 208n50; as authors and readers, 1–2, 53, 58–59, 66–67, 71; compliance from, 108, 109, 110; as customers, 96, 104, 106, 109, 112, 120, 156; as datasets, 2; empowerment of, 2, 6, 120, 216n68; long-term, 107–9; talking back in literary tradition, 223–24n165
Pavlov, Ivan, 176
penetration, medical, 112–13
performance, by doctor, 60–61
pharmaceutical advertising, 93, 103, 109, 215n50, 215n55, 217n69
pharmaceutical companies, 120, 214n36, 216n68; Soviet, 222n132
pharmaceuticals, 213n8
Pharmageddon (Pasqui), 121
Philoctetes (fictional character), 62
phrenology, 30
physical education (*fizkul'tura*), 131
physicians, 21, 47–48, 55, 215n62; as authors, 22, 24–25, 43–44; palliative-care, 53
physician-writers, Russian, 196n5
physiognomy, 30
physiological and pathological, 106
pineal gland, 162
Pirogov, Nikolai, 47–48
Pirogova, Anna Stepanovna, 87, 212n105

INDEX

plague, Black Death, 45
plays, sanitary, 146–47, 155
plot, 3, 4, 19, 21, 82, 126; death and, 15–16, 17, 23, 44; diagnoses as, 1; readers and, 65; treatment as, 1–2; virtual, 65–66, 69. *See also* emplotment
politics: geo-, 190; hygiene and, 138
Pollock, Anne, 159–60
posthuman, 11, 187, 224n2
postmortem examination, 23, 27, 29, 30, 44, 87; narration and, 23–24
power, 144–45; health and, 111
Praskovia Fyodorovna (fictional character), 51, 52, 56
Prescribing by Numbers (Greene), 211n92, 214n34
"Prescription Maximization" (Dumit), 110
present, the, 85, 86
prevention, 105; of disease, 80, 99–100; of illness, 92
preventive medicine, 120–22, 127–28, 138, 214n34
previvors, 79; cancer, 81
prognosis, 9, 10, 67. *See also* time horizon
propaganda, 191; healthcare, 144; medical, 157; public-health, 174; Sanprosvet, 151; Soviet health, 142–43, 158
prosthetics, 159
prosti ("forgive me"), 61–62
protection, health, 127–28
psychiatry, 9, 204n79
psychoanalysis, 157, 197n10
psychology, 9
public health, 126, 192; geopolitics and, 190; goals for, 2, 106; language of, 127; narratives for, 97; socialist, 140; Soviet, 218n93, 218nn88–90, 228n39
public-health campaigns, 7, 93, 101, *102*, 104, 107, 121–58, 219n98
public-health maps, *133*, *134*, *135*–36
public-health policies, 190
public-health propaganda, 174
punishment. *See* crime and punishment theories
Pushkin, Alexander, 77

quack doctors, 95, 121, 213n14
quack medicine, 148, 153–55

railroad worker (fictional character), 73, 75
RAN. *See* Russian Institute of Economic Strategy
Raskol'nikov (fictional character), 34, 35, 37–38, 87
reader-response theorists, 65
readers, 71; patients as, 44, 53, 58–59, 66–67, 71; plot and, 65
Reading for the Plot (Brooks), 18–19
Reassembling the Social (Latour), 172
reductionism, 37, 52
reflections, end-of-life, 59–60
regeneration, 164
Régis, François, 113, 114
rejuvenation operations, 164, 182
relativization, 76, 88
Renovating Russia (Beer), 219n100
Republic of Suffering, This (Faust), 46
Resurrection (Tolstoy), 41–42, 49
revolution, and the arts, 219n95
Revolutionary Experiments (Krementsov), 227n34
rhetoric, medical, 94, 100, 101, 125
Rhetoric of Fiction, The (Booth), 8, 196n7
Ricoeur, Paul, 3, 19, 43–44, 64
risk, 4, 80–81, 91–92, 110, 211nn92–93, 213n8, 214n34
Romains, Jules, 6, 9–10, 92, 213n11; *Doctor Knock, or The Triumph of Medicine*, 93–100, 103–11, 116–25, 152, 157–58, 213nn12–13; *Donogoo-Tonka, or The Miracles of Science*, 95, 125–26, 218n85; *Men of Good Will*, 114
Röntgen, Wilhelm Conrad, 196n4
Rosenberg, Charles, 54
Rougon-Macquart cycle, 32–33
Rozentul, M. A., 148, 149
Russian formalism, 10, 15, 126, 184
Russian Institute of Economic Strategy (INES RAN), 17
Russian medicine, 7–8, 48
Russian physician-writers, 196n5

Sacks, Oliver, 198n15
sanitary enlightenment, 124, 142–43, 144, 151, 221n125
sanitary plays, 146–47, 155
sanitation education, 223n143
sanitation films, 222n142
sanitation mock trials, 147–48, 154–55
Sanprosvet propaganda, 151
scapegoating, 190–91
Scarry, Elaine, 55–56, 207n29
science fiction, 207n30
Science of a Healthy Society (Semashko), 128, 131–32
"Scientific Organization of Labor" (NOT), 131
Scientific Revolution, 122
Semashko, Nikolai A., 124, 127, 218n94; *Science of a Healthy Society*, 128, 131–32; *Social Illnesses and the Fight Against Them*, 131
Sense of an Ending, The (Kermode), 79
serialized narrative, 66–67, 69, 209n57
Sharik (Sharikov) (fictional dog), 176–83, 185–86, 229n51
Sheldon, Richard, 126
Shklovskii, Viktor, 6, 9–10, 85, 126, 184
Sirotkina, Irina, 204n80
skulls, 29–30, 35. *See also* craniology
Slap in the Face of Public Taste, A (futurist manifesto), 129
smert'. *See* death
Snowden, Frank, 230n2
Social Bodies (Horn), 223n145
social hygiene, 128–29, 218n93
Social Illnesses and the Fight Against Them (Semashko), 131
socialism, 140, 229n51; alcoholism and, 141–42
social medicine, 128
society, 67, 122; living space and, 128
"Society Must Be Defended" (Foucault), 122–23
sociology, medical, 216n65
Sontag, Susan, 57
Sophocles, 62
Soviet aesthetics, 129, 130, 175
Soviet experiment, 196n6

Soviet health propaganda, 142–43
Soviet state, 5, 121, 126–28, 139, 185, 222n135; capitalism and, 145; children in, 220n105; healthcare in, 145; industrialization and, 130–31; pharmaceutical companies in, 222n132
specimens, anatomical, 30
spectatorship, 74
speech, deathbed, 16, 46
speech disorders, 26
Starks, Tricia, 142, 219n100
Starr, M. Allen, 201n29
state, as machine, 142
state-as-body, 10, 88, 127, 138, 224n6
state control, over health, 6, 93, 124
Steinach, Eugen, 164
Steinach-Film, Der (film), 164, 175
Storytelling and the Sciences of Mind (Herman), 195n2
streaming video, 64, 65
Structure of the Artistic Text, The (Lotman), 215n49
subjectivity, 88, 161
succession narrative, 19–25, 43–44
surgical techniques, 132
surveillance, 6, 144, 192, 221n119; peer, 111, 121, 155, 157
survivors, cancer, 81
Svevo, Italo, 187, 224n19; *Continuations*, 164; "Doctor Menghi's Drug," 4, 167–74, 184–85, 186; *Zeno's Conscience*, 164, 167–68
Sydenham, Thomas, 20
symptoms, 51, 101, 110
syphilis, 132

Tarde, Gabriel, 123
Taylorism, 174, 184
technology, medical, 17, 23, 122–23, 196n4
teleology, 44; in *Anna Karenina*, 68, 69, 73; in *The Death of Ivan Ilych*, 49–63
television series, 64, 65–66
temporality, 6, 19, 44, 64, 71, 78; in *Anna Karenina*, 73–74, 83

testing, genetic, 79–80, 81
"Theater and Theatricality as Components of Early Nineteenth-Century Culture, The" (Lotman), 145–46
theatricality, 145–48
theme, Frankenstein, 4
theorists, reader-response, 65
therapeutic emplotment, 86
thing theory, 160, 224n2
Three Songs About Lenin (film), 174–75
thyroid, 162–63, 164, 168, 225n9, 226n11, 226n19
time horizon, 4, 6, 11, 63–69, 84, 86–88
Todd, William Mills III, 66, 67
Tolstaia, Sofia Andreevna, 87, 212n105
Tolstoy, Leo, 5–6, 9, 32, 39, 46, 48; *Anna Karenina*, 44, 47, 63–87, 209n63, 210n82; on death, 205nn6–7; *The Death of Ivan Ilych*, 44, 49–63, 68–69, 190, 206n13, 206nn17–20; diaries of, 85–86, 205n8; health of, 49; on medical practitioners, 213n15; narrative and, 84–85; *Resurrection*, 41–42, 49; *What Is Art?*, 41
Tom Jones (Fielding), 24–25
Topographical Anatomy of the Human Body (Pirogov), 47–48
totalitarianism, 7, 125–26
trains, 210n71
traits, of criminals, 29–30, 31
Treatise of Man (Descartes), 162
treatment, 1–2, 105; diagnosis and, 116; income and, 112; long-course, 4, 6, 63, 73
Tret'iakov, Sergei, 183–84
trials. *See* mock trials
Trotsky, Leon, 176
Trump, Donald J., 190
Turgenev, Ivan, 37
"Tyranny of Diagnosis, The" (Rosenberg), 54

unanimes (collective beings), 117
unanimism, 117

understanding (*Verstehen*), 3
unreliable narrator, 8, 101, 207n27, 216n64

Verstehen (understanding), 3
Vertov, Dziga, 222n142
Villella, Giuseppe, 29–30
virtual plot, 65–66, 69
viruses, 191
vnenakhodimost' (outsideness), 10
vocabulary, political, 177
Voronoff, Sergei, 163–64, 224n12
Vronsky (fictional character), 74–75, 77

war: medicine and, 132; metaphors, and medicine, 57, 131, 132
Ward No. 6 (Chekhov), 118–19, 124
warfare maps, 113, *113–14*, 115
We (Zamiatin), 129
Wedding Director, The (film), 16–17
Welles, Orson, 63
wellness, 89–91
well people, 89–91
Wernicke, Carl, 26
What Is Art? (Tolstoy), 41
When Breath Becomes Air (Kalanithi), 64–65
When Species Meet (Haraway), 160–61
When the Babka Treats the People, She Ruins Them (Iushkov), 148–49, 151–54
White, Hayden, 16, 24
Williams, William Carlos, 199n16, 207n30
Will to Knowledge, The (Foucault), 122
women: empowerment of, 82–83; narrative of, 211n94
writings, clinical, 19–20

Young Doctor's Notes, A (Bulgakov), 227n35

Zak, Sofiia, 149, *150*, 151
Zamiatin, Evgenii, 129
zemstvo doctors, 47, 147
Zeno (fictional character), 164, 167
Zeno's Conscience (Svevo), 164, 167–68
Zola, Émile, 32–33

GPSR Authorized Representative: Easy Access System Europe, Mustamäe tee 50, 10621 Tallinn, Estonia, gpsr.requests@easproject.com

www.ingramcontent.com/pod-product-compliance
Lightning Source LLC
Chambersburg PA
CBHW021939290426
44108CB00012B/898